Communication Theories in Action

An Introduction

FROM THE WADSWORTH SERIES IN SPEECH COMMUNICATION

THIRD EDITION

Communication Theories in Action

An Introduction

Julia T. Wood

Lineberger Distinguished Professor of Humanities
The University of North Carolina at Chapel Hill

WADSWORTH
CENGAGE Learning

Australia • Brazil • Japan • Korea • Mexico • Singapore • Spain • United Kingdom • United States

WADSWORTH
CENGAGE Learning™

**Communication Theories in Action:
An Introduction, Third Edition**

Julia T. Wood

Publisher: Holly Allen

Assistant Editor: Amber Fawson

Editorial Assistant: Breanna Gilbert

Technology Project Manager: Jeanette Wiseman

Marketing Manager: Kimberly Russell

Marketing Assistant: Neena Chandra

Advertising Project Manager: Shemika Britt

Project Manager, Editorial Production: Mary Noel

Print/Media Buyer: Rebecca Cross

Permissions Editor: Elizabeth Zuber

Production Service: Vicki Moran, Publishing Support Services

Copyeditor: April Wells-Hayes

Cover Designer: Brittney Singletary

Compositor: Pre-Press Company

For product information and technology assistance, contact us at
Cengage Learning Customer & Sales Support, 1-800-354-9706

For permission to use material from this text or product,
submit all requests online at **cengage.com/permissions**
Further permissions questions can be e-mailed to
permissionrequest@cengage.com

Exam View® and Exam View Pro® are registered trademarks of FSCreations, Inc. Windows is a registered traddemark of the Microsoft Corporation used herein under license. Macintosh and Power Macintosh are registered trademarks of Apple Computer, Inc., used herein under license.

Library of Congress Control Number: 2003100505

ISBN-13: 978-0-534-56639-5

Student Edition with InfoTrac College Edition: ISBN-10: 0-534-56639-1
Student Edition without InfoTrac College Edition: ISBN-10: 0-534-56640-5

Wadsworth
25 Thomson Place
Boston, MA 02210
USA

Cengage Learning is a leading provider of customized learning solutions with office locations around the globe, including Singapore, the United Kingdom, Australia, Mexico, Brazil, and Japan. Locate your local office at: **international.cengage.com/region**

Cengage Learning products are represented in Canada by Nelson Education, Ltd.

For your course and learning solutions, visit **academic.cengage.com**

Purchase any of our products at your local college store or at our preferred online store **www.ichapters.com**

Printed in the U.S.A
9 10 12 11 10

This book is dedicated to my Aunt Frances,
who is family and more.
She always was, and she remains,
an important presence in my life.

About the Author

Julia T. Wood is the Lineberger Distinguished Professor of Humanities and a Professor of Communication Studies at the University of North Carolina at Chapel Hill. Since completing her Ph.D. (Pennsylvania State University) at age 24, she has conducted research and written extensively about communication and personal relationships and about gender and communication.

In addition to presenting more than 150 papers at conferences and publishing more than 70 chapters and articles in major journals, she has authored or co-authored fourteen books and edited seven others. She has won eight awards for teaching excellence and nine awards for research.

Professor Wood lives with her partner, Robbie (Robert) Cox, who is also a professor of Communication Studies at the University of North Carolina. When not writing and teaching, Professor Wood enjoys traveling, legal consulting, and spending time with students, friends, and family.

Contents at a Glance

Contents

Chapter Two   *Understanding Communication Theories   30*

Chapter Three   *Building and Testing Theory   51*

Part Two   **Communication Theories**

Chapter Six   *Theories About Performance   116*

Chapter Seven   *Theories About How People Construct Meaning   140*

Preface

I wrote *Communication Theories in Action* because I wanted to show students that communication theories, as well as the process of theorizing, are interesting and relevant to everyday life. In these opening pages, I explain my goals for writing this book and the pedagogical features that I've woven into the text.

Goals

For years I have been troubled by many students' belief that theories are obscure and removed from "real life." This belief may be fueled by the ways in which theories are often presented. Some textbooks employ technical language and advanced concepts that are not translated for people who don't have background in theories. The level and the language of these books confirm many introductory students' impression that theories have little to do with their lives. Other theory textbooks cover such a range of theories that students can easily be overwhelmed. When a great many theories are presented, it's difficult, if not impossible, to examine any in detail. Cursory discussion of numerous theories also discourages students from exploring interrelationships among theories. As a result, students may mistakenly think there is little coherence in the field of communication.

Making Theories Accessible and Relevant to Students' Lives

I hope to provide a book that offers an alternative to the foregoing models of theory textbooks. One goal of the book is to introduce students to theories in a way that demonstrates that theories are directly relevant to their everyday lives. I hope this book also excites students about theories and theorizing. Toward that end I encourage students to understand the process of theorizing as not only a formal, academic activity but also an informal practice in which we all engage. In approaching theories as paths to understanding experience and interacting more effectively, this book invites students to use communication theories in their lives.

Selective Presentation of Theories

I've chosen to focus on a limited number of communication theories in preference to providing superficial coverage of numerous theories. My own experiences in teaching convince me that providing rich discussion of selected theories increases students' appreciation of the process of theorizing and—equally important—increases their interest in applying theories to their lives. Rather than overwhelming students with encyclopedic coverage, I've selected 23 theories that illustrate the breadth of the communication field as well as the different intellectual traditions that have informed it.

The book is organized to provide students with foundations for understanding theorizing and opportunities to explore and apply those foundations in relation to particular theories. Part I (Chapters 1–3) introduces the field of communication and discusses foundations of theorizing and criteria for evaluating theories. In Part II (Chapters 4–14) each chapter presents two or three theories that focus on a particular type of communication (mass media), a specific context of communication (organizations, relationships), or an aspect of communication (creating meaning, critiquing cultural life). The final chapter summarizes and integrates discussion of theories.

Critical, Integrative Coverage

My third goal is to encourage students to think critically and integratively about theories. I explain each theory's key assumptions and concepts so that students can grasp and evaluate the foundations informing specific theories. Following this, I explore criticisms of the theory. This brings students into the debates that fuel progress in theorizing. In addition, presenting criticisms of theory encourages students to adopt critical attitudes when thinking about theories.

Equally important to the coherence of this book, I highlight connections between theories, and I invite students to reflect on how claims of one theory relate to those of other theories. I hope this approach helps students see that theories generally draw from and build on previous work. This approach should also enhance students' awareness of the "multiple truths" that coexist in human experience.

Pedagogical Features

I have already mentioned three features that distinguish *Communication Theories in Action* from other communication theory textbooks: emphasis on the relevance of theories to students' lives, discriminating selection of theories, and critical, integrative discussion of theories. In addition to these features, I've included features to enhance students' engagement with the book and with theories.

Conversational Tone

I've written this book in a conversational style to make theories accessible to introductory students. Rather than using formal writing style, I adopt an informal tone. For instance, I often use contractions (we're, don't) instead of more stilted terms (we are, do not). I also refer to myself as "I," rather than "the author." I hope that this style of writing encourages students to feel they are in a conversation in which their responses and ideas are welcome. I avoid jargon whenever possible and provide clear definitions of specialized terms.

To further animate writing, I offer practical examples that relate to students' concerns, relationships, and everyday activities. Through the conversational tone and real-life examples, I invite students to engage the material in this book personally and to see themselves as participants in the ongoing discussions of theory that keep the communication field vital.

Practical Application

In addition to using language and examples that are practical, two features encourage students to work with theories and to engage them personally. Each chapter includes several "Try It Out" exercises that allow students to discover how a theory works in action. The Try It Out exercises may be used as in-class activities or assigned as homework or entries for a journal.

Each chapter also includes a number of "Reflections," which encourage students to think further about ideas and about connections among theories. The Reflections can be assigned for journal entries or short papers, or they can serve as springboards for class discussion.

Additional Resources

To assist instructors who adopt this book, there is an *Instructor's Guide*, co-authored by Michelle Violanti and me. It includes suggestions for organizing the course, creating an engaging classroom climate, and developing major assignments. In addition, it provides activities to apply material and sample test items. Also, computerized testing is available to instructors who adopt this book. These supplements are available to qualified adopters; please consult your local sales representative for details.

With Michelle Violanti, I've written a *Student Companion* for this book to extend what is covered in the text. The *Student Companion* includes exercises, activities, chapter summaries, and self-test items so that students can evaluate their command of material covered.

New to This Edition

This edition of *Communication Theories in Action* retains the basic structure and vision that characterized the first and second editions. At the same time, I've revised this edition in response to feedback from students and faculty who used the previous editions.

To ensure that this edition of *Communication Theories in Action* reflects important emerging theoretical lines, I've added discussion of several emergent theories. I've incorporated critical race theory and white studies into Chapter 10's discussion of standpoint theories. I've also added coverage of multiracial feminist theory to Chapter 12's coverage of feminist theories. Finally, because postmodern theories are increasingly important in the field of communication, I've added a chapter devoted to them, Chapter 13.

At the request of faculty who adopted the first and second editions, I have more strongly highlighted key concepts in this edition. At the end of each chapter is a list of primary concepts discussed in that chapter. Also at the request of faculty who used previous editions, I have more explicitly highlighted connections between different theories so that students can appreciate the ways in which theories are both related and different.

This edition of *Communication Theories in Action* also includes over 100 references. Since the second edition was published, there have been developments that add to our understanding of theories covered in this book.

Acknowledgments

Although I am listed as the author of this book, many others contributed to it. I am particularly grateful to my colleagues at the University of North Carolina at Chapel Hill and to communication scholars around the nation whose research and theorizing inspired *Communication Theories in Action*. I hope I have done justice to the creativity and quality of their ideas.

I am also grateful to the superb publishing team at Wadsworth. Members of our team are true professionals who blended imagination and rigor in developing this book. I am especially grateful to Deirdre Anderson, former Executive Editor of Communication at Wadsworth, for her support of my work. Others who contributed to the development of this edition are Vicki Moran of Publishing Support Services, production; April Wells-Hayes, copy editor; Mary Noel, project editor; Breanna Gilbert, editorial assistant; Amber Fawson, assistant editor; Jeanette Wiseman, technology project manager; and Kimberly Russell, marketing manager.

I acknowledge the generous and insightful reviews of drafts of the first edition of this book that were provided by Bill Balthrop, the University of North Carolina at Chapel Hill; Judy Bowker, Oregon State University; James Chesebro, Indiana State University; Bill Owen, California State University, Sacramento; Jack Perella, Santa Rosa Junior College; Charles Roberts, East Tennessee State University; James Sahlman, Angelo State University; Donna Vocate, Boston University; and Denice Yanni, Fairfield University.

I would also like to thank the reviewers of the second edition of this book: Randy K. Dillon, Southwest Missouri State University; James M. Gotcher, Austin Peay State University; George W. Musambira, Western Kentucky University; Peter Oehlkers, Emerson College; and Della Pollock, the University of North Carolina at Chapel Hill.

Reviewers for this third edition who gave me very valuable feedback are James A. Herrick, Hope College; Deirdre D. Johnston, Hope College; Patricia Kearney, California State University at Long Beach; Phaedra Pezzullo, Indiana University; Linda M. Pledger, University of Arkansas at Little Rock; Jeanne Posner, Western Connecticut State University; and Ted Striphas, Ohio University.

Finally, I thank the people to whom I am closest. Invariably, my work reflects the support and stimulation I receive from my intimates. At the top of that list is Robbie Cox, my partner for 30 years and, we hope, for many more to come. Along with Robbie, my friends Todd, Shelly, Nancy, and Linda Becker, and my sister and friend, Carolyn, enrich my life and my work with their support, challenges, and thoughtful responses to my ideas.

Julia T. Wood
Spring 2003
The University of North Carolina
at Chapel Hill

Communication Theories in Action

Introduction

When I was a child, my father devoted much time and energy to making sure I knew our family history. He told me vivid stories of his spirited and strong mother, Miss Sal, whom I never met. I heard about Luther and Mary, who were important members of his family though unrelated by blood. I was captivated by tall tales about my father's brother Arch, who died young but not before stirring up considerable mischief—a talent my father claimed I inherited directly from Arch. My father also told me stories of his father, who stoically endured the Great Depression, and his grandfather, who taught him to respect animals and to value compassion in dealing with others.

Sometimes I was bored by my father's narratives of people long dead. I wondered why I had to know about them. With the impudence and ignorance of a young child, I once demanded, "What do any of these people and stories have to do with me?" His reply was fast and firm: "To understand who you are, you have to know your family history." Although I didn't fully appreciate his wisdom at the time, in the years that followed I listened with greater respect to the steady stream of family stories that poured forth from my father. As a result, I feel I *know* personally many of the people he brought alive for me. And as I have matured, I've realized that my own identity is intricately tied to my foremothers and forefathers.

Just as we learn our family histories to understand who we are, we learn the history of an intellectual discipline to appreciate its identity. An academic field of study bears the traces of the people, ideas, and events that have been part of it. To understand the modern discipline of communication, then, it's necessary to explore the people and ideas that have contributed to its historical and current character. Communication, like all fields, has constructed a history of its identity—the people, ideas, and events that have shaped what it is today.

Reprinted by permission of Tribune Media Services

Central to the history of the field's identity are the theories that define its scope and cultivate insight into human interaction. The concerns and knowledge of the communication discipline reflect a history of discoveries, conceptual developments, and modes of inquiry. Consequently, what the field is today can be fully appreciated only by understanding its historical journey and the theories that were developed along that journey.

Values of Studying Communication Theories

Knowledge of the Field

There are many reasons to study communication theories. I've already noted that one value is a better understanding of the field's present concerns and knowledge. The disciplines studied in the modern university do not exist apart from their histories; each can be fully understood only within the context of what has come before. Learning about the theories that have influenced the communication field historically will enhance your insight into the issues, principles, and problems that characterize the discipline today. By extension, learning about theories that are influential now will help you anticipate future developments in communication research and teaching.

Practical Value

In addition to expanding your knowledge of the field, studying theories has practical value. Because theories of communication describe and explain what happens when people interact, they will enlarge your understanding of experiences in your personal life and the lives of those around you. Studying theories will also give you insight into patterns in cultural life. In other words, communication theories are directly pertinent to real life.

Each theory that we will explore offers us valuable tools for understanding our everyday lives, our relationships with others, and the ways in which communication shapes and reflects cultural values. This highlights the fact that theory and practice are not distinct concerns. Good theories inform and improve practical life, and practical activities are the focus of theories.

What you learn in this book will have immediate, practical value. You will gain skill in developing and testing theories in your own life. If that statement surprises you, it may be because you share the common misunderstanding that theorizing is restricted to academic scholars. Actually, all of us—academics, writers, nurses, attorneys, salespeople, parents—are theorists who continually try to describe, explain, understand, and control our experiences in communicating with others.

Perhaps in your relationships you've sometimes been confused by competing desires to be close to and separate from another person. If so, dialectical theory (Chapter 8) will help you understand that both autonomy and connection are normal and constructive impulses that surface in most personal relationships. Maybe you've noticed there are ritualized patterns of communication at mixers ("Hi, what year are you?" "What's your major?" "Do you like this band?"), in exchanges with store clerks ("How are you today?" "Fine—you?" "Thank you; have a nice day."), and on first dates ("Where are you from?" "Do you like Mediterranean food?"). Rules theory (Chapter 7) describes these sorts of regularities in interaction so that we understand why they occur, what they mean, and what may happen if we disrupt them. If you've ever wondered why many men and women tend to differ in some of their communication behaviors, then you'll want to pay particular attention to Chapter 10. In that chapter, we discuss standpoint and speech community theories, both of which shed light on gendered dynamics in communication.

Communication theories also give us insight into the public sphere. As I was writing this book, corporate scandals were rocking the country. First we learned of the accounting deception at Enron. Then reports came out about similar accounting misrepresentations at Tyco, WorldCom, and Xerox. Theories of organizational culture (Chapter 10) provide a framework for explaining how members of organizations develop shared understandings about normal business practices and about what is ethical. After the terrorist attacks on the United States on September 11, 2001, many Americans were unable to understand the suicide bombers; how, they wondered, could anyone believe it is good, patriotic, and religiously right to kill others? Chapter 7's discussion of rules theory helps us understand the suicide bombers in the context of the meanings that formed them and informed their actions. If you have ever noticed that some public figures are more skillful than others in generating commitment to themselves and their ideas, then you'll want to read about Kenneth Burke's work. His dramatistic theory focuses on ways that people use symbols, primarily language, to create identification with others. Each theory in this book gives you insights into human communication in its many forms and contexts. In turn, these insights empower you to understand and function more effectively in your own life and to appreciate more fully the complexities of communication in society as a whole.

Although everyone is a theorist, not everyone is equally skilled at theorizing. Like any other activity, theorizing can be done well or poorly. Effective theorizing is based on knowing what theories are and how to evaluate their validity and value. In the chapters that follow, you will learn how to test and assess theories. In turn this will allow you to theorize more effectively about communication in your life. Thus, you will enlarge your ability to understand and control your interactions with others.

The Focus of *Communication Theories in Action*

Communication Theories in Action explores a number of theories that have charted the communication field's evolution and led to its current status as an intellectually vibrant, socially relevant area of study and practice. As you learn about theorizing and specific theories of communication, you should gain an enlarged appreciation of the complex, multifaceted process of human communication.

Selective Focus on Theories

Like all histories, the history provided in this book is incomplete. Over the years, communication scholars have advanced hundreds of theories. Don't worry—you won't encounter all of them in the pages that follow! Rather than trying to cover a large territory superficially, we'll concentrate in depth on a limited number of theories that have shaped the character of the field. I believe the 23 theories discussed in this book will give you a good introduction to the breadth of the field and the diversity of approaches, concerns, and assumptions that communication theorists make.

Attention to the Process of Theorizing

Beyond what you will learn about specific theories presented in this book, you may develop an appreciation of the *process* of theorizing as an intellectual activity. As a result of your study, you should gain insight into the concerns and goals that motivate scholars to develop theories. You will also learn about the special challenges and constraints that confront scholars as they generate and test theories in the real world of practical situations and concrete activities.

Tensions Among Theories

In learning about the process of theorizing, you will discover that theories and theorists vary widely not only in what they study but also in the fundamental assumptions they make about human nature, knowledge, communication, and the goals of theory. Although I point out disagreements among theories, I've made no effort to disguise differences in order to fabricate a false consensus among communication scholars. Rather, I encourage you to struggle with tensions among theories so that you may appreciate the multiple, sometimes conflicting, views of human beings, communication, and theorizing that coexist within the field.

I firmly believe that theories are not dull, irrelevant abstractions that matter only to academics. I see theories as vibrant, fascinating perspectives on personal and social life. In writing *Communication Theories in Action*, I've tried to bring important communication theories to life for you so that you can share my excitement about their value, interest, and relevance. Perhaps some of the theories you study in this book will become as real and alive to you as Miss Sal and Uncle Arch are to me. If so, then you'll have a living link to your academic family history.

CHAPTER ONE

Communication as a Field of Study

Cass stumbles across the room to silence her alarm clock. Last night she had moved it away from the bed so that she wouldn't cut it off and go back to sleep as she had done the last three mornings she'd had an 8 A.M. chemistry class. Yawning, Cass promises herself that she not only will make it to the class today but also will keep her attention focused on what the professor is saying. Her mind always seems to wander in that class.

As Cass dries her hair, she thinks about Jason, her boyfriend. Sometimes she feels so close to him and can't see enough of him, but at other times she feels crowded and wants some distance and time away from him. That just doesn't make sense if she really loves him.

Turning on the television, Cass hears a reporter recount two assaults. She shrugs and thinks to herself, "So what else is new? It's a mean world out there." While she dresses, Cass runs through the schedule for the day: first the chemistry class, and then classes in anthropology and communication. Later in the afternoon she'll meet with the project group in her psychology class. She dreads that meeting because one member of the group, Nelson, is overbearing and dominant; he always pushes his ideas on others. He is from a very well-off family, and he acts like he's better than everyone else. Cass is intimidated by Nelson's style of communicating, and she becomes virtually silent when she's around him. The final item on her list for today is a presentation to the residence hall association for programming this spring. She has only five minutes to explain her ideas, and she's not sure how to be effective.

As she thinks about her uneasiness around Nelson, Cass wonders if there's something odd about her. Sometimes she feels like a real misfit at this school. She comes from a working-class family in a small rural town in the South, and almost everyone here is middle- or upper-class. And white. Cass is African-American on a predominantly white campus. Do her communication problems with Nelson and others on this campus stem from differences in race and class?

Like most of us, Cass is involved in communication continually. We talk with ourselves to organize our time and prod ourselves to do what we should (like pay attention in chemistry class), interact with friends and romantic partners, tune into mass communication, work in groups, and present our ideas to others. Communication is fundamental to our everyday lives.

Because you've been communicating all your life, you might wonder why it's necessary to study communication formally. One answer is that the better we understand something, the more effective we can be. For example, some individuals have a natural aptitude for singing or playing basketball. Their innate talent allows them to sing or play basketball fairly well. They become even more effective, however, if they take formal voice training or study theories of offensive and defensive play. Likewise, even if you already communicate well, learning about communication will make you still more effective in your everyday communication.

Another reason to study communication theories is that they help us make sense of interaction. You may think you don't want to learn any theory, because it is boring and removed from real life. Before you decide this, however, consider how helpful theories can be. For instance, Cass is confused by her contradictory feelings about her boyfriend, Jason. Sometimes she loves being with him, yet at other times she wants her own space. Relational dialectics, a theory we'll discuss in Chapter 8, explains that it is normal for Cass to feel what she does. All of us have needs for intimacy, or closeness, on the one hand and for autonomy, or independence, on the other hand. Understanding and managing the tension between these conflicting needs are constant challenges in personal relationships.

Cass might also figure out why she becomes quiet around people like Nelson, if she learns about muted group theory (Chapter 12), which explains that dominant social groups tend to silence members of nondominant groups. Theories of symbols and meaning, such as Burke's dramatism and Fisher's narrative theory (Chapter 5), could help Cass design a persuasive presentation for the residence hall association. Theories about speech communities and standpoint theory, which we'll explore in Chapter 10, could shed light on the reasons Cass sometimes feels out of place with people of different races and socioeconomic classes. And cultivation theory, which you'll study in Chapter 11, would inform Cass of ways in which violence on television persuades many people to believe the world is more violent than it is. Cass can maximize her effectiveness in each communication activity in her day by gaining theoretical insight into different kinds of communication.

*How do you think race
and class affect your
communication?*

Because communication is basic and important, we need to understand how it works and how it affects personal, interpersonal, professional, and cultural life. *Communication Theories in Action* will help you gain this understanding by increasing your insight into how communication works, or doesn't work, in a wide range of contexts. In Part I, we will lay the foundation for thinking about communication theories. This chapter and the following two introduce you to the field of communication and the processes of building, testing, and evaluating theories.

In Part II we'll look at a variety of communication theories that provide perspectives on meaning, language, performance, interaction in relationships, communication dynamics, mass communication, and the reciprocal influence of communication and culture. Studying these theories will enhance your understanding of human communication and your ability to communicate effectively in your daily life.

The goal of this opening chapter is to give you a broad understanding of the field of communication. To do so, we'll pursue five questions: What is communication? What are the values of communication? What is included in the field? What are the foci of scholarship and teaching in communication? What careers are open to individuals with strong backgrounds in communication?

A Definition of Communication

So far we've been using the word *communication* as if it meant the same thing to everyone. That's probably not very wise, as there are many different definitions of communication. In 1970, Frank Dance, a communication theorist, counted over 100 definitions of communication proposed by experts in the field. In the two and a half decades since then, even more definitions have emerged. So that we have a shared understanding of its meaning, however, let's choose one definition. Because our goal is to study a range of theories, the definition we use should be broad enough to include diverse perspectives on communication and ways of studying it. A narrow definition might exclude communication in some contexts and communication that serves particular purposes. To maximize the scope of theories we can consider, then, we will define **communication*** as "a systemic process in which individuals interact with and through symbols to create and interpret meanings."

---

* Boldfaced terms are in the glossary at the end of the book.

The first important idea in this definition is that communication is a **process**, which means it is ongoing and always in motion. It's hard to tell when communication starts and stops, because what happened long before we talk with someone may influence our interaction, and what occurs in a particular encounter may have repercussions in the future. The fact that communication is a process means it is always in motion, moving ever forward, and changing continuously. We cannot freeze communication at any one moment.

Communication is also **systemic**, which means that it involves a group of interrelated parts that affect one another. In family communication, for instance, each member of the family is part of the system. In addition, the physical environment and the time of day are elements of the system. People interact differently sitting in a formal living room and sunning on a beach, and we may be more alert at certain times of day than at others. Communication is also affected by the history of a system. If the family in our example has a history of working out problems constructively, then a son is unlikely to evoke defensiveness by saying, "There's something we need to talk about." On the other hand, if the family has a record of nasty conflicts and bickering, then the same comment might arouse a high level of defensiveness.

The third key idea in our definition is the use of **symbols**, which are abstract, arbitrary, and ambiguous representations of other things. Symbols include all of language and many nonverbal behaviors as well as art and music. Anything that abstractly signifies something else can be a symbol. We might symbolize love by giving someone a ring, saying "I love you," or taking the person out for a special dinner. Later in this chapter, we have more to say about symbols. For now, just realize that human communication depends on symbols.

Finally, our definition focuses on **meaning**, which is the heart of communication. As we will see in this and later chapters, meaning is not intrinsic to experience. Instead, we create it, typically in the process of communication. We talk with others to clarify our own thoughts; we decide how to interpret nonverbal behaviors; we label feelings and hopes to give them reality. In all these ways, we actively construct meaning by working with symbols.

The Values of Communication

We spend more time communicating than doing anything else. We talk, listen, have dialogues with ourselves, watch television and listen to radio, participate in group discussions, browse the World Wide Web, interview or are interviewed, send electronic messages, and so forth. From birth to death, we communicate to meet personal, professional, relationship, and social goals.

Personal Impact

George Herbert Mead (1934), whose theory we'll encounter in Chapter 5, said that humans are talked into humanity. He meant that we gain personal identity through communicating with others. In our earliest years our parents told us who we were: "You're so strong," "You're so cute," "You're such a funny one." Mead theorized that we first see ourselves through the eyes of others, so their messages are extremely important in forming the foundations of self-concept.

Later in life we interact with peers and teachers, who communicate how they see us, and we filter their impressions into our own self-image. Interactions with friends and romantic partners provide additional insight into how others see us and thus how we come to see ourselves. Mass communication, including radio, television, and films, also influences our understanding of ourselves and the world.

The profound connection between identity and communication is dramatically evident in children who are deprived of human contact. Case studies of children who were isolated from others for a prolonged period reveal that they seem to have little sense of themselves as humans, and their mental and psychological development is severely hindered by lack of language. One of the most extraordinary cases was Ghadya Ka Bacha, or "the wolf boy." In 1954, outside a hospital in Balrampur, India, a young boy was found. He had calloused knees and hands, as if he moved on all fours, and he had scars on his neck, suggesting he had been dragged about by animals. Without interaction with others, children cannot learn what it means to be human and cannot develop their identity as humans. Ramu, which was the name the hospital staff gave the child, showed no interest in people but became very excited when he visited a zoo and saw wolves. Ramu lapped his milk from a glass instead of drinking as we do, and he tore apart his meat. Some of the doctors who examined Ramu concluded he was a "wolf boy" who had grown up with wolves and who himself acted like a wolf, not a person (Shattuck, 1980). Others thought Ramu had not been raised by wolves but clearly had been deprived of interaction with other humans.

Reflection

Was Ramu human? What does your answer imply about your definition of human nature?

Communication with others not only affects our sense of identity but also directly influences our physical well-being. People who lack close friends have greater levels of anxiety and depression than people who are close to others (Hojat, 1982; Jones & Moore, 1989). Heart disease is also more common among people who lack strong interpersonal relationships (Ruberman, 1992). Steve Duck (1992), a scholar of interpersonal communication, reports that people in disturbed relationships tend to have lower self-esteem and more headaches, alcoholism, cancer, sleep disorders, and other physical problems. Medical researchers at my university recently reported that arthritis patients who have good relationships with friends and loved ones have less severe symptoms and live longer (Whan, 1997). Again and again research confirms the link between good relationships and physical and mental health (Bolger & Eckenrode, 1991; Bolger & Kelleher, 1993) and, conversely, that social isolation and lack of intimates are correlated with increased problems in physical and psychological well-being (Cohen, 1988; House, Umberson, & Landis, 1988).

Relationship Impact

Communication also critically affects our relationships. We build connections with others by revealing our private identities, remembering shared history, planning a future, and working out problems and tensions. Marriage counselors have long emphasized the importance of communication for healthy, enduring relationships (Beck, 1988; Gottman & Carrère, 1994; Scarf, 1987). They point out that troubles and problems are not the primary reason some marriages fail, as those are common to all relationships. A primary distinction between relationships that endure and those that collapse is effective communication. Couples who have worked to understand each other and who talk through problems have the potential to adjust and refine their relationships so that they remain healthy over time. Good communication in intimate relationships involves listening skillfully, expressing your own ideas clearly, and responding with empathy and understanding.

But communication is more than a way to solve problems or make personal disclosures. Steve Duck (1994b, p. 52), who studies personal relationships, says that "talk is the essence of relational maintenance." The mundane, routine talk between friends and romantic partners continuously weaves their lives together. More than the big moments, such as making the first statements of love or surmounting a major crisis, it is the unremarkable, everyday interaction between partners that sustains the "conversation of marriage" (Berger & Kellner, 1964). Through small talk, gossip about mutual acquaintances, nonverbal exchanges, and discussions of clothes and other mundane topics, partners embody their relationship. The importance of communication to relationships was emphasized in a recent national poll. Regardless of sex, age, ethnicity, or income level, Americans said that communication problems are the number one cause of divorce. You can review results of this poll at the Web site for the National Communication Association (http://www.natcom.org). The importance of ongoing communication to healthy relationships explains why couples involved in long-distance romances say the biggest problems are missing the nonverbal communication that occurs in face-to-face interaction and not being able to share small talk (Gerstel & Gross, 1985).

Professional Impact

Communication skills affect professional success. The importance of communication is obvious in professions such as teaching, business, law, broadcasting, sales, and counseling, in which talking and listening are central. Many attorneys, counselors, businesspeople, and teachers major or minor in communication before pursuing specialized graduate training. What they learn about presenting ideas and responding to others allows them to be persuasive, effective professionals.

In other fields, the importance of communication is less obvious but nonetheless present. Even highly technical work, such as computer programming, accounting, and systems design, requires a variety of communication skills. Specialists must be able to get along with others and explain their ideas, particularly technical ones, to people who lack their specialized knowledge. An IBM manager stated that, when he considers applicants for positions as computer programmers, he looks for those who get along well with people and express themselves effectively. The manager went on to point out that applicants who lack skills in computer programming can learn them on the job, but no company is prepared to teach employees how to deal with people and communicate effectively (McBath & Burhans, 1975).

Success in most professions requires communication skills. Members of work teams must learn to coordinate meanings so that they share understandings, an issue of primary concern in rules theory (Chapter 7). In addition, they must understand the rituals and specialized language that define their group, a topic considered by organizational culture theory (Chapter 10). Individuals in caregiving professions must be able to empathize and respond in ways that provide comfort. This topic has been explored in depth by research relying on constructivist theory (Chapter 7). Careers involving organizing—from the grassroots level to national political campaigning—require an understanding of power relationships in society and ways that existing power hierarchies can be challenged. This is a focus of cultural studies theories, which we consider in Chapter 12. It's virtually impossible to think of a career that doesn't involve communication and can't be more successfully pursued by studying relevant communication theories.

Cultural Impact

Communication skills are also important for the health of our society. To be effective, citizens in a democracy must be able to express ideas and to evaluate the ideas of others. A routine event in presidential elections is one or more debates between candidates. To make informed judgments, viewers need to listen critically to candidates' arguments and to their responses to criticism and questions. We will also be more enlightened citizens if we're familiar with communication theories that explain how media shape our perceptions of events, people, and issues. We'll consider two theories of mass communication in Chapter 11.

Good communication skills are also the essence of social life. As our culture becomes increasingly pluralistic, we must all learn to interact with people who differ from us and to learn from them in the process. This means we need to understand the different verbal and nonverbal communication styles of distinct social communities. In Chapter 10 we'll consider speech community theory, which sheds light on the different ways women and men and people of different ethnic backgrounds learn to communicate. We should also be critical of media representations of social groups, because sometimes these representations are stereotypic and distorted. Our study of cultivation theory in Chapter 11 will sharpen your awareness of how media shape perceptions.

The performance theories that we'll discuss in Chapter 6 will enhance your ability to appreciate the ways in which individuals and social groups enact identities and, in so doing, reiterate or challenge conventional views of who they are and where they fit in the culture. Both civic and social life depend on our ability to listen thoughtfully to a range of perspectives and to communicate in a variety of ways.

Communication, then, is important for personal, relationship, professional, and cultural reasons. Because communication is a cornerstone of human life, your choice to study it will serve you well.

The Breadth of the Communication Field

More than 2,000 years ago, when the study and teaching of communication began, the field focused almost exclusively on public communication. Both Aristotle (384–322 B.C.) and his teacher, Plato (approximately 427–347 B.C.), viewed communication as a practical art—one that aimed to have an impact, to do something. Aristotle's pragmatic concern was teaching citizens persuasive skills so that they could participate in the Athenian democracy. Plato had a broader view of communication, regarding it as linked to human nature and our philosophical ways of approaching life. Plato insisted that a solid theory of communication must attend not only to speakers but also to listeners and the means of affecting their perceptions, values, and actions. Other ancient theorists, such as Quintilian (approximately A.D. 35–95), were primarily educators who synthesized centuries of thinking about human communication.

The modern field of communication reflects the work of ancient theorists and also extends it. In 1914 the National Association of Teachers of Public Speaking was formed to promote public speaking education as a profession. In the years since, that organization has changed in response to the ever-widening scope of the communication field. Its name has also changed to reflect changes in focus. It became the Speech Association of America, the Speech Communication Association, and, most recently, the National Communication Association, which is its name today. You can find out more about this organization and the resources it offers to students interested in communication by going to its Web site: http://www.natcom.org. The modern field of communication includes eight major areas.

Intrapersonal Communication

Intrapersonal communication is communication with ourselves, or self-talk. You might be wondering whether the term *intrapersonal communication* is just jargon for *thinking*. In one sense, intrapersonal communication does involve thinking, as it is a cognitive process that goes on inside of us. Yet because the process relies on language, it is also a kind of communication. Intrapersonal communication involves dialogues we have with ourselves—those conversations that continually go on in our heads. This area of the field is reflected in many books, most recently one by Donna Vocate (1994), that focus exclusively on intrapersonal communication.

One school of counseling focuses on enhancing self-esteem by changing how we talk to ourselves about negative feelings (Ellis & Harper, 1977; Rusk & Rusk, 1988; Seligman, 1990). For instance, you might say to yourself, "I blew that test, so I'm really stupid. I'll never graduate and, if I do, nobody will hire a klutz like me." This kind of talk lowers self-esteem by convincing you that a single event (blowing one test) proves you are totally worthless. Therapists who believe that what we say to ourselves affects our feelings would encourage us to challenge negative self-talk by saying, "Hey, wait a minute. One test is not a measure of my intelligence. I did well on the first test in this course and have a good overall record at the college. I shouldn't be so hard on myself." What we say to ourselves can enhance or diminish self-esteem.

TRY IT OUT For the next day, pay attention to the way you talk to yourself. When something goes wrong, what do you say to yourself? Do you put yourself down with negative messages, blaming yourself for what happened? Do you generalize beyond the specific event to describe yourself as a loser or as inadequate?

The first step in changing negative self-talk is to become aware of it. The second step is to challenge it when it occurs.

We engage in self-talk to sort out feelings and ideas, plan our lives, rehearse different ways of acting, and prompt ourselves to do or not do particular things. For example, Cass used self-talk to motivate herself to listen more attentively in her chemistry class. Intrapersonal communication is how we remind ourselves to eat in healthy ways ("No saturated fats!"), show respect to others ("I can't let my boss see that I'm peeved at her."), and check impulses that might be destructive ("I'll wait until I've cooled off before I say anything.").

Intrapersonal communication also helps us rehearse alternative scenarios to see how each might turn out. Cass might consider telling Nelson to shut up, suggesting the group adopt a rule that everyone should participate equally, or taking Nelson out for coffee and privately asking him to be less domineering. She'll think through the various ways to approach Nelson, weigh the likely consequences of each, and then choose one to put into practice. We engage in internal dialogues continually as we sort through ideas and test alternative courses of action.

Interpersonal Communication

A second major emphasis in the field of communication is **interpersonal communication**, which deals with communication between people. In one sense, all communication is between people, so all communication is interpersonal. Such a broad definition, however, doesn't create any useful boundaries for the area of study.

There is growing consensus that interpersonal communication is not a single thing but rather exists on a continuum from highly impersonal to highly interpersonal (Wood, 2000). The more personally we interact with another as a distinct individual (versus communicating in a general social role), the more interpersonal the communication is. Using this criterion, we would say that a deep conversation with a friend is more interpersonal than a casual exchange with a sales clerk.

Since the late 1960s, interest in interpersonal communication has mushroomed, making it one of the most vibrant branches of the field. Scholars focus on how communication creates and sustains relationships (Duck, 1994a,b; Spencer, 1994), how partners communicate to deal with the normal and extraordinary challenges of maintaining intimacy over time (Canary & Stafford, 1994; Duck & Wood, 1995; Wood & Duck, 1995a,b), and how media shape our expectations of and communication in relationships.

Interpersonal communication researchers also study how communication is influenced by gender (Vavrus, 2002; Wood, 1986, 1993c,d, 1994a,b, 1996a, 1998b,c, 2003; Wood & Inman, 1993), ethnicity (Gaines,

1995; Houston & Wood, 1996), and sexual orientation (Huston & Schwartz, 1996; Wood, 1994c).

Group and Team Communication

A third important area of the field is communication in small groups and teams. Small group communication involves a range of topics such as leadership, member roles, group structure, task agenda, and conflict. Several of the theories we'll consider in this book shed light on how communication affects groups and teams.

Scholars such as Dennis Gouran (1990) and Randy Hirokawa and Scott Poole (1996) study how communication both fosters and interferes with effective group decision making. Other scholars (Bormann, 1975; Bormann, Putnam, & Pratt, 1978) focus on how group cohesion and identity often crystallize through **fantasy themes**, which are chains of ideas that spin out in a group and capture its social and task themes. For example, the talk of many politicians suggests that they view their parties as warring opponents. When politicians speak of "attacking" the other side's plan, "defending" their agenda, and "refusing to give ground," they create a fantasy chain that defines the parties as warring factions. Fantasy themes frame how group members think about what they are doing and how they define success. A compromise is unlikely if parties define themselves as at war, where only one side wins.

Public Communication

Although public speaking no longer defines the scope of the field, it remains an important branch of communication theory, research, and practice. Even though most of us may not seek careers that involve frequent formal speaking, all of us will have opportunities to speak to others. My editor speaks to her sales representatives to spotlight important features of new books. I recently coached my doctor, who was asked to address her colleagues on an important development in the treatment of renal disease. My sister relies on public speaking skills when she's trying cases in court and when she's persuading companies to support the battered women's center in her town. My plumber talks with his staff about new developments in plumbing and new regulations that affect what they do. He once told me that the main reason his business has grown while others have gone under is that he takes time to keep his staff informed. My editor, doctor, sister, and plumber don't consider themselves public speakers, but public speaking is a part of their lives, and doing it effectively is important to their success.

Scholars of public communication focus on the related subjects of critical evaluation of speeches and principles for speaking effectively. Rhetorical critics study important communication events such as the Reverend Martin Luther King, Jr.'s "I Have a Dream" speech and public arguments for and against reproductive freedom. Critics often take a role in civic life by evaluating political debates and speeches to help voters understand how well candidates support their positions and respond to challenges from opponents.

Scholars of public communication are also interested in discovering and teaching principles of effective public speaking. By now we have learned a great deal about what makes speakers seem credible to listeners and how credibility affects persuasion. Research has also enlightened us about the kinds of argument, methods of organizing ideas, and forms of proof that listeners find effective. If Cass had studied this body of research, she would have gleaned useful guidelines for preparing her remarks for the residence hall association.

Performance

Both historically and today, performance occupies an important place in the field of communication. For well over two thousand years both scholars and laypeople have appreciated the ways in which performance can move us to tears, laughter, and new knowledge. In the field of drama, performance operates under the authority of the playwright, whose vision actors and directors are supposed to embody. In performance studies, however, the textual authority of a script is not as binding on actors and directors. Performance studies often remove the aesthetic distance that theater demands, inviting actors, directors, and audiences to interact with each other and a text to open myriad possible meanings (Diamond, 1996, p. 2).

Performance studies scholars are also increasingly interested in phenomena other than remarkable events and people and closed narratives, which are associated with drama. Linking their work to critical engagement with cultural life, many performance studies scholars today study how individuals and groups perform identities in everyday life and how they use rituals and other communicative practices to reflect, sustain, and sometimes alter social relations. This focus leads a number of performance studies scholars to view performance as political action, which has the potential to critique and change oppressive practices in cultural life.

Media and New Technologies of Communication

One of the most exciting areas of the modern field of communication is media and new technologies. For some time, communication scholars have studied mediated communication such as films, radio, and television. From substantial research we understand a great deal about how different media work and how they represent—or misrepresent—particular cultural values.

Media reinforce cultural stereotypes about race and ethnicity. For example, African Americans are most often cast in supporting roles rather than principal roles. In addition, black males are frequently portrayed as lazy and unlawful and are typically cast as athletes or entertainers (Evans, 1993; "Sights, Sounds, and Stereotypes," 1992). Robert Entman (1994), a communication professor at Northwestern University, points out that major networks are more likely to show black defendants in mug shots without names but to offer names and multiple pictures of white defendants. This difference may contribute to perceptions of blacks as an undifferentiated group. Hispanics and Asians seldom appear in prime time; when they do, it is usually as villains or criminals (Lichter, Lichter, Rothman, & Amundson, 1987).

Reflection

Do media have a responsibility not to foster stereotypes of social groups?

To the extent that media shape our understandings of ourselves and our society, misrepresentations can be dangerous. Communication scholars who study media heighten our awareness of how media inform and entertain us as well as how they sometimes distort reality. In Chapters 11 and 12 we'll explore theories that describe and criticize the ways in which mass communication functions and affects us.

A more recent focus in the area of media is new and converging technologies of communication. We are in the midst of a technological revolution that provides us with the means to communicate in more and more ways, faster and faster, with greater and greater numbers of people throughout the world. How do new technologies and the accelerated pace of interaction influence how we think, work, and form relationships? Some scholars caution that new technologies might undermine the kind of human community formed through face-to-face talk (Hyde, 1995; Potter, 2001; Urgo, 2000), whereas others celebrate the increased social contact, productivity, and modes of thinking and interacting that technology allows (Chesebro, 1995a).

Reflection

To what extent do new technologies affect the content, as well as the form, of communication?

The verdict on media's effects is not in and will not be for some time. Meanwhile all of us struggle to keep up with our increasingly technological world. Overnight mail services, fax machines, and electronic mail make it possible for us to communicate almost immediately with people on the other side of the world. Whereas previous generations of students had to physically go to libraries to conduct research, today's students often rely on the Internet and the World Wide Web to find and read reference works.

From the *Wall Street Journal*—Permission, Cartoon Feature Syndicate

Communication scholars will continue to study whether emerging technologies merely alter how we communicate or actually change how we think about interaction and the human connections we build.

Organizational Communication

Communication in organizations is another growing area of interest in the field of communication. As we saw earlier in this chapter, communication skills facilitate advancement in most careers. Communication scholars have identified verbal and nonverbal communication skills that enhance professional success; they have traced the impact of various kinds of communication on morale, productivity, and commitment in organizations.

In addition to continuing to study these topics, organizational scholars have begun to focus substantial attention on organizational culture and personal relationships in professional settings. The term **organizational culture** refers to understandings about identity and codes of thought and action that are shared by members of an organization (Conrad & Poole, 2002). For instance, some organizations think of themselves as families. This understanding of who they are is reflected in rules for interacting with each other and working together.

Studies of organizational culture also shed light on the continuing problem of sexual harassment. Many institutions have a culture that normalizes sexist comments and treatment of women as sex objects. Mary

Strine (1992), a critical scholar in communication, has shown how some institutions trivialize complaints about sexual harassment and sustain abusive environments by adopting a culture that says, "This is how we do things around here." Other communication scholars have identified ways organizational cultures allow or discourage sexual harassment (Bingham, 1994; Conrad, 1995; Taylor & Conrad, 1992).

Another area of increasing interest for organizational scholars is personal relationships among coworkers (Zorn, 1995). As we expand the hours we spend on the job, it is natural for personal relationships among coworkers to increase. Further, because the majority of women work full- or part-time outside the home today, romantic and sexual relationships have increased opportunity to unfold. Obviously this adds both interest and complications to life in organizations.

Because women and men increasingly interact in the workplace, they need to understand each other's language. In a number of ways women and men tend to communicate differently, and so they may misunderstand each other. For example, women tend to make more "listening noises," such as "um," "uh huh," and "go on," than men do. If men don't make such noises when listening to women colleagues, the women may think the men aren't paying attention. Conversely men are likely to misinterpret the listening noises women make as signals of agreement rather than indicators of interest. Some scholars of organizational communication study and conduct workshops on effective communication between the sexes (Murphy & Zorn, 1996).

TRY IT OUT Interview a professional in the field you plan to enter, and find out what communication perspectives and skills she or he thinks are most important for success. Which of the perspectives and skills do you already have? Which ones should you learn more about? How can you use this book and the accompanying course to develop the understandings of communication that will help you be effective in your career?

Intercultural Communication

Finally **intercultural communication** is an important focus of research, teaching, and training. Intercultural communication refers to communication between people from different cultures, including distinct cultures within a single country. Although intercultural communication is not a new area of study, its importance has grown in recent years. Demographic shifts in the last decade have enlarged the diversity that has always marked life in the United States. Increasing numbers of

Asians, Indians, Latinas and Latinos, and people from other nations are immigrating to the United States and making their homes here. With them they bring cultural values and styles of communicating that differ from those of citizens whose heritage is European-American. Understanding different modes of verbal and nonverbal communication can help us learn how to live, socialize, and work effectively with an ever-increasing range of people (Wood, 1998b).

Scholars of intercultural communication increase awareness of different groups' communication goals, styles, and meanings. For example, a Taiwanese woman in one of my graduate classes seldom spoke up and wouldn't enter the heated debates that characterize good graduate classes. One day after class I encouraged Mei-Ling to argue for her ideas when others challenged them. She replied that she could not be so impolite. In her culture, unlike in the West, it is disrespectful to argue with others or to assert oneself. I would have been mistaken had I interpreted her deference as lack of confidence or involvement in the class.

A particularly important recent trend in the area of intercultural communication is research on different communication cultures within a single society. Cultural differences are easy to perceive, for example, in communication between a Nepali and a Canadian. Less obvious are cultural differences between people who speak the "same" language. Within the United States there are distinct communication cultures based on race, gender, affectional preference, and ethnicity.

Two of the leading writers about intercultural communication are Larry Samovar and Richard Porter (1994). Their book, *Intercultural Communication*, reveals distinctive styles of communication for women, men, blacks, whites, Native Americans, gays, individuals with disabilities, and other groups in our country. For example, women, more than men, tend to disclose personal information and to engage in emotionally expressive talk in their friendships (Wood, 1993c, 1994a,d, 1998b,c, 2003). African Americans belong to a communication culture that encourages dramatic talk, rapping, verbal duels, and signifying (indirect comments), which have no equivalents in Caucasian speech communities (Houston & Wood, 1996). Recognizing and respecting different communication cultures increases effectiveness in a pluralistic society.

Reflection

If communication differs in different cultures, can we have universal criteria for effectiveness in communication?

After reading about the major branches of the modern field of communication, you might think that the field consists of unrelated areas of interest. Actually this isn't at all the case. The overall field of communication is unified by a persisting interest in language, in nonverbal behavior, and in the ways we construct meaning for ourselves and our activities.

Communication as a Field of Study

Seemingly disparate areas such as intrapersonal, organizational, and relational communication are unified by central concerns with symbolic activities and meaning. These two themes underlie research and teaching in different branches of the communication field.

Symbolic Activities

Symbols are the basis of language, thinking, and much nonverbal behavior. You may recall that we defined symbols as arbitrary, ambiguous, and abstract representations of other phenomena. For instance, a wedding band is a symbol of marriage, the name *Julia* is a symbol for me, a smile is a symbol of friendliness, and the word *cat* is a symbol for one species of animal.

Symbols represent, or stand for, other things, but they are not the things for which they stand. Symbols are like a map, which represents a territory but isn't itself the territory. Symbols are abstract, which means they aren't concrete or tangible. On a map the term *Iowa* is not the concrete state but an abstract representation of that state. Symbols are also arbitrary, which means they have no intrinsic, or natural, relation to what they represent. There's no natural reason to call one of our states Iowa; we could just as easily call it Whitby. Similarly, there's no necessary connection between your name and who you are, and no intrinsic reason why shaking hands is a greeting in the United States and kissing cheeks is a greeting in other countries. Symbols are arbitrary conventions that allow us to agree on what things mean. Finally, symbols are ambiguous, which means their meanings are less than clear-cut. For example, imagine asking a friend if a course in Third World film is tough. *Tough* might mean that the course is challenging, or that the tests are demanding, or that a major paper is required, or that the course is graded on a strict bell curve. What *tough* means is not transparent. We have to think about the word and assign meaning to it.

Symbols allow us to name experiences, which is a primary way we give meaning to our lives. It's hard to think about and understand things we cannot name. For instance, prior to the 1970s, there was no legal term for unwanted and unwelcome sexual attention in the workplace and educational institutions. A number of people, especially women, were subjected to sexist comments, demeaning suggestions, unwanted touching, and overt propositions for sexual activity. However, there was no serious term to name what was happening, so victims of unwelcome sexual attention tended to think, "He went too far," or "What have I done to invite this?" (Wood, 1992). When the term *sexual harassment* was coined, victims had a socially recognized label for their experiences, one that blamed the harasser.

Reflection

Can you think about something without relying on symbols?

Because we humans are symbol users, we are not confined to the concrete world of the here and now. Symbols make it possible to call up memories and to dream of the future. We cast ourselves into real and possible futures when we speak about "after I graduate," "next summer," and "when I win the lottery." We revisit former moments when we talk about "yesterday" and "when I was a child." Symbols enable us to live continuously in all three dimensions of time and to do so simultaneously so that past and future infuse the present (Dixson & Duck, 1993).

Symbols also allow us to reflect on ourselves and to monitor our activities. Many philosophers and academics claim that humans are the only species capable of self-reflection. We are able to think about who we are, to have a self-concept, and to view ourselves and our activities from the perspectives of others. Feelings such as shame and pride are possible because we can reflect on ourselves. Symbolic interactionism, a theory we'll consider in Chapter 5, concentrates on explaining the relationships between symbols and self-identity.

Monitoring is observing and managing our own thoughts, feelings, and actions. As you sit in class, your mind wanders, you realize the teacher could think you're not paying attention, and you refocus your eyes on her or him and nod in understanding. This is an example of monitoring. You looked at how you were acting and decided to adjust your behaviors to project the image you wanted—in this case, that of an attentive student. We monitor all the time: reminding ourselves not to interrupt, prodding ourselves to be more assertive, warning ourselves not to raise our voices, checking an impulse to criticize a friend, suppressing a look of disapproval or a snicker. We audit our communication continuously and adjust it to be more effective. Monitoring is possible because we think symbolically and point out our behaviors to ourselves, reflect on them, and direct ourselves to adjust them.

Finally, symbols allow us to share with others ideas and feelings they have not directly experienced. Words allow us to tell others about events and people in our lives and to express how we feel about them. A friend may not know your parents, but she or he can grasp your relationship with them if you explain what happens between you and your parents and how you feel. If we couldn't communicate, each of us would have no way to share our own private experiences with others.

Whether we are interested in intrapersonal, group, organizational, or intercultural communication, symbols are always central. Thus, symbols and the mental activities they allow are a unifying focus of study and teaching about all forms of communication. Symbolic interaction theory, dramatism, and semantics are theories we'll study that focus especially on symbols as an essential foundation of meaning.

Meaning

Closely related to the communication field's focus on symbols is its persisting concern with **meaning**. Meaning is significance that is conferred on experiences and phenomena. The human world is one of meaning. We don't simply exist, eat, drink, sleep, and go through motions. Instead we imbue every aspect of our lives with significance, or meaning. When I fill my cat Sadie's dish, she eats her food and then returns to her feline adventures. For her, eating is a necessary and enjoyable activity but not one that has meaning beyond consuming food.

For humans, however, food and the activity of eating are layered with significance. Food can symbolize special events or commitments. For example, kosher products reflect commitment to Jewish heritage; eating turkey with all the trimmings is a widely observed Thanksgiving ritual in the United States (though vegetarians have to generate alternative ways to symbolize the holiday); eggnog is a Christmas tradition; and mandel brot is a Hanukkah staple. Birthday cakes celebrate an individual, and we may fix special meals to express love for others. Unlike Sadie, for us the activity of eating takes on significance as a result of how we define what we are doing and what it means.

Because we are symbol users, we actively interpret events, situations, experiences, and relationships. Many communication theorists argue that we humans don't react passively or unthinkingly to our world but proactively construct its meanings. Symbols are the foundation of meaning because they enable us to name, evaluate, reflect upon, and share experiences, ideas, and feelings. Using symbols, we can construct organized systems (called *cognitive schemata*) for perceiving and making sense of our experiences. In the process of communicating with others, we define our relationships: Do we have a friendship, or something more? How serious are we? Is this conflict irresolvable, or can we work it out and stay together?

To study communication, then, is to study how we create meaning in our lives. Communication scholars see relationships, groups, cultures, media, and organizations as human constructions to which we create and assign meaning in the process of interaction (Andersen, 1993; Wood, 2000).

Leslie Baxter (1987, p. 262) says that "relationships can be regarded as webs of significance" spun as partners communicate. In Chapter 5 we'll look at three theories that focus specifically on communication and meaning, and we'll also see attention to meaning in many of the theories covered in other chapters.

Careers in Communication

Studying communication is good preparation for a wide array of careers. As we've seen, most professions require good communication skills. In addition there are a number of careers for people whose primary backgrounds and interests are in communication.

Research

Communication research is a vital and growing field of work. Much research is conducted by academics whose careers combine teaching and scholarship. In this book you'll learn how academic research is designed and conducted as well as the knowledge it generates.

Businesses also conduct research to determine how people respond to different kinds of advertisements, logos, and even labels for products. Before naming a new cereal or beer, companies extensively test market reaction to various names. Their bottom line depends on understanding how customers will interpret different communication strategies. In addition, businesses research the audiences reached by different media such as newspapers, magazines, radio, and television. Individuals who understand communication and who have research skills can pursue careers in communication research.

Public Relations and Advertising

Communication specialists are also in demand for careers in advertising and public relations. People who understand how communication works can use their knowledge to help companies develop effective strategies for media advertising. Expertise in communication also allows individuals to pursue careers in public relations, in which the "product" to be advertised is a particular company or corporation. In 1994, Intel's much-touted Pentium chip was revealed to have a defect. To control the damage, Intel ran full-page ads in major newspapers assuring customers that it would repair or exchange any Pentium-powered computer. Intel's corporate image was restored because an event that could have impugned the company's integrity was managed well. Public relations professionals help companies define their images and protect them when there are problems.

Education

I am biased toward education as a career because I've had a 28-year love affair with teaching communication. I find nothing more exciting than opening students' eyes to the power of communication. Across the nation, opportunities are growing for communication teachers at all levels. There are communication classes and often whole curricula in secondary schools, junior colleges, colleges, universities, technical schools, and community colleges.

The level at which a person is qualified to teach depends on how extensively she or he has pursued the study of communication. Generally, a bachelor's degree in communication education and certification by the Board of Education are required of teachers in elementary and secondary schools. A master's degree in communication qualifies a person to teach at community colleges, technical schools, and some junior colleges and colleges. The Ph.D., or doctoral degree, in communication is usually required for a career in university education, although some universities offer short-term positions to individuals with master's degrees.

Although generalists are typically preferred for many teaching jobs, at the university level individuals can focus on areas of communication that particularly interest them. For instance, my research and teaching focus on gender and communication and on communication in personal relationships. My partner, who is also on the faculty in my department, focuses his work on environmental advocacy and social movements. Other faculty members concentrate on areas such as oral traditions, intercultural communication, family communication, organizational dynamics, performance of literature, and symbolic development in children.

Not all communication educators make their homes in academic departments of communication. In recent years, more and more individuals with advanced degrees in communication have taken positions in medical schools and business schools. Good doctors have not only specialized medical knowledge but also good communication skills. They know how to listen sensitively to patients, explain complex problems and procedures, and provide comfort, reassurance, and motivation. Similarly, good businesspeople not only know their business but also know how to explain it to others and how to present themselves and their company or product favorably. Increasing numbers of medical and business schools are creating permanent positions for communication specialists (Mangan, 2002).

Consulting

Consulting is another field that increasingly welcomes individuals with backgrounds in communication. Businesses need to train employees in effective group communications, interview techniques, and interpersonal interaction. Some large corporations, such as IBM, have entire departments devoted to training and development. Individuals with communication backgrounds often join these departments and work with the corporation to design and teach courses or workshops that enhance employees' communication skills.

In addition, communication specialists may join or form freelance consulting firms that provide communication education to a variety of organizations. One of my colleagues consults with corporations across the country, training men and women in how to understand each other's language and work together effectively. Another colleague consults with organizations to help them develop work teams that interact effectively. Other communication specialists work with politicians to improve their presentational style and sometimes to write their speeches.

I consult with attorneys on cases of sexual harassment and sex discrimination. I help attorneys understand how particular communication patterns and actions create hostile, harassing environments, and I collaborate with them to develop trial strategy. In addition, I sometimes testify as an expert witness on whether sexual harassment or sex discrimination has occurred. Other communication specialists work with attorneys to make jury selections and to advise about dress and nonverbal behaviors that might affect jurors' perceptions.

Human Relations and Management

Because communication is the foundation of human relations, it's no surprise that many communication specialists build careers in human development or human relations departments of corporations. Individuals with solid knowledge of communication and good communication skills are effective in careers such as personnel, grievance management, customer relations, and development and fund raising.

Communication degrees also open the door to careers in management. The most important qualifications for successful managers are not technical skills but communication skills (Goleman, McKee, & Boyatzis, 2002). Good managers know how to listen, express their ideas, manage conflict constructively, create supportive work environments, build teams, and balance task and interpersonal concerns in workplace relationships. These are all communication skills, so specializing in this field provides a firm foundation for a career in management.

Summary

In this chapter we've taken a first look at the field of human communication. We've seen that theories can help us understand how communication works and how we can be effective in our own communicative endeavors. We've also explored the personal, relationship, professional, and cultural values of communication. Third, we've surveyed the breadth of the communication field, noting that it ranges from intrapersonal to public and from organizational to intercultural.

What holds these seemingly diverse areas of study together is abiding interest in symbolic activities and meanings, which together form the foundation of personal, interpersonal, professional, and social life. Finally, we've considered some of the many career opportunities open to individuals who choose to specialize in communication. The modern field of communication is growing, and it offers an array of exciting career paths.

Key Terms

communication

fantasy theme

intercultural communication

interpersonal communication

intrapersonal communication

meaning

monitoring

organizational culture

process

symbol

systemic

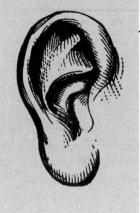

CHAPTER TWO

Understanding Communication Theories

Recently I visited my sister, Carolyn, and her family. One morning my nephew Harrison, who was then three years old, said I could have a sip of his juice if I would play Ghostbusters with him.

———

A few years ago my partner, Robbie, served as president of the national Sierra Club. His responsibilities required him to travel much of the time, so we were separated more than we had been since marrying. In the past we had tended to work on our individual projects on weekends, but during his presidency we usually spent time together any weekend he was home.

———

In 1993 I served as an expert witness in a sexual harassment trial. The facts of the case were ambiguous: There had definitely been some sexist treatment of a woman hired to lead an organization, but whether that explained her dismissal was unclear. Jennifer, the attorney with whom I consulted, wove all of the evidence and known facts into a coherent story that painted her client as the victim of a systematic campaign of sexual harassment. Opposing counsel offered other explanations of individual pieces of evidence, but he didn't create an overall story that convincingly offered a counterexplanation. We won the case. Later Jennifer told me that she always prepared her closing statements in the form of a story. She said, "You have to give jurors an account that makes sense and holds together; whichever attorney creates the better story is going to win."

———

Each of these situations involves communication theory. Each situation also shows that people act on theories, often without realizing it, in their everyday lives. Harrison's strategy for getting me to play with him reflects social exchange theory, which claims that people like equal rewards in relationships. Although he didn't realize he was using a theory, Harrison nevertheless applied the principles of exchange when he reasoned that giving me a sip of orange juice might induce me to help him chase down ghosts (it did).

The changes in my relationship with Robbie can be explained by dialectical theory, which asserts that people have needs both for connection, or closeness, and for distance, or autonomy. As long as Robbie and I lived together most of the time, our connection needs were satisfied by our normal daily interaction. Once his work took him away from our home, however, our needs for connecting were unsatisfied, and we had to generate other ways to be together.

The attorney with whom I consulted relied on narrative theory, which maintains that human beings have a natural capacity to tell and listen to stories. In other words, we think in terms of characters, settings, plots, and motives. Although Jennifer had not formally studied narrative theory, she had learned from experience that jurors were best persuaded by a good story that provided a coherent explanation for the evidence and what happened in a case.

Jennifer, Harrison, Robbie, and I use communication theories in our daily lives. You also use communication theories, whether or not you realize it. All of us are everyday theorists. This means that, in taking a course in theories, you are not studying something that is removed from your normal life. The formal study of theory allows you to be more careful and effective in your own theorizing. As we'll see in this and later chapters, theories are directly relevant to practical life. Theories guide how we act, respond to others, and make sense of our experiences. In this chapter we'll explore the nature of theorizing. We'll ask what theories do, why they matter, and how we can use them in our lives. In addition we'll consider how to evaluate the worth of theories. By the time you have completed this chapter, you should have a basic understanding of what theories are, what they do, and how to judge them. This will provide you with a firm foundation for reading Chapters 4 through 13, in which we consider specific communication theories.

The Goals of Theory

The simplest way to define *theories* is to say that they are attempts to make sense of things. A **theory** offers an account of what something is, how it works, what it produces or causes to happen, and what can change how it operates. Put another way, theories are human constructions—symbolic ways we represent phenomena. The fact that theories are human constructions implies that they are neither objective descriptions of reality nor necessarily true. Instead, theories represent points of view. As we'll see, however, not all points of view are equally sound. We'll discuss ways to evaluate the quality of various theoretical points of view.

Theories pursue one or more of four basic goals: description, explanation, prediction or understanding, and reform. We'll consider each of these objectives and see how it operates in the context of particular theories.

Description: What Is It?

The foundation of a theory is **description**, which is a process of using symbols to represent phenomena. Before we can figure out how something works, we must first describe it. Thus, the first task in building a theory is to identify features of some phenomenon and describe any variations in them. Descriptions, of course, are not neutral reflections of some objective reality. They are necessarily subjective because what a theorist perceives and emphasizes is affected by personal background, sensory skills, values, and so forth. Ecologists identify important features of environments and describe how they may vary. For example, a wetlands area includes marshes and the vegetation and animal life supported by the marshy environment. The marshes and the life they support vary in response to rainfall, erosion, and weather. Geneticists have identified 23 pairs of chromosomes as the basis of individual characteristics. Chromosomes vary in response to the chromosomal structure of parents and other factors.

Like environmental scientists and geneticists, communication theorists begin by identifying key features of communication and describing how those features may vary. For example, elsewhere (Wood, 2000) I have described personal relationships as made up of five features: individuals, social contexts, communication, relational culture (the private world of intimates), and time. Each feature in this model of relationships affects all others. Thus, when Robbie travels frequently and meets new people, communication between us changes. As Robbie's involvement with the Sierra Club accelerated, we placed greater emphasis on time together than we had when we were continuously together in the same place.

Reflection

What features would you include in a description of human communication?

In the 1940s Claude Shannon and Warren Weaver developed one of the earliest models of the communication process. At the time Shannon and Weaver were working on their theory, the United States was captivated by scientific ideas in general and by mechanical and technical explanations in particular. We would expect a theory developed in this historical context to emphasize information flow and accuracy. That is precisely what Shannon and Weaver's model of communication did.

Understanding Communication Theories

Figure 2.1

*The Shannon–Weaver Model
of Communication*

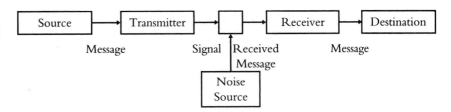

Claude Shannon was a research scientist who worked for Bell Labs, and Warren Weaver was a member of the Rockefeller Foundation and the Sloan-Kettering Institute for Cancer Research. With Shannon working out the mathematics behind the theory and Weaver in charge of translating it into understandable language, the two men developed a model that described what happens when people communicate. They described communication as the flow of information from one person's mind (a source) to the mind of another person (a destination).

The person who is a source creates a message and transmits it by voice or with the aid of a telephone or microphone or other transmitting equipment. The message is then received by an ear or a piece of receiving equipment, and it is interpreted by the person who is a destination. As messages move from source to destination, there is a potential of loss of information due to noise in the communication system. Noise could be static on phone lines, competing sounds such as television or stereo, or distractions such as smoke or odors in the environment of one or both communicators.

Since 1949, when Shannon and Weaver published their comprehensive statement on the information theory of communication, there have been many criticisms. One of the strongest indictments is that this model misrepresents communication by portraying it as a one-way process in which information flows in a linear sequence from a source to a receiver. The model also labels each communicator as either a sender or a receiver, instead of acknowledging that all communicators are both senders and receivers. When Sharon talks with Molefe, the latter smiles, frowns, wrinkles his brow, and nods. All of these nonverbal messages are communication. When Michelle bargains with me for my bracelet, she watches my nonverbal behaviors as she speaks, and I send her cues as I listen.

Reflection

*What do you perceive
as the strengths and
limitations of Shannon
and Weaver's
description of the
communication process?*

In 1967 Norbert Weiner, an MIT scientist, refined Shannon and Weaver's ideas by adding two new features to their model. First he emphasized feedback as an essential feature of effective communication. In Weiner's view, feedback was information about past performance that could be used to adjust future activity. For example, if I wrinkle my brow and shake my head when Robbie mentions a trip he's planning to make, that feedback will tell him I'm not pleased with his plan. Based on my feedback, he may adjust what he says next: Perhaps he'll suggest I join him for the trip, propose doing something together before he leaves, or explain why it is important for him to make this particular trip.

Weiner's second addition to the information model of communication was an emphasis on ethics. He was very concerned that technological systems of communication could be used to control and manipulate human beings, and he saw this as undesirable. In his book *The Human Use of Human Beings* (1967), Weiner cautioned that technical systems of communication should be used to control only things, not people.

A second criticism of the Shannon–Weaver model, one that hasn't been resolved by later research, is that a communication theory that focuses only on information overlooks important dimensions of human communication. Shannon and Weaver's theory doesn't describe or help us understand feelings, motives, needs, history, and other factors that affect how we communicate and how we interpret the communication of others. The fact that Shannon and Weaver's research was funded by Bell Labs may explain the mechanical focus of their theory. It's doubtful that the model offers a useful description of many kinds of communication, such as romantic interaction, team building, mass media, and conflict management.

The Shannon–Weaver model of communication is one of many ways to describe the features of communication. Other theories that we will encounter later provide alternative descriptions of what happens when people interact. For example, Leslie Baxter's theory of relational dialectics, which we'll discuss in Chapter 8, offers a far more dynamic and interactive view of communication than the Shannon–Weaver model does. Ethical aspects and uses of communication are of primary concern in critical theories, which are covered in Chapter 12. Although theorists offer different descriptions of communication, all theories begin with a description of the features of communication and how they vary.

Explanation

The second objective of theory is **explanation**, which is an effort to clarify how and why something works. After describing what makes up communication, a theorist asks how the parts interact and work together. An ecologist might explain how commercial development causes specific damage to wetlands environments. A geneticist might explain how certain drugs affect chromosomal structure in developing fetuses. And a communication theorist wants to explain why communication works as it does: Why does Harrison's strategy to get me to play Ghostbusters succeed or fail? Why and how does Robbie's travel affect communication between us? Why are juries persuaded by a good story?

Mary Lund (1985) wanted to explain what caused commitment between romantic partners. Previous research had focused on love as the basis of enduring relationships, and love was viewed as the result of receiving rewards in a relationship. Thus, the common belief was that we love and stay with people who reward us with positive experiences, support, and other things we value. Lund, however, thought that love might not be the real glue of romantic relationships. In a sophisticated study, Lund discovered that commitment, which she defined as the intention to continue in a relationship, was a better predictor of whether a relationship lasts than was love.

Lund also found that commitment is heightened by investments in a relationship, whereas simply receiving positive outcomes may not enhance commitment. To explain why relationships endure or fail to endure, Lund said that personal choices to invest time, energy, material resources, and feelings heighten commitment, and commitment in turn predicts relational continuity. Although love often accompanies commitment, it is not the basic glue of lasting intimacy.

Lund's theory offers a convincing explanation of why some relationships endure and others wither. In addition, Lund's work provides a good example of the practical value of theory. You can use her theory to analyze your own relationships: What have you invested? What has your partner invested? Have the two of you invested equally? Asking these questions is a way for you to apply one theory to your everyday life.

Reflection

How does Lund's theory add to your understanding of a current or past romantic relationship in your life?

Prediction, Control, and Understanding

A third objective of theories is to allow us to understand and/or predict and control what will happen. **Prediction** involves projecting what will happen to a phenomenon under specified conditions or exposure to particular stimuli. **Control** is the use of explanations and predictions to govern what a phenomenon actually does.

For some theorists, prediction and control are primary objectives. Scholars who adopt this position believe that a good theory is one that allows us to forecast what will happen under certain conditions and/or if certain other actions are taken. Prediction is related to control in that we can control outcomes if we can predict what causes them. An environmental scientist could construct a theory to predict what will happen in wetlands areas if commercial development takes place. Control would be exercised by allowing or precluding commercial development adjacent to wetlands areas. Similarly, geneticists have been able to predict the probability that children will have various genetic qualities (ranging from hair color to conditions such as Tay-Sachs disease) based on the genetic structure of their parents. Narrative theorists explain that stories are persuasive because they provide coherence and bring order to a jumbled set of facts.

Other scholars, often ones who define themselves as humanists, are less interested in prediction and control; instead, their goal is **understanding**, which may not require prediction and control. They evaluate the value of a theory by its ability to provide insight into why something is as it is or why certain things happen. An environmental scientist would want to understand in detail how wetlands are altered by natural and human interventions. A geneticist would seek to understand why chromosomes occasionally deviate from the XY and XX structure for males and females, respectively; why do some individuals have XO, XYY, or XXY sex chromosomes, and what do these variations mean? A communication theorist might try to understand why humans seem to like fairness in their relationships and why they count certain exchanges as fair or unfair.

Different communication theories place more or less emphasis on the objectives of prediction, control, and understanding. For example, assume that two communication theorists are interested in the relationship between parent–child interaction and a child's self-concept. The scientific theorist who seeks prediction and control will be satisfied only if she or he discovers how to use communication to enhance self-concept. The humanistic theorist would be more likely to focus on understanding why some children develop more positive self-concepts than others and the subjective impact of differing self-concepts.

Reflection

What is your personal evaluation of the goals of prediction, control, and understanding?

The goals, though distinct, are not necessarily incompatible. Prediction and control on the one hand and understanding on the other hand often overlap. Understanding how parents' communication affects children's views of themselves is the basis of being able to predict and control parent–child interactions. Conversely, even if understanding is all a theorist seeks, the understanding she or he gains may inform predictions.

Despite the fact that understanding and prediction often go hand in hand, the two goals are distinct. The goal of science is objective explanation, whereas humanism strives for subjective understanding of humans and how they operate. Although these distinct goals can go together, sometimes they do not. For example, suppose you notice that a friend of yours likes it when you talk about how she feels about a problem but doesn't appreciate it when you give her advice on how to solve a problem. Maybe you don't understand why she likes to talk about feelings more than solutions to problems. Just being able to predict that she will be hurt if you offer solutions when she shares a problem is sufficient for you to interact effectively with her.

It's also possible to understand something that you cannot predict or control. For instance, I understand that Robbie and I have needs for both autonomy and togetherness, and I know we become uncomfortable whenever either need is unsatisfied. Even with this understanding, however, I can't always predict or control when we will seek more distance from each other or more intimacy with each other. Also, I understand the typical stages in children's development, so I have insight into some of Harrison's antics, but I have virtually no control over his developmental patterns.

Reform

A fourth goal of some theorizing is **reform**, or active pursuit of positive social change. At the outset of discussing this goal, we need to recognize that not all theorists and not all theories are interested in reform. Many theorists see description, explanation, prediction, and control as the proper goals of theorizing. These scholars believe theorists have no responsibility and possibly no right to try to change social behavior. It is primarily critical theories, which we'll explore in Chapter 12, that regard social change as a major goal of theorizing.

Emphasis on reform is a relatively new trend in theoretical scholarship. Traditionally description, explanation, and prediction were the foci of theory. That is because, historically, theorizing has been regarded as an objective process in which a theorist is and should be detached from what he or she studies. In recent years, however, a number of scholars have challenged these conventional views of theorizing. Many current scholars argue persuasively that theories should make a difference in the real world—that they should improve the lives of humans in concrete ways. In addition many theorists today reject the idea that scholars are or should be removed from what they study. Instead they believe that scholars are part of the world—not removed from it—and that their work is informed by who they are and the experiences they have had (Wood & Cox, 1993).

Reflection

Do you believe theorists should try to affect social policy and social life?

Critical theorists study how communication oppresses or liberates individuals and social groups. One impressive line of critical theorizing has come from feminist scholars who have shown how prevailing communication practices often silence women (Campbell, 1995; Foss & Foss, 1991; Kramarae, 1981). Another important focus of critical theorizing is the impact of the media in sustaining a social order that privileges some people and oppresses others (Hall, 1982, 1989a,b). Other subjects of critical theory are communicative structures and practices that make sexual harassment seem normal and acceptable (Bingham, 1994; "Telling Our Stories," 1992) and that sustain patterns of abuse between intimates (West, 1995). In each case, the theories attempt to point the way to reform of social practices that are oppressive and sometimes deadly. Critical theorists believe that it is not enough to describe, explain, or even predict the incidence of wife battering. We also need to change the social and personal circumstances that allow it to happen.

It's important to realize that theorists interested in the goal of reform seldom dismiss the values of more traditional theoretical goals. Although critical theorists don't consider description, explanation, prediction, and control to be sufficient theoretical goals, they often find them necessary to their larger goal of inducing positive social change. After all, it's very difficult to reform a process unless we first understand what it is and how it works. It's also the case that reform can be thought of as a kind of control—an effort to influence what happens.

In summary, we've discussed four goals that may guide theory. The first two goals, description and explanation, are objectives of all theories, since understanding what communication is and how it works is the basis of any further theoretical work. A third goal of theory is either to predict and control communication or to understand communication. Although these two can overlap or work in tandem, they aren't synonymous or necessarily joined. We can understand phenomena that we can't predict or control, and we can predict and control phenomena that we don't fully understand. The final goal of theorizing, social change or reform, goes beyond prediction and even control to focus on theorists' responsibilities to better the world, an objective that requires a firm foundation of understanding.

Stop for a moment and reflect on how you view the different goals of theorizing. Do you value prediction and control more than understanding? Do you think theorists have a moral responsibility to be agents of positive social change? As you read later chapters in this book, you'll discover that how you answer these questions has considerable bearing on which theories you appreciate and which ones you find uninteresting or pointless.

Standards for Evaluating Theories

Now that we understand what theories are and the goals they pursue, we can turn to the question of how to evaluate theories. How can you tell whether a theory is good or bad, important or trivial, helpful or useless, sound or defective? Over the years theorists have developed five criteria for evaluating theories.

Now that you're familiar with the goals of theory, put them in practice by constructing a theory of your own. Develop a theory of communication in your communication theory classroom.

1. Identify and describe the most important features of communication in your classroom.

2. Explain how the features interact and what happens as they do.

3. Offer an understanding of what the communication in your classroom means and how it is subjectively experienced by individuals in the class.

4. Predict what will happen in the future, and define ways you could control future events in the classroom.

5. Identify what should be the case for communication in your class. Are there any communication practices that oppress or discriminate against certain members of the class? If so, what needs to be changed to end or reduce the disadvantage? Does the communication that takes place support the goals of learning fully? If not, how should it be changed to improve learning?

Scope: How Much Does the Theory Describe and Explain?

The first question to ask about any theory is how large a scope it has. **Scope** refers to the range of phenomena a theory describes and explains. Theories vary in their scope; some focus on very narrow realms of communication, and others advance grand perspectives on all human communication. Symbolic interactionism and dramatism, which we discuss in Chapter 5, are among the broadest in the field of communication: each of them claims to offer a theory of communication in general, that is, a range of diverse contexts. Interactional theory (Chapter 8), on the other hand, has a much more limited scope—it attempts to describe and explain only communication in the context of families. The theories discussed in Chapters 4 through 13 will give you opportunities to examine theories of diverse scope.

A good theory provides a good description and explanation of events, processes, or behaviors. Although descriptions and explanations don't offer completely objective representations of phenomena, we can still assess the value of the particular representation of communication a theory offers. To do so, we ask how well a theory answers the *what* question (What is it?) and the *how* or *why* question (How does it operate? Why does this happen?).

In describing a communication phenomenon, a theory clarifies what it considers essential in communication. For example, Shannon and Weaver's information model concentrated on features such as source, message, noise, and destination. Shannon and Weaver cast the spotlight on only a few of the many factors that are part of communication and affect how it works. In so doing they directed our attention to those features and not others. My model of personal relationships focuses attention on five features: individuals, social systems, communication, relational culture, and time. It does not emphasize other aspects of relationships, such as partners' feelings or rewards and costs.

All theories are partial in focusing on some aspects of a phenomenon and not others. The question for the critic is whether the features a theorist highlights are the most important ones. As we saw, Shannon and Weaver's model was criticized for not including feedback and ethical considerations, which are part of communication. If you, like Norbert Weiner, believe that feedback and ethical implications are important in communication, then you too would judge Shannon and Weaver's description of communication as inadequate.

We also evaluate theories according to how well they explain communication. Generally, a theory that provides incomplete description is weak in its explanatory power. A theory that rests on a good descriptive base, however, may or may not result in a satisfying explanation. A good explanation requires not only that we understand what's involved in communication, but also that we know how the parts work together and what results follow from their interaction.

Theorists use two broad types of explanations. One relies on universal laws to explain why things happen. **Laws-based explanations** argue that anytime x happens, y will follow, or that x and y are usually related. This form of explanation seeks to discover universal or very probabilistic laws that explain human communication in a wide range of situations. For example, one communication theory claims that uncertainty (not knowing what is happening in a relationship) fosters increased communication (efforts to figure out what is happening). This is a law about communication.

Reflection

Can you state some laws of human communication that are universal?

Laws-based explanations may be either **causal** or **correlational**. A causal law states that x causes y or y happens because of x. For example, we might say that uncertainty causes communication. A correlational claim, on the other hand, says only that two things go together but does not assert that one causes the other. We might note, for instance, that uncertainty and increases in communication go together. It's possible that uncertainty actually causes communication; alternatively, it's possible that uncertainty causes some other factor (interest, curiosity), which in turn results in increased communication. It is also possible that one or more other factors cause both uncertainty and communication—different cultural backgrounds, for example, might increase both uncertainty in interaction and efforts to

communicate. If two things go together but the cause is unclear, then the relationship between the two things is correlational. If it can be demonstrated that one thing directly causes another, then the relationship is causal.

In *The Structure of Scientific Revolutions* (1970), a highly influential book on the nature of theory, Thomas Kuhn contended that a mature science has a universal paradigm, theory, or model that explains its phenomena. For many years communication scholars as well as academics in other fields tried to achieve the universal theories that Kuhn claimed were the earmark of a mature science. However, their attempts to produce universal laws of communication failed. It seems that communication, like other human activities, is so complex and varies so greatly across situations that it cannot be covered by universal laws.

A second form of explanation identifies rules that explain why people in particular circumstances communicate as they do and why certain consequences follow. **Rules-based explanations** do not claim to offer any universal laws about human communication. Instead, they aim to articulate the patterns that describe and explain what happens in a specific type of communication situation or relationship. Thus, rules have a more restricted scope than laws. For example, there are rules (or regularities) that friends follow in their communication, but these rules may not surface in communication between members of work teams.

Don't make the mistake of thinking that rules explanations are entirely idiosyncratic and can only account for what happens in a single case. Therapists may be concerned only with understanding and helping a particular client, but theorists have broader aims. A theorist who relies on rules-based explanations attempts to explain how communication operates in a defined sphere of activity. For example, theorists of group decision making don't claim that the communication rules in groups necessarily extend to public speaking situations. They do, however, believe that there are some communication rules common to how most groups function. Similarly, theories of communication between romantic partners may not tell us a great deal about political rallies and speeches.

When evaluating how well a theory explains communication, we should ask whether it provides an account that incorporates all known data and makes sense. One basic question to ask about any theory is this: Does it make sense? A good theory should make sense and provide a reasonable account of all known data.

Testability: Is It Testable?

A second important criterion for evaluating theories is **testability**, which asks whether the claims advanced by a theory can be investigated to determine their accuracy. If a theoretical claim or prediction is faulty, we should have a way to detect this. We should also be able to verify theoretical predictions that are correct. If we can't test a theory, we can rely only on faith, guesswork, or personal experience to evaluate its accuracy.

A testable theory is clearly and specifically stated. For example, we can test the proposition that increased communication always accompanies uncertainty. The accuracy of the theory can be tested by conducting observations or experiments to determine whether communication always follows uncertainty and whether increased communication ever occurs when uncertainty isn't present. On the other hand, it would be difficult to test the proposition that honesty is a good thing in relationships. We'd have trouble testing this claim because we don't have a precise definition of "a good thing"; is it something that makes partners feel good, something that is right by particular moral precepts, or something that has concrete effects on trust, love, and commitment? We also don't have a clear definition of "relationships"; does this refer to romantic relationships, friendships, family connections, professional associations, or all of these? Finally, our ability to test the claim that "honesty is a good thing in relationships" requires us to evaluate honesty, which might prove very challenging. How could we tell for sure whether a person was being honest or dishonest? It is extremely difficult to test predictions that are general, vague, or ambiguous.

Reflection

Can you think of ways other than testing to assess a theory's accuracy? What assumptions of Western culture underlie the idea that testing determines accuracy?

Let's return to Lund's (1985) theory of commitment. She predicted that the greater the investment a person makes in a relationship, the higher will be the person's level of commitment to continuing the relationship. She also predicted that investment would be a stronger influence than love on relational continuity. To test these predictions, Lund studied college students.

Because college romances are most likely to deteriorate during times of transition, Lund measured the students' reported feelings of love and commitment in February of their senior year and in the summer following their graduation. Her findings were very clear: Those students who expressed the greatest intention to continue a relationship (commitment) in February were the most likely to be together the following summer. The amount of love expressed by students in February was not nearly as good a predictor of which couples would remain together. She tested her prediction empirically and found convincing support for its accuracy.

Reflection

Look back at the theory of classroom communication that you developed. Can it be tested? If it is too vague or general to be tested, how might you revise it to make it testable?

Parsimony: Is It Appropriately Simple?

When it comes to theory, complexity is not necessarily desirable. The term **parsimony** refers to appropriate simplicity. Among theorists it is widely believed that the best theory is the simplest one that is capable of describing, explaining, understanding, and perhaps predicting future events or instigating change. This doesn't mean that theories should be simplistic or omit important ideas. What it does mean, however, is that a theory should be as simple as possible without sacrificing completeness. Thus, if we have several theories that provide equally useful explanations, the most parsimonious one is the best.

Sometimes theorists get caught up with complexity and offer explanations that are more involved than is necessary to understand the phenomena that interest them. Of course, a theory must be complete in order to meet the criterion of providing sound description and explanation. However, theories that are unnecessarily cumbersome fail to meet the criterion of parsimony. As you encounter theories in this book, you can ask whether they include irrelevant material and whether they are more complex than they need to be. The general rule is that, if two theories shed equal light on the same phenomenon, the simpler one is better.

Utility: Is It Useful?

Theories are also measured by their **utility**, or practical value. Years ago, a distinguished social psychologist named Kurt Lewin said that there is nothing so practical as a good theory. By this Lewin meant that a good theory should have practical use. It's fair to ask how much a given theory applies to practical life.

Evaluation of utility should be based on the goals of that particular theory. A theory that seeks to predict and control communication is measured by how well applying it achieves the desired results. A theory that seeks to understand subjective aspects of communication, however, is not appropriately measured by whether it allows prediction and control. Instead, a theory that aims to enhance understanding is gauged by whether it achieves that. The utility of critical theories rests on their ability to motivate or actually direct positive social change.

Reflection

What is the practical value of your theory of classroom communication? What does it do that matters?

Heurism: Does It Generate New Thought or Insights?

The final criterion for evaluating a theory is **heurism**, which refers to the degree to which a theory provokes new ideas, insights, thinking, and research. A theory is judged to be heuristic if it sparks new thinking. By this criterion, Shannon and Weaver's information theory was good because it generated an enormous amount of research on how communication works. Weiner's emphasis on feedback and communication ethics might never have surfaced if Shannon and Weaver hadn't introduced their theory. Lund's theory of commitment also has triggered substantial research that has elaborated knowledge about the bases of commitment and relational endurance.

A Summary of Criteria for Evaluating Theories

1. Does the theory provide a full description and explanation of communication?
2. Can the theory be tested?
3. Is the theory as simple as it can be?
4. Does the theory have practical utility?
5. Does the theory generate new thinking?

Reflection

How would you rank-order the five criteria for evaluating theories?

Balancing Criteria for Evaluating Theories

We have discussed five criteria for evaluating theories. It may have occurred to you that a particular theory can fare well on some criteria and poorly on others. For instance, Shannon and Weaver's information theory doesn't offer a full description of communication, yet it is highly heuristic. It is not unusual for a theory to meet some evaluative standards better than others.

As an analogy, think about how we evaluate apples, broccoli, pizza, bagels, and eggs. One criterion might be low fat and cholesterol; the apples, bagels, and broccoli would come out well on this measure. A second criterion for evaluating foods is sodium content; again, the apples, bagels, and broccoli fare well, and so do eggs. We might also assess a food by the amount of protein it supplies; the egg and the pizza come out best by this measure. Which is the best food? It depends on which criterion or set of criteria you use to evaluate the foods. This implies that evaluating theories is not an objective activity. Instead, the criteria we use to judge theories reflect our subjective values, preferences, perspectives, and goals.

Theories, like foods, can be assessed in different ways that lead us to different conclusions about their merit. Ideally, a good food would be low in sodium, fat, and cholesterol and high in protein and taste. Ideally, a good theory would provide full description and explanation and also would be easy to test, parsimonious, useful, and heuristic. However, just as most foods don't meet all criteria for merit, some theories don't fully satisfy all five criteria for value. This is one reason why scholars often disagree about the worth of a particular theory: they use different measuring sticks to assess it.

Each criterion we discussed measures theories along one dimension. No one criterion is the only or the most important standard. As you study theories in this book, keep in mind all five criteria, and apply them to each theory. Doing this will give you insight into which criteria you consider most important in judging the worth of theories.

A Perspective for Studying Theories

So far we've examined the various goals that motivate theory and the standards for evaluating the worth of theories. Drawing from what we've already discussed, we can develop guidelines for thinking about the theories you'll encounter in subsequent chapters. As you consider specific theories, keep in mind that theories are points of view, not absolute truths. You'll also want to remember that any theory is limited in scope and that different theories may fit well together.

Theories Reflect Points of View

Students who are new to the study of theory often find it confusing that there are different theories of communication. They want to know which is "the right one." The desire to know which theory is right is understandable, but it isn't a realistic or useful attitude to hold when studying theories.

A theory expresses a point of view. It is a way of making sense of experiences, situations, events, or other phenomena. A majority of scholars recognize that theories do not (and cannot) offer absolute truth. Instead, theories offer perspectives on reality, and those perspectives reflect the particular human beings who build theories and the specific historical and cultural contexts in which theories are built.

Because human beings create theories, the theories include points of view that keep them from being absolutely objective descriptions of reality. Let's consider just a few of the ways in which theories reflect the particular interests, values, assumptions, and contexts of the people who develop them. In working to understand communicative phenomena, individual theorists make choices about which phenomena to emphasize and which to neglect. The choice of what to study involves several kinds of decisions. First, theorists choose which kind of communication to focus on—talk between intimates, interaction in groups, public speaking, cross-cultural communication, mass media, and so forth.

Second, theorists make different choices about what they will focus on in studying a particular kind of communication. For example, Leslie Baxter and Steve Duck both concentrate on communication in personal relationships. Yet Baxter (1990, 1992, 1993, 1994) rivets her attention on the tensions between contradictory impulses such as the need for autonomy and the need for togetherness. Duck (1994a,b), on the other hand, focuses his energy on understanding how ordinary, routine talk between intimates creates the meaning of relationships. Both Baxter and Duck are theorists of communication in personal relationships, but they emphasize different facets of intimate interaction. Recall that Shannon and Weaver emphasized the flow of information in their theory of communication. Other relationship scholars have focused on different aspects of interpersonal communication, including sharing meaning, creating identification between people, and developing feelings of trust and commitment.

Theorists also vary in the goals they pursue. A scholar interested in prediction and control will develop a theory quite different from that of a scholar whose primary interest is understanding. Critical theorists, who see the ultimate goal of theory as producing positive social change, will not be satisfied to develop a theory that describes, explains, and predicts how communication works but does nothing to make it more constructive for humans.

Finally, theorists differ in what they regard as a good explanation. Whereas some theorists adhere to the traditional quest for universal or near-universal laws, others seek to understand rules that guide communication in specific contexts. A lawful explanation will not be persuasive to a theorist who believes there are no universal laws of human behavior. Conversely, a rule-based explanation will seem inadequate to a theorist who believes in universal laws.

Different theorists focus on different types of communication and different facets of communication within each type. Consequently, we shouldn't be surprised to find that there are many different theories of communication, each reflecting the views, values, and interests of the person or persons who developed it. As you study the different theories in this book, try to resist the urge to pick one as the right one. Instead, approach each theory on its own terms and consider when, where, and for whom it might be useful. Each theory we will study offers a perspective that can help us understand particular aspects of what happens when certain people communicate in defined situations.

Different Theories Are Not Necessarily Incompatible

We've already seen that theories, even theories about a single kind of communication, vary. This leads to the question of whether different theories are compatible or separate and irreconcilable perspectives. The answer to that question is, "It depends."

Some theories cannot work together because they reflect fundamentally opposed views of human beings or of knowledge. We'll look more closely at these issues in Chapter 3. For now, it's important to understand that, when the foundations of two or more theories are inconsistent, they are incompatible. Let's consider a concrete example to clarify this point. Scholars who believe humans have no free will try to identify the external stimuli that cause human behaviors. Operating on the assumption that human behavior is determined, a scholar might develop a theory that claims the external factors of job stress and middle age cause male midlife crisis. A theory of this sort would suggest that we should lessen job stress to reduce the incidence of male midlife crisis.

A theorist who believes that humans have free will would reject the idea that male midlife crisis is caused by external factors. Instead, a theorist who believes in free will might explain the increasing incidence of middle-aged men who have identity crises as the result of cultural attitudes that undercut personal responsibility for one's actions. If individuals internalize a cultural view that we aren't responsible for what we do, then they are more likely to act in ways that could be judged irresponsible. The theorist who believes human behavior is determined focuses on external stimuli that precede certain actions, while the theorist who believes in free will concentrates on the meanings and values that individuals ascribe to what they do. The two perspectives are not compatible.

Yet some theories do work well together. This is the case when the theories are concerned with the same kind of communication and when they have common fundamental assumptions about human nature and knowledge. For example, in Chapter 5 we will examine symbolic interactionism, which is very broad. The value of this theory is that it provides an overall perspective on the process whereby individuals learn the symbols and the meanings of their culture. What symbolic interactionism doesn't do is explain precisely how individuals create meaning in various specific contexts. Two other theories covered in Chapter 7, constructivism and rules theory, supplement the broad view of symbolic interactionism with more detailed explanations of how individuals create meanings. Rules theory highlights the personal, relationship, and social rules that structure communication between people. Complementing this emphasis is constructivism, or attention to the cognitive processes individuals use to organize and interpret communication. These three theories work well together, and in combination they provide a fuller understanding of the human process of creating meaning than does any of the theories on its own.

Theories Have Limited Focus and Scope

A theory asks particular questions. Its scope is defined by the specific aspects of communication it seeks to describe and explain. No theory can address all communication or even all facets of a single type of communication. Brant Burleson's (1984, 1986, 1991) work on comforting behaviors provides enormous insight into the ways we communicate comfort and support to others. It tells us nothing, however, about constructive methods of managing conflict or ways of dealing with power and manipulation. Burleson isn't trying to explain power or conflict, and it's not appropriate to judge his scholarship by whether it sheds light on power and conflict. Those issues are beyond the scope of his theory.

A theory should be considered and evaluated on how well it does what it sets out to do. It's entirely reasonable to decide that a certain theory's focus doesn't interest you or isn't of value in your life. It is not reasonable, however, to criticize a theory for not doing something it doesn't attempt to do. The fact that there are hundreds of theories of communication tells us that any theory is limited in scope. Thus, each theory should be appraised in terms of whether it enlarges our knowledge about the particular contexts and facets of communication that are its focus.

As you consider theories in this book, keep in mind that theories are human constructions, and therefore they reflect points of view, not statements of objective truth. Also realize that theories with compatible basic assumptions often work well together to provide richer understandings of human communication than any single theory can offer. Third, recognize that theories have limited scope and can be judged only on whether they increase knowledge about the specific domain of communication that is the theory's focus. Finally, I hope you'll keep an attitude of curiosity as you study communication theories. Learning about many different perspectives on human communication introduces you to points of view and modes of understanding other than your own. This allows you to grow personally and intellectually.

Summary

In this chapter we've considered the foundations of communication theory. We began by examining the goals that guide theory. Description and explanation are the basic building blocks of all communication theories.

Beyond those two goals, theories also attempt either to predict and control or to increase understanding of communication phenomena. A fourth goal, most often embraced by critical theorists, is to produce positive social change. As we noted, these are not mutually exclusive goals; they often work together. Description is necessary for explanation; explanation allows prediction, control, and/or understanding; and positive social change grows out of a foundation of understanding.

The second section of the chapter concentrates on criteria for evaluating theories. To judge the value of a theory, we ask five questions: (1) Does it offer a full description and explanation of the communication it studies? (2) Is it testable? (3) Is it appropriately parsimonious, or simple? (4) Does it have practical utility? (5) Is it heuristic in generating new thoughts, research, and/or insights? Most theories will not fully meet all five of these evaluative criteria. Thus, you must decide which criterion or criteria are most important to your evaluations of theories.

In the final pages of this chapter we discussed guidelines for studying theories in this book. Perhaps the most important one is to realize that communication theories are human constructions. As such, they reflect individuals' perceptions, values, needs, experiences, and goals, as well as the social, temporal, and intellectual currents of particular contexts in which theorists live and work. Realizing this allows us to understand that theories are not objective truths but perspectives on reality.

A second guideline for your study of theories is to recognize that different theories that share common fundamental assumptions may complement one another and work well together. Theories with contradictory views of human nature and knowledge, however, are not compatible. Third, it's important to recognize that theories have limited scopes. No communication theory explains all communication in all contexts, and it would be unrealistic to expect this of a theory. What is reasonable is to ask whether a given theory does a good job of explaining and enhancing knowledge about the communication on which it focuses. Finally, I've suggested that it's valuable to adopt an attitude of curiosity toward the range of theories we'll discuss in this book. You're most likely to gain new insights into your own communication as well as communication in general if you keep your mind open to points of view that differ from your own. This allows you to learn about people and contexts that are beyond your current personal experiences.

In Chapter 3 we will continue to consider how theories are developed and tested. There we will examine different assumptions that underlie and shape theories and ways of doing research to test theories. Following this are nine chapters that introduce a variety of communication theories. As we discuss each theory, we will describe its goals and scope, examine research that has tested the theory, and critically assess strengths and weaknesses of the theory. This should provide you with a basic understanding of each theory and some insight into its particular values and limitations.

Key Terms

causal	prediction
control	reform
correlational	rules-based explanation
description	scope
explanation	testability
heurism	theory
laws-based explanation	understanding
parsimony	utility

CHAPTER THREE

Building and Testing Theory

If you tell a two-year-old child that the world is round or that the moon will not appear tonight, the child is likely to ask, "How do you know?" or to say, "Prove it."

Children's skeptical attitude toward claims is very much like the attitude scholars take toward theories. We don't accept an account of communication just because someone advances it. Instead, we ask, "How do you know?" and we demand, "Prove it." The question of how you know concerns how the theory was developed and what assumptions the theorist has made. The demand to prove it asks for evidence that supports the claims a theory makes.

In this chapter we'll see how theories are developed, refined, and tested. We'll begin by discussing the building blocks of theory: assumptions about human beings, knowledge, and the research process. Next we'll consider diverse methods that scholars use to test and refine theories. By the end of this chapter you should have a good working understanding of alternative foundations on which theories are built and various methods by which they are tested.

The Building Blocks of Theory

Do theories of human communication describe how humans actually communicate, or do they reflect individual theorists' perceptions and perspectives? When people communicate, are they reacting to external stimuli or making personal choices? Are theories based on objective knowledge or subjective interpretations? Do they tell us about communication behaviors or about the meaning of communication? Do they provide universal truths or situated accounts? Each of these questions is answered in different ways by various theorists. Just as there is no single theory of communication, there is no single view of the foundations of theory. In this section we will consider four building blocks of theories and varying points of view on each of them.

Reflection

As a framework for reading the rest of this chapter, state your personal opinions regarding the preceding questions

Views of Human Nature

The basis of any theory is its view of human nature. Different theorists subscribe to different views of human nature, and you will find you agree with some views more than others.

One of the continuing controversies in philosophy concerns **ontology**, or assumptions about human nature. The crux of the controversy is whether or not humans have free will and, if so, how great the latitude of free will is. How you answer this question makes a great deal of difference in the theories you find credible and in how you act in everyday life. For example, if you think people don't have free will, it makes no sense to blame individuals for bad behavior or praise them for good behavior; in neither case do they control what they do. On the other hand, if you think that humans do have free will, you're likely to hold people responsible for their actions.

Despite all the effort and energy devoted to figuring out the nature of human beings, we still don't know whether we have free will and, if so, how much. Consequently, the assumptions theorists make about humans can't be proved or disproved scientifically; they are matters of faith or belief. Theorists are divided in terms of whether they assume individuals react to external stimuli or act from free will and thus exercise intentional choices.

Reflection

What practical differences does it make whether we believe human behavior is determined or personally willed?

Determinism **Determinism** assumes that human behavior is governed by forces beyond individual control, usually the twin forces of biology and environment. Whatever we do is the inevitable result of genetic inheritance, environmental influences, or a combination of the two.

Freud is famous for having said, "Biology is destiny." By this he meant that biology determines sex, and sex determines phenomena such as fear of castration in males and penis envy in females. From this point of view, each of us is prewired by sex chromosomes to have certain feelings and fears. How we behave is inevitable and unavoidable given the determining force of biology.

Many more modern thinkers draw a sharp distinction between sex and gender (Basow, 1992; West & Zimmerman, 1987; Wood, 1993c, 1994e, 1995a, 2003). *Sex* refers to biological qualities determined by the sex chromosomes and hormones. *Sex* designates whether a person is biologically male or female. *Gender,* on the other hand, refers to socially constructed views of men and women—that is, the meanings assigned to the sexes at a particular time in a given society. Most scholars believe that the vast majority of differences between women and men are learned (a matter of gender), not biologically determined (a matter of sex). Thus, to explain differences between the sexes, they focus on social practices that prescribe how women and men are expected to think, feel, act, and be.

Free Will   At the other end of the ontological spectrum is the belief that humans have free will and that they make choices about how to act. Theorists who believe in free will assume that individuals interpret experiences and create meanings, which then guide what they think, believe, say, feel, and do. These theorists reject the idea that human behavior is an unthinking, automatic response to conditions and stimuli around us.

Belief in free will is sometimes misunderstood as the notion that people have complete control over their lives. Most scholars and laypeople who assume individuals have free will are not so naive as to believe that will is boundless and unqualified. Instead, the majority of theorists who assume that humans have and exercise will recognize that we do so within definite constraints. In writing about the impact of social structures on personal relationships, Graham Allan (1989) noted that our relationship choices are not entirely free. Instead, he pointed out, we make them within the limitations of biological and social forces that undeniably affect our lives and our perceptions of our options in any situation. Realizing that biological and social forces *affect* what we do is quite different from assuming they *determine* what we do.

Many years before Graham Allan's time, the philosopher Martin Heidegger (1927/1962) advanced the idea that individual freedom is constrained by what he called "thrownness." For Heidegger, **thrownness** refers to the fact that we are thrown into a multitude of arbitrary conditions that influence our lives and opportunities. For example, a Caucasian woman born in the United States in 1812 would not have been allowed to pursue professional training, own property, or vote. African Americans born in Georgia in 1850 were likely to be slaves, an identity that severely restricted their life chances and opportunities. A woman who seemed to have extrasensory perception would have been burned, hung, or drowned if she had been thrown into Salem, Massachusetts, in the late 1600s. A woman born in India at the turn of the last century—and in some regions of India today—would be thrown into the custom of arranged marriage.

The Building Blocks of Theory

In each of these cases the individual's free will is constrained by his or her throwness—the arbitrary social conditions of the time and place in which they live. Each of us is also affected by our throwness in a society that has particular beliefs about gender, race, age, sexual orientation, ethnicity, physical ability, socioeconomic class, and so forth.

Those who believe in human will do not think the fact that will is constrained means it is nonexistent. Instead, they argue that, within the constraints of biological and social influences, there remains substantial latitude for choice about what we believe and do and to shape our own destinies. How we are thrown into the world is not within our control. Each of us does, however, have some control over what we do with our throwness.

Individual control over how to deal with throwness is evident in the different choices individuals with social and biological constraints make. For example, in the early 1800s, women in the United States were legally defined as the property of their fathers or husbands. Many women accepted social views of themselves as dependent on and inferior to men. Yet other women responded differently to their throwness. Individuals such as Elizabeth Cady Stanton, Sojourner Truth, and Susan B. Anthony challenged prevailing restrictions on women's identity and rights. Eventually their actions, along with those of hundreds of others who didn't accept existing views of women, altered the legal rights available to women.

Reflection

Describe your throwness. How does it limit your ability to exercise will?

Another example of exercising choice within the constraints of throwness comes from the 1960s civil rights movement. In the United States blacks were treated as subordinate members of the society. They were not given equal opportunities in careers, and they were forced to attend fewer schools with more meager resources, to ride in the back of buses, and to use restaurants, hotels, and public bathrooms separate from those used by whites.

Although many blacks were resigned to the racist attitudes that held sway at the time, others refused to accept them. The Reverend Martin Luther King, Jr., was one of the leaders who emerged to champion the cause of racial equality. His choice to challenge racism influenced what thousands of other African Americans saw as their options for resisting racism. Even among those who argued against racial discrimination, there were differences. The Reverend Martin Luther King, Jr.'s advocacy of civil disobedience and passive resistance was far removed from the confrontational rhetoric of Malcolm X or the fiery politics of Stokley Carmichael or the quiet, behind-the-scenes organizing of Ella Baker. Each individual

Building and Testing Theory

made distinct choices about how to challenge racial discrimination and how to instigate change in society.

In addition to presenting historical examples of outstanding individuals, proponents of free will have marshaled persuasive evidence that ordinary individuals make choices that have concrete impact on themselves and their activities. Recent research demonstrates that individuals adopt different perspectives on their relationships, which affect how they see themselves and how they act in relation to others (Duck & Pond, 1989; Fletcher, Rosanowski, & Fitness, 1992; Honeycutt, 1993). For example, people who choose to focus on positive aspects of relationships and to downplay dissatisfactions have more comfortable, more gratifying relationships than partners who choose to concentrate on negative features and to downplay what is good about their relationships (Bradbury & Fincham, 1990; Fletcher & Fincham, 1991). This implies that we can change how we see our relationships by changing how we think about them.

TRY IT OUT To understand how your beliefs about human nature affect what you say, do, think, and feel, try this out:

1. First, think about a situation in which another person hurt you. Did you attribute the other person's action to biological qualities (men/women always act that way) or environmental factors (he/she had a rough day, was stressed, and so on)? Or did you attribute the other person's action to her or his own choices (she/he intended to hurt me; she/he was being mean)?

2. Now try explaining what the other person did in a different way. If you explained the behavior as determined, redefine it as a personal choice; if you regarded the behavior as the result of free will, try perceiving it as determined by forces beyond the person's control.

3. Conclude this exercise by describing how your assumptions about human nature affect how you feel about the person and what happened.

In summary, the most basic foundation of any theory is its ontological premise. Whether theorists view human behavior as determined by social and/or biological forces or as personally willed, within the constraints of thrownness, affects all other aspects of theorizing. What theorists study and how they explain their findings inevitably echo their ontological assumptions.

Ways of Knowing

At some time in your life you probably entertained this question: If a tree falls and nobody hears it, does it make a sound? That question is part of a

The Building Blocks of Theory   **55**

larger philosophical debate about the nature of knowledge. **Epistemology**, the branch of philosophy that deals with knowledge, is concerned with how we know. Is knowledge based on the existence of phenomena (the falling tree) or on human perceptions (hearing it fall). As you might suspect, there are different opinions about what counts as knowledge and how we come to know what we think we know.

Epistemological assumptions are the second building block of theory. Along with ontological premises, all theories include epistemological propositions that state what knowledge is and how we acquire it. The continuum of epistemological assumptions ranges from belief in an objective truth that humans can discover to belief that humans create meanings and therefore many meanings are possible. We'll consider each end of the epistemological continuum.

Discovering Truth   Some people, scholars as well as individuals removed from academia, believe that there is a singular truth. This viewpoint is called **objectivism**, which is the belief that reality is material and external to the human mind. For objectivists, truth or reality is material, external, independent of feelings, and the same for everyone. For the ancient philosopher Plato the ultimate truth was the idea or ideal of something rather than any concrete instance of the thing. For others truth is external, resolute reality. Those who believe in a singular, objective truth assume that it is independent of human feeling and motives and is discovered through direct observation. In other words, through our senses we should be able to see, hear, taste, smell, and/or touch the reality "out there." Our senses do not alter or affect objective reality. Within this perspective, knowledge is assumed to be objective and discoverable by humans.

Scholars who assume there is an objective truth also regard theorizing and research as objective activities. **Objectivity** is the quality of being uninfluenced by values, biases, personal feelings, and other subjective factors when perceiving material reality. According to researchers who believe that inquiry can and should be objective, a theorist's values and subjective feelings should not affect science. Instead, good scholars detach themselves from their values in order to maintain objectivity and discover reality. The result of detached scholarship, these individuals think, is real knowledge that is uncontaminated by human subjectivity.

Believers in objective truth presume that the true nature, or meaning, of any act of communication can be determined. They think that a single, correct truth, or meaning, exists and that we can discover it if we have all the relevant information, including understanding of the context in which communication occurs. For objectivists, different views of communication (or other phenomena) are not equally valid. Objectivists believe that there

is a single correct or true view and other views are erroneous because they
are based on less than full information. Thus, people may perceive things
differently, but only one perception is ultimately correct, or true. Only one
is consistent with the "real world."

Creating Meaning   At the other end of the epistemological spectrum
are people, again both scholars and nonacademic individuals, who do not
believe in an objective truth. Instead, they assume there are multiple views
of reality, no one of which is intrinsically more true than any other. They
believe that what we call reality is a subjective interpretation rather than an
objective truth. Because individuals have different experiences, values, perceptions, and life situations, their realities and their meanings vary widely.
Further, even with great effort we may not be able to uncover all of the
meanings people hold, since some meanings are less than conscious and
others may be ones they conceal to avoid embarrassment.

   Let's consider three examples of communication in everyday life. In
some situations you might interpret "You look wonderful today" as a

The Building Blocks of Theory   **57**

compliment. However, if it were said by Tom Clarence, who has a history of sexually harassing Hillary Ann, then Hillary might perceive the words as threatening, debasing, and cause for alarm. Calling someone a "queer" might be interpreted as an insult in most circumstances. In recent years, however, many gays have reappropriated that word as a positive self-description that they use among themselves. What calling someone "queer" means differs depending on whether it is uttered by a straight person or said by one gay man to another. Finally, most of us would agree that "I love you" is generally affectionate communication. Yet in some circumstances it can be manipulative. For example, children often proclaim love when they want something from the person they claim to love. Individuals who batter their intimates often follow violence with pledges of love that are intended to keep the abused partner from leaving or reporting the crime. In this context, "I love you" might not be regarded as an expression of affection.

Those who believe that there are multiple realities would regard it as entirely reasonable that different people interpret communication in varying ways. A good illustration of this perspective is found in **standpoint theory**, which we will discuss in detail in Chapter 10. The starting premise of standpoint theory is that the material, social, and symbolic circumstances of a social group shape what its members experience, as well as how they think, act, and feel (Harding, 1991; Wood, 1993e, 1995a). Thus, someone from the underclass has experiences with deprivation, hunger, and poor housing that a middle- or upper-class person doesn't have. The two individuals have different knowledge about what it means to be hungry, homeless, and so forth. Similarly, in the United States, members of racial minorities have experience with prejudice and discrimination that most European Americans don't have. Can different racial groups have the same knowledge of what racism is and means?

One group of communication scholars ("Telling Our Stories," 1992) explored the multiple meanings of sexual harassment. Their analyses dramatically illustrated the difference between what women and men in general consider sexually harassing. One reason that women are more likely to be offended by sexually oriented remarks and nonverbal behaviors is that they have been the victims of harassment more often than men. The danger that offensive remarks and behaviors could lead to more serious kinds of sexual intrusion may also be more salient to women than to men. The sexes' disparate standpoints explain some of the differences in how they interpret communication of a sexual nature. For theorists who assume there are multiple, legitimate realities, differences in interpretation are normal and to be respected. They are not evidence that some people can't recognize "real truth."

The epistemological question of how we know is a foundation of theories. Some individuals believe truth is an objective phenomenon that humans can discover through careful observation or other scientific methods. Other people think that reality is ultimately subjective and that what we know is intimately tied up with who we are. The stances theorists take on this issue influence how they conduct research, interpret findings, and advance claims.

Purposes of Theory

The third building block of theory concerns the purpose of theory. We first encountered this issue in Chapter 2, and now we will examine it in greater detail. A basic controversy about the purpose of theory is whether theories should generate universal laws that apply in a broad range of circumstances or whether theories should articulate rules that describe patterns in more limited spheres of activity.

Universal Laws   As we saw in Chapter 2, some theorists believe there are universal laws of human behavior. A **law** is an inviolate, unalterable fact that holds true across time and space. For example, you are familiar with the law of gravity, which states that objects are pulled toward the earth. The law of gravity explains everything from the fact that a pen dropped from your hand hits the floor to the fact that an airplane whose engines fail falls to the ground. The law of gravity is true across all situations within the scope of the earth's atmosphere (but the law of gravity doesn't hold in outer space). It's also universally true that mixing two molecules of hydrogen and one molecule of oxygen will unvaryingly produce water. Consuming large quantities of arsenic will inevitably cause death. These are all laws that remain true across a variety of circumstances.

Universal laws may be more applicable to natural science than to human behavior, including communication. Most laws of communication are probabilistic—they specify that certain kinds of communication are likely to occur in specific situations or in response to particular stimuli. Statistical tests, as well as other measures, allow researchers to define levels of probability very specifically. For instance, a researcher might report that judgmental communication in the workplace evokes defensive responses 95% or 99% of the time.

Beliefs about the purpose of theory are related to ontological assumptions, which we discussed earlier in this chapter. If human behavior is determined by biological and social forces, then we would expect to be able to predict behavior with relative certainty. In other words, if human behavior is determined by something other than personal will, then patterns of behavior will occur in response to specific stimuli; they will not vary as a result of personal wishes, commitments, or perceptions.

Situated Rules   Some theorists scoff at the idea that theories of human behavior should generate universal laws. Instead, they assume there are no laws that explain human communication across all time and circumstances. Theorists who adopt this position tend to see the purpose of theory as the articulation of rules that describe patterns in human behavior rather than the formulation of laws that explain its causes.

As you'll recall from Chapter 2, a second way to explain human behavior is by identifying rules that guide how we act in particular situations. Rules-based explanations of communication aren't assumed to hold true across all situations and people. Instead, they are believed to describe regularities in how some people act in specific circumstances. For example, most of us follow turn-taking rules when we talk with others (Nofsinger, 1991). When we speak, we expect not to be interrupted; when we're through speaking, we signal this by looking at others to indicate that the conversational floor is open again. When we want to speak, we wait until the person speaking finishes. Within Western culture, it is considered rude for one person to monopolize a conversation and not let others have their say. The turn-taking rule is a convention that we learn in the process of becoming socialized. Moreover, turn taking isn't equally important in all cultures. Thus, theorists who believe in rules regard turn taking as a rule-governed activity, not a behavior caused by any universal law.

Theorists who rely on rules to describe human activity tend to assume that humans have at least some degree of free will. They argue that our behavior is guided by rules or follows rules rather than absolutely determined by laws beyond our control. This suggests that our actions represent choices rather than automatic responses to external stimuli. Presumably we could communicate differently by adopting different rules to guide us. Rules-based accounts assume that regularities in human behavior reflect rules that are arbitrary, learned, and subject to change. Thus, they search not for lawlike explanations but for reasons that shed light on why people follow particular patterns in their communication.

The Focus of Theorizing

The final building block of theory is the focus, or content, that theories address. Once again we'll see there are different schools of opinion on this matter. We'll also see that a theorist's stance on the issue of focus is related to her or his ontological and epistemological assumptions.

The basic division on this issue is whether theories should focus on behavior, on the meanings behind behavior, or on a combination of the two. Most theorists who believe that human behavior is determined and that knowledge is objective also believe that the proper focus of theories is behavior. Theorists who assume that human behavior is sculpted by free will and that knowledge is subjective and variable are more likely to see the appropriate focus of theories as meanings. This doesn't necessarily mean that theorists who assume a degree of free will ignore behaviors, for studying behaviors may help us understand meanings. Many theorists who focus on observable behavior do not assume that this is all there is to humans.

Behavioral Focus   Traditionally, science has been concerned with observable phenomena. Thus, scientists have sought to describe, explain, predict, and control behavior. Many researchers focus on observable behaviors but do not necessarily assume that there is nothing other than what can be observed. Some scientists assume, however, that behaviors are all there is or all that matters. This view is **behaviorism**, a form of science that focuses on observable behaviors and that assumes meanings, motives, and other subjective phenomena either don't exist or are irrelevant. Behaviorists believe that scientists can study only concrete behaviors, such as what people do or say. Human motives, meanings, and intentions are beyond the realm of behavioristic investigation. In fact, behaviorists would consider such explanations idle speculation rather than scientific activity.

B. F. Skinner (1971) was a staunch behaviorist who believed that human behavior is a response to external stimuli. Skinner is particularly well known for referring to the mind as a "black box" the contents of which cannot be known and which are irrelevant to science. Skinner believed that understanding what happens in the human mind is not necessary for a theory of human behavior. The mind and its activities, such as wanting, hoping, dreaming, intending, fearing, and so forth, are irrelevant.

Skinner regarded free will as a romantic illusion that many people find comforting but that really has nothing to do with how we behave. He thought concepts such as human freedom and responsibility and feelings such as pride, shame, hope, and commitment were humanistic fictions that allow people to believe they control their fates when in fact they do not. This may explain why Skinner (1971) titled his book on behavioral science *Beyond Freedom and Dignity*. For Skinner, as well as other behaviorists, all

The Building Blocks of Theory

that matters and all that can be measured is concrete, objective behavior. Meaning, motive, and intentions, even if they exist, aren't measurable, so they aren't within the province of science.

It would be erroneous to assume that all researchers who study behaviors are strict behaviorists who think humans' mental activities are irrelevant. Skinner was a radical behaviorist; that is, he studied only outward behavior and also argued that any unobservable behavior (if it exists) is unimportant. Many communication scholars who study observable phenomena do not share Skinner's assumption that human mediation and intention are romantic fictions. These scholars study behavior because it can be observed and measured, whereas feelings, motives, and other internal activity are not outwardly visible. They do not, however, share Skinner's assumption that subjective experiences are nonexistent or irrelevant.

Meanings   Many scholars aren't convinced that behaviorism is desirable. They reject both behaviorism's ontological assumptions and the idea that science should confine itself to the study of observable, concrete behaviors. Theorists who reject behavioral views of science believe that the crux of human activity is meaning, not behaviors themselves. Because this group of scholars claims to be interested in what is distinctively human—namely, free will, the ability to make choices, and the capacity to create meanings— they are often called *humanists,* and the form of science they pursue is called **humanism**.

Humanists see external behaviors as the outward signs of mental and psychological processes. For them, what we perceive, think, and feel directly affects what we do and what we assume it means. Thus, the reasons for human behavior lie with what happens inside of us. These scholars believe that cognitive and psychological processes offer the most insight into why we do what we do and what our behaviors mean.

A number of years ago, a scholar named John Searle (1976) wrote an important book called *Speech Acts*. In this small volume he made the distinction between **brute facts** and **institutional facts**. Brute facts are objective, concrete phenomena—the observable behaviors that behaviorists study. Institutional facts, in contrast, are what brute facts mean—what humanists wish to study. To illustrate the difference between these two kinds of facts or activities, Searle used the example of a football game. He offered this amusing account of the brute facts an observer would use to describe football:

> Our observer would discover the law of periodical clustering: at statistically regular intervals organisms in like colored shirts cluster together in a roughly circular fashion (the huddle). Furthermore, at equally regular intervals, circular clustering is followed by linear clustering (the teams

line up for the play), and linear clustering is followed by the phenomenon of linear interpenetration. (p. 52)

This account describes the concrete behaviors in a football game. Yet, as Searle pointed out, no matter how much data of this sort we collect and no matter how many inductive generalizations we make from the data, we cannot describe football by relying on these raw behaviors. Brute facts alone tell us little about what the game means. To understand the meaning of football, we turn to institutional facts that explain the social meanings of head and shoulder gear, lines on the field, the ellipsoidal object, and so forth.

In a sharp repudiation of behaviorism, Searle asserted that brute facts offer little insight into human activity because behaviors alone have no intrinsic meaning. Instead, humans assign meanings to them, and this requires interpretation. Interpretation is not evident in concrete behaviors, and it cannot be reduced to physical motion. In 1995 Searle published *The Construction of Social Reality,* which extended the ideas he developed in his earlier book, *Speech Acts.* In the more recent book Searle emphasized that social reality grows largely out of the functions that we assign to things. He uses the example of a screwdriver, whose use is not intrinsic to its material nature. Humans assign the function of screwing screws to the screwdriver.

TRY IT OUT Apply Searle's ideas to your own experiences. For each of the following communication activities, provide a description based on only brute facts and a second description based on institutional facts.

1. A marriage ceremony

2. A person interacting in a chat room

3. Two friends engaging in a game of friendly insults and put-downs

4. Children watching Saturday-morning cartoons

5. Interaction between a person from Buffalo, New York, and a person from Kathmandu, Nepal, neither of whom speaks the other's language

How well do brute facts and social facts describe these five activities? How are social facts influenced by the standpoint of the person using them? What does each type of fact explain and fail to explain?

The four building blocks of theory involve decisions about human nature, ways of knowing, the purpose of theory, and the focus of theory. Taken together, these are the foundation on which theories are developed. We turn now to a discussion of alternative ways of doing research and the kinds of data and knowledge that each method generates.

The Building Blocks of Theory

Let's assume that as a theorist you have worked out your starting assumptions. You have clear ideas about human nature and knowledge, and you have decided what the purposes and focus of theories should be. Based on your starting assumptions, you develop a theory.

Hypotheses and Research Questions

Perhaps you have heard that women and men have different communication styles, but your own experience doesn't support that. Thus, you want to develop and test your theory that women and men engage in conversation in similar ways. The first step in developing and testing a theory is to pose some hypotheses or questions for study. **Hypotheses** are testable predictions about relationships between communication phenomena. As a theorist, your goal is to develop hypotheses that allow you to test whether the sexes talk in similar or different ways:

H1: Women and men interrupt with equal frequency.

H2: Women and men make equally frequent efforts to involve others in conversation.

H3: Women and men find it equally satisfying to talk about issues in a shared relationship.

If you don't have a clear basis for making predictions, then you might prefer to avoid formal hypotheses. A second option for studying men's and women's communication is to generate **research questions**, which specify the phenomena of interest but do not predict relationships between the phenomena. For instance, you might generate these research questions to guide your study:

RQ1: How frequently do women and men interrupt in dialogues with each other?

RQ2: How frequently do women and men make efforts to involve others in conversation?

RQ3: How satisfying do women and men find it to discuss issues in their relationships?

Before moving ahead with your research, you have one further task: You need to define terms in your hypotheses or questions. So that others can understand your research, you must specify exactly what you are studying. For the study in our example, we need to define terms such as *interruption* (Is it any comment made when another is speaking or only comments that initiate new lines of talk?), *satisfaction* (Is it defined by individuals, a research instrument, or another measure?), *efforts to involve others in conversation* (Do these include only verbal or both verbal and nonverbal efforts? Questions of others, comments to others, or both?), and *discussing their relationship* (Do discussion topics cover problems, good features, small talk, history?).

Operational definitions are precise descriptions that specify the phenomena of interest. For example, operational definitions for your theory would define what counts as an interruption, as satisfaction, and so forth. If the concepts of interest in a theory have been studied by others, it's a good idea to consider their definitions. This allows different researchers to use concepts in the same way, and thus their findings can be compared and related.

To grasp the importance of consistent operational definitions for research concepts, consider the confusion that can result when researchers in a particular area rely on diverse definitions. In a recent report, Mary Rohlfing (1995) noted that various researchers have variously defined the concept of "long-distance relationships" as "living more than 250 miles apart," "visiting less than once a month," and "being in situations in which partners find it difficult to see each other every day." Given these discrepant definitions, it's no wonder that some researchers report that long-distance couples are frustrated (those living many miles apart) and other researchers report that long-distance couples are content!

Now that you know your basic assumptions and have generated testable hypotheses or researchable questions with key concepts operationally defined, you confront the question of how to find out if your predictions are accurate or not. In this section, we'll consider three broad types of research that scholars use to test theories. As we examine each approach to research, we'll discuss examples related to the three hypotheses and questions we just generated.

Quantitative Research

Many scholars use **quantitative methods** to conduct research. They gather information that can be quantified and then interpret the data to make arguments about what the numbers reveal about communication behaviors and relationships among communication phenomena. Three of the most popular quantitative methods are descriptive statistics, surveys, and experiments.

Descriptive Statistics   As the name implies, **descriptive statistics** use numbers to describe human behavior. They describe populations, proportions, and frequencies of behavior. To investigate your first hypothesis or question, which focused on the frequencies of interruptions by women and men, you might observe natural conversations and count the number of interruptions made by members of each sex. This simple frequency count would give you information about how often each sex interrupts. Communication researcher Victoria DeFrancisco (1991) did just that in her study of interruptions in conversations between wives and husbands. She found that husbands interrupt wives far more often than wives interrupt husbands. Relationship therapist Aaron Beck (1988) observed the same pattern in couples he counseled.

But suppose you want to know whether the pattern of interruptions DeFrancisco and Beck found holds true in contexts other than marital conversations. To discover the scope of your findings, you would need to count interruptions in a variety of situations. Work by other communication scholars shows that the interruptions DeFrancisco and Beck noted between spouses also occur in group communication (Baird, 1976; Eakins & Eakins, 1976) and in face-to-face interaction between men and women who aren't married (Brandt, 1980; Mulac, Wiemann, Widenmann, & Gibson, 1988). Numbers are like brute facts—alone they mean very little. We attribute meaning to numerical data, deciding whether it is important that men interrupt more often than women do. Numerical observations are meaningless until we interpret them.

You could also use descriptive statistics to test your second hypothesis or pursue your second question, which concerns the frequency of women's and men's attempts to include others in conversation. You might count the number of times women and men in varying communication contexts invite others into conversations. Existing research indicates that women are more active than men in doing what is called "conversational maintenance," which is involving others in conversations (Beck, 1988; Fishman, 1978; Tannen, 1990). Descriptive statistics would not be very helpful in testing your third hypothesis (that women and men find it equally satisfying to talk about relationship issues). We can't count satisfaction because it isn't an overt behavior.

Descriptive statistics are useful to describe patterns and frequencies in communication behavior. Although they can't tell us much about the causes of communication or about subjective states such as satisfaction, descriptive statistics can give us valuable profiles of what happens.

Surveys A second quantitative method is the **survey**, an instrument, questionnaire, or interview that asks respondents to report on their experiences, feelings, actions, and so forth. You could devise a questionnaire to get data relevant to all three of your questions or hypotheses. You might ask 100 women and 100 men to report how frequently they interrupt others, how often they try to include others in conversations, and how satisfying they find it to talk about relationship issues with partners. Alternatively, you could survey 100 members of each sex about their perceptions of men's and women's conversational behaviors. Because both self-reports and observers' perceptions are fallible, collecting both forms of data would provide you with greater information than either form of data alone.

Responses to surveys are raw data. We have to do something with the data to understand their significance. In other words, scholars construct what significance means. They have established a number of statistical tests that can be used to determine whether there are significant differences in quantitative data about perceptions of women's and men's conversational styles. A basic statistics course or textbook will explain these tests to you.

There are limits to what survey research can tell us. Surveys can demonstrate patterns and even relationships, such as an association between interruptions and satisfaction with relationship talk. As we noted in Chapter 2, however, correlational data can't prove causation. Thus, finding that satisfaction is lower in relationships in which there are many interruptions doesn't tell us whether interruptions cause dissatisfaction. It's entirely possible that dissatisfaction causes interruptions or that the two simply accompany each other while some other variable, such as relationship history, causes both of them.

Reflection

Can you think of correlational phenomena in your communication? What is the value of recognizing correlational patterns?

A popular form of survey is the self-report, in which respondents report on their activities, feelings, perceptions, and so forth. Some scholars consider self-reports suspect for several reasons. First is the possibility of **social desirability bias**, which occurs when participants in research give responses that they think are socially acceptable but which may not be totally honest. For example, a person might think it was unacceptable to state the honest feeling that "I find it boring to talk with my partner about our relationship," so the person might self-report that she or he feels relationship talk is important. Second, participants may want to "help" researchers and may provide the responses they think researchers want. Third, respondents may have inaccurate or selective perceptions of what they and others do, feel, and so forth. We might selectively notice all the times we are interrupted but fail to perceive instances in which we interrupt others. Despite these limitations, self-reports provide valuable insight into how individuals perceive themselves, others, and communication encounters.

Finally, surveys often ask respondents to recall past behaviors and feelings. There is the possibility that respondents edit retrospective experience to fit with current knowledge. For example, if you have read reports that say men interrupt more frequently than women, this knowledge may affect how you recall your own experiences with interruptions. This doesn't mean that retrospective data are useless. Quite the contrary. As Steve Duck and Kris Pond (1989) have pointed out, retrospective accounts are very important sources of information about how people currently think about, feel, and perceive experiences. Retrospective data may not accurately reflect what actually happened in the past, but they can tell us how people presently perceive their past experiences. Particularly if you assume that there is no singular, absolute reality, then retrospective data are good sources of information.

Can you generate two hypotheses or research questions whose value outweighs the limitations of retrospective data?

Experiments   An **experiment** is a controlled study that systematically manipulates one thing (called an independent variable) to determine how that affects another thing (called a dependent variable, for what it does depends on the independent variable). One of the greatest strengths of experimental methods is that they provide control so that only the variables of interest are present. This is also a major limitation of experiments: because human interactions are seldom controlled, relationships found in a laboratory, where so many conditions are controlled, may not tell us much about what happens in real communication.

Linda Acitelli (1988) conducted an experiment that provides information about the third hypothesis. She had men and women read descriptions of talk between husbands and wives. In half the situations, couples discussed a conflict or problem in their relationship. In the other half, couples talked about the relationship in general when no particular problem was present. After participants in her experiment had read the descriptions, Acitelli asked them how satisfying they thought the husbands and wives in the descriptions found the conversations. Her assumption was that participants would rely on their own feelings and experiences to rate the satisfaction of the spouses in the scenario.

Acitelli found that both partners found it satisfying to talk about the relationship when there was a problem. When no conflict or difficulty existed, however, the wives in the scenarios were perceived as being more satisfied with conversation about the relationship. Acitelli's finding is consistent with a great deal of research that reports that in general women enjoy talking about relationships more than men do (Aries, 1987; Schaef, 1985; Wood, 1993c, 1994c, 1996a, 2003).

Qualitative Analysis

Not all communication can be measured quantitatively, and quantitative data cannot provide substantial insight into the texture and meaning of experiences. **Qualitative methods** of research are valuable when we wish not to count or measure phenomena but to understand the character of experience, particularly how people perceive and make sense of their communication experience. This involves interpreting meanings and other unobservable dimensions of communication. We will consider two widely used forms of qualitative research.

Textual Analysis   Textual analysis, also called *interpretive analysis,* involves describing communication **texts** and interpreting their meaning. In scholars' vocabulary, texts are more than written documents or presented speeches. Texts include all symbolic activities that are written, oral, or nonverbal. Examples of texts are a presidential address, a discussion between friends, the AIDS quilt, the Vietnam Veterans War Memorial, cartoons, and secret handshakes exchanged between members of a club.

Textual analysts aim to mine the meanings of texts by studying them closely. Linguist Deborah Tannen (1990) uses textual analysis to understand gendered conversational dynamics. By scrutinizing interactions between women and men, Tannen has discovered a number of sex differences in conversational behaviors. Relevant to our research topic, Tannen's analysis of conversational texts reveals that men do interrupt more often than women and that women invest greater effort than men to include others in conversations.

Textual analyses are especially powerful in identifying patterns of meaning in communication. For instance, William Foster Owen (1984, 1985) and a research team to which I belonged (Wood, Dendy, Dordek, Germany, & Varallo, 1994) used thematic analysis of texts to discern broad patterns of meaning and significance in romantic partners' accounts of their relationships. Our goal wasn't to identify and classify particular communication acts, for which quantitative methods might have been more useful. Instead, we wanted to decipher threads of meaning that ran through intimates' perceptions of their relationships.

Using textual analysis, several communication scholars have identified differences in the kind of interruptions that women and men typically make. Men, it seems, often interrupt to challenge others or to assert themselves. Women's interruptions are more likely to support others or to indicate interest in what others are saying (Aries, 1987; Mulac et al., 1988; Stewart, Stewart, Friedley, & Cooper, 1990). This finding enriches our understanding of the brute fact of interruptions by helping us recognize qualitative differences in what interruptions do and mean.

Ethnography Another qualitative method that is gaining increasing popularity is **ethnography**, an interpretive approach to meaning (Geertz, 1973). Ethnography attempts to discover what things mean to others by sensitive observation of human activity. Typically, ethnographers rely on **unobtrusive methods**, which are means of gathering data that intrude minimally on naturally occurring interaction. Rather than constructing an artificial experiment or interrupting natural interaction with a survey or other instrument, unobtrusive data gathering takes place within the existing flow of activity. The goal is for the researcher to fade into a situation so that participants act as they normally do when not being observed. For example, a researcher might sit in the break room of a company every day for two weeks before formally gathering data on communication in the break room. By making herself or himself part of the setting, the researcher's presence is less obtrusive.

A guiding principle of ethnography is to discover what behaviors mean to people on their own terms, not those of the researcher. Thus, ethnographers try not to impose their perceptions, meanings, and views on the activities of others. Instead, they aim to discern meanings that others attach to communication, which may be quite different from their own meanings. This implies that they need to do more than record brute facts of communication. In addition they need to become enough a part of interactional settings to have insight into institutional facts that shed light on how participants in the scene attribute meaning to particular activities (Philipsen, 1992).

Ethnographic studies have long been a mainstay in anthropological research. Because anthropologists seek to understand other cultures, they must avoid imposing their views, values, and perceptions on people in societies different from their own. In other words, the brute facts of particular customs and rituals in a culture become meaningful only when we have insight into cultural perspectives that establish institutional facts. Only by understanding the perspective of members of other cultures can we learn the meaning and social significance of activities.

In recent years ethnographic methods have been increasingly adopted in fields outside anthropology. Many communication researchers find ethnography an especially valuable way to gain insight into communication practices of diverse social groups. For example, Westerners regard eye contact as a sign of respect and interest, so making eye contact is considered polite. In other cultures, including many Asian ones, eye contact is regarded as rude and intrusive. If an American researcher judges Nepalese nonverbal communication by American standards, she or he will misinterpret the lack of eye contact. Instead, the researcher must figure out what eye contact means to Nepalese people.

Ethnographic research directs attention toward rituals, myths, stories, customs, beliefs, and talk that reflect meanings shared by members of particular social groups. Relying on ethnography, communication researchers have been able to identify distinctive communication practices typical of feminine and masculine speech communities (Tannen, 1990; Wood, 2003), differences in how women and men experience and express closeness (Riessman, 1990; Wood & Inman, 1993), and dissimilar meanings that women and men attach to talk about relationships (Acitelli, 1988; Beck, 1988; Tannen, 1990; Wood, 1994c). We risk misinterpreting masculine communication if we evaluate it according to standards of feminine communities. Conversely, we may misunderstand the meaning of much feminine communication if we judge it by criteria appropriate for masculine talk. We will discuss ethnography in greater detail in Chapter 6.

Critical Scholarship

A third approach to research is **critical analysis**. An increasing number of communication scholars believe that research should not be confined to the ivory tower but should make a real difference in the lives of human beings. Critical scholarship is one important way to change oppressive or wrong practices in the world. Thomas Nakayama (1995, p. 174) insists that "communication scholarship can (and should) make a difference in the everyday lives of people." These critical theorists aren't satisfied to understand what happens in communication or even the meanings of various communication practices. Instead, they see the goal of their research as critiquing communication practices that oppress, marginalize, or otherwise harm people. Criticism raises awareness of inequities and problems and thus can motivate change. In addition, critical scholarship can illuminate paths to change by identifying and arguing for alternatives to present conditions, practices, and processes.

Critical theorists often begin with other research methods to determine what is happening and what it means. However, they go beyond description and explanation of communication to argue for changes in communicative practices that disadvantage some social groups. For example, assume our tests of the hypotheses on women's and men's conversational styles revealed that men interrupt women and don't make efforts to include them in conversations. We might use what we learned about techniques of dominance to suggest how men should alter their communication styles to be more egalitarian, and/or to advise women on ways they might resist efforts to interrupt their communication.

Analysis that reveals how communication supports unjust social relations instigates change on two levels. On a personal level, knowledge of oppressive practices allows individuals to notice and resist subtle communicative manipulations. On a social level, understanding of oppressive strategies can be used to revise social policies and practices. Deliberately and unapologetically partisan, critical scholars engage themselves in their work and aim for positive social change.

Reflection

How does involvement with social problems enhance and limit researchers' insights into communication?

Assessing Research

A theory isn't necessarily good simply because researchers have conducted a series of studies and reported their findings. We have to judge how the research was framed, conducted, and interpreted to decide how useful it is and whether it supports a theory. The scholarly community has developed three basic criteria for judging both individual research projects and theories.

Validity   **Validity** refers to the truth or accuracy of a theory in measuring what it claims to measure. Concern with validity does not imply an objectivist ontology, as multiple truths can be regarded as reasonable. The basic issue of validity is whether a theory studies and tests what it intends to study and test.

There are two primary forms of validity. **Internal validity** is the degree to which the design and methods used to test a theory actually measure what they claim to. In regard to our example, we might ask how we know that asking questions is a means of including others in communication. Could questions equally reflect either a kind of pressure or conversational dominance? Another example of internal validity concerns research on communication apprehension. For years, many scholars studied communication apprehension by measuring how much individuals communicated in various situations. Then a key distinction was made between being unwilling and being unable to communicate. A person who isn't motivated to communicate may speak infrequently but may not be apprehensive about communicating. Thus, an internally valid test of communication apprehension has to measure anxiety about communicating.

External validity refers to the generalizability of a theory across contexts, especially ones beyond the confines of experimental situations. In other words, the concern of external validity is whether a theory applies in the real world. The artificiality of an experimental laboratory may affect how we behave, so actions observed in an experiment may not generalize to real life. For example, people may be less likely to interrupt when they are being observed than in ordinary conversations. If so, then a laboratory study of interruptions might lack external validity.

Reliability   A second criterion for evaluating theoretical research is **reliability**, the consistent accuracy of measurement over time. *Accuracy* is generally defined as "consistency of occurrence of a given relationship, behavior, or pattern." If the speedometer in your car registers 60 mph when you are driving 50 mph, 60 mph, and 70 mph, it is unreliable. (It may also earn you a speeding ticket.) If your doctor's arm cuff registers 150/110 as your blood pressure one day, 100/80 a second day, and 190/138 a third day, then something is wrong. It is possible that your blood pressure is actually fluctuating substantially. It's also possible that your doctor's pressure cuff is unreliable, because it doesn't measure your blood pressure accurately on different occasions. Developing good communication theories demands that we use reliable methods of research—ones that measure communicative phenomena with consistent accuracy.

Significance   A third criterion for evaluating research and theory is **significance**, the conceptual or pragmatic importance of a theory. A good theory is useful. It allows us to do something we could not do without the theory. The utility of a theory depends on whether it allows us to explain, predict, control, or change communication behavior and/or conditions that affect it. Research might discover that laughing is correlated with crinkled eyes, leading to the theory of eye crinkling. Even though the theory might accurately describe and predict a behavior, we would be likely to raise questions about the significance of the theory. What difference does its claim make to anyone other than perhaps plastic surgeons?

Quantitative research, qualitative study, and critical analyses are all valuable methods of studying communication. Each form of research is useful in providing particular kinds of insight and limited in revealing other information. The research method or methods scholars use should be appropriate to the questions they are asking and the assumptions they hold about human beings, knowledge, and the research process. Thus, when you read a research report, you should ask whether it is based on methods that suit the goals of that specific investigation.

Summary

In this chapter we've learned how theories about communication are developed and tested. The building blocks of theories are fundamental assumptions that frame researchers' perspectives on human beings. The most basic assumption a theorist makes concerns ontology, or the nature of humans. Whereas some scholars believe human communication is determined by social or biological forces, others assume it reflects the free will, or intention, of sentient agents. The second assumption underlying theories is an epistemological belief either that knowledge is the discovery of objective truth or that it is the interpretation of multiple realities. Third, theorists make assumptions about whether the purpose of research is to generate universal laws of human communication or situated accounts of communication practices in particular circumstances. Finally, theorists differ in whether they assume the focus of research and theory building is communication behavior itself (brute facts) or the meaning of communication behaviors (institutional facts). These four assumptions are the foundation that supports theory.

We examined three broad approaches to research: quantitative, qualitative, and critical methods. The methods differ in what they can tell us and in the fundamental theoretical assumptions with which they are compatible. Despite differences among them, all of the methods we discussed are valuable tools for unlocking knowledge about human communication. Each way of doing research helps us test and refine theories so that they are continually bettered.

Key Terms

behaviorism	objectivity
brute fact	ontology
critical analysis	operational definition
descriptive statistics	qualitative methods
determinism	quantitative methods
epistemology	reliability
ethnography	research question
experiment	significance
external validity	social desirability bias
humanism	standpoint theory
hypothesis	texts
institutional fact	thrownness
internal validity	unobtrusive methods
law	validity
objectivism	

CHAPTER FOUR

An Early Communication Theory

In this chapter we'll make an initial foray into the world of communication theories by examining one of the first theories advanced in the field. Because this is our first effort to consider a specific theory, we will examine only one. Chapters 5 through 13 discuss two or more theories each. As you read this chapter, keep in mind the various goals of theories and the criteria for evaluating them. These are tools that will help you make sense of theorizing in general and specific theories in particular.

General Semantics

In Chapter 1 we noted that today the discipline of communication includes everything from dialogues with ourselves (intrapersonal) to organizational and intercultural communication. In the second decade of this century, however, the scope of the field was much narrower. Rhetoric was the unquestioned center of the communication field; professors studied great speeches and speakers and devoted their primary teaching energies to improving students' public speaking skills.

In this era young I. A. Richards was a novice member of the field who found himself at odds with the emphasis on public speaking. Richards regarded oratory as contemptible because, in his opinion, public rhetoric had sunk to a low level of quality. He also believed that studying classical rhetoric and historical speeches was largely a waste of time. Richards disdained the idea of teaching public speaking, whether in classes to students or in workshops for professionals. He was skeptical of what in later years (1955) he called "sales talk" and equally skeptical of those who would teach persuasive skills.

Despite his criticism of the prevailing emphasis in his field, Richards was not uninterested in communication, nor was he uncommitted to teaching communication skills. He believed, however, that the field needed to redirect its energies to study misunderstandings that plague everyday communication and discover ways to fix them. Richards criticized the focus on public speakers and the process of persuasion and instead advocated a focus on listeners and the process of understanding.

Richards's challenge to trends in the field in the 1920s was instrumental in altering the directions, emphases, and content of both scholarship and teaching in communication. His insistent criticism of the narrow focus on public rhetoric expanded thinking about the scope of communication contexts. His lack of interest in persuasion paved the way for the study of a fuller range of communicative processes.

Richards was one of many scholars called general semanticists. This group of theorists embraced the goal of improving everyday communication by discovering the ways in which words distort, obscure, and complicate understanding between people. If they could discover the sources of misunderstanding, general semanticists thought, they could develop ways to avoid or correct them and thus improve communication. To understand the point of view of Richards and other general semantic theorists, we'll explore their primary ideas about language and some of their proposed remedies for misunderstanding.

The Special Character of Symbols

When a cat hisses, it's a signal of anger and warning of possible attack. Red berries are signals that a plant might be poisonous. Lightning is a signal of thunder. In each of these cases, the signal (hissing, red berries, lightning) is directly connected to what it signifies. Signals, then, are naturally related to what they represent. Because of this natural relationship between signals and their referents, little effort is needed to understand signals—their meanings are relatively clear, unvarying, and unambiguous.

Symbols Are Arbitrary

General semanticists recognized that symbols are different from signals. Symbols such as words, art, and music have no direct or natural relationship to what they represent. The word *cat* is not intrinsically related to furry critters like Sadie, who is sitting on my shoulder as I write. We could as easily call her a kudzu, hetap, or magpie. *Cat* is an arbitrary symbol that we use to refer to a particular species of animal. Like the word *cat*, all symbols are

Figure 4.1

The Semantic Triangle

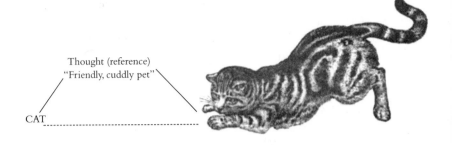

Thought (reference)
"Friendly, cuddly pet"

CAT

conventions that members of a culture agree to use to represent other things. As such, they are arbitrary ways of representing reality, not necessary or natural ones.

In their book *The Meaning of Meaning* (1923), Ogden and Richards used the semantic triangle pictured in Figure 4.1 to illustrate the arbitrary and indirect relationship between words and their referents. Notice that the line between the symbol "cat" and the actual referent of a particular cat is dotted to indicate the two are only indirectly related. There is no natural, absolute connection between the symbol and the referent. The other two lines in the triangle, however, are unbroken. This reflects the direct linkage between our thoughts and both symbols and referents. Once someone who likes cats thinks the word *cat*, she or he has fond thoughts about friendly pets. Because humans tend to think in words and images, our thoughts (references) are directly connected to the words we've learned to use to describe phenomena. Likewise, our thoughts about cats are directly connected to the actual furry creatures we call cats, which are the referents for the word *cat* and thoughts about cats. But the relationship between the word *cat* and the actual referent of the furry animal is arbitrary. Symbols are connected to referents only by indirect, agreed-on conventions of how to use words.

Symbols Are Abstract

In addition to being arbitrary, symbols are abstract because they are not concrete or tangible. They stand for ideas, people, situations, and so forth, but they are not themselves the concrete ideas, people, and situations. Instead, symbols are imperfect, partial ways of designating the raw reality of experience. When we rely on symbols to refer to actual phenomena, we abstract or move away from those phenomena.

Abstractness is a matter of degree, so symbols can be more or less abstract, depending on how general and removed from concrete referents

The Special Character of Symbols **77**

Figure 4.2

The Ladder of Abstraction

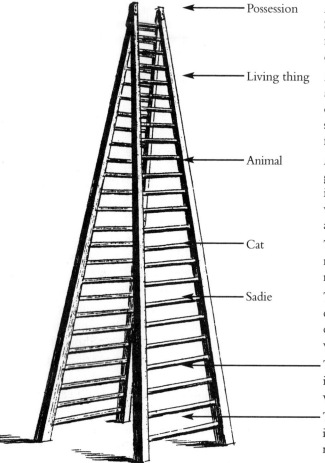

Possession — A very abstract way of describing the particular cat Sadie. At this level of abstraction we've left out almost all references to the features of the specific cat.

Living thing — *Living thing* is an even more abstract term than *animal*. This label calls attention to what Sadie has in common with all living phenomena but fails to specify how she differs from dogs, people, trees, or flowers.

Animal — At this level of abstraction the label is even more general. The word *animal* recognizes what Sadie has in common with all other animals but fails to note what is distinctive about her or even her species of animal.

Cat — This species label abstracts what is common to all members of the species known as cats. Thus it is a more abstract, or less specific, designation of Sadie.

Sadie — The name we give to the particular cat. The name captures only some of the qualities that we perceive in her and obscures other features of her that we could notice.

— The cat Sadie as we perceive her. Out of the totality that she is, we abstract only certain features that we identify as Sadie.

— The chemical, biological, and physical creature that is Sadie has specific qualities and makeup that cannot be fully appreciated by human perception.

they are. Because there are concrete referents for it, the word *table* is less abstract than words like *love*, *honor*, and *dignity*, which don't refer to tangible phenomena. To illustrate varying levels of abstraction in language, general semanticists developed a model called the ladder of abstraction (Hayakawa, 1978) (see Figure 4.2).

Symbols Are Ambiguous

Symbols are also ambiguous because their meanings are unclear and variable. Whereas signals have uniform and absolute meanings, the meaning of a symbol is not absolute and fixed. The word *cat* means one thing when used in reference to an animal, and it means something quite different when used to describe a person. We say "I love you," "I love broccoli," and "I love this course," but the word *love* means different things in each usage.

TRY IT OUT Write your definitions of each of the following words or phrases:

1. Committed relationship

2. Faith

3. Prejudice

4. Welfare

5. Affirmative action

Compare your definitions with those of other students in your class. How do your meanings differ? How might your and others' standpoints explain the differences?

Symbols are arbitrary, abstract, and ambiguous. These three qualities account for the mystery, majesty, and power of language. At the same time, as we will see, these qualities explain the potential for misunderstandings when we use words to communicate.

Reflection

Would we be better off if we could develop a language that was concrete, clear, and based on natural ties between referents and symbols?

Meanings Are Contextual

General semanticists claimed that the arbitrariness, abstractness, and ambiguity of symbols account for why people have different meanings for the same words. This led to a still-popular communication axiom: Meanings are in people, not in words. Richards (1936) argued that the key to understanding (and misunderstanding) is context because meaning changes as symbols move from one context to another.

For Richards and other general semanticists, context was a very broad concept. It refers to more than specific sentences or communication situations. Context also includes thoughts and feelings we have in a situation, history between communicators, the relationship in which communication occurs, and so forth. Context, then, is the entire field of experience that is related to communication. To complicate matters, each of us has a unique field of experience. Because no two individuals have precisely the same field of experience, it's impossible for them to have exactly the same meanings for words.

If fields of experience shape our interpretations of communication, then perhaps we could decrease misunderstandings by working on our

The Special Character of Symbols 79

fields of experience. General semanticists were interested in this solution to misunderstanding. Among them was Alfred Korzybski, a Polish American scientist, linguist, and philosopher who founded the Institute of General Semantics in Connecticut in 1929. One of the better-known ideas from the general semanticists is captured in their phrase "the map is not the territory," which is meant to emphasize the difference between concrete referents (the territory) and symbols that represent them (the map).

Korzybski's training as a physical scientist inclined him to appreciate the precision of science and the importance of careful, empirical observation. That scientific perspective is embodied in Korzybski's book *Science and Sanity* (1958), which attempted to use scientific principles to reduce misunderstandings in communication. A major emphasis of this book, as well as much of the work by general semanticists, was on finding ways to distinguish maps from territories in our thinking and communication.

Korzybski believed that communication problems often occur when we rely on our maps, or words, to assign meanings instead of referring to the territories, or actual phenomena of experience. To distinguish between these two routes to meaning, Korzybski referred to intensional and extensional orientations. **Intensional orientations** to communication and meaning are based on internal factors, or what's inside of us—our own definitions, associations, and fields of experience related to words we speak, hear, and read.

Extensional orientations, in contrast, are based on observation and attention to objective particulars that distinguish phenomena from one another. Korzybski believed we would have fewer misunderstandings if we adopted more extensional orientations and kept "checking the facts" behind words. In other words, Korzybski thought the problems caused by intensional orientations were inherent in language—we could escape them only by getting out of language and back into the extensional world to which language refers. For example, intensional language such as "She's politically liberal" should be replaced with more extensional language such as "She supports efforts to reduce racial discrimination." Table 4.1 summarizes the differences between the two orientations to communication.

Perhaps you've had the experience of being fooled by language because you didn't check to see what the territory was. For example, a group of communication researchers (Stacks, Hill, & Hickson, 1991, p. 85) recounted a clever advertising tactic invented by a fast-food store. Noticing that many customers refused to order milkshakes because milkshakes are fattening, this store named its milkshake a "Skinny Shake." Sales of milkshakes/Skinny Shakes soared because people who wanted to avoid high-calorie foods assumed the label "Skinny Shake" meant the beverage was

An Early Communication Theory

Table 4.1

Intensional and Extensional Orientations

Intensional	Extensional
Notices generalities and classes	Notices particulars and uniqueness
Relies on preset beliefs and values to assign meaning	Observes reality to determine what it is and means
Begins with assumptions about meaning	Begins with observations of phenomena
Doesn't question the assumed meaning of words	Compares words with concrete referents

Source: Adapted from Korzybski, A. (1958). *Science and sanity: An introduction to non-Aristotelian systems and general semantics.* Lakeville, CT: Institute of General Semantics.

appropriate for them. In reality the very same ingredients in milkshakes were used to make Skinny Shakes.

A less amusing example of being fooled by words because we don't check on the facts occurred in the early 1990s. At that time, Congress was debating a bill designed to increase job opportunities for citizens who had not participated fully in the labor market. Those who opposed the bill dubbed it the "quota bill," and it was soundly defeated. When questioned about the reasons for their votes, many politicians reported that they were against quotas and wouldn't support any legislation that imposed quotas on hiring. A check of the extensional facts, the actual language in the bill, however, revealed that the bill did not mandate quotas. In fact, there was a provision in the bill that explicitly banned quotas. In this case, the label "quota bill" shaped meanings more than the facts did.

Reflection

What ethical implications do you perceive in using language that inaccurately represents "the facts"? Can symbols ever be really "accurate"?

Another example of uncritical reaction to a word occurred in 1999, when David Howard, a top aide of Mayor Anthony Williams of Washington, used the word *niggardly* to describe the funds given to his office. A black staff member confused the word *niggardly*, which means *miserly* or *stingy,* with the similar-sounding racial epithet. Howard apologized for the misunderstanding and for using a word that could be confused with a racial slur. Ever alert to political currents, Mayor Williams accepted Howard's resignation. However, the public outcry against Howard's resignation was fierce. Even NAACP chair Julian Bond called pressuring Howard to resign ridiculous. To make his point humorously, Bond said he thought Mayor Williams had been "niggardly" in his judgment (Clemetson, 1999). Perhaps Bond heeded general semanticists' advice and refused to be confused about what a word does—and does not—mean.

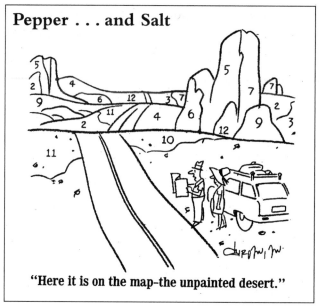

Pepper . . . and Salt

"Here it is on the map-the unpainted desert."

From the *Wall Street Journal*—Permission, Cartoon Features Syndicate.

Remedies for Misunderstanding

General semanticists were firmly committed to practical application of their ideas. Reminding ourselves that "the map is not the territory" prompts us to check the facts behind words. We will, however, discuss three of the more popular techniques for understanding that they advocated.

Etc.

According to general semanticists, we get ourselves in linguistic trouble when we forget that symbols are abstract and therefore partial representations of phenomena. We can never say all there is to say about anything. To remind ourselves of the incompleteness of symbols, we should use the term *etc.* continually. For example, we should say "That was a great class, etc.," "I met an interesting person, etc.," "General semantics theory is exciting, etc." Using *etc.* is a way of indicating to ourselves and others that we know we haven't said all that can be said about a class, person, or theory. Reminding ourselves that language abstracts only part of reality was so important to general semanticists that they named their professional journal *Et Cetera.*

Events in recent history provide a dramatic example of the general semanticists' point that we can never say everything about anything. In late summer of 1991 in Crown Heights, a suburb of Brooklyn, a young black child was killed when he was struck by a car in Rebbe Menachem

An Early Communication Theory

Schneerson's motorcade. Some African Americans thought the child had been deliberately murdered because of racial prejudice, so they retaliated by killing a Jewish student. Anna Deavere Smith, a performance artist you will meet again in Chapter 6, went to Crown Heights, where she interviewed over 200 members of the community, some of whom had been eyewitnesses to the death of the black child. Smith (1993) then created a one-woman show called *Fires in the Mirror*, in which she presented the views of members of the community using the words and gestures those people had used in her interviews of them. Smith's performance was remarkable in its refusal to offer resolution in the sense of which views were "right." Instead, Smith let her performance show that each position and each set of words spoken by and through her was both legitimate and incomplete (Martin, 1993). The fuller story of Crown Heights surfaced in the lack of closure, the deliberately portrayed incompleteness of any single set of words. Her performance embodied the principle that we can never say all there is to say about anything.

Indexing

Have you ever been frustrated because someone, perhaps a parent, refers to you in a way that reflects who you used to be but not who you are now? As a child and teenager, I was not responsible with money. If someone gave me a dollar, I spent it as fast as I could on some short-lived pleasure such as ice cream. In my twenties, however, to put myself through college and graduate school, I worked 40 hours a week. This experience taught me to budget, save, and be financially responsible. Yet, well into my thirties, my father continued to lecture me about savings and to refer to any purchases I made as frivolous extravagances. I felt hurt and angry that he didn't recognize the financial responsibility I had developed.

General semanticists would say that my father's misunderstanding of me was a common problem that resulted from the use of a single, unchanging word to refer to phenomena that change and evolve. The word *Julia* labeled me at 5, 15, 25, 35, and 45 years of age. Because my parents had an unchanging label for me, their thoughts about me were similarly fixed (notice this reflects an intensional orientation). To remedy the fixity of symbols, general semanticists recommended that we index terms to specific dates, situations, and so forth. For example, we could say that $Julia_{1958}$ was irresponsible with money, but $Julia_{1995}$ was responsible about finances. Using the dates reminds us that when we refer to others, we are referring to them at particular times, and people change. We can also index situations. We might say that $Zuriin_{social\ situations}$ is outgoing and dynamic, but $Zuriin_{one\text{-}to\text{-}one\ conversations}$ is quiet and pensive. **Indexing** is a way to remind ourselves that meanings vary and change across time and circumstances.

TRY IT OUT Experiment with indexing in your thinking and communication. For one hour, use indexes to specify a date and/or situation for every noun you use. How does doing this affect the meanings you have for the nouns you use in thought and communication?

Feedforward

You've heard the term *feedback,* which refers to a response to communication. General semanticists coined the term **feedforward** to describe the process of anticipating the effects of communication and adapting to these anticipated effects in advance of actually communicating with others. Their thinking was that, if we were more thoughtful in planning communication, we would have fewer misunderstandings that require repairing.

At the age of 75, nearly half a century after he had begun his career, Richards (1968) reflected on the most important things he had learned. Of all the insights he had gained into communication and all the solutions to misunderstandings he and others had developed, feedforward was the one that seemed most valuable to Richards. He wrote that feedforward is a method of taking into account the fields of experience of those with whom we communicate and adapting our communication accordingly. Feedforward, in other words, is anticipatory feedback.

Reflection

How might David Howard (discussed on page 81) have used the principle of feedforward to prevent misunderstanding in his situation?

Richards advised us to take the perspectives of others, to think through what we plan to say and how we plan to say it, and to ask whether the planned communication will mean to others what we intend it to mean. If Jerome walks into his apartment planning to hole up to write a paper that's due tomorrow, he might feel angry on hearing his roommate's stereo blaring. Jerome might immediately think, "I'm going to tell him to shut that ★★!!!##! music up so that I can work." Using feedforward, however, Jerome would realize that demanding and cursing may express his personal feelings, but they are unlikely to motivate his roommate to cooperate, much less to preserve friendly relations. Thus, Jerome might modify his communication and say to his roommate, "Hey, guy, could you turn it down for tonight? I have to get a paper written in time for my 9 A.M. class tomorrow." This request is likely to be more effective than the original communication Jerome conceived.

Reflection

Can you identify aspects of situations and relationships that enhance or restrict the ability to engage in feedforward?

Although general semantics is no longer a dominant communication theory, the idea of feedforward has survived rather well. Using varying language, many theorists emphasize the importance of considering the perspectives of those with whom we communicate as a prerequisite for creating effective communication. In several books I have used the term *dual perspective* to capture the idea that good communication requires awareness of our own and others' perspectives (Phillips & Wood, 1983; Wood, 1998b, 2000). I have also written of monitoring—observing, evaluating, and adapting our communication throughout the communication process. Constructivism, which we discuss in Chapter 7, uses the concepts of person-centeredness and perspective taking to emphasize the same process. George Herbert Mead, whose theory of symbolic interactionism we'll study in Chapter 5, wrote about taking the role of the other in order to interact effectively. Theories that we will examine in later chapters also stress the importance of considering others' viewpoints.

Critical Assessment of General Semantics

The heyday of general semantics was the 1920s through the 1940s. Since then, it hasn't prospered, nor does it receive much attention from most modern scholars and teachers. This is somewhat surprising, as many of the basic ideas that originated with general semantics inform current theory and teaching. For instance, the notion that the map is not the territory is an axiom found in current textbooks, and the advice to distinguish between facts (extensional orientation) and inferences (intensional orientation) is a basic premise taught in many introductory communication courses. Given the endurance of some of the concepts that general semanticists developed, why has the theory not withstood the test of time?

Too Simplistic

One reason general semantics no longer has many followers is that many scholars regard the theory as simplistic. They charge that general semantics oversimplifies communication and advises quick and easy fixes for highly complex problems. Further, some critics assert that, for all of its commitments to practical applications, the theory is not very practical. How realistic is it to follow everything we think or say with "etc." or to index everything?

Misrepresents the Character of Symbols and Language

A second and particularly important criticism of general semantics is that the theory misrepresents the complex character of symbols, specifically language. From what you've read, you realize that general semantics views language as representing the extensional world, or concrete reality. Thus, theorists who adopt this perspective seem to suggest that all language does is represent what is—what already exists.

Many communication scholars reject the view that language is only representational (Billig, 1987; Shotter, 1993; Stewart, 1991; Wood & Duck, 1995a). Instead, they argue, language is also presentational in that it presents images, ideas, and perspectives. In other words, language not only reflects reality, it also creates the reality in which we believe. From this point of view, one of the most powerful functions of language is to create meanings—this is far different from the general semanticists' presumption that language represents a concrete and objective reality. When you say "I love you" for the first time to another person, something happens. You are not just describing an objective phenomenon. You are changing your identity and the relationship you have with the other person. This suggests that identities and social experiences arise in discourse. If language is presentational, not merely representational as general semanticists claimed, then this theory fails to offer a good description of communication.

Lacks Applied Value

Related to the criticism that general semantics neglects the presentational power of language is the charge that some of the correctives advised by general semanticists can't be applied to many kinds of human communication. Why might this be so? Because symbols are inherently abstract and ambiguous, they often do not have extensional referents. For example, what are the concrete referents for symbols such as love, honor, idea, loyalty, friendship, family values, arrogance, and fear? What these symbols mean to you depends on your own experiences, values, and perceptions, and those may not be the same as others' experiences, values, perceptions, and meanings for the symbols. Meaning, in other words, often isn't based on concrete, material phenomena. Thus, it isn't always possible to follow the general semanticists' advice to "check the facts" by referring to objective, concrete phenomena.

Despite criticisms, some scholars continue to regard general semantics highly and to work to advance its principles. Research and theory relevant to general semantics continues to appear in *Et Cetera*, which was founded in 1943. If you would like to learn more about current thinking in general semantics, as well as biographical information on Korzybski, visit the Institute of General Semantics Web site: http://www.general-semantics.org/.

Summary

Even though general semantics is no longer influential in the field of communication, it made and makes valuable contributions to our understandings of what happens when people talk to one another. Basic ideas such as "the map is not the territory" and "meanings are in people" are shorthand references for very important insights. If we realize that words are slippery and have great potential for multiple meanings, then we are more likely to use them carefully and to check with others to see whether meanings are shared.

The general semanticists were concerned about misunderstandings that arise because of the slippage in language. Their goal was to discover and teach methods of enhancing clarity and reducing misunderstandings in communication. Because general semanticists saw context in the broad sense as the source of meanings, their theorizing focused on describing and explaining contextual sources of misunderstanding, and the practical applications they generated emphasized habits of thought and communication that minimize misunderstandings between people. As we explore more modern theories of communication in later chapters, keep in mind the central concerns of general semanticists. You will see the issues that commanded their attention resurface in various ways in theories developed in more recent years.

Key Terms

extensional orientation

feedforward

indexing

intensional orientation

CHAPTER FIVE

Theories About Symbolic Activity

Because symbols are at the heart of communication, scholars have generated many theories about symbolic activity. In this chapter we'll consider three that, although distinct, are compatible in their basic assumptions about human nature and the importance of symbols in human experience. Although the theories differ in important aspects, they share an interest in understanding the ways in which we use, misuse, and abuse communication.

Symbolic Interactionism

Although George Herbert Mead never completed his Ph.D., for many years he lectured at the University of Chicago, which was a hub of intellectual life in the United States in the 1920s and 1930s. Trained in both philosophy and social science, Mead was fascinated by the human ability to use symbols. His observations and reflections over many years led him to believe that human symbolic activities account for the distinct character of human thinking, for individual identity, and for the persistence of society through the behaviors of individuals.

Mead thought that symbols were the basis of individual identity and social life. In his opinion, individuals can acquire identity only by interacting with others. As we do so, we learn the language and the perspectives of our social communities. Because Mead regarded symbols as the foundation of both personal and social life, the theory he developed is called **symbolic interactionism**.

Throughout his academic career Mead continually refined his ideas about the ways humans create meaning for objects, situations, experiences,

89

others, and themselves. During his lifetime Mead was an enormously popular teacher and a widely respected intellectual leader. Given his influence, it is surprising that Mead himself published very little during his life. After his death, however, his students collaborated to create a book based on his lectures. That book, *Mind, Self, and Society* (1934), is the bedrock of symbolic interactionism. In the 60 years since Mead formulated symbolic interactionism, the theory has continued to inspire scholars in a range of fields, including communication. To understand Mead's ideas, we'll examine five of the key concepts in symbolic interaction theory.

Mind

Mead believed that at birth humans have neither minds nor selves. Both, he argued, are acquired in the process of interacting with others. In the earliest period of life, infants can interact with others only by behaving and responding to the behaviors of others. According to this theory, there is no way for a four-week-old baby to share ideas with others. Once a child learns language, however, she or he can communicate meanings with words. Instead of using the behavior of crying to signal a desire for food, an infant who has acquired language can say "food," "din din," or some other symbolic code to communicate the desire for food. Also, once a child understands language, others can communicate ideas to him or her. Instead of punishing a child after the fact for throwing food, a parent can issue a verbal warning, "If you throw your food, you're going into quiet time."

Mead described **mind** as the ability to use symbols that have common social meanings. As children interact with family, peers, and others, they learn language, and concurrently they learn the social meanings attached to particular words. In Mead's view, social life and communication between people are possible only when we understand and can use a common language. The ability to use symbols that have common meanings allows individuals to share ideas and to communicate about ideas rather than simply behaving toward one another as animals do.

Because language expresses social meanings, in learning language individuals also learn the meanings of a society. Every culture has its own meanings for various feelings, actions, concepts, and other phenomena. In Western society, the word *dog* means "a four-footed animal that is usually friendly and often a cherished pet." Yet in some cultures dogs are eaten. Thus, children in different cultures might both learn the symbol for dog, but they would learn different meanings for it. In Western society, the word *individualism* has positive connotations of personal strength, initiative, and self-reliance. Most Asian cultures emphasize family and community above individuals, so individualism is considered selfish and unbecoming (Ferrante, 1995). In the process of acquiring language, individuals learn the common meanings of their culture. This is what it means to acquire a mind.

Self

Like mind, **self** doesn't exist at birth. Also like mind, self is developed through interaction with others. Mead regarded self as the ability to reflect on ourselves from the perspective of others. Before children develop a concept of themselves, they first experience others acting toward them, labeling them, defining them. Children learn how others see them through comments such as "You're a good boy," "You're always creating trouble," "You're smart," "You're dumb," "You were an accident," or "You're the apple of my eye." The views of us that others communicate are the basis of our initial meanings for ourselves—our understanding of who we are.

The concept of the **looking glass self** clarifies Mead's view of the human self. Symbolic interactionists explain that we learn to see ourselves mirrored in others' eyes. In other words, our perceptions of how others see us are lenses through which we perceive ourselves. We learn to see ourselves in terms of the labels others apply to us. Those labels shape our self-concepts and behaviors.

Reflection

To whom do you look for reflections of yourself? How do the views of you that they reflect affect how you see yourself?

Mead's views of self give us insight into the phenomenon of **self-fulfilling prophecy**, in which individuals live up to the labels others impose on them. Perhaps you have known people who believe they are unattractive, although you think they're nice looking, or who think they are not very smart, although you perceive them as bright. How others see us may be so powerful that it dictates how we see ourselves and how we live our lives, regardless of whether others' perceptions are reasonable.

I and ME

In analyzing the self Mead was fascinated by the fact that humans have the distinctive ability to be both the subjects and the objects of their experience. We can both act and observe ourselves in the process of acting. Mead referred to the part of the self that is an acting subject as the **I**. The I is impulsive, creative, spontaneous, and generally unburdened by social rules and restrictions. Thus, the I is the source both of creative genius and individuality and of criminal and immoral behavior. The **ME** is the socially conscious part of the self, who reflects on the I's impulses and actions. (Notice that Mead employed his own theory of language in giving names—and thus social significance—to these two aspects of the self.) The ME is analytical, evaluative, and above all aware of social conventions, rules, and expectations. The I might think it would be great fun to go skinny-dipping on a crowded beach, but the ME would probably remind the I that skinny-dipping is not generally socially approved. The I may wish to tell off a friend or parent, but the ME imposes social guidelines.

Mead saw the I and the ME as complementary, not opposing, parts of the self. He emphasized that the I is the source of personal creativity and social invention and progress. The I's impulsive, imaginative talents are important to individuals and societies. At the same time, Mead thought, if we acted only from personal whim, desire, and impulse, collective life would not be possible. We would live in anarchy or chaos. When the two parts of the self work well together, the ME edits and channels the I's creativity in socially acceptable ways, and the I refuses to let the ME turn it into a carbon copy of other people.

Reflection

Identify two examples of how your I and ME interact in your everyday activities.

Role Taking

According to symbolic interactionists, the ME, or the socially aware aspect of the self, consists of the perspectives of others. As we interact with others, we come to understand the meanings they attach to situations, behaviors, people, ideas, values, and so forth. We then import, or take inside ourselves, the perspectives of others, which become our (for the ME part of us) own perspectives on the world.

Symbolic interactionists claim that our meanings for things reflect the perspectives of both **particular others** and the **generalized other**. Particular others are individuals who are significant to us. The first particular others for most of us are family members. Later, friends, romantic partners, and work associates may also become significant people in our lives. As we interact with particular others, we gain an understanding of what things mean to them and how they make sense out of various experiences, situations, and people. Mead described this process as importing others' perspectives into ourselves. Once we import, or internalize, the perspectives of particular others, we are able to see the world through their eyes. In other words, we invoke the perspective of a particular other or several particular others to guide how we think and act. The process of internalizing others' perspectives and viewing experience from their perspectives is called **role taking**.

My mother was a very compassionate woman who remains one of my models of caring for others. I often rely on my mother's perspective when I am trying to comfort a friend or student. My father was an accomplished negotiator and a very creative prankster. I find myself taking his perspective when I am negotiating business and when I am plotting a practical joke. The cast of particular others in my head also includes a teacher whose perspective I often assume when thinking about teaching, a friend whose knowledge of art is excellent and whose perspective I use when I look at works of art, and a partner whose sense of social responsibility has formed much of my own view of social issues and my contributions to my community and the planet. All of these particular others are included in the ME aspect of my self. They provide lenses through which I view both the world and myself.

Reflection

Which particular others' perspectives have you imported into your ME?

In addition to particular others, individuals also use the perspective of the generalized other to decide what things mean. Mead described the generalized other as the viewpoint of a social group, community, or society as a whole. It includes rules, roles, and attitudes that are shared by members of the society or community in which an individual lives. The generalized other is an organized composite of all of the particular others who belong to a particular society or social community. In addition, the generalized other reflects our understandings of society in general based on direct interactions with others, exposure to media, and observations of social life.

To clarify how particular others and the generalized other are distinct as well as how they work together, Mead relied on the analogy of a baseball game. He noted that at first a new player understands only his or her own role in the game. The player recognizes what's required to be a pitcher, first-base player, or catcher. Gradually the new player grasps the perspectives of other particular players in the game. Even when our player is in the role of batter, she or he understands the role of pitcher enough to know that the pitcher will try to get her or him to strike at bad balls. At this point the player grasps the perspectives of particular others. Finally, said Mead, our novice player understands the game of baseball as a whole. This involves realizing how all of the players interact and how their coordinated activities create the overall game. When our player comprehends the big picture, she or he understands and can use the perspective of the generalized other.

Let's consider an example to illustrate the symbolic interactionist view of how individuals create meanings for their activities. One of my closest friends is a man. We both understand that our relationship is neither romantic nor sexual but is a very warm friendship. Both Bert and I are people who express affection by touching, so we're inclined to hug each other and engage in other nonverbal communication to express our fondness for each other. Our friends and families understand what Bert's and my relationship is and is not, and they realize that we are each firmly committed to other romantic partners. Because we understand the perspectives of our families and friends and they understand ours, Bert and I don't worry about being misinterpreted if we embrace or touch each other when we are with these people.

Yet when we are together in public settings with people who don't know us well, Bert and I restrain nonverbal expressions of affection. We understand that the perspective of the generalized other in Western society is that a man and a woman who are physically affectionate are romantically and/or sexually involved. Consequently, we (the ME parts of us) edit our behavior in public contexts. When we adopt the generalized other's perspective toward nonverbal signs of affection between women and men, we understand that others are likely to misinterpret hugs between us. Like Bert and me, all of us learn to see ourselves and our communication from the perspectives of particular others and the generalized other.

Let's summarize the symbolic interactionist view of how individuals create meaning. First, symbolic interactionists believe that people act on the basis of what things mean to them. Thus, meanings are the basis of behavior, including communication. Second, symbolic interactionists claim that meanings are formed in the process of interacting symbolically with others in a society. This implies two important ideas: (1) that symbols are the foundation of meaning; and (2) that individuals' meanings aren't strictly personal but always carry social overtones. Third, symbolic interactionists believe that the meanings individuals confer on experiences, feelings, events, activities, other people, and themselves reflect the internalized perspectives of particular others and the generalized other.

As you may have realized, symbolic interactionism views individuals as interpretive beings whose mental activities, rather than external stimuli, direct their behaviors. Herbert Blumer (1969), a theorist who extended Mead's original work, insists that individuals construct their actions through a process of personal interpretation. Although the perspective of the generalized other may be strong and even compelling, it does not determine individuals' meanings or actions. Instead, their interpretations of others' perspectives—not those perspectives themselves—guide individuals' meanings and choices of how to communicate in particular situations.

Mead was very clear about the kinds of research he thought were appropriate and inappropriate for symbolic interactionism. He firmly rejected behavioristic views of individuals as unthinking, unwilling reactors to external stimuli. Mead also scorned experimental research because he believed that it and most other quantitative methods were incapable of getting at the meaning behind observable actions (Blumer, 1969; Denzin,

2001). Participant observation, ethnographic study, and interpretive textual analysis are favored methods of symbolic interaction theorists.

T R Y   I T   O U T   Apply the criteria for evaluating theory (see Chapter 2) to symbolic interactionism. How well does this theory measure up on each criterion?

1. Does the theory provide a full description and explanation of how individuals create meaning?
2. Is the theory testable?
3. Is it appropriately simple?
4. Does it have practical utility?
5. Is the theory heuristic?

Critical Assessment of Symbolic Interactionism

As is true of most theories, symbolic interactionism has both admirers and detractors. Those who find fault with this theory tend to focus on three shortcomings.

The Theory Has Conceptual Inconsistencies   First, a number of scholars complain that Mead is inconsistent in his description of key concepts such as self, mind, and generalized other. The response of symbolic interactionists to this criticism is twofold. First, they point out that Mead himself never formally wrote out his theory. It was only years after his famous lectures at the University of Chicago that his students synthesized their lecture notes to compile the manuscript of *Mind, Self, and Society,* which is often called "the Bible of symbolic interactionism." Second, say proponents of the theory, the concepts Mead emphasized are inherently complex and appropriately take on different nuances in varying contexts. For instance, in describing the generalized other as both society and social groups in different portions of his book, Mead was faithful to the complicated and multifaceted nature of social life.

The Theory Is Too Vague and Broad   A second charge is that symbolic interactionism is too vague and general to be useful. Critics assert that Mead's ideas are highly abstract and don't provide much insight into the specific processes by which individuals construct meanings and sculpt communication behaviors. Responding to this, symbolic interactionists argue that the criticism is unfair because it disparages Mead and his followers for not doing something they never set out to do. Mead's goal was to understand how "society got into individuals" so that they constructed meanings with reference

Calvin and Hobbes

by Bill Watterson

to the ones commonly endorsed in the culture as a whole. Mead was successful in providing a coherent account of the role of symbols in socializing individuals and allowing meanings to be shared by members of a society.

The Theory Neglects Self-Esteem   The third indictment of symbolic interactionism is that it virtually ignores self-esteem, which many communication scholars consider a centrally important concept. Symbolic interactionism describes how we come to see ourselves but has little to say about how various experiences and others' labels for us enhance or diminish self-esteem. Symbolic interactionists agree that self-esteem is not a focus, but they don't agree that this is a weakness of the theory. Instead, they point out that Mead's goals were to describe and explain how society gets into individuals. He was not attempting to provide a critical theory. Thus, he didn't offer critical analysis of processes that affect self-esteem, and he didn't criticize ways in which the generalized other's perspective can oppress individuals and groups outside of the cultural mainstream. Like all theorists, Mead limited his attention to only some dimensions of communication and social life.

To place these criticisms in perspective, it's important to recognize that symbolic interactionism has remained healthy, vibrant, and popular for over 60 years—a record that few theories can match. In addition, this theory provides the foundation for countless other, more specific communication theories. In this book, you'll hear echoes of symbolic interactionism as you study dramatism, narrative theory, constructivism, rules, cultural studies theory, theories of mass communication, muted group theory, and standpoint theory. The scope and endurance of symbolic interactionism's influence are impressive.

Dramatism begins with the premise that life is a drama and that it can be understood in dramatic terms. Thus, communicators involved in situations are seen as actors performing dramatic scenes on the metaphorical stage of life. Dramatism includes both rhetorical and sociological theories. Probably the best-known tradition in sociology is Erving Goffman's dramaturgy, which studies individuals as always engaging in the presentation of self in everyday life. We will examine Goffman's (1967) perspective in Chapter 6.

Our exploration of dramatism will focus on the work of Kenneth Burke, a giant among symbolic theorists. Burke's theory accords a central position to symbolic action; thus it is particularly pertinent to the study of communication. Burke sees life as a drama, which involves conflict and division that threatens some existing form of order. For example, a strike by workers creates (or makes visible) the division between workers and factory owners and threatens the existing order, in which owners define the terms of work in ways that suit them. Burke also believes that drama involves scenes that invite or discourage specific action by actors. For example, a news conference called by workers invites actions that highlight their grievances and condemn owners' lack of concern and respect for workers. Management–labor negotiation behind closed doors is a different scene, which invites more cooperative forms of communication and discourages purely one-sided views. Burke believes that the conflict inherent in drama results in suffering and gives birth to new ways of understanding self, others, and situations. Thus, in Burke's view dramatic conflict opens new possibilities for humans.

Kenneth Burke is as unorthodox a theorist as we will meet. He spent his early adult years in Greenwich Village, a New York community that has long attracted beatniks, hippies, and others who didn't fit or want to fit into the social mainstream. Unlike most of the theorists we've studied, Burke never earned an undergraduate degree. Despite this, he educated himself well in literary criticism and later in philosophy, communication, sociology, economics, theology, and linguistics. Clearly he loved learning and education, even if he didn't find academic institutions the best context for his education. In midlife Burke taught for nearly two decades at various colleges, including Harvard, Princeton, and the University of Chicago. His time at the University of Chicago may explain the consistency between many of Burke's ideas and those of George Herbert Mead, who for years was one of the luminaries on the faculty at the University of Chicago. Unlike Mead, Burke has published prolifically. Since 1931 he has published eight books as well as numerous articles and chapters in books. His work is widely quoted and, even when not directly cited, often is reflected in the perspectives of many communication scholars.

Burke's theory has been called the most comprehensive of all theories of symbolic action. Because Burke himself is so well read in many fields, his ideas are complex, nuanced, and sometimes very confusing. The originality and depth of his insights into human nature and human communication, however, make it worth our while to try to understand Burke's dramatistic theory. We'll do so by examining two of the central concepts in his theory and the method that he invented to analyze human symbolic behavior.

Identification

Burke launches his theory by announcing that we must recognize that all things have **substance**, which he defines as "the general nature or essence of a thing." Each person is a distinct substance, a holistic essence derived from the interaction among all aspects of that individual. Burke believes that the distinct, or unlike, substance of each person is the basis of human communication. There is a degree of overlap between the substances of individuals, but it is not complete, so we remain apart. Because people are not identical, we are divided from one another. Communication becomes the primary means by which we seek to transcend our divisions and enhance our **consubstantiality**, or identification with each other (Burke, 1950).

For Burke, consubstantiality is what makes communication possible. We can understand one another only because there is some overlap in individuals' substances (experiences, language, goals). At the same time, communication can't be perfect, because there are also differences and divisions that keep individuals from being completely consubstantial. Communication is the primary way that we increase our identification, or consubstantiality, with others and diminish our division, or separateness, from others.

Whether a public speaker is trying to persuade a large audience or a couple is trying to work out a conflict, division is always present and is the impetus for communication that seeks to build identification. In all cases, Burke thought, there is an order that is threatened by divisions between people. We may fail to live up to the order, or ideal, of friendship, in which case we experience guilt and must find a way to redeem ourselves. These are the interlocking moments in the unfolding drama of human communication. Identification is sought because we feel division; division makes us aware of the need for identification.

Guilt

Burke (1965, 1966) argues that **guilt** is the central motive for human action, specifically communication. Guilt, however, is defined broadly as "any tension, discomfort, sense of shame, or other unpleasant feeling that humans experience." In Burke's judgment, we continuously feel guilt and are continually attempting to purge ourselves of the discomfort it causes. In other words, guilt is the primary motivation for human action. According to Burke, the ability to feel guilt is uniquely human and is possible only because we are symbol-using animals. He identifies three ways in which symbolic abilities give rise to guilt in humans, and one consequence of our capacity to experience guilt (1965, 1966).

Hierarchy   Language allows us to create categories and evaluations that are the basis of social hierarchies, such as socioeconomic classes, titles in organizations, and degrees of status and power. In turn, social hierarchies create division among people, and division provokes guilt. Guilt can be aroused both by being above some people and by not being higher ourselves in the social **hierarchy**. In both cases, we're divided from others by our position in the hierarchy. Hierarchy explains the human propensity for war and conquest, which were major concerns of Burke's social criticism. Whether as individuals or nations, we want to be on top, the winner, the conqueror rather than the conquered. At the same time, the human quest for consubstantiality makes us uncomfortable with conqueror–conquered and have–have not relationships.

Perfection   In defining humans, Burke says we are "rotten with perfection" (1966). By this he means that our symbols allow us to conceive and name perfect forms or ideals that are at the top of the hierarchy: a flawless relationship, a completely egalitarian society, your ideal weight, a perfect LSAT score, a world free of war. Guilt arises because of the gap between what is the case (personal shortcomings, imperfections in relationships, social inequities) and the **perfection** that we can imagine. Because we can identify perfection yet can never achieve it, we feel rotten. If we couldn't conceive of perfection, we wouldn't feel guilty about falling short of ideals.

The Negative   Humans, says Burke, invented the idea of the **negative**, by which he means the moral capacity to say "no," "not," and "thou shalt not." Our ability to name the negative, or what should not be, is the basis of moral judgments, which other animals do not seem to make in any sophisticated way. Because we have invented a great many negatives and judge ourselves by them, it's difficult to avoid guilt about disobeying some rule we've created or believe in. For example, we think, "We should lose weight to be attractive," and we simultaneously think, "It's wrong to deprive ourselves of pleasure." You believe that "I shouldn't be selfish when close friends and family want my company and time," yet you also believe that "it's wrong to let others define my life." You believe everyone should have basic medical care and decent living conditions, yet you also think your tax dollars should not be used to support other people. Which "should" should you follow? Which "should not" should you disobey? In Burke's view, conflicts such as these are basic to the human condition.

TRY IT OUT   List five "shalt nots" in which you believe. Select ones you consider important to your personal code of morality. Now list particular situations in which you violated some of your shalt nots. Can you identify an alternative rule that specifies a shalt not that was honored by transgressing the rule you listed?

Purging Guilt   If guilt is the primary human motive, reasons Burke, then purging guilt becomes the principal goal of communication. Two methods of ridding ourselves of guilt are available. First, we may engage in **mortification**, which is blaming ourselves. We do this by confessing our failings and asking forgiveness. The statements "I'm sorry," "Can you overlook what I did?" and "America was wrong to interfere in the internal affairs of another country" are examples of ways we engage in mortification. A more formal method is the Catholic ritual of confession followed by penance to regain grace.

A second way to purge guilt is to engage in **victimage**, which involves identifying an external source for some apparent failing or sin. The two-year-old says, "She pushed me first," whereas the 40-year-old says, "I was really stressed out by work." Either way, some source other than the individual is blamed for a wrongdoing. Victimage often takes the form of **scapegoating**, the placing of sins into a sacrificial vessel whose destruction serves to cleanse an individual or group of sin. In biblical times a sacrificial goat carried all the sins of people, and the slaughter of the goat cleansed them. In secular activities an individual is often sacrificed to redeem many others. For example, in 1994 a nominee for a high post in the Clinton administration was found to have failed to pay social security taxes for a domestic employee. She became the sacrificial scapegoat for a great many economically privileged people who hadn't paid social security taxes for their domestic employees. Once this individual was sacrificed, all prominent officials were symbolically redeemed from the sin of not having paid taxes.

Scapegoating was attemped again in 2002. America faced a rash of corporate scandals—Enron, WorldCom, Tyco, and others. As stories broke, executives of the companies engaged in wrongdoing scrambled to deflect blame from themselves and onto others. Enron officials tried to blame Arthur Andersen, the accounting firm that had audited Enron's finances. WorldCom executives denied any wrongdoing and blamed others.

TRY IT OUT   To see Burke's theory in practice, examine articles on people accused of some kind of wrongdoing that are reported in the first section of a state or national newspaper during one week. How do the reports and the statements made by those accused of misbehavior illustrate mortification and victimage? Are there any accounts of wrongdoing that don't fit into one of the means of redemption Burke identifies?

The Dramatistic Pentad (Hexad)

To show how his theory could illuminate symbolic activities, Burke (1945) devised a method of analysis that relies on the **dramatistic pentad**. The pentad is a tool that provides a structure for analyzing human actions. The pentad does not perform actual analysis—it provides only the terms for conducting analysis. As the name suggests, the pentad consists of five aspects that Burke considered central to understanding and analyzing human symbolic activity. The **act** is what is done by a person (insult, caress, explanation of behavior, request for forgiveness, statement of common ground). The **scene** is the context in which interaction occurs (the physical situation, the cultural setting, the historical era). The third element of the pentad is the **agent**, which is the individual or group that performs an act (the character, history, personality, occupation, family ties). **Agency** refers to the means an agent uses to accomplish an act (channels of communication, message strategies, storytelling, physical violence). Finally, the **purpose** is the goal of the act (to gain forgiveness, to highlight common ground, to scapegoat another).

Many years after Burke developed the pentad for conducting dramatistic analysis, he added a sixth element to his model of human action, thereby revising the pentad into a hexad. **Attitude** refers to how an actor positions herself or himself relative to others and the contexts in which she or he operates (Burke, 1968). Attitude is incipient action that shapes the disposition of an actor in relation to action, specifically communication. If you've ever interacted with a person who acts superior, then you understand the importance of attitude to the overall meaning of human activity. Examples of attitudes include egalitarianism, fairness, suspicion, respectfulness, vengeance, and arrogance. Because these attitudes underlie and shape our communication, we need to consider them in analyzing particular symbolic activities.

Dramatistic analysis of rhetorical actions involves two steps. First, it's important to identify each of the elements in a particular situation: What is portrayed as the act? (What is represented as the primary issue? What is defined as not an issue?) What scene is represented as the context for action? Who is presented as the agent? (It is not always the one speaking—as, for example, in the statement, "He made me do it.") What is the agency of communication? (How is the act implemented?) What is the purpose of the act? (What rationale or goal is claimed?) What is the attitude of the agent? (How does the person or group position itself in relation to others, the scene, and the act?) Asking these questions gives us insight into the dramatic structure of a particular symbolic interaction.

Dramatistic analysis also may focus on **ratios** between various elements in Burke's model. A ratio is a proportion. For example, 1:10 describes a 10% proportion. In dramatistic analysis of ratios, we ask how prominent each element is in relation to the others. How often is the agent emphasized? How often is attention called to scene, act, purpose, agency, and attitude? Analyzing ratios among elements of the human drama allows us to see which elements prevail in a particular situation, and this tells us something about dramatic emphasis and point of view. In addition to considering ratios, analysts may focus on points of conflict or division (Burke called these *agon*) and progression in a drama from order to division to suffering to purging of guilt and finally to redemption.

The value of dramatistic analysis is illustrated by rhetorical critic David Ling's (1970) study of Senator Edward Kennedy's speech to the people of Massachusetts in 1969. In this speech Kennedy wanted to persuade his constituents that he was not primarily responsible for the death of Mary Jo Kopechne, a political aide who drowned when Kennedy drove his car off a bridge. In addition, he wanted to convince his constituents to grant him forgiveness in the form of supporting his continuation as their senator. In his analysis, Ling shows how Kennedy skillfully transformed himself from an agent of Kopechne's death to a helpless victim of circumstances. After transforming the agent from himself to circumstances, Kennedy then redefined the agent as the people of Massachusetts. He offered to resign if that was their wish or to stay on as their senator if that was their desire, thereby casting the voters as the actor and their decision as the primary action in the situation. Dramatistic analysis helps us see why Kennedy's speech was remarkably effective. By understanding the metamorphosis of agent during the course of his address, we gain insight into why his constituents refused to blame him.

Critical Assessment of Dramatism

Burke's dramatism is widely regarded as the most comprehensive theory of symbolic action. This is a source of both praise and criticism. Although serious challenges to Burke's overall views have not been advanced, two reservations have been voiced.

The Theory Is Obscure and Confusing   The most frequent criticism of Burke's theory is that it is complicated, confusing, and extremely difficult to comprehend (Foss, Foss, & Trapp, 2001). Unquestionably Burke's writing is dense and difficult to follow. In part this is because he commands and uses the language of many different perspectives to develop his ideas. On a single page he may mix the vocabularies of linguistics, psychology, and religion and garnish his discussion with liberal literary allusions. Readers who don't have Burke's vast knowledge are likely to be bewildered. For people who are committed to understanding Burke's grand theory, however, the struggle to follow his ideas can be most rewarding.

The breadth of Burke's theory also leaves it open to the charge that it lacks focus. In one sense this is a valid criticism. In later chapters we'll examine tightly focused theories such as uncertainty reduction, which concentrates on the relationship between communication and uncertainty. For Burke such a narrow focus is restrictive and inadequate for understanding the many forms of communication. His aim is to explore the expansive terrain of human society, and that means studying symbolic activity wherever, however, and whenever it occurs (Gusfield, 1989). Whether the deliberate breadth of his theory is a weakness or a strength depends on your point of view. In Burke's view it is clearly an asset.

Is Guilt All There Is?   A more specific criticism of dramatism is its claim that guilt is the basic motive that underlies most (or all) human action. Are there no other important human motives that impel us? Are we not motivated by love, patriotism, compassion, desire for esteem, and a desire for community? Celeste Condit (1992) suggests that Burke's emphasis on purging guilt and specifically engaging in victimage reflects his knowledge of Christian theology. She suggests that there may be different basic motives for human conduct in, for example, Buddhist societies. It is possible that Burke's emphasis on universality hindered him from recognizing much of the diversity in human experience and motives (Chesebro, 1992).

Although Burke might not dismiss the idea that there could be other important human motives, he would argue that guilt ultimately underlies them. Compassion, esteem, and love, after all, reflect awareness of division and a desire to transcend it. According to Burke, these motives reflect guilt, which he sees as the crux of any tension. If we accept Burke's broad definition of guilt, then perhaps it is the ultimate human motive and thus the basis of human communication.

Difficult, frustrating, imaginative, dense, confusing, fascinating—Burke's theory is all of these. It is also an extraordinarily original analysis of the motives and manifestations of human communication. Considered by many to be the preeminent symbolic scholar of this century, Burke himself says he's a "gypsy scholar" and a "word man."

Narrative Theory

Kenneth Burke isn't the only "word man" among communication theorists. As an introduction to another such theorist and the theory he developed, read the four passages below and consider what they have in common:

- Once upon a time there were three bears. There was a great big bear called Papa Bear, and a middle-sized bear called Momma Bear, and a little bear called Baby Bear. . . .

- *Question:* How did your day go?

  Answer: I had a really interesting experience. I was walking to my 11 o'-clock class when a guy who is in the class came up to me and started talking. It turns out that we're both juniors and both from small towns, and we both feel overwhelmed by this huge campus. We talked more after class, and we're going out this weekend.

- Mommy, my shirt got dirty outside, so now we have to wash it and make it clean again. Then we can put it back in my closet for another day.

- Professor Smith, I want to explain why my paper isn't ready to hand in today. I have been working on it for the last two weeks, not waiting until the last minute. Then just when I was finishing it last night, there was a power surge and the file got scrambled. I have an appointment after class today to work with the computer support office to retrieve the file. As soon as I do that, I'll print it out and give it to you.

What do these four communications have in common? Each one is a story. "The Three Bears" is a fairy tale told to many Western children. The other three scenarios are also stories, although they are less formal ones than the fairy tale. When asked about the day, the respondent in the second example tells a story. She doesn't just say "I met a new guy." Instead, she recounts their meeting by telling a story with a plot, a climax, and a beginning, middle, and end. The child in the third example also tells a story, a progressive account of events that begins by defining a starting event (the shirt got dirty), moves on to identify what must be done (wash it), and casts forward in time to predict what will then happen (it will be clean and can be hung in the closet). In the fourth exchange, a student tells the professor a story (perhaps a figurative as well as a literal one) that explains why a paper is not ready on time. The student could have simply said, "My paper isn't ready, but I will have it for you soon," but instead a story is woven to give reasons for the delay. According to communication theorist Walter Fisher, humans are natural storytellers (1978, 1984, 1987). We continually weave discrete events and experiences together into coherent wholes that have all the features of stories: a plot; characters; action; a sequence of beginning, middle, and end; and a climax.

In Chapter 3 we discussed different ontological beliefs of theorists. In addition to opinions about whether human behavior is determined from outside or motivated by free will, ontological assumptions concern the essence or crux of human nature. Mead, for instance, believed that humans are defined by their ability to use symbols. General semanticists also saw symbolic abilities as the crux of human nature. In Chapter 7 we'll learn about coordinated management of meaning theory, which points to the capacity to invent, understand, and follow rules to create meanings as definitive of human nature, and constructivism, which regards the ability to form and use knowledge schemata to interpret experiences as the essence of what it means to be human.

Walter Fisher thought there was something more fundamental about humans than the capacities highlighted by other theorists. He argued that humans are by nature storytelling beings and that the narrative capacity is what is most basic and most distinctive about humans. According to Fisher, humans are storytelling animals. Fisher (1987) believed that we make sense of our experiences in life by transforming them into stories, or narrative forms. In addition, he maintained that most of our communication takes a storylike form with plot, characters, and sequences of action. To appreciate Fisher's narrative theory, we'll consider the concepts central to this perspective.

Reflection

What are the practical implications of defining humans as storytellers?

The Narrative Paradigm

Calling his theory the **narrative paradigm**, Fisher defined *narration* as "symbolic actions—words and/or deeds—that have sequence and meaning for those who live, create, or interpret them" (1987, p. 58). As you probably realized immediately, this is a very broad view of narration. If we accept this definition, it's difficult to identify communication that *doesn't* qualify as narration. That, thought Fisher, is exactly why it is appropriate to describe and explain communication as storytelling. In his view, storytelling is not an occasional activity; instead, it's the continuous processes by which we perceive the world and communicate with others. Storytelling, in other words, is an ongoing human activity, one as natural and nearly as continuous as breathing.

The word *story* is often associated only with formal kinds, such as novels, films, fairy tales, and ballads. Departing from this restrictive view of stories, Fisher claimed that narrations abound in everyday life. You go to a church, temple, or synagogue, and a religious leader tells stories. Christian preachers often weave sermons out of parables, which are much of the content of the Bible. Buddhist priests tell *teichos*, which is translated in English as "teaching stories"—tales designed to teach a moral lesson. Science professors describe inventions and discoveries in terms of the sequence of research and thinking that led to new insights. History professors weave stories about events in former times and the effects they had. Lawyers, too, tell stories when they give jurors accounts of what happened and why and who is to blame (Bruner, 2002). Legal consultants used to focus on helping attorneys pick juries and dressing to sway jurors' opinions; today, however, many legal consultants spend at least as much time coaching lawyers in storytelling techniques (Felsenthal, 1996).

In conversation with friends, you share experiences by creating sequences out of discrete events (plots); dramatizing good and bad individuals (heroes and villains); imputing motives to what you and others do, think, feel, and believe (character development); and deferring the point of a discussion or the revelation of an experience until the end (climax). Stories, stories, stories—they're woven throughout our lives (Abbott, 2002; Charon & Montello, 2002; Flundernik, 1996; Landa & Onega, 1996).

Reflection

How persuasive do you find technical evidence, logical reasoning, and compelling stories?

Good Reasons

In Western cultures, rationality is considered extremely important. We are taught to evaluate the worth of ideas and arguments by judging how much evidence is adduced, how many facts support a claim, and how well links among evidence and claims are reasoned. Fisher thought the Western emphasis on "pure logic" and conventional rationality was excessive. He also thought that logic or strictly rational thinking don't always explain why we believe what we do.

In his original statement about narrative theory, Fisher (1978) claimed that telling a compelling story is more persuasive than scads of statistics, expert testimony, and logical deduction. He believed that, because we are naturally storytellers, we are most persuaded by good stories. Nearly a decade after introducing his narrative paradigm, Fisher (1987) wrote a book elaborating his view that compelling stories are the basis of persuasion. In that book, Fisher contrasted what he called "the rational world par-

Table 5.1 Rational World and Narrative Paradigms	Assumptions of the Rational World Paradigm	Assumptions of the Narrative Paradigm
	• People are basically rational beings. • We make decisions and form beliefs on the basis of arguments. • Arguments are determined by the nature of specific speaking situations. • Rationality is evaluated by the quality of knowledge and reasoning. • Life consists of logical relationships that can be discovered through rational logic and reasoning.	• People are basically storytelling beings. • We make decisions and form beliefs on the basis of good reasons. • What we consider good reasons depends on history, culture, personal character, and biography. • Narrative rationality is evaluated by the coherence and fidelity of stories. • Life is a set of stories; in choosing to accept some stories and to reject others, we continuously re-create our lives and ourselves.

adigm" and "the narrative paradigm." The distinctions between the two approaches are summarized in Table 5.1.

The paradigm shift that Fisher advocated opens up new ways of thinking about communication, persuasion, and belief. If we accept the rational world epistemological position, then evidence and reasoning alone should guide what we believe and do. Values, emotional arguments, and aesthetic considerations should make no difference in what we believe and do. If we adopt the epistemology of the narrative paradigm, however, then a compelling story is the basis of our beliefs and actions. Within the narrative paradigm, values, beliefs, and actions are assumed to be influenced by emotional arguments and by aesthetic matters such as verbal style and dramatic flourishes.

Narrative Rationality

Although Fisher argued that we are all natural storytellers, he didn't believe that we are all equally skilled or that all stories merit equivalent belief. To answer reservations that the narrative paradigm provided no standards for judging the quality of various stories, Fisher presented the concept of **narrative rationality**. He claimed that not all stories are equally compelling; that is, not all stories have the same power to gain our belief. We judge stories on the basis of a distinctively narrative form of rationality, which Fisher saw as quite different from conventional criteria of rationality (those in the rational world view). Fisher identified two standards for assessing narrative rationality: **coherence** and **fidelity**.

Coherence   The first question to be asked about a story (remember, Fisher meant this to refer to most, if not all, communication) is whether it is coherent. Do all parts of the story seem to fit together believably? Does the outcome of the story make sense given the plot and characters? In short, the coherence criterion asks whether a story makes sense.

How do you decide whether a story makes sense? Fisher suggested that we first ask whether a story has internal coherence. We judge whether the storyteller has told us all of the important details so that the outcome is believable. We try to figure out if the storyteller has distorted parts of the story. We ask whether the characters behave consistently as they should, given what we know about them and how the storyteller has portrayed them and their motivations. If we find holes in a story or think it doesn't quite hang together, we will judge it to be incoherent and thus not compelling of our belief.

The importance of narrative coherence was highlighted in a study that Erin Shank-Krusiewicz and I conducted (Shank-Krusiewicz & Wood, 2001). We interviewed adoptive parents to learn how they told their adopted children about their entrance into the families. Again and again, the parents told us that they worked to heal the broken narrative that children experience when their birth parents give them up or die. Adoptive parents struggled to create stories of their children's lives that offered a coherent narrative in which the birth parents had loved the children and had made sure the children would be with other parents who also loved them.

The second way we assess coherence is to compare a specific story we are told with other stories about the same or similar situations, events, and so forth. Perhaps you have been friends with a couple who broke up. If so, you may have heard two decidedly different accounts of what happened. Pat says the relationship ended because Leigh was selfish and demanding; Leigh says it ended because Pat was unresponsive and unwilling to invest in the relationship. Although there may be some truth to each account, we usually find one more compelling than the other. To evaluate the stories and decide which one is more believable, we rely on our knowledge of each person in the couple and of people in general, and on our perception of each story's coherence.

In the fall of 1991 we witnessed a dramatic example of conflicting stories and efforts to assess the coherence of each. As you may recall, Clarence Thomas had been nominated to be a member of the Supreme Court when law professor Anita Hill came forward to charge that he had sexually harassed her years before when they worked together. The two main characters told radically different stories about what happened. Anita Hill recounted a series of vulgar remarks, inappropriate sexual impositions, and sexist and sexual activities that she alleged Thomas had committed. She portrayed him as a man with perverted sexual interests who used gutter language and harassed her. He countered with a story that portrayed him as an honorable professional and Anita Hill as a sexually provocative, hysterical feminist.

How were the Senate committee and the millions of viewers around the nation to decide between these two dissimilar stories? Many who followed the hearings, both senators and laypeople, were swayed by Orrin Hatch and other defenders of Thomas who argued that Hill's story was incoherent. They claimed that, if Thomas had actually done to her what she claimed he had, it would not be consistent for Hill to have continued to work for him or to wait years to bring charges. The Senate committee apparently found this a credible attack on the coherence of Hill's testimony, as it confirmed Thomas's appointment to the highest court in the land.

However, communication scholars who analyzed the hearings point out that the reason Hill's story seemed incoherent to the committee was that all members of the Senate committee were male, powerful, and white (see Bingham, 1994, 1996; "Telling Our Stories," 1992). White men, more than men of color or women, have limited experience of being trivialized and abused by others. These researchers argued that Hill's behaviors were consistent—that they made sense for a young black woman working for a powerful, older black man.

A more recent example that gives us insight into evaluating the comparative coherence of differing narratives comes from the Enron episode in 2002. After the Enron accounting scandal was exposed, Enron officials claimed that they had not known of the fraudulent accounting practices that were used to conceal the company's shaky finances and that they had never ordered shredding of incriminating documents. However, some middle- and lower-level Enron employees testified that the practices had been widely known and that employees had been given direct orders to shred documents. Which story is more believable—that of the executives who would face criminal penalties if they had done what they were charged with, or that of the employees who had nothing to gain by testifying?

Fidelity Fisher's (1987) second standard for narrative rationality is fidelity, which he defined as "the extent to which a story resonates with listeners' personal experiences and beliefs." Fidelity concerns whether a story rings true to listeners in terms of their own experiences, values, beliefs, and self-concepts. This is reminiscent of the general semanticists' emphasis on fields of experience as the filters through which we interpret the meaning of communication. According to narrative theorists, we find stories believable when they are consistent with experiences in our lives, and we find characters believable when they act as we do or as we would like to see ourselves acting. If you've ever felt irrelevant to the world, then you can identify with Willie Loman in *Death of a Salesman*. If you see yourself as an adventurer who boldly goes into new territories, then you may identify with many of the characters in *Star Trek: The Next Generation*.

In the case of the Hill–Thomas hearings, the members of the Senate committee didn't find Hill credible, because she didn't act as they would have under similar circumstances. To powerful men who have never been sexually harassed, it simply didn't make sense that Anita Hill would tolerate the egregious behaviors she charged Thomas with committing. It wasn't believable that she wouldn't have brought charges at the time she alleged he sexually harassed her. Many women of all races, however, found Hill's tolerance of abominable harassment and her ensuing silence credible. They knew, many from personal experience with sexual harassment, that victims can't always leave a job or complain officially. Judgments of fidelity, then, may differ according to personal experience and standpoint.

Fisher explains that the standard of fidelity involves judging the values in narration. When we identify with a character, we regard her or his actions as admirable, worthy, or reasonable. When we accept a story as true and right, we judge it to reflect the values in which we believe and the ways of the world as we have experienced them. Those people who identify with the idea that black men have been subject to vindictive, violent racism may identify with Thomas's portrait of the hearings as a "high-tech lynching." People who have experienced sexual harassment and learned that superiors will not respect their complaints are more likely to perceive fidelity in Anita Hill's story.

Reflection

With which film and television characters do you identify? What does this tell you about how you see yourself and the values in which you believe?

From the perspective of narrative theory, a crucial moment in the 1991 hearings came when Thomas proclaimed that the hearings were a "high-tech lynching." Thomas issued this charge in the form of a story of the history of injustices to black men. He chronicled discrimination against African Americans, from enslavement to violent lynchings to racist treatment and attitudes in general. In likening the hearings to a "high-tech lynching," Thomas created a story that was compelling to many who heard it. The story made sense to some listeners in terms of history, culture, biography, and character—the criteria Fisher lists for good reasons.

In 1995 communication scholar James Baesler created an empirical way to measure coherence and fidelity, the two criteria of narrative rationality. When Baesler tested the relative impact of coherence and fidelity, he found that both affected the persuasiveness of stories but that coherence was the greater influence. This suggests that listeners place somewhat more weight on the internal consistency and comprehensiveness of stories than on the extent to which stories resonate with their own experiences and beliefs.

The narrative paradigm has had considerable influence in the field of communication. In 1985 one of the major communication journals devoted an entire issue to discussing the narrative paradigm ("Storytelling and Narrativity in Communication Research" in the *Journal of Communication, 4,* 1985). Seven years later, in 1992, the *Journal of Applied Communication Research* published a symposium entitled "Telling Our Stories," in which members of the field who had been sexually harassed gave accounts of their experiences. Prior to the symposium, articles on sexual harassment had been restricted to reporting the frequency of sexual harassment, analyzing personal and organizational dynamics that legitimized sexual harassment, and identifying characteristics of victims and harassers. Breaking from these traditions, "Telling Our Stories" didn't offer conventional evidence about sexual harassment. Instead, it offered compelling personal accounts of what sexual harassment is and how it affects victims. Many readers reported that the 30 stories in the symposium were more persuasive and more compelling than all the facts and statistics they had encountered in prior research. That's one example of the power of storytelling.

TRY IT OUT Test Fisher's claim that narration is the basis of all communication by viewing television advertisements and deciding whether they tell stories.

1. Pick two nights during which you will watch television for several hours. For each commercial, record who the characters are and how they are portrayed. Then offer your opinion of the believability or fidelity of the characters.

2. Next, summarize the plot of each advertisement. What is the sequence of events, and is it coherent? Do the characters and plots of commercials lead you to believe in the products advertised or the claims advanced by the advertisers?

3. Which commercials do you find most compelling? Using the concepts of coherence and fidelity, explain why.

Critical Assessment of Narrative Theory

What's the verdict on the narrative paradigm? As is the case with any theory, it depends on which criteria we use to assess it. If we judge it by heuristic power, it fares very well indeed. Fisher's ideas are original, and they have provoked new ways of thinking about communication, the nature of reasons, and the bases of judging rationality. The theory also measures up to the criterion of parsimony, since it uses a limited number of concepts to explain communication. Even with these strengths, the narrative paradigm has been criticized in three ways.

Incomplete Description   First, some scholars are skeptical that the theory really provides, as it claims to, a comprehensive description of all communication. Is Fisher right that all communication is narrative? Robert Rowland (1989) argues that some forms of communication are not narrative and don't attempt to be. For example, he points out that science fiction and science fantasy stories don't attempt to make sense in terms of most people's experiences and values. The very purpose of science fiction and science fantasy is to challenge prevailing values, experiences, and ways of being in the world. We might also ask whether storytelling is at work in exchanges between customers and clerks, in business meetings, and in technical articles in scientific and professional journals.

There are two specific kinds of communication that scholars have identified as not within the articulated scope of narrative theory. First, Kirkwood (1992) argues that Fisher's view of narrative fails to explain how stories create new possibilities, new visions of ourselves and social life. Surely some storytelling, such as that by the Reverend Martin Luther King, Jr., holds forth new ways of being that are sufficiently compelling to change how people see themselves and act. James Chesebro (1995b) also believes that the narrative paradigm seems unmindful of the metaphorical power and harmful social consequences of storytelling. For example, narratives of injustice and the right to revenge can incite riots and killing. In developing his theory, Fisher has not fully accounted for the power of stories to create new visions or to instigate evil.

Too Broad   A second criticism of the narrative paradigm is just the opposite of the foregoing charge. This criticism is that Fisher's theory is too broad. You may recall encountering this criticism in our previous discussions of symbolic interactionism and dramatism. If Fisher is right that all communication is narration, he simultaneously says everything and nothing.

If all communication is narration, then defining communication as narrative fails to distinguish among different types of communication. Do we wish to lump public speaking, group discussion, intimate talk, intercultural dialogues, and organizational negotiations into one large heap called "communication" or "stories"? Such a sweeping view of communication, charge the critics, doesn't help us recognize important distinctions among myriad forms of communication.

Conservative Bias   A final criticism of the narrative paradigm is that it has a distinctly conservative bias. In the context of evaluating theory, *conservative* doesn't refer to political stands or social beliefs. Instead, it refers to preservation of existing or established values and practices. According to William Kirkwood (1992), Fisher's idea of good reasons gives privilege to prevailing values and attitudes and accords less attention to the ways in which stories can promote positive changes in the human condition. This is an important criticism. Remember that Fisher says one criterion for judging narrative rationality is fidelity, which he defines as how well a story resonates with listeners' beliefs, values, and experiences.

This may explain why we find some stories more credible than others, but does it amount to a sound or adequate criterion for evaluating the goodness of a story? Kirkwood thinks not. He argues that this standard of judgment encourages us to say only what will square with others' experiences and to avoid challenging prevailing views, values, and the status quo in social life. Rather than seeing his ideas as a direct challenge to Fisher's theory, Kirkwood thinks they extend it by acknowledging the power of stories to create new possibilities for people.

Fisher denies the charge that narrative theory perpetuates the status quo. Even before Kirkwood published his critical article, Fisher (1987) wrote that humans are wonderfully creative and imaginative beings. Extending this, he claims we are able to invent and accept new stories when they better explain our lives or offer better directions for future living than the stories we have grown up hearing and believing. This may account for the stunning shift in opinion over time about the stories told by Hill and Thomas. During and immediately after the Hill–Thomas hearings, national polls reported that a majority of people found Thomas's story more credible than the one Anita Hill told. However, a year after the hearings, when people had thought more about the stories, a majority of those polled reported that they believed Anita Hill's account. Given time to consider and weigh both stories, people came to believe one that initially they had not found credible. This shift suggests that the criterion of fidelity may not be fixed at one time but may shift in response to additional experience and/or reflection.

There is certainly ample evidence that we are able to do more than retell old stories and respond to stories that are familiar. History is full of examples of humans who created original narrations and people who were captivated by stories that departed from customary values, experiences, and ways of acting. Most of the major advances in social life have come about because people told new stories that contested popular views and established ideas about life.

In the late 1800s and early 1900s India was oppressed by English rule. Mahatma Gandhi rose to leadership and gained a following through a narrative that was different from the ones used by most rebel leaders. Gandhi taught his followers to engage in nonviolent resistance. He told them that the principle of an eye for an eye is wrong. As he put it, an eye for an eye leaves all people blind. Acting on the new story Gandhi offered, the Indian people eventually freed themselves from British rule.

Following Gandhi's philosophy, the Reverend Martin Luther King, Jr., told stories about nonviolence to his followers, whose own lives had been riddled with incidents of violence in which they were both victims and perpetrators. The stories King told gave many African Americans another way of thinking about how to resist injustice. His stories were powerful not because they reflected existing experiences of African Americans but because they created a compelling alternative to what they knew.

Similarly, feminists in the 1800s and 1900s did not argue for women's rights by telling stories that resonated with existing values and experiences. Instead, their narratives were of new ways of seeing women and new kinds of relationships between the sexes. Environmental rhetoric too is most successful when it offers a counterpoint to attitudes and practices that have prevailed historically. Narratives that tell of recycling, simplifying, living lightly on the planet, and respecting rather than dominating the earth invite us to see the world and ourselves in new ways.

Summary

In this chapter we've studied three theories of how language works. Although all three theories are centrally interested in language, they offer distinct, yet compatible views—stories, Fisher would say—of what happens when people use language to communicate.

Symbolic interactionism and dramatism are especially broad theories, which means they rate well on the criterion of theoretical scope. Both theories offer expansive descriptions of relationships between individuals and social life. Whereas Mead concentrates on how symbolic interaction allows individuals to acquire minds and selves, Burke focuses on the ways in which we use language to create identifications and purge ourselves of guilt. Both of these theories call attention to the crucial role of communication in our perceptions of others, situations, and ourselves.

Walter Fisher, on the other hand, is not particularly interested in the development of self and mind or in the motives of human symbolic behavior. His theory is an effort to explain how language bewitches, beguiles, and compels belief. Whereas general semanticists urged people to be more rational and more attentive to evidence and the empirical world, Fisher claims we already accord too much emphasis to conventional rationality. He advocates greater awareness of and respect for a new kind of logic—narrative rationality—in which good reasons, culture, history, character, and aesthetics are recognized as having a legitimate influence on how we interpret communication and on how we ourselves create communication.

In different ways, symbolic interactionism, dramatism, and narrative theory enlarge understanding of how we use and misuse words and why they affect us as they do. Perhaps the theories are not incompatible but are distinct in the aspects and effects of language they describe and explain.

Key Terms

act

agency

agent

attitude

coherence

consubstantiality

dramatism

dramatistic pentad (hexad)

fidelity

generalized other

guilt

hierarchy

I

looking glass self

ME

mind

mortification

narrative paradigm

narrative rationality

negative

particular other

perfection

purpose

ratio

role taking

scapegoating

scene

self

self-fulfilling prophecy

substance

symbolic interactionism

victimage

CHAPTER SIX

Theories About Performance

When I was in my doctoral program, a group of students, faculty, and townspeople met weekly to play penny poker. One of the players was a retired chief of police from New York. Before our poker game one evening, this man spent an hour instructing all the students in how we should behave to minimize the chance we would be assaulted. He taught us to walk with confidence, to meet the eyes of others to show we were assertive but not confrontational, and to hold our heads and use our arms to suggest that we were totally in charge of ourselves. In essence, he taught us to perform a don't-mess-with-me identity.

All of us create and project images that suit our purposes in various moments. We know how to appear self-confident in job interviews, contrite when we have offended others, and interested even if we are bored. The distinguished anthropologist Victor Turner (1986) defined humans as *homo performans* (p. 81) to emphasize that humans are defined by their participation in rituals, social drama, and improvisational, creative performances in daily life. For us, as Shakespeare observed, all the world's a stage and we are all players on the stage.

Within the field of communication, performance has a long and distinguished history, founded on the premise that performance is an important way of both knowing and being. In other words, performances are a means to knowing about experiences, and they are also ways in which we define our personal, social, and cultural identities.

Early work in performance studies tended to emphasize what is sometimes called "high art"—events and experiences that were removed from everyday life. In fact, performance studies scholar Mary Frances Hopkins (1995) recalls that, traditionally, detachment from ordinary life was "one factor that qualified a performance as an aesthetic event" (p. 229). In addition to continued attention to "high art," many performance studies scholars today are also keenly interested in the dramatic structures and performances of everyday life.

Currently, performance studies includes a diversity of work, ranging from the study and performance of literature to the use of performances to achieve political impact—to criticize, challenge, or change social systems and practices. Knitting these diverse interests together is an abiding fascination with how performances work in a variety of ways, often in ordinary, everyday contexts. One theoretical focus is **dramaturgy**, which is particularly concerned with performances in everyday life. Another research emphasis, called **performance ethnography**, explores how social communities are sustained and their values expressed and sometimes changed through performative practices such as rituals, ceremonies, rites of cultural practice, and oral history. Other performance studies scholars study the power of performance to critique and reconfigure culturally inscribed identities and traditions that underlie social inequities.

In a single chapter, it is impossible to discuss the range of theories and research associated with an area as richly diverse as performance studies. Rather than attempting a superficial survey of all theoretical perspectives on performance, we'll focus on three significant currents in the area today.

First we'll examine the dramaturgical approach, which is well captured in the title of one of Erving Goffman's books, *The Presentation of Self in Everyday Life* (1959). Next we'll look at performance ethnography, which includes personal narratives and the study of performances that reflect and sustain various cultural practices and values. In the third section of the chapter we consider performance as political action that aims to make injustices known and precipitate change. Although they have distinct emphases, these three theoretical inclinations share many common assumptions about social life's intimate reliance on human communication, specifically performance. Thus, you will find greater compatibility among these theories than among theories in some areas of the communication field. You will also discover that the lines between these three theoretical inclinations are more blurred than clear-cut—for example, performance ethnography often blends into politicized commentary.

Dramaturgical Theory (Performance in Everyday Life)

In Chapter 5 we discussed Kenneth Burke's dramatistic theory. In addition to his influence on understanding the dramatic structure of language, Burke contributed significantly to performance studies. His dramatistic theory helps us understand the dramatic aspects of everyday social interaction, and his method of pentad or hexad analysis focuses our attention on the dramatic elements of act, agent, agency, scene, purpose, and attitude. Erving Goffman also developed theoretical insights into the drama inherent in routine social life. Because we have already explored Burke's ideas, in this discussion we will focus on Erving Goffman, a sociologist who skillfully observed and theorized how people perform in everyday life.

Like Burke, Goffman was schooled in symbolic interaction theory. He extended Mead's basic insights by viewing everyday human behavior as distinctly dramatic, or theatrical. Goffman (1983) once wrote that "it is social situations that provide the natural theatre in which all bodily displays are enacted and in which all bodily displays are read" (p. 4). This comment emphasizes Goffman's focus on how physical, or bodily, actions are used performatively to craft and project impressions of individuals and to define the nature of particular situations.

Although Goffman's theory is not currently the strongest force in performance studies, his theorizing, along with Burke's, is important because it provided a theoretical basis for understanding the performative character of human action and interaction in everyday life. The theoretical insights that grew out of Goffman's interest in performance in everyday life are a legacy that informs more current work in performance studies.

Goffman was fascinated by the ways in which people work to craft and sustain impressions in their ordinary day-to-day activities. For Goffman, our efforts to manage the impressions we create are not fakery or attempts to manipulate others unethically. Instead, he viewed them as normal, perhaps unavoidable, because humans are social and therefore must coordinate their identities and actions with those of others. To appreciate Goffman's ideas, we'll explore three central concepts in his theory.

The Dramaturgical Model

Goffman is the person most associated with what has become known as the **dramaturgical model** of social interaction. As the name suggests, this model likens ordinary social interaction to theatrical performance. Thus, the setting, or context, of interaction is viewed as a stage. The people who are acting are actors; those who watch are the audience. The roles people (or actors) take in interaction are performances strategically crafted to project particular images to others, the audience. Within a drama are a number of specific scenes, each of which must be managed correctly for the overall drama to be successful.

Goffman (1974) also wrote about **frames**, which are models we rely on to make sense of experience. Building on Mead's symbolic interaction theory, Goffman theorized that we rely on frames to define situations for ourselves and others. We learn many frames through interaction with the generalized other, or society as a whole. Thus, members of a society or a social community share many common frames for interaction. Despite differences that arise from personal experience and membership in diverse social communities, most Americans share a basic frame for interactions such as first date, wedding, applying for a job, funeral, and so forth.

Because frames typically reflect cultural knowledge, they vary from culture to culture. For instance, most members of a specific culture share an understanding of the frame for classes: we know the range of behaviors that are normal for teachers and students. In the United States, students are often rewarded for being assertive and participative in classes. In other countries, such as China, students understand their role as more deferential and less participative. To a large extent, the frames we use to define situations are shaped by our membership in particular cultures and social communities.

Reflection

What connections do you notice between Goffman's ideas and vocabulary and those of Kenneth Burke?

Using his dramaturgical model, Goffman studied how people present themselves and their activities to others. His theory describes how people shape others' impressions of them as well as how people convince others to adopt certain, and not other, definitions of a situation. What can a person do and not do to sustain a particular image? For example, what does a teacher do to project her- or himself as knowledgeable and interested in students? What can a teacher not do if she or he wants to convince students of this image? What do students do to convince teachers that they are engaged in learning? What might students do that would invalidate this image of them in the eyes of teachers?

TRY IT OUT Describe a first date using Goffman's dramaturgical model.

1. What impression do you want to project to your date?

2. What definition of the situation (the first date) do you want your date to accept?

3. How do you manage your dress, gestures, and words to project that impression of yourself?

4. How do you control the setting (or stage) to support the image of yourself and the situation that you want to project to your date?

5. What can you *not* do if you want to sustain the desired impression of yourself?

Impression Management

As hinted at in the foregoing paragraphs, Goffman was especially interested in **impression management**, which is the process of managing setting, words, nonverbal communication, and dress in an effort to create a particular image of individuals and situations. According to Goffman (1959), our efforts to create and project certain impressions may be either highly calculated or unintentional. Goffman also noted that sometimes an individual may be highly strategic in crafting an image but unaware that he or she is creating an impression.

Reflection

Is it unethical or harmful to engage in impression management?

On first learning about impression management, many people think it is manipulative and deceitful. Of course, it can be deceptive and unethical. Goffman (1959) realized this and cautioned against managing impressions in ways that are harmful to others. However, impression management can also be highly constructive because it allows us and others to behave in socially appropriate and beneficial ways. If you doubt this, think for a moment about what would happen if all of us acted exactly as we wanted without any regard for others' feelings. Social life would be impossible without the ordinary courtesy and politeness that most of us extend to others by engaging in impression management.

Goffman argued that all of us manage the impressions we create. We are sometimes more effective than at other times in convincing others to accept the impressions of us that we desire, but we're always managing how we come across. Think about all of the ways you manage your impression in everyday life:

- Some women remove hair from legs, underarms, and other parts of their bodies.
- People dress differently when at work, on dates, and relaxing with friends.
- You might drink from a carton of juice if you are alone in your home but not if you are visiting the family of your girlfriend or boyfriend.
- You might confess doubts about your career skills to a close friend but not to a job interviewer.
- In a class that you find boring, you periodically look up at the professor and write in your notebook to give the impression you are taking notes.
- In front of a young child, you curb what you say to avoid harsh language or curse words.
- While you are in the checkout line in a grocery store, the clerk asks, "How are you today?" and you resist giving an honest response, which would be "I have a bad cold, I didn't sleep last night, I have two exams tomorrow and I feel like —— !"

In each of these instances, you manage the impression you project in an effort to achieve certain goals, including persuading others not to perceive you as odd or obnoxious. As we interact with others, we adopt roles and present ourselves as specific characters. Not drinking juice from a carton when others are present is an effort to establish the character of a mannerly person. Shaving legs and underarms may be an effort to establish oneself as a conventionally feminine character. Managing your actions to seem attentive in class helps you establish your character as a serious student. Choosing not to impose your frustrations on the clerk is a way of creating the impression that you are polite and socially competent.

Dramaturgy doesn't necessarily require us to assume that people are aware that they are performing roles, managing impressions, and so forth. The theory views life as a theater, but does not claim that people/actors are conscious of being on stage or of creating performances (Messinger, Sampson, & Towne, 1962).

Front Stage/Back Stage

We've already noted that Goffman regarded the setting of social interaction as a stage. Yet he went farther to distinguish between **front stage** and **back stage**. The front stage is what is visible to an audience, whereas the back stage includes all that is not visible to an audience. The back stage is where actors can act in ways that might undermine their front stage performances. When you attend a dramatic presentation, you see the actors performing on stage. What you don't see is all that is happening backstage to make the frontstage performances believable. You don't see grips working on scenery, lighting, and other physical aspects of the set. You don't see actors rehearsing lines and gestures. You don't see directors guiding how the actors perform. You also don't see an actor who is playing a religious leader cursing at stage hands, and you don't see an actor who is playing a mean-hearted character cuddling a child.

Just as in the theater, everyday life occurs on both front stage and back stage. To illustrate this, Goffman used the example of servers who work in a restaurant. Frontstage behavior in a restaurant involves being polite and attentive to diners, showing concern for quality of food, and ensuring sanitation. Backstage behavior, however, may include servers dropping food on the floor, picking it up, and putting it on a plate to be served to a diner on front stage. On the back stage, servers may sample diners' meals, remove mold from a wedge of cheese before putting it on a plate to be presented to a diner, or ridicule customers.

To fully appreciate how social interaction works as drama, we must recognize both the front stage and the back stage of the theater. Backstage behavior allows people to vent feelings safely so that they don't interfere with frontstage performances. Backstage behaviors may also enhance solidarity among members of a group (servers in a restaurant, for instance) and allow them to plan effective frontstage presentation. Competent commu-

Dramaturgical Theory

nicators know how to keep backstage behaviors out of view of the audience so they don't invalidate the frontstage performance. If a diner sees a server nibbling food from a customer's plate, the server is no longer credible in his or her frontstage role. Conversely, knowing there is a back stage where we can let our hair down and relax helps us tolerate the sometimes stressful frontstage work we do.

TRY IT OUT Identify one role you perform in everyday life, the audience of your performance, and the frame for that role. For example, you might focus on being a good student (role) in the perceptions of a professor (audience) within the classroom or an office conference with your professor (frame). List the frontstage and backstage behaviors you engage in within that role. Also predict what would happen if your backstage behaviors were observed by your audience.

Frontstage Behaviors	Backstage Behaviors	Predictions
_____	_____	_____
_____	_____	_____
_____	_____	_____
_____	_____	_____

In our discussion we have focused on Erving Goffman's work so that you could understand it in some depth. However, dramaturgical theory and research is not the sole province of Goffman or even of sociology. Scholars in a range of fields embrace the dramaturgical model and use it to guide their work. As we will see in our critical assessment, that fact is sometimes perceived as indicating that the theory lacks intellectual coherence.

Critical Assessment of Dramaturgical Theory

Many people find Goffman's dramaturgical theory both accurate and useful. For them, the metaphor of life as drama is a useful way to make sense of actions and interactions in everyday life. Not everyone, however, shares this favorable opinion of dramaturgical theory. We'll review three criticisms of dramaturgy.

Metaphor or Reality?   One criticism of dramaturgical theory is its lack of clarity—whether it claims to offer a metaphor for life or a factual description of life. Do dramaturgical scholars claim that people really are actors and spectators, that we really do engage in performances, and that settings of interaction really are stages? Or are they offering theater as a metaphor that provides one useful perspective on people's communication?

Bruce Wiltshire (1977) argues that theater is useful as a metaphor but limited as a description of social life and interaction among people. It allows us to see more clearly than we otherwise might how we work to create and sustain impressions. Yet highlighting impression management may obscure other, perhaps equally or more important, aspects of human interaction. Does the dramaturgical perspective help us realize or understand that people feel empathy, speak spontaneously, and make ethical choices? If not, then the dramaturgical perspective is, if not inaccurate, at least limited.

Reflection

How does thinking of social interaction as performance direct and limit your insight into human communication?

Too Speculative   Another criticism of dramaturgy is that it is more speculative than empirical. The claim that people adopt roles and give performances is difficult to prove or disprove empirically. How would we know if someone were performing a role instead of being an authentic, unplanned self? How could we even identify an "authentic self"? If there is no firm proof (or even a way to obtain proof), then the theory is weak according to the criterion of testability. Further, the validity of the theory cannot be demonstrated if it defies testing. As we noted in earlier chapters, validity is one test of a theory's worth.

Goffman's response to this criticism is that people are actors. He adopts the idea that life *is* drama rather than the softer claim that life is in some ways *like* drama. Although Goffman and others (Messinger et al., 1962) don't assume that people are conscious of being on front stage and giving performances, they believe that people are nonetheless involved in creating and presenting performances in their daily lives.

An Interest Group, Not a Theory   Dramaturgical views of social life are embraced by scholars in a wide range of fields, including anthropology, communication, philosophy, political science, psychology, and sociology (Gronbeck, 1980). Some critics think that the diversity of disciplines employing a dramaturgical perspective suggests that dramaturgy is not a unified theory. Instead, argue some critics, dramaturgical scholars are an interest group loosely unified by a shared metaphor (life is drama) but not by an integrated, consistent theory. Even some (Combs & Mansfield, 1976) who enthusiastically embrace dramaturgical work question whether dramaturgical scholars have yet developed the kind of systematic set of covering laws or rules that theories are generally expected to produce.

Because dramaturgical scholars do not share common theoretical terms, methods of research, or principles of inquiry, there is no single theory or theoretical vocabulary. Instead, scholars who define themselves as dramaturgists tend to have their primary training in specific fields, such as communication or sociology, and they rely on the terms, methods, and principles of their fields when doing dramaturgical research (Gronbeck, 1980). Their results, therefore, may not lead to integrated theoretical knowledge about the theater of life.

Performance Ethnography

Dwight Conquergood (1985), one of the preeminent performance ethnographers, explains that, "ethnographers study the diversity and unity of cultural performance as a universal human resource for deepening and clarifying the meaningfulness of life" (p. 1). Conquergood's point is that cultural performances are an intimate, universal aspect of human experiences; thus, studying them gives us insight into cultural life.

Performance ethnography attempts to understand how symbolic behaviors actually perform—and sometimes challenge—cultural values and personal identities. In other words, individual and group performances reveal some things about how we see ourselves and about the values, traditions, and customs that make up our culture or social community. In illuminating cultural views, performances simultaneously reconstruct or reproduce them (Conquergood, 1998; Phelan & Lane, 1998). For example, graffiti consist of symbols that reflect the values, issues, and identities important in particular cultures or social communities. Graffiti can be said to perform in the sense that they make statements about life in specific social communities. Graffiti also form values, identities, and issues of consequence to those who produce them. And graffiti also inform others of values, identities, and issues important to a particular social group. We'll examine key concepts in performance ethnography and then explore how those are used by scholars of performance studies.

Ethnography

To understand performance ethnography, we must learn about **ethnography**, a method of interpreting actions in a manner that generates understanding in the terms of those performing the actions. We cannot understand the rituals of Taiwanese people by relying on Western values and assumptions. If we want to understand what particular rituals mean to natives of Taiwan, we must get inside Taiwanese systems of meaning. This is precisely what ethnographers do when they work to understand a particular group, be it Taiwanese villagers or street gangs in Chicago.

Clifford Geertz, an anthropologist at Princeton University, is one of the most influential ethnographers. The form of ethnography that he prefers relies on what he calls **thick description**, in which the ethnographer gradually develops the ability to represent cultural practices from the point of view of people who are native to the culture. To clarify what this means, Geertz (1973, 1983) distinguishes thick description from thin description. The latter involves description that doesn't really get at meaning. Thin description gives a shallow description of activities, but thick description gives a fuller account by working to understand the meanings of activities from the perspective of those engaged in them.

Recall our discussion in Chapter 3 of John Searle's (1976) distinction between brute facts and institutional facts. Brute facts are observable, concrete behaviors; institutional facts are the meanings of brute facts—their social significance. Thin description is similar to brute facts, whereas thick description is more like institutional facts. Distinguishing ethnographic research from conventional social science, Dwight Conquergood (1991) wrote, "The once dominant ideal of a detached observer using neutral language to explain 'raw' data has been displaced by an alternative project that attempts to understand human conduct as it unfolds through time and in relation to its meanings for actors" (pp. 179–180). From the perspective of Conquergood and other ethnographers, human action is not simply "raw data" that can be gathered objectively; instead, it is filled with meaning that can be grasped only by an in-depth understanding of the social context in which action occurs.

The in-depth understanding sought by performance ethnographers cannot come from the ethnographer alone. She or he must be in intimate contact with other people and cultures, and this means that members of those cultures are central to the ethnographic method and the knowledge it generates. Emphasizing this point, Henry Glassie (1982) insists that "ethnography is interaction, collaboration" (p. 14). Agreeing, Conquergood (1985) explains that, in ethnographic study of others, "instead of speaking about them, one speaks to and with them" (p. 10). The ethnographer and the people being studied work together to generate knowledge of identities and cultural life.

Direct, Bodily Experience

How does an ethnographer manage to get outside his or her own cultural interpretations and into those of other groups in order to provide rich description? According to Conquergood (1991), to do this an ethnographer engages in **participant-observation**, the distinctive method of ethnography. By being not only an observer but also an active participant in a culture and sometimes even an activist on behalf of that culture, an ethnographer gains understandings in much the same way that members of indigenous groups do—through direct experience, through being involved in the life of the group in body as well as mind. An ethnographer must learn to speak, listen, and act with members of the culture or group being studied. This leads Conquergood to refer to ethnography as "embodied practice" (p. 180).

Ethnographers who commit to the moral posture described by Conquergood operate between the extremes of identification with others and distance from them. On the one hand, the ethnographer must identify enough with others to understand them on their terms, not terms imposed from other perspectives. Yet, if the ethnographer identifies totally, she or he ceases to see how she or he is different from those being studied. Performance ethnographers can perform others' lives in richly textured, complex ways only if they can navigate between feeling one with the others and acknowledging difference from them (Madison, 1999).

The Hermeneutic Circle

Through bodily involvement in a social community, an ethnographer engages in an extended process, in which he or she moves within the **hermeneutic circle**, which consists of near-experience and distance-experience concepts and meanings (Geertz, 1973, 1983). Near-experience meanings are those that have significance to members of a particular culture or social community.

Distance-experience meanings are those that have meaning to people outside of that particular culture or social community. To render a thick description, an ethnographer first observes behaviors and tries to understand them from his or her own perspective, which is distance-experience because it is removed from the point of view of members of the group. As an outsider, the ethnographer cannot understand the meaning of the actions she or he observes. As the ethnographer spends more and more time with the group, he or she progressively gains some understanding of the meaning systems that operate in it, thus creating near-experience meanings. Then, the ethnographer must translate the insider meanings into ones that can be understood by others who are outside of the group being studied.

Harold Garfinkel (1967), another prominent ethnographer, also describes the process of figuring out meaning as circular. According to him, interpretation of phenomena is not solely the province of scholars, because regular people use the same process in their everyday lives. We rely on our working models and expectancies (much as theorists rely on premises, axioms, and so forth) to understand what specific events and actions mean. At the same time, the expectations and models we have are modified by encounters with new experiences, especially those that don't fit our preconceived ideas. So it is specific events that allow us to grasp underlying patterns and models; conversely, underlying patterns and models of the world allow us to interpret specific events (Potter, 1996).

Figure 6.1

The Hermeneutic Circle

Near-experience meaning, in which the ethnographer progressively gains appreciation of behaviors from the point of view of those behaving

Distance-experience meaning, in which ethnographer tries to understand behavior using concepts, assumptions, and so forth that are removed from the context of study

Translation of near-experience meaning into distance-experience meanings for outsiders, while preserving the near-experience meanings

Behavior observed by people who are outside of the ethnographer's culture or social community

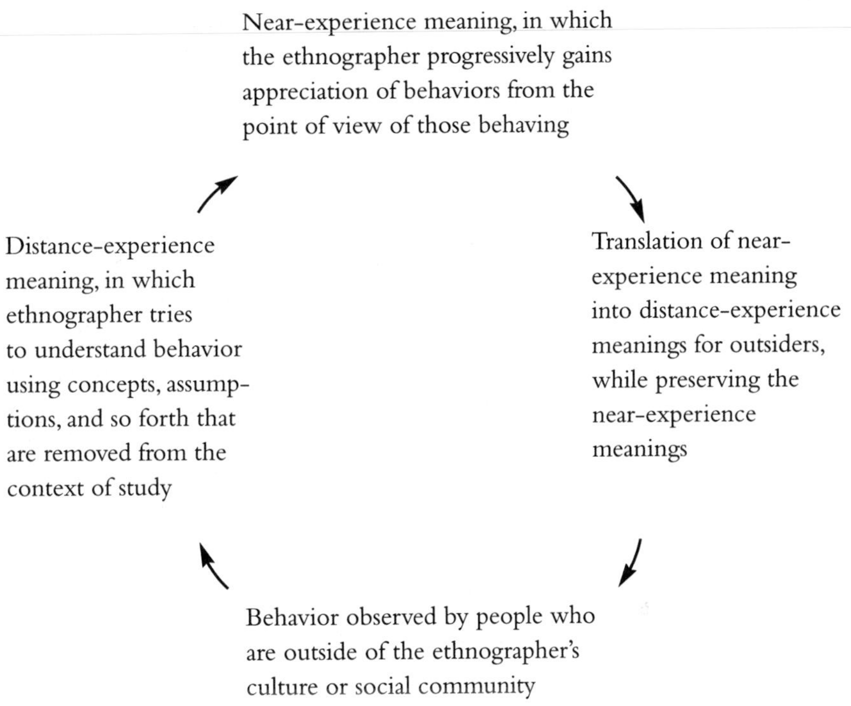

Soyini Madison, a performance studies scholar at the University of North Carolina, launched her scholarly career by studying the lives and experiences of black domestic workers and sharecroppers. In one publication (1991), Madison focused on the life of Mrs. Alma Kapper as told through her stories of life in the early and middle parts of the 20th century. Reflecting on this project, Madison wrote that she had worked to understand Mrs. Kapper's stories and life from Mrs. Kapper's perspective and to explain Mrs. Kapper's life using "specialized knowledge, the knowledge by 'experts'" (pp. 229–230). Madison also noted that intellectual black feminist consciousness is inherently divided between deeply felt ties to community and family and the knowledge and ways of thinking that mark "expert" authority. Madison's comment exemplifies what it means to enter and operate within the hermeneutic circle.

Personal Narrative

As Madison's study of Alma Kapper's narrative suggests, some performance studies scholars are interested in understanding and performing personal and oral histories, including ones told by regular people (not renowned individuals) in everyday contexts (not dramatic settings) about ordinary events (not momentous occurrences in cultural life). You and I and everyone tell stories about who we are, what we've done, what we stand for, and how we operate in our world. These are the personal **narratives** that interest many scholars in performance studies. They also serve as oral histories, not just of individual lives but also of traditions and experiences that define a culture or social community.

Performance studies scholars Eric Peterson and Kristin Langellier (1997) note that personal narratives are not objective representations of experiences or identities. Rather, they say, a narrative is "a strategic practice in its occurrence" (p. 141). By this they mean that, when we tell stories about ourselves and our experiences, we do so to achieve some effect in a particular context: we may want to persuade others to see us as adventurous, honest, loyal, engaging, and so forth; we may intend to convince others that our view of a situation is the correct one; we may want to convince others that we live interesting lives; we may want others to regard us as standing up for the right values; we may want others to gain some insight into experiences we have had but they have not. Whatever our intentions in presenting narratives, we do so for some purpose. To achieve a particular goal, we may accent or embellish certain parts of a narrative, gloss over or abridge other parts, and creatively revise still other parts. Thus, personal narratives are strategic in their effects in specific contexts.

Personal narratives entail **testimony**, which consists of statements based on personal experience about what someone, some activity, or something is, did, believes, feels like, and/or means. To testify is to act as a witness, to stand up and speak about something that the teller believes should be heard by others. For this reason, stories involve a risk for the teller—the risk of exposing one's own experiences, feelings, and thoughts to others in the hope that those others may better understand and perhaps act on the knowledge gained from the story. But others (ethnographers and audiences) may not understand our narrative in our terms. They may distort our experiences and misrepresent them in performance. This is the risk for those who share their personal narratives.

There is also risk for those who listen to stories. Arthur Frank (1995) notes that "listening is hard, but it is also a fundamental moral act . . . The moment of witness in the story crystallizes a mutuality of need, when each is *for* the other" (p. 25). To listen mindfully and openly to personal narratives is to place in jeopardy what we have believed and felt previously. For those who listen, the risk is of being affected, changed by what is heard.

What of the "truth" of personal narratives? What makes a story true or false? Can an experience become true in the process of telling it? Can it change in that process? Many narrative theorists think that a personal narrative is its own truth, which may or may not correspond directly with what the story ostensibly represents. As Frank explains, "The truth of stories is not only what *was* experienced, but equally what *becomes* experience in the telling and its reception" (p. 22). In telling our stories to others, we—as well as they—are affected.

Reflection

How do coherence and narrative fidelity (criteria in narrative theory) apply to personal narratives?

Responsibility

Responsibility is one important aspect of the performance of narratives and oral histories. Writing about personal narratives of illness, Frank (1995) notes that the core morality of personal narratives is a dual responsibility to self and others. Frank explains that "storytelling is *for* an other just as much as it is for oneself. In the reciprocity that is storytelling, the teller offers herself as a guide to the other's self-formation" (p. 18). When the teller of a story and the listener accept this responsibility, each has the potential to enter the other's life and to be changed by that entry. To be responsible to a story requires us to do more than treat it as merely cognitive content to be analyzed critically. We—whether tellers or listeners—must also try to live with the story or walk in the words of another (Smith, 1993).

TRY IT OUT   Discover for yourself what it means to walk in the words of another. Select a person who is very different from you in terms of ethnicity, sexual orientation, experience, or other factors. Talk with that person about his or her identity; probe to learn what it means *to that person* (not to you) to be of that ethnicity, to have had a particular experience, etc. Also spend time with that person in his or her normal daily life and the contexts that are part of his or her world.

After talking and being with the person, write a one-page identity statement that represents that person's identity *in his or her terms;* use the words of that person as much as possible. Then commit the statement to memory and perform it for others. Your performance should capture the words and feelings of the other without commentary or critique from your own perspective. What do you learn from walking in the words of another?

Let's consider one example of the power of performance of oral histories. Historian Jacquelyn Hall and her colleagues (Hall, Leloudis, Korstad, Murphy, Jones, & Daly, 1987) interviewed over 300 former cotton mill workers in the South. What they learned about mill workers' lives—the hardships and joys, the daily rhythms and values—was published in the book *Like a Family: The Making of a Cotton Mill World.*

In collaboration with Hall and 12 students, performance studies scholar Della Pollock (1990) created a performance based on narratives in Hall's book. Using transcripts from Hall et al.'s interviews with cotton mill workers, Pollock created a moving performance in which audiences learned about a world and way of living that was unfamiliar to them. They came to appreciate deeply the ties within families and community and the perseverance of mill workers during hard times. The performers, too, gained new insights; many said that they came to identify deeply with some of the experiences, values, and issues in the lives of mill workers. Reflecting on how performing *Like a Family* affected the student performers, Pollock (1990, p. 35) notes their "constantly renewed curiosity—the meaning of the mill world emerged in the process of performative exchange."

The culmination of Pollock's work came when she took the performance to six mill communities in the Piedmont region of Appalachia. In those communities Pollock's performance was given back to people whose stories Hall and her colleagues had gathered through interviews. Those people recognized themselves in the performance of their narratives, and they also saw themselves in new ways as a result of how the performance presented sharpened and shaped aspects of their lives. In addition, some of the mill workers talked back to the performers, disagreeing vehemently with their interpretations of cotton mill workers' lives and experiences. This exemplifies the dialogic character of performance, in which both performers and audiences make and contest meanings (Cohen-Cruz, 1998; Denzin, 2001). Pollock's project also underlines the power of narrative performances to affect all who are involved in them.

Performance ethnography is not restricted to personal narratives. Many performance ethnographers are particularly interested in cultural practices of groups as expressed and understood through performances. Rather than trying to study a total culture or society, some performance work focuses on local practices, people, and embodied activities. Influenced by anthropologist Victor Turner (1975, 1986), who was passionately interested in village life, some performance ethnographers (Cohen-Cruz, 1998; Denzin, 2001) seek to understand how particular communities create and sustain meanings through rites, rituals, and other performances.

One of the leading scholars in this area is Dwight Conquergood (1985, 1986a,b, 1988, 1998), who teaches at Northwestern University. Conquergood's performance ethnography has led him to study theater in Thai refugee camps in Southeast Asia, gang culture in America, and Laotian refugees living in Chicago. To provide a thick description of street gangs in Chicago, Conquergood (Conquergood, Friesema, Hunter, & Mansbridge, 1990) spent 20 months living in an apartment in a neighborhood largely populated by refugees and immigrants from Mexico, Puerto Rico, Iraq, Laos, Cambodia, Poland, and Lebanon. After those 20 months of fieldwork, Conquergood continued his study and interpretation. This should make us appreciate the depth of ethnographers' commitment to understanding groups in which they are not natives.

Critical Assessment of Performance Ethnography

Performance ethnography is open to criticism of two sorts.

Tension Between Ethnography and Representation of Others
Some question whether performance ethnography can accurately represent others and their experiences in those others' own terms. Sociologist Judith Stacey (1991), for instance, asserts that "it is the researcher who narrates, who 'authors' the ethnography" (p. 114). It is the ethnographer who decides whom to study, how to study them, and which aspects of their identities and experiences to highlight and diminish in a performance. In response, ethnographers acknowledge that their work is necessarily a construction of others' identities and experiences. Yet they also point out that, unlike researchers who claim objectivity and distance from their studies, ethnographers are aware of their involvement in research and performances—they acknowledge and reflect on how they affect both the ethnographic process and the performances that grow out of it. The self-reflexive character of ethnography makes it more aware of the limits of subjectivity and the dangers of misrepresentation than methods that claim complete objectivity.

Attempting to discourage misrepresentation of others' lives, Conquergood (1985) cautions against what he calls "curator's exhibitionism" (p. 7), in which a performance ethnographer creates a performance that presents those studied as the exotic other, primitive and alien. Conquergood warns that this performative stance emphasizes only the difference of the other, not the similarity of the other to us and not the universal aspects of humans. Yet Conquergood is equally wary of the danger of presuming too much universality, which would erase real differences among groups and their experiences.

Reflection

Should detachment be a goal of performance ethnography? What would be gained and lost if detachment were possible?

Misuse of Ethnography
As originally developed, ethnography was intended to be a method that allowed researchers access to meanings of unfamiliar groups. The purpose of ethnography was to understand groups to which we don't belong. The purpose was not to change the groups or the contexts in which they exist. Performance ethnography, however, sometimes pushes beyond the goal of understanding. It may ask audiences (as well as performers and those who are performed) to rethink their views of and attitudes toward individuals and groups whose identities are performed.

Although this departs from the explicit goals for which ethnography was developed, changes that grow out of new understandings may not be incompatible with ethnographic values and assumptions. If performance ethnography fosters better understandings of others, then changes in action and attitude may be a natural result. In fact, a good response to this criticism might be that any new understanding inevitably provokes some kind of change. If we understand something about a group of people that we did not previously understand, how can our attitudes *not* be affected?

Performance as Political Action

A third focus of performance studies scholars is performance as a political act. The emphasis here is on appreciating how performers and performances interact with audiences, communities, and cultures to name, contest, and sometimes alter social processes, practices, and relations. In a landmark essay on performance studies, Mary Susan Strine, Beverly Whitaker Long, and Mary Frances HopKins (1990) noted that some performances are "sites of political action" that "dramatize real-life situations so as to move audiences to action" (p. 188). Can performance do political work? If so, how?

Augusto Boal (1974) opens his book *Theatre of the Oppressed* with this sentence: "This book attempts to show that all theater is necessarily political" (p. ix). Boal sees performance as a "weapon for liberation" (p. ix). Agreeing with Boal, Janelle Reinelt (1996) argues that "performance is transformative social practice" (p. 1). Performance studies scholars who share Boal's and Reinelt's view seek to understand the political power of performance and also to use performances to instigate change in social and political practices. Their answer to the question of whether performance can do political work is a resounding "yes!" Their answer to how performance accomplishes political work might be that it does so by dramatizing oppression, injustice, and other problems in ways that not only inform audiences but also move them to action.

Reflection

What connections do you see between viewing performance as political and Kenneth Burke's dramaturgical perspective on language and action?

Performativity

Performativity is a key concept both for performance studies scholars who embrace the political character of performances and for scholars in other branches of performance work. Before considering a formal definition of performativity, let's discuss a concrete example. Judith Butler's analysis of gender provides an especially illuminating introduction to the meaning of performativity. According to Butler (1990), gender is not a quality that is in individuals. Rather, she says, gender comes into being only as it is performed. We are not genders, but rather we *do* gender, says Butler.

Theories About Performance

Bizarro

In this instance, performativity is both the doing of gender (the performance) and that which is performed (social norms and expectations regarding women and men). It's important to note that, without social conventions that prescribe masculinity and femininity, we could not perform gender.

Elin Diamond (1996) calls performativity "the theoretical partner of performance." Although scholars disagree about some aspects of performativity, they generally concur that the concept emphasizes the extent to which performance realizes, or makes real, identities and experiences. In other words, actions and identities are real only to the extent that they are performed; the performativity of actions and identities is crystallized in specific performances. This implies that performativity is not the mere representation of preexisting identity (or other reality); performativity means that it is in performance that we enact, or generate, the very phenomenon to which performativity refers (Butler, 1990; Diamond, 1996).

Della Pollock (1998) elaborates this by emphasizing that performativity highlights "the process by which meanings, selves, and other effects are produced . . . the embodied process of making meaning" (p. 20). It is both a doing (the act of performing) and what is done (the result of the act, which may change in the process of performance). Pollock (1999) also notes that, in the act of performance, behavior that is typically constrained by social norms may be loosened, and prescribed identities may be challenged and remade in inventive, unconventional ways.

Diamond (1996) points out that performativity "must be rooted in the materiality and historical density of performance" (p. 5). So, for example, in doing gender our performance of masculinity or femininity materializes the social and linguistic patterns that frame understandings of what it means to be a man or a woman. Yet these conventional understandings are not static. The conventions that embody femininity and masculinity at any moment in a given culture's life are negotiated by and in the material bodies of performers.

Reflection

Can you think of any way to perform gender that does not rely on social norms and conventions?

Performativity is not a single act. As Butler (1990, 1993) emphasizes in her analysis of gender, performativity is a *reiteration of a norm or set of norms*. We recognize a particular action as masculine or feminine precisely because it echoes widely established and accepted social norms. It is those norms—not actions themselves—that prompt us to perceive specific acts as signifying masculinity or femininity. Performance, then, is the materialization of performativity through the embodiment of widely held and recognized social conventions.

In her book *Exceptional Spaces* (1998), Della Pollock provides additional insight into the concept of performativity. She emphasizes the active, collaborative role of audiences in producing the meaning of performance. To recognize gender, for example, audiences must be aware of cultural expectations and conventions. They may then accept or resist those, as may the performers. Thus, Pollock notes that performance has the potential both to reinscribe and to resist what it represents—cultural practices, identities, and relationships. More concisely, Pollock (1999) says that "it is performance that challenges performativity—and makes change possible."

Cultural, Political Critique

As we've already noted, those who endorse the political power of performance seek to do more than use performance simply to represent existing social meanings for identities such as gender. Performance is also a primary means of critiquing social meanings and the identities and practices they foster. The cultural and political critique offered by performance as political action challenges the very social conventions and norms that frame—and perhaps limit—individual identities and social relations.

Theories About Performance

Why is it that women cannot curse, spit, or be aggressive without running the risk of being labeled "unfeminine?" Why is it that men cannot cry, care for children, or enjoy makeup without transgressing cultural meanings for masculinity? Why is sexuality defined as fixed and as limited to heterosexual, gay, lesbian, or bisexual? Could there be additional forms of sexuality? Could there be substantial fluidity among different sexualities? Why must individuals choose between masculinity and femininity, as if gender were absolutely fixed and binary? Is it possible that there are multiple genders instead of just the two recognized by Western culture? In asking these questions, performance studies scholars who are interested in the political power of performance invite audiences (as well as performers) to reflect critically on the meaning-making systems that operate in societies and that frame personal identities and social relations.

Reflecting on the move in performance studies to use performance for political work, Conquergood (1991) asked, "What is the relationship between performance and power? How does performance reproduce, enable, sustain, challenge, subvert, critique, and naturalize ideology? How do performances simultaneously reproduce (and thus highlight) and resist (and thus invite change) hegemony? How does performance accommodate and contest domination?" (p. 190).

An example of performance as a site for political action was one focused on the AIDS crisis, presented at a meeting of the Speech Communication Association (A. Martin, 1988). Based on research on people with AIDS and on attitudes toward AIDS and its victims, the performance was an aesthetic argument against demonization of those who suffer from AIDS. In the performance, people with AIDS were presented in their full humanness—not merely as patients with a life-threatening disease. Many who saw the performance left with changed views of both people with AIDS and widely held negative judgments about them. The performance disrupted conventional meanings and invited those involved with it to rethink identities and attitudes and the social processes that shape them.

Another example of performance as political action is the work of Anna Deavere Smith, an actress and playwright and also the head of Harvard's Institute of the Arts and Civic Dialogue. (She also has a continuing role on *The West Wing*.) In an interview, Smith stated that her performance work grows out of her belief that "in addition to finding the world inside us, we had to have techniques that were about going outside of the self, to find the other" (Woods, 1999, p. 1C).

Smith is best known for her one-woman performances that grapple with social tensions by giving voice to the perspectives of multiple social communities. Smith's first major one-woman show was titled *Fires in the Mirror* which dealt with the ethnic turmoil in Crown Heights, Brooklyn, that followed after a black child was killed by a car in the motorcade of a

Jewish leader. (We looked at this event and performance more closely in Chapter 4.) Later, Smith created a one-woman show called *Twilight: Los Angeles, 1992* about the riots that erupted in Los Angeles after a jury acquitted the police officers who were accused of beating Rodney King. To create her show, Smith interviewed many people connected with the Rodney King incident. These included Reginald Denney, the white truck driver who was beaten by black youths, and Paul Parker, the brother of one of the men who beat Reginald Denney.

The one-woman performance that grew out of her interviews includes 46 characters, each of whom she represents in his or her own voice (based on the interviews). The show does not attempt to weave a coherent narrative in which it is clear who are the "good guys" and "bad guys" or what is "right" and "wrong." Instead, Smith deliberately performs fragments—sometimes disunited, often conflicting—to upset the possibility of any single resolution of complex racial relations that were embodied in the beating of Rodney King and the jury's acquittal of those accused of the beating. Of Smith's performance, scholar Beverly Whitaker Long says that she "allows all the parties involved in these struggles a very fair hearing. She truly speaks for the other" (Woods, 1999, p. 1C).

Reflection

What might fragments achieve that a coherent narrative cannot?

In an interview with Carol Martin (1993), Smith tried to explain why she believes performing others' words is so powerful. She said, "My grandfather told me that if you say a word enough, it becomes you" (p. 51). After extensive interviews with people representing different perspectives on and stakes in issues such as the Rodney King beating and the ensuing trial, Smith tries to walk in their words. She lends her voice and her body to others who travel through her to speak. Yet in doing this Smith does what her grandfather said—she becomes the words and the others. "Acting is becoming the other," says Smith. And yet, she realizes that "to acknowledge the other, you have to acknowledge yourself" (Martin, 1993, p. 51).

Critical Assessment of Political Performance Theory

We will consider two criticisms of currents in performance studies theory.

Lacks a Coherent Theoretical Foundation Performance studies may be faulted for lacking a coherent theoretical foundation. Dramaturgy springs from the work of sociologist Erving Goffman; performance ethnography is informed by the work of anthropologists, sociologists, philosophers, and scholars in other fields; and performance as political action seems especially influenced by postmodern and poststructural theories (covered in Chapter 13).

In one sense this criticism is well founded. No single theory unifies and informs all the work that has been done in the area of performance studies. However, the same observation could be made of work in interpersonal communication, mass communication, and other areas in the field of communication. Likewise, other disciplines draw on a wide range of theories and also generate diverse theories. There is, after all, no single theory that unifies the discipline of psychology or political science.

Most performance studies scholars do not find this criticism particularly troubling. They are likely to reject the value of any singular theoretical foundation on the grounds that it would be limiting. Instead, like scholars in any area of inquiry, they study theories that can help them do their work, and they generate theoretical insights that pertain specifically to their activities. If there is no unifying theory, perhaps that is because performance studies surveys the vast terrain of human experience and cultural life, which surely cannot be described or understood fully by any single theory.

Misuse of Art   Another criticism is that performance as political action errs in using art to do political work. Traditionally performance has been thought of as an artistic creation that amuses, entertains, and moves audiences. Politics, on the other hand, is generally understood to be concerned with public and civic life. If art and politics are totally separate, then perhaps it is mistaken to use art to do political work. But are art and politics really separate? Should they be?

Reflection

Has any kind of art ever changed you in important ways?

Art of all sorts has a long and established tradition of entering into politics. Historically, sculptures, paintings, and performances have commented on political issues. The alliance of performance with politics is especially evident in Bertolt Brecht's (1961, 1964) theory of drama. Brecht assumes that performance can and should motivate political change. He believes effective drama should not provide easy catharsis (or an "emotional orgy"), because that relieves us of the distress and discomfort that motivate rethinking and change. He believes that unresolved tensions—such as those in Anna Deavere Smith's work—have greater potential than catharsis to motivate change. Brecht calls on performance to transform the world and make it more just. Brecht argued that performance has a responsibility to help people see how society should progress and how they can help it do so.

Agreeing with Brecht, those scholars who regard performance as political would argue that the arts have always been involved with politics and that this remains true today. Della Pollock (1998) celebrates the extraordinary ways in which performance "ruptures and rattles and revises history" (p. 27).

Performance as Political Action   **137**

The many kinds of communication have multiple purposes and potentialities. Interpersonal communication can bring people closer, and it can poison relationships. A public speech can inspire us to idealistic beliefs and actions, and it can fuel our basest, most hateful attitudes and behaviors. Mass communication can inform, entertain, and mislead us. Why, performance theorists might ask, should performance be any different in this respect from other forms of human communication? Why can performance not preserve and revere history and tradition, on the one hand, and undermine tradition and challenge history on the other?

Summary

In this chapter we've explored several of many currents in contemporary performance studies. Departing from a view of performance as an aesthetic event that is removed from everyday life, performance studies scholars today tend to be at least as interested in ordinary life and cultural practices as in what conventionally have been considered "high" cultural events. The early work of Erving Goffman led to dramaturgical theory, which focuses on how people engage in performances in their daily lives. Goffman's theory invites us to understand the contexts of our lives as a stage and our actions as performances. This theoretical perspective heightens awareness of the extent to which we engage in strategic (although not necessarily conscious) efforts to manage the impressions we create and the interactions in which we engage.

Performance ethnography is a second current in performance studies today. Building on ethnographic research that seeks to understand others on their own terms, performance ethnographers work to understand others and their experiences by engaging in thick readings of cultural life. Following that, performance ethnographers create performances that are designed to give audiences access to the meanings of those studied.

Performing oral histories and personal narratives is one means of giving voice to others, often individuals and groups that lie outside of the mainstream in social life.

The third current we examined in this chapter is performance as political action. In this area, scholars seek to create performances that serve political goals, such as highlighting social injustices, calling into question accepted social norms and relations, and contesting practices that oppress individuals and groups. The power of performance to resist sedimented traditions that undermine an equitable society and to instigate reflection on cultural life and alternatives to its current form is a particularly exciting trend in contemporary performance theory.

Key Terms

back stage

dramaturgical model

dramaturgy

ethnography

frames

front stage

hermeneutic circle

impression management

narrative

performance ethnography

performativity

testimony

thick description

CHAPTER SEVEN

Theories About How People Construct Meaning

Erik meets a new person and notices that she's bright, friendly, politically liberal, and concerned about social issues. Erik assumes she votes Democratic and does volunteer work in her community.

———

At work, Carlos's supervisor tells him teamwork is expected on the new project to which he's been assigned. Carlos understands this means he's expected to share information and coordinate with others rather than make himself stand out as an individual.

———

Shennata and her partner have a disagreement. When she sees her partner's jaw clench, Shennata knows from past experience to drop the subject for now. She's learned to wait until her partner's anger blows over before dealing with the conflict.

———

On what basis does Erik make predictions about his new acquaintance's patterns of voting and community service? How does Carlos translate the abstract term *teamwork* into a specific behavioral script that will guide his future actions? What leads Shennata to believe it is wiser to delay discussing a touchy subject with her partner?

All these questions revolve around the process by which individuals construct the meanings of communication. Communication theorists have generated a number of impressive theories to account for the ways we go about making sense of interactions.

In this chapter we will consider two of the most prominent and widely endorsed theories about how individuals construct meaning. The two theories, **rules theory** and **constructivism**, extend the general premises of symbolic interactionism by providing more detailed accounts of how individuals construct meanings. These two theories are compatible with each other, and both reflect the basic framework of symbolic interactionism, which we studied in Chapter 5. Although constructivism and rules theory work well together, that isn't necessarily the case for all theories. These two theories are compatible because they have a common philosophical foundation and share intellectual roots in symbolic interactionism.

Rules Theory, or the Coordinated Management of Meaning

Rules theory is concerned with how humans construct meaning for their communication. One prominent rules theory is called coordinated management of meaning (CMM) theory, to emphasize that we use communication rules to coordinate meanings in interaction with others. CMM emerged in the 1970s and has been continuously refined and elaborated since then. This theory owes an intellectual debt to symbolic interactionism, whose fundamental assumptions it shares and uses to develop its own claims.

CMM is an interpretive theory that assumes human communication is rule guided and rule following. Rules theorists do not believe human behavior is strictly determined by external forces. Instead, they think that we learn broad social patterns of interpretation that are woven into cultural life, and that we use those to guide our communication. You should recognize immediately the link between this ontological premise and symbolic interactionism's emphasis on learning social meanings through interaction with others. To understand CMM, we'll focus on its three key concepts.

Hierarchy of Meanings

Barnett Pearce and Vernon Cronen (1980) believe that we rely on a **hierarchy of meanings** to interpret experiences. The hierarchy consists of multiple levels of meaning, and each level is contextualized by higher levels in the hierarchy; that is, how we interpret experience at a lower level of meaning is influenced by higher, or more general, levels of meaning in the overall hierarchy.

Rules theorists have identified six levels of meaning in the hierarchy. They are quick to note, however, that there may be additional levels of meaning that have not yet been recognized.

Content   Consider a simple comment: "You are a jerk." The words "You are a jerk" are the **content** of communication, the lowest level of meaning in the hierarchy. We understand the dictionary meanings of *you*, *are*, *a*, and *jerk*, but that doesn't tell us how to interpret the statement. What does it mean when someone says, "You are a jerk"? To construct the meaning of this content, we must refer to higher levels of meaning in the hierarchy.

Speech Act According to CMM theorists, communication is action. In other words, we do things when we speak: we plead, demand, promise, threaten, joke, apologize, and so forth. The action emphasis of CMM is captured in the concept of speech acts, which are "actions we perform by speaking" (Pearce, 1994, p. 104). Speech acts provide a context for interpreting the raw content of communication. They tell us how to view particular comments.

If a friend says, "You are a jerk" and smiles while speaking, you're likely to interpret the comment as the **speech act** of joking. If you've just told a sexist joke, and a woman friend says, "You are a jerk," you would probably interpret her comment as the speech act of scolding or reprimanding. But if you bump into a stranger on the street and he says, "You are a jerk," you might decide he's engaging in the speech act of hostility or threat. Of course, *which* speech act is performed isn't always clear. That's why we need higher levels of meaning in the hierarchy.

Episode Episodes are larger frames for interpreting speech acts. An **episode** is a recurring routine of interaction that is structured by rules and that has boundaries. For example, in the episode of "friendly banter," it is acceptable to say, "You are a jerk" in a joking manner. It's within the rules for friends to exchange playful insults, but it is outside of the rules to be cruel or to inflict real hurt. It violates the rules of friendly banter to attack a friend in areas where you know he or she feels vulnerable. "You are a jerk" takes on a different meaning if it is said within the episode of an ugly argument, in which case it would probably not be interpreted as playful and friendly. Episodes are frames that help us determine what is inside and outside of a given interaction routine (Pearce, 1994).

Relationships The fourth level in the hierarchy is **relationships**, the somewhat scripted ways we interact with particular others. In some relationships it is understood that exchanging friendly insults is a form of playing, so "You are a jerk" is appropriate within those relationships. In other relationships, that understanding may not exist. If you and a particular friend haven't established the rule that insults aren't offensive, then "You are a jerk" may be interpreted as the speech act of serious insult rather than play. How we define a given relationship provides a context for interpreting particular content, speech acts, and episodes within it.

Jonathan Shailor (1994), a student of Barnett Pearce, explains that we define relationships as including certain rights, exclusions, freedoms, and responsibilities. Thus, I think my partner, Robbie, has a right to complain if he feels I'm not spending enough time with him. I don't grant that same right to my neighbors. If both Robbie and a neighbor I know only casually said, "I want you to spend more time with me," I would interpret the two statements differently because of the distinct understandings I have of the two relationships. I might interpret Robbie's communication as the speech act "requesting intimacy" and decide it was an example of the episode "feeling distant," which each of us has experienced in our many years together. The same statement from a casual neighbor, however, I might interpret as the speech act of "being pushy" and regard it as inappropriate in the episode of neighborly interaction.

Reflection

What happens in communication when communicators don't define their relationship in the same way or when they don't agree about the episode they are in?

Autobiographies   Originally Pearce labeled the fifth level in the hierarchy "life scripts." Later, however, he and other CMM theorists refer to it as "autobiographies." An **autobiography** is an individual's view of himself or herself that both shapes and is shaped by communication. In other words, how you see yourself influences how you communicate; at the same time, communication with others influences how you perceive yourself. The link to symbolic interactionism is clear here, since Mead argued that we gain a sense of self in the process of interacting with others.

Your definition of who you are influences communication in many ways. You regard some speech acts as consistent with your sense of self and others as inconsistent. For example, helping others, being responsible, and arguing about ideas are three speech acts that are consistent with my sense of who I am. Consequently, I am comfortable in episodes and relationships that I perceive as allowing or requiring these speech acts. Being rude, ignoring others, and deferring are speech acts that are not consistent with how I view myself. As a result, I feel uncomfortable when I am in relationships and episodes that evoke being rude, ignoring others, or being deferential.

Just as we see certain speech acts as consistent or inconsistent with our identities, so too do we see episodes, relationships, and even specific content as congruent or incongruent with who we are. The comment "You are a jerk" may be consistent with the autobiographies of people who perceive themselves as playful and sassy. The "same" words may be incongruent with the autobiographies of individuals who see themselves as formal and conventionally polite.

All the speech acts and episodes that are consistent with an individual's sense of self make up the whole autobiography. It describes a person's overall pattern of communicating, responding, and acting in the world.

Some individuals consistently act out of a tragic script in which they view events as trials, focus on losses or problems, and represent themselves as martyrs, downtrodden, or otherwise victims of a tragic cosmos. Other people operate out of a comic life script in which they approach problems with a sense of humor, appreciate the irony in events, and represent themselves as jesters. My autobiography is defined by adventure. Consistently, I approach challenges, problems, and relationships as adventures: I'm always looking for new discoveries and experiences.

Reflection

How has your autobiography been shaped by communication, and how does it influence your patterns of communicating?

Cultural Patterns   The final level of meaning that has been identified is cultural patterns. A **cultural pattern** is an understanding of speech acts, episodes, relationships, and autobiographies that is shared by particular social groups or societies. "You are a jerk" is more likely to be interpreted as friendly and acceptable among college friends than among business associates: the two social groups have understandings that distinctly affect how the "same" words are likely to be understood. Social groups develop distinctive ways of interpreting experiences, and these make up the cultural patterns on which members of those groups rely to construct meanings.

Because different social groups develop distinct cultural patterns, communication between cultures is often laced with misunderstandings. For example, what would you think if you asked a classmate how her job interview went, and she replied, "Damn! I'm good. I was so terrific that they will be begging me to take that job. They won't even look at anyone else." If you are a European American, you might identify this as the speech act of bragging within the episode of obnoxious, egotistical behavior. On the other hand, a person who grew up in traditional African-American communities might recognize this as the speech act of braggadocio, which is intended as humor, not serious boasting (Gates, 1987; Houston & Wood, 1996; Smitherman, 1977), and recognize that it fits in the episode of joking and displaying wit. Different speech communities have different cultural patterns that affect how they communicate and what the various forms of communication are understood to mean. We'll learn more about this in Chapter 10, which presents theories that focus on communication cultures and social communities.

Native English speakers who were socialized in Western culture are generally highly individualistic. The content of native English speakers' communication includes references to *my* school, *my* parents, *my* country, and so forth. The individualism that is a cultural pattern in the West is not prominent in many Eastern cultures. A greater sense of family, community, and collectivity infuses most Eastern cultures. The collectivism that is a cultural pattern in many other cultures explains why the content of their communication includes phrases such as *our* school, *our* parents, and *our* country (Ferrante, 1995).

TRY IT OUT Apply the hierarchy of meanings to analyze the levels of meaning you rely on in your own communication. Think about the last time that you had a disagreement with a friend. Now recall a specific verbal statement made in that situation.

1. What did you regard as the content?
2. How did you define the speech act?
3. What did you consider the episode?
4. How did you perceive the relationship?
5. How do you describe your autobiography?
6. What cultural patterns can you identify that influenced this specific communication?

Notice that, in each of the foregoing questions, you are asked how you defined, interpreted, described, and perceived levels in the hierarchy. You aren't asked, "What was the episode?" or "What is your autobiography?" This highlights the important point that *we* construct the meaning of communication by the ways in which we define levels in the hierarchy of meanings. The levels are not objective phenomena.

Rules

The hierarchy of meanings provides the basis for social interaction. Yet to coordinate the different levels in the hierarchy, we need some ways to connect the six levels (Figure 7.1). **Rules** allow us to make sense of social interaction and guide our own communication so that we coordinate meanings with others. CMM theorists refer to two kinds of rules: constitutive and regulative.

Constitutive Rules **Constitutive rules** define what counts as what. Like the institutional facts that Searle (1976) discussed, constitutive rules tell us what certain actions constitute or mean. For example, many people count hugging, kissing, and giving support as showing affection; listening and responding often are counted as being attentive; preparing an agenda and guiding discussion count as group leadership; and dating someone other than your regular partner may count as betrayal.

Figure 7.1

The Hierarchy of Meanings

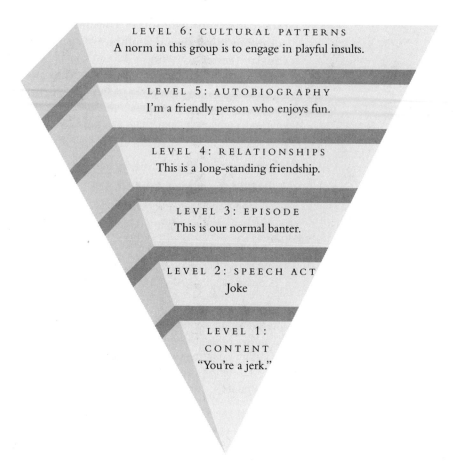

LEVEL 6: CULTURAL PATTERNS
A norm in this group is to engage in playful insults.

LEVEL 5: AUTOBIOGRAPHY
I'm a friendly person who enjoys fun.

LEVEL 4: RELATIONSHIPS
This is a long-standing friendship.

LEVEL 3: EPISODE
This is our normal banter.

LEVEL 2: SPEECH ACT
Joke

LEVEL 1:
CONTENT
"You're a jerk."

We learn constitutive rules in the process of interacting with others. Consequently, our constitutive rules reflect the cultural patterns of our particular social groups rather than universal rules of meaning. Developing shared understandings of constitutive rules is essential if we are to coordinate meanings with others. Many romantic partners have difficulty coordinating their constitutive rules. A common example of this difficulty concerns rules for conflict. One partner thinks that disagreement counts as disruption and that avoiding discussion of problems counts as being loving, and the other partner thinks that constructively confronting tensions counts as loyalty to the relationship.

Reflection

According to your constitutive rules, what does conflict count as?

Regulative Rules   To coordinate communication, we also rely on **regulative rules** to guide interaction. Regulative rules tell us when it's appropriate to do certain things and what we should do next in an interaction.

Theories About How People Construct Meaning

In the episode of playful banter, friends follow a regulative rule that says it is appropriate to match an insult with an insult. Classroom communication often follows regulative rules, such as students should raise hands before speaking, you can (or must) speak when a professor calls on you, and it is not appropriate to insult teachers or other students.

TRY IT OUT Apply CMM theory by identifying constitutive and regulative rules that operate in your family of origin.

Constitutive Rules

1. What counts as affection?

2. What counts as rudeness?

3. What counts as responsibility?

4. What counts as respect?

Regulative Rules

1. Is heated discussion appropriate during meals?

2. Is it appropriate for children to challenge or disagree with parents?

3. If a parent criticizes a child's behavior, what should the child say?

4. Is it appropriate to talk about personal topics?

When constitutive and regulative rules are coordinated, interaction tends to run smoothly and comfortably. That's because the individuals agree on what various communications mean and on how to sequence their activities. But when individuals operate according to different constitutive and regulative rules, friction and misunderstandings often result.

Consider this example from research. Studies show that men interrupt more frequently than women and that men give minimal responses ("um," "yeah") to others, whereas women typically give more extensive responses (DeFrancisco, 1991; Wood, 1994a). In a conversation among men, frequent interruptions and minimal responses may be seen as normal interaction. Women, however, may operate by constitutive rules that define interruptions as rude and minimal responses as showing indifference. This is one of many gender differences in communication. We'll learn more about these in Chapter 10.

Logical Force

As we've noted, rules theorists do not endorse a deterministic view of human nature. They view rules not as absolute and unchanging but as fluid

Jump Start reprinted by permission of United Feature Syndicate, Inc.

patterns that humans construct and that are more or less open to change. Some of the rules we use to guide our communication and to interpret others' are relatively flexible, and we may choose not to follow them at times. Yet other rules we rely on feel too important to abandon.

Cronen and Pearce (1981) use the concept of **logical force** to describe the felt obligation to act. The term *force* refers to the degree to which we feel we must act or cannot act in particular ways. The term *logical* reminds us that our sense of obligation is tied to the logic of our overall hierarchy of meanings. We decide what we may, should, or must say based on our understandings of speech acts, episodes, relationships, autobiographies, and cultural patterns. The assumption that higher levels of meaning contextualize lower levels implies that we feel more bound by rules that involve higher levels in our system of meanings. Thus, you might deviate from a regulative rule about how you should respond in a particular episode, but you would be unlikely to disregard a constitutive rule that is tied to your autobiography. For example, Zarina might choose not to be attentive in class (episode), but she would resist communicating in ways that undermine her view of herself as a supportive friend (autobiography).

Logical force concerns the extent to which we feel certain actions are logical, appropriate, or required in specific situations. There are different sources or types of logical force. Sometimes we feel we must do something because of prior actions, such as promises we've made. We may also feel logically forced to act because of desired outcomes we think will result from acting in particular ways. For example, mischievous children often become atypically well behaved shortly before their birthdays in the expectation that good behavior will result in more or better presents.

Situational demands are a third basis of logical force. For instance, imagine that you attend the funeral of a relative whom you didn't like, and someone who loved the deceased says to you, "Such a wonderful person, don't you think?" The logical force of the funeral context is likely to compel you to agree that the deceased was a very fine human being.

Finally, rules theorists say that sometimes we feel impelled to change situations that are other than we think they should be. People who grew up in dysfunctional families often take it upon themselves to create very different patterns of communication in the families they create as adults. This kind of change could alter the relationship level (family) in the hierarchy of meanings. Logical force, then, comes in four different forms but has the common feature of leading us to feel that certain kinds of communication are right, appropriate, or required.

Strange Loops   Pearce's student Robert Branham and Pearce (1985) extended the theory by identifying what they called **strange loops** in interaction. Strange loops are internal conversations by means of which individuals become trapped in destructive patterns of thinking. Meanings at different levels in the hierarchy interact to sustain a repetitive cycle of behavior from which an individual seems unable to escape. Using this concept, therapists have helped clients deal with eating disorders and other problems.

Let's consider an example of a strange loop. Repeatedly, Marla drinks too much and suffers a hangover and impaired ability to function the next day. Marla defines her behavior as the act of getting drunk in the episode of college partying. Finally, Marla decides to get control of her problem and resolves not to drink. After three weeks without alcohol, Marla concludes she can control her drinking and thus doesn't have a problem. So she drinks at the next party, and the whole cycle begins anew.

Is Marla forever trapped in this destructive cycle? Not necessarily. CMM theorists would argue that, if Marla wants to escape from this strange loop, she must revise her hierarchy of meaning. Perhaps Marla should redefine drinking episodes as "problem behavior" instead of "college partying." As long as Marla interprets her drinking as routine college partying, she's likely to regard it as acceptable and normal. It might also help Marla escape the strange loop if she redefined "college partying" as "drinking scenes" and redefined her own participation in parties as "abstaining from alcohol." Marla might also consider redefining her autobiography to include the view of herself as alcoholic or predisposed to have problems with alcohol. By altering the meanings she assigns to her drinking and to herself, Marla might be able to escape from a strange loop that is dangerous and potentially debilitating.

Let's summarize what we've learned about CMM or rules theory. The fundamental premise of the theory is that individuals create meanings by relying on an organized system of meanings in which higher levels contextualize lower levels of meaning. In interaction, individuals rely on constitutive and regulative rules to guide how they communicate and how they interpret the communication of others. Like symbolic interactionism, CMM assumes that people make sense of their experiences by assigning meanings to them. Also like symbolic interactionism, CMM assumes that the meanings we assign are not entirely unique to individuals but are nestled within larger frames of reference and meaning that operate in cultures.

Originally, CMM theory was envisioned as a theory of interpersonal communication. Since the theory's birth, however, it has been applied to intrapersonal, organizational, therapeutic, and intercultural communication. Jonathan Shailor (1994) relied on CMM principles to analyze uncoordinated communication between spouses engaged in dispute mediation. Several scholars have used CMM theory to describe and explain various aspects of communication in institutions and organizations (Barge, 1985; Harris, 1979; Williams, 1989). This theory has also illuminated lack of coordination between people from different cultures (Cronen, Chen, & Pearce, 1988).

Critical Assessment of CMM Theory

Criticism of CMM has tended to focus on three issues.

Unclear Meaning of *Rule*
One problem is that not all rules theorists agree on the meaning of the key concept of rules. Susan Shimanoff (1980, 1985) asserts that rules deal exclusively with observable behaviors. On the other hand, Pearce and his colleagues (Cronen, Chen, & Pearce, 1988; Cronen & Pearce, 1981; Pearce, 1989; Pearce & Cronen, 1980) claim that rules pertain to internal, subjective interpretation as well as to overt activities.

Because the term *rule* is used to mean different things, it's difficult to coordinate findings from rules theorists' research. Of course, the deeper issue underlying terminological confusion concerns epistemological assumptions. If we assume that only observable behaviors can be known, then we would agree with Shimanoff's definition of *rule*. If, however, we think that behaviors that aren't overt also matter and deserve scholarly attention, we're likely to find ourselves more comfortable with Pearce and his colleagues' definition.

Too Ambiguous   Rules theories have also been criticized for their ambiguity. Not only is there no agreed-on definition of *rule,* but theorists have not advanced a precise definition of how to identify whatever it is they count as rules. In other words, what are the constitutive rules for defining rules? This ambiguity leads to the related question of whether rules theory deals well with unexpected forms of communication. If rules are based on the hierarchy of meanings and are influenced by logical force, then what accounts for creativity, innovation, and violations of convention? Ambiguous responses—such as the assertion that violations follow different rules—are not convincing. Rules theorists have not developed or identified precise rules for violations, so creative behaviors remain difficult to analyze within the framework of this theory.

Too Broad in Scope   The most common criticism of CMM theory is that it is too broad in scope. Critics have asserted that CMM tries to explain the whole universe, from problems between cultures to difficulties in intimate relationships (Brenders, 1987). In attempting to explain such diverse phenomena, critics charge, the theory fails to achieve sufficient precision to permit insight into specific communication activities.

Reflection

Based on the foundations of theory that you endorse, what do you perceive as values of CMM theory?

CMM theorists do not deny the charge that the theory is extremely broad. They do, however, reject the idea that this is a problem or a weakness of the theory. One of the primary theorists, Vernon Cronen (1991), replies to the criticism by asserting that a good humanistic theory should shed light on the overall human condition, not just on isolated facets of human activity. CMM theorists argue that the theory is meant to offer an expansive view of human action and should be assessed in terms of whether it achieves that goal. If that is the criterion of evaluation, then CMM fares rather well. Unquestionably it gives us new insights into how we create meanings and how our patterns of making meaning guide our communication.

Symbolic interactionism gives us a broad picture of humans as interpretive beings who actively engage in the process of constructing meanings for their activities. Yet it doesn't explain in a precise way exactly how we go about interpreting the world to assign meanings to people, events, behaviors, and so forth. Constructivist theory attempts to do this. Working from the fundamental assumptions of symbolic interactionism, constructivist theorists have developed an account of the interpretive process.

The roots of constructivist theory are symbolic interactionism and psychologist George Kelly's (1955) personal construct theory. Both of these foundations of constructivism focus on cognitive processes that we use to create meaning. Extending those foundations, communication theorists have elaborated the relationship of cognitive processes to communication (Delia, O'Keefe, & O'Keefe, 1982). Before studying this theory, respond to Figure 7.2, which is an abbreviated version of the basic research tool used by constructivists (Crockett, 1965).

Figure 7.2

Role Category Questionnaire

Think of people about your own age whom you know well. Select one person you like and one person you dislike. Spend a moment to mentally compare and contrast them in terms of personality, habits, beliefs, and the way they treat others. Don't limit yourself to similarities and differences between the two; consider all the qualities that make them who they are.

Please take about five minutes to describe the person you like so that a stranger would have an accurate picture of him or her. Don't describe physical characteristics, but do list all of the attributes, mannerisms, and reactions to others that identify the person. Use phrases and single words to describe the person; full-sentence descriptions aren't necessary.

When you've finished describing the person you like, repeat the procedure for the person you dislike.

Liked person _____   **Disliked person** _____

1. _____   1. _____

2. _____   2. _____

3. _____   3. _____

4. _____   4. _____

5. _____   5. _____

To understand constructivist theory, we will discuss three of its primary concepts. As we do so, you'll discover how constructivist theorists would interpret your descriptions of a liked and a disliked peer and what they would conclude about your ways of constructing meaning.

Cognitive Schemata

In his original theoretical statement, George Kelly (1955) claimed that personal constructs are the building blocks of individuals' interpretations of experience. Substantial research done since Kelly's formulation of the theory has supported his basic insight and identified three additional kinds of knowledge structure or **cognitive schema** (plural *schemata*). We'll consider each of the four schemata and how they work together to help us make sense of our experiences.

Prototypes   **Prototypes**, the broadest cognitive structures, are ideal or optimal examples of categories of people, situations, objects, and so forth (Fehr, 1993). You have prototypes of "great teachers," "nasty supervisors," and "good friends." For each category, your prototype is the person who most exemplifies the whole category—the ideal teacher, the nastiest boss you ever worked for, and the best friend you ever had. That person who embodies the category is your prototype. We use prototypes to interpret others who fit into particular categories. Thus, when you begin a new class, you don't interpret the professor only in terms of what he or she does. Instead, you compare that person to your prototypes of teachers.

Personal Constructs   **Personal constructs**, the second-broadest knowledge structures, are building blocks that Kelly (1955) originally identified. Kelly defined a *personal construct* as a "mental yardstick" that allows us to measure a phenomenon on a particular dimension. Personal constructs are bipolar, or opposite, scales of judgment. Examples of personal constructs many people use in judging others are *intelligent–unintelligent, interesting–uninteresting, attractive–unattractive, ethical–unethical,* and *kind–unkind.*

Each of these bipolar scales serves as a measuring stick against which you interpret others and compare people to one another: Konya and Allison are both intelligent, and Konya is more intelligent than Allison. Whereas prototypes help us place a person or experience in a particular category (both Konya and Allison are intelligent), personal constructs allow us to go further and assess the person or experience in depth and in comparison to others along particular dimensions we consider relevant (Konya is more intelligent).

Reflection

What personal constructs are salient in your initial impressions of people?

Stereotypes **Stereotypes**, the third type of knowledge structure, are predictive generalizations. Stereotypes go beyond the description that prototypes and personal constructs provide and make predictions about how a person will behave. When we stereotype a person, we prophesy what she or he will do based on the general group into which we have classified the individual (notice that we classify people, so that, too, is part of our interpretive construction of meaning). For example, because you've defined Aaron as liberal, you predict he votes for pro-choice candidates; because you've interpreted Margo as an ambitious person, you predict she isn't committed to homemaking and mothering. Your predictions may be correct or incorrect; either way, they are part of how you interpret others and decide who they are.

Scripts The final cognitive schema is **scripts**, which are guides to action, much like the episodes that we read about in CMM theory. A script is a routine, or action sequence, that we have in mind about a particular interaction. You have scripts for most of your daily activities, such as how to talk to clerks in stores, how to discuss classwork with professors, and how to interact with friends or roommates. You also have scripts that define what kinds of behaviors and sequences of behaviors are appropriate in contexts such as classes, parties, and visits with family. Scripts define how particular kinds of interactions are supposed to proceed—what happens, what comes first, second, and so forth. Thus, they help us organize interaction.

Among college students, researchers have found broad agreement on scripts for dating: Men are still expected (by both sexes) to initiate dates and plan activities, and women are still expected (by both sexes) to defer to men's initiatives except in the realm of sexual activities (Pryor & Merluzzi, 1985). Leslie Baxter (1992), an interpersonal communication scholar, reports that playfulness and "hanging out" with no particular purpose are important scripts for friendship. Steve Duck and Paul Wright (1993) also found that talking and working together on a project are among the most common scripts for women's and men's friendships.

Reflection

What is your script for a first date? How does your script compare with the scripts of others in your class?

Prototypes, personal constructs, stereotypes, and scripts organize how we think about others and situations and help us make sense of interpersonal experiences. These four knowledge structures provide a simple, concise description of how we interpret phenomena.

Theories About How People Construct Meaning

Think about a relatively common communication activity in your everyday life. Examples are meeting with a professor to discuss your work in a class, having lunch with a close friend, and visiting with your family over the holidays.

Once you have the specific activity in mind, answer the following questions:

1. What prototypes do you apply in interpreting the activity and other people?
2. What personal constructs are salient in your thinking about the other people?
3. What stereotypes do you make about how specific others will act? What is the basis of your predictive generalizations?
4. What script do you follow in this activity? Has your script ever not worked? What happened?

Cognitive Complexity

Although four kinds of knowledge structures have been identified, only one has been the focus of substantial research by constructivist scholars in communication. Personal constructs are the centerpiece of constructivist theory building, perhaps because they are the most specific interpretations we make of others.

Constructivists believe that people vary in the complexity, or sophistication, of their interpretive processes. Some of us, they claim, have more elaborate ways of organizing perceptions and interpreting phenomena. The concept of **cognitive complexity** refers to how elaborate or complex a person's interpretive processes are along the three dimensions of differentiation, abstraction, and organization. We'll discuss each of the three.

Differentiation   The first facet of cognitive complexity is **differentiation**. It is measured by the number of distinct interpretations (in this case, constructs) an individual uses to perceive and describe others. Presumably, more cognitively complex individuals use more constructs to interpret others than do less cognitively complex individuals.

Constructivist theorists don't emphasize average numbers of constructs that are used by more and less cognitively complex individuals. Thus, there are no absolute scores that tell us how complex a person is. However, you can get a rough idea of how your own cognitive complexity would be scored by counting the number of distinct constructs you used in the descriptions of liked and disliked peers in Figure 7.2. Do not count as separate constructs adjectives and adverbs that are attached to a descriptive term. For example, *kind, very kind,* and *always kind* would count as one construct, not three. Also, don't count separately items that are repetitious. If you described your liked peer as *interesting* twice, that

Constructivism   **155** counts as only one construct. More than 30 constructs is above average in cognitive complexity.

Abstraction   The dimension of cognitive complexity referred to as **abstraction** is the extent to which a person interprets others in terms of internal motives, personality traits, and character. Describing George as quiet because he doesn't talk much shows less cognitive complexity than interpreting George's quietness as stemming from personal insecurity. The latter explanation is rooted in internal processes that are less visible and more abstract than concrete descriptions of the surface interaction. It's important to note that abstractness isn't necessarily related to accuracy. Abstractness is concerned simply with a person's ability to base interpretations on mental or psychological qualities.

To assess your abstractness, consider how many of the descriptive terms you used in Figure 7.2 are surface-level observations (*quiet, attractive, physically active*) and how many are psychological impressions (*secure, compassionate, spiritually centered, inconsiderate*).

Organization   The final facet of cognitive complexity is **organization**, which is the degree to which a person notices and is able to make sense of contradictory behaviors. For example, perhaps you know a person who is outspoken and assertive in classes but quiet and deferential in social situations. How would you reconcile these seemingly contradictory observations? A person who is not very complex cognitively might simply record all observations without recognizing tensions among them.

Another cognitively unsophisticated interpretation is, "Sometimes Logan is outspoken, and sometimes he is not." That may be true, but it provides little insight into the psychological dynamics behind the surface observation. A cognitively more complex explanation would be, "Logan is outspoken and assertive in academic contexts where he feels confident, but he is quieter in social situations where he feels unsure of himself." This explanation reconciles the two observations by linking both to the psychological dynamic of confidence or security.

Most constructivist research has measured cognitive complexity primarily or entirely in terms of the one facet of differentiation. Obviously, this is a convenient and easy aspect of complexity to measure, since all we have to do is count the number of distinct constructs a person uses to interpret others. But does a measure of differentiation tell us anything about cognitive abstractness and organization? According to proponents of differentiation, it does. They point out that early efforts to measure all three facets demonstrated that differentiation is moderately positively correlated with abstractness and organization (Burleson & Waltman, 1988; O'Keefe &

Theories About How People Construct Meaning

Sypher, 1981). Thus, claim the theorists, measuring all three is redundant and unnecessary to determine the cognitive complexity of individuals.

Person-Centeredness

According to constructivists, cognitively complex people are more capable of engaging in sensitive communication that is tailored to particular others. They refer to this as being **person-centered**. Here's the reasoning: A person who is not cognitively complex doesn't perceive many nuances in others, misses subtle differences among people, and doesn't understand surface behaviors in terms of internal, psychological dynamics that provide insight into people. On the other hand, a cognitively complex individual interprets others in detailed ways, distinguishes people from one another on multiple dimensions, and has insight into the psychological reasons behind specific behaviors and communication patterns (Burleson & Waltman, 1988).

If this is true about cognitively complex individuals, then the interpretations such people make might allow them to adapt their communication to others' particular styles, needs, tendencies, and so forth. Consequently, they would be more persuasive and effective in personal and professional interactions (Applegate, 1990; Zorn, 1991). Suppose Rodriguez is a supervisor who has to have performance appraisal conferences with two of his subordinates, John and Suchen. If Rodriguez is not highly complex cognitively, he may express criticism and identify areas for improvement in much the same way to both subordinates. However, if Rodriguez is cognitively complex, then we would expect him to use different communicative strategies with his two subordinates. Perhaps he would be very explicit about desired changes in talking with John, whom Rodriguez perceives as a concrete thinker and someone who needs considerable guidance. He must be much more supportive and spend more time emphasizing positive aspects of Suchen's job performance, since Rodriguez perceives her as overly critical of herself. The ability to adapt communication to particular others is an earmark of effectiveness.

Reflection

Describe a person you consider person-centered in his or her communication and a second person you think is not person-centered in her or his communication. How do their different levels of person-centeredness affect your relationships with them?

The research inspired by constructivist theory is impressive and growing. The studies conducted so far have largely supported the theoretical claims advanced by constructivism. One firm conclusion from existing research is that the link between cognitive complexity and person-centered communication is clear and strong. In a specific extension of work on person-centered communication, Brant Burleson has studied comforting communication (Burleson, 1989; Burleson, Albrecht, & Sarason, 1994). His studies indicate that more cognitively complex individuals are more skilled than less cognitively complex individuals in creating messages that are comforting to particular others.

Another important line of constructivist inquiry concerns the development of cognitive complexity in children. Ruth Ann Clark and Jesse Delia (1977), who are among the foremost constructivist theorists, first measured young children's cognitive complexity by giving them the Role Category Questionnaire (RCQ) to which you responded in Figure 7.2. After taking the RCQ, the children were asked to create persuasive messages for three different listeners. The more cognitively complex children showed greater flexibility in adapting their communication to listeners of different ages and interests. The less cognitively complex children either didn't recognize that listeners might differ from them, or realized the differences but didn't tailor their communication to address these differences.

Critical Assessment of Constructivist Theory

Three significant criticisms of constructivist theory and research have been advanced.

Internal Validity Is Questionable   First, questions have been raised about the internal validity of constructivist theory. Not all scholars are satisfied with the adequacy of the RCQ, which is the single measure on which constructivists rely in developing and testing their theory. One question is whether the RCQ actually measures what ordinary people think of as cognitive complexity (this is referred to as validity—see Chapter 2). Some scholars believe that the RCQ largely measures vocabulary rather than the actual complexity of an individual's interpretations.

According to this criticism, a person with a large vocabulary could provide more elaborate, wordier descriptions of liked and disliked others than a person with a limited vocabulary. There is doubt about whether the number of different words a person uses to describe others reflects the complexity of her or his thinking about others. Further, we should ask if it is appropriate to measure cognitive complexity by only one of three facets that have been theorized.

Pragmatic Utility Is Weak   A second criticism is that constructivist work has not addressed practical issues. Not only has applied research received little attention so far, but the leaders of the theory seem to think this trend will and should continue. Jesse Delia, who is acknowledged as the founder of the theory, argues that applied research detracts from a concern with pure theory. He sees developing and testing constructivist theory as the primary, if not the exclusive, goal of future research.

As we noted in Chapter 2, many scholars believe that a good theory should have practical value—it should make a difference in the real world. Those who regard pragmatic utility as an important assessment criterion reproach constructivists for ignoring practical applications. Others, including many prominent constructivists, argue that there is value in purely theoretical research. They claim that a good theory will eventually have practical applications. Yet they maintain that focusing on practical implications is not what pure theorists should do.

Theoretical Scope Neglects Communication   Related to the second criticism is the recurrent charge that constructivist research and theory are more concerned with cognitive processes than with actual communication. As you read about this theory, you probably noticed that it emphasizes cognitive operations involved in perceiving and interpreting interpersonal phenomena. Although it seems safe to assume a link between how we think about others and social situations and how we communicate, that link has been little explored so far.

Reflection

Must all scholars concerned with theory attend to pragmatic issues?

In response to this criticism, some constructivist researchers are conducting studies that advance understanding of how cognitive processes affect actual talk between people. Ted Zorn (1995) has integrated constructivism with other theories to examine how people make sense of interactions in the workplace. Brant Burleson's (1984, 1991) studies of comforting communication also apply constructivist theory and use constructivist research methods to enlarge understandings of how cognitive schemata influence our efforts to communicate comfort.

Summary

In this chapter we've examined two theories that are centrally concerned with how individuals create meanings. Asking how we make sense of the world, ourselves, and interactions, these theories offer keen insights into ways in which we sculpt the lines of action for ourselves and assign meaning to the actions of others.

Both CMM theory and constructivism build on the rich foundation provided by symbolic interactionism. Each theory assumes that humans are interpretive beings who actively work to make sense of experiences, which explains why these theories focus less on external phenomena than on how individuals process impressions. CMM theory is an ambitious effort to explain the multiple levels of meaning we rely on to make sense of experiences and coordinate communication. Constructivist theory emphasizes different aspects of cognition (personal constructs and cognitive complexity instead of rules and the hierarchy of meaning) in its quest to describe and explain how we organize perceptions in ways that affect our communication.

Because CMM and constructivism share ontological and epistemological assumptions, the two theories are generally compatible. Each offers a particular viewpoint of the overall question of how we go about the complex, difficult, and fascinating process of deciding what things mean in our lives. Despite the high degree of compatibility between CMM and constructivism, the two theories are distinct. Theorists of the two schools identify and pursue different goals. Whereas constructivists have historically been less interested in pragmatic applications of the theory than in developing the theory itself, CMM theorists have consistently highlighted the ways in which their theory applies to real-life situations. Whether you regard immediate utility as a key goal of theorizing will affect how you judge these two theories.

Key Terms

abstraction

autobiography

cognitive complexity

cognitive schema (plural *schemata*)

constitutive rule

constructivism

content

cultural pattern

differentiation

episode

hierarchy of meanings

logical force

organization

personal construct

person-centeredness

prototype

regulative rule

relationship

rule

rules theory

script

speech act

stereotype

strange loop

CHAPTER EIGHT

Theories About Interpersonal Dynamics

Although most communication theories deal at least indirectly with interpersonal dynamics, only some theories focus specifically and directly on them. These theories try to get at the *how* and *why* of communication phenomena. They ask questions such as these: How does communication operate? How does communication affect satisfaction in relationships? How are patterns of communication formed and changed, and how do they affect people and relationships? How do facets of communication affect one another? In this chapter we'll consider two theories that concentrate on communication dynamics: interactional theory and dialectical theory.

Interactional Theory

In 1967 three clinicians named Paul Watzlawick, Janet Beavin, and Don Jackson wrote a very important book entitled *The Pragmatics of Human Communication*. In it the authors advanced an original and bold **interactional theory** (also called pragmatic theory) of communication. Both immediate and long-term responses to interactional theory have been positive, and it remains influential in the field three decades after it was first formulated.

Watzlawick, Beavin, and Jackson had spent years counseling troubled families. Their clinical experiences led them to new insights about family communication. Working at the Mental Health Institute in Palo Alto, California, Watzlawick and nearly two dozen other clinicians developed interactional theory. Although the original theorists were most interested in family interaction and applied their theory to family contexts, other scholars have extended the theoretical principles of interactional theory to other types and environments of communication. To understand interactional theory, we'll discuss four of its central concepts.

Communication Systems

Before interactional theory was developed, many communication professionals had concentrated on isolated aspects of communication or individual communicators: the verbal behavior of group leaders apart from the behaviors of other members and the context in which the group meets; the behaviors of an individual labeled "dysfunctional" independent of the interpersonal situation; conflict episodes divorced from other communication patterns in relationships.

According to interactional theory, focusing on individuals is misguided. Interactional theorists believe that any useful insight into communication must consider the contexts in which it occurs, because those contexts affect communication and what it means. Interactional theorists claim we can't understand group leaders, so-called dysfunctional individuals, or conflict episodes unless we examine them in the contexts of the relationships in which they exist.

Reflection

In what ways do you think general semanticists would agree or disagree with the idea that communication can be understood only within contexts?

The idea of contexts did not originate with Watzlawick. A Viennese professor of biology named Ludwig von Bertalanffy pioneered the idea under the name **general systems theory.** Shortly after emigrating to Canada in 1949, von Bertalanffy founded the Society for the Advancement of General Systems Theory. Von Bertalanffy's biological research led him to puzzle over basic questions about life: Why does a live sponge that is forced through a sieve spontaneously reorganize itself? Why does transplanting certain cells from the leg of a newt to its tail result in growth of a second tail instead of a new leg? Why, when one organ is injured or destroyed in a living creature, do other organs compensate by replacing the functions of the damaged organ (Hampden-Turner, 1982, p. 158)?

After many experiments and years of thinking, the scientists concluded that these things happen because life forms are organized wholes that seek to sustain themselves (von Bertalanffy, 1951, 1967). In other words, organisms function and continue to exist as a result of organized, dynamic interaction among parts. An organism seeks to sustain its wholeness or structural integrity. This is why the newt grows only tails and not legs in the tail area of its body. If the original wholeness of an organism is disrupted or no longer possible, the organism generates an alternative

Theories About Interpersonal Dynamics

form of holistic organization. This is why other organs take over for damaged ones and why live sponges reconstitute themselves after being reduced to pulp.

Reflection

Is the hierarchy of meaning discussed in Chapter 7 an organized whole or system? If so, how do principles of general systems theory apply to CMM theory?

You may be wondering why we're discussing newts and sponges in a book on communication theories. The reason is that von Bertalanffy's insights were not restricted to biology. He believed that all life forms, social as well as biological, can be understood only as complex, organized wholes that he called systems. Von Bertalanffy's insights earned him a nomination for a Nobel Prize just before his death in 1971 (Hampden-Turner, 1982).

The Palo Alto group of therapists used von Bertalanffy's ideas about life systems as the foundation of their interactional theory of communication. Systems thinking also quickly found its way into communication research and teaching (Fisher, 1982). Most concisely defined, a communication system is a group of interrelated and interacting parts that function as a whole. The systems view of communication rests on four propositions.

All Parts Are Interrelated   The elements of communication systems are not just a random heap of parts that happen to be together. Instead, the parts are interrelated and interacting. Because the parts of a system are interdependent, they affect one another. This explains one of the axioms of interactional theory: If you change any part of a system, you change the entire system.

Anyone who has had a child understands how one new part (the baby) in a system (the family) changes all aspects of the system, including how parents interact with each other, when meals are served, and what kinds of recreation are pursued. Drawing an example from CMM theory, if you change how you define episodes and autobiographies, you may be able to extricate yourself from strange loops. The general semanticists we discussed in Chapter 4 relied on this systems principle (though they used different terminology) when they advised people to replace intentional orientations with extensional ones to improve the accuracy of communication.

Systems Are Organized Wholes   This second proposition of systems theory emphasizes the idea that we cannot understand any part of a system in isolation from the other interrelated parts. Because systems are organized wholes, they must be seen and studied as a totality of interacting elements (Hall & Fagen, 1956). By extension, each element of the system must be understood within the context of the overall system.

Interactional Theory   **163**

Prior to the Palo Alto group's insights, therapists often worked with disturbed members of families and tried to "fix" the individual who supposedly was the problem disrupting family life. Thus, an alcoholic might be separated from his family and given therapy to reduce the motivation to drink and/or to increase the desire not to drink. Often, however, the alcoholic who was "cured" resumed drinking shortly after rejoining his family.

Systems theorists believe this result is almost inevitable when therapists fail to deal with the entire family system. In many troubled families, the "problem person" is abetted by other family members. Perhaps the alcoholic's wife denies he has a problem, and his children try to cover for his lapses to minimize friction in the family. The problem isn't the individual but the whole system in which the individual's alcoholism interacts with other family members' behaviors.

Now assume that the man has individual therapy and then returns to his family. If he says he is an alcoholic, his wife may deny it because this is her patterned way of acting in the family system. When the man acknowledges he has a drinking problem and his wife denies that he does, the children are anxious about the friction between their parents. Consequently, they engage in their patterned responses to tension by trying to excuse or cover up for their father. With everyone else telling him he doesn't have a drinking problem and criticizing him for causing discord by saying he's an alcoholic, the man returns to drinking. He does so not because the therapy was ineffective in changing his attitudes but because individual therapy didn't address or alter the overall family dynamics that sustain his drinking.

Reflection

Does focusing on an overall family system when dysfunction exists relieve individuals of personal responsibility for their actions?

The Whole Is More Than the Sum of Its Parts   This third proposition is an effective way to remind ourselves that living systems are more than the aggregate parts that make them up. Living systems such as families, groups, organizations, and societies evolve, change, discard old parts and patterns, and generate new parts and ways of interacting. Over time the changes in a system result in something that is more than the sum of its original parts.

A concrete example will help us understand the idea that in living systems the whole is more than the sum of its parts. Hannah and Damion meet in October and are attracted to each other. By January each of them has come to trust the other, and they have developed a number of interaction routines. On Wednesdays they study together in the library and then go out for a snack. Damion fixes a meal for them on Saturday night, and then they either talk or go out to a film. On Sunday mornings they attend services together, and then Hannah treats them to lunch. By this point in their relationship, Damion understands that Hannah values constructive conflict and expects him to be up-front when he's upset about something. Hannah has learned that Damion has trouble dealing with conflict and needs time before he can talk about it.

Originally, this relationship was a system consisting of only two elements: Hannah and Damion. Their interactions, however, gave birth to new elements in their relationship: trust, routines, roles, dual perspective or person-centeredness, and insights into each other's meanings. All of these features that are part of the relationship system in January grew out of, but are different from, the two original parts of Hannah and Damion that were present in October. Thus, we should understand that systems include not only their original parts but also interaction among those interrelated parts and what is created as a result of the interaction.

Living systems vary in how open they are. **Openness** is the extent to which a system affects and is affected by factors and processes outside of it. Most human relationships are fairly open. Damion and Hannah's relationship is affected by their interactions with families, work associates, and friends as well as by the norms and practices in their environment. Some tribal communities, such as those in the imperiled rain forests, are virtually, but not completely, closed systems in which interaction with people and events outside their community is extremely limited. The more open a system is, the more factors can influence what happens in it.

Systems Strive for, but Never Achieve, Equilibrium

This is a paradoxical but important premise about systems. On the one hand, living systems seek to achieve a state of equilibrium, or **homeostasis**. Hannah and Damion developed a number of routines to create stable, predictable patterns of interaction in their relationship. They also generated ways of balancing responsibilities for meals: Damion cooked one night and Hannah paid for lunch on another day. The family we discussed earlier had developed stable ways of living with an alcoholic member. In fact, the members were so committed to the balance they had achieved in the system that they pulled the man back into those patterns and thus back into alcoholic behavior.

Yet absolute balance or equilibrium isn't possible for living systems. Change is inevitable and continuous. Sometimes it's abrupt; at other times it's gradual. Sometimes change comes from outside a system; in other cases it arises within the system. To maintain function and to meet the system's objective of survival, members of the system, like the sponge, must continuously adjust and change. Perhaps Hannah has to quit working in order to spend more time on her studies. Without her earnings, she can't afford to buy lunches every week. She might decide she'll cook lunches on Sundays as a less expensive way of providing her half of their joint meals. Alternatively, Hannah might ask Damion to pick up the cost of lunches, a choice that would disrupt the equity they had previously maintained. Hannah and Damion could adapt in a variety of ways to her diminished finances, but change of some sort is inevitable. Because parts of systems are interrelated, a change in any one reverberates throughout the whole system.

TRY IT OUT How do you deal with changes in your relationships? Think about one specific relationship—perhaps a long-standing friendship or a serious romantic bond or your family. Recall a time when something major happened—you and your friend or romantic partner had to separate because of jobs or school, your parents divorced or remarried, a baby was born, and so on.

The following questions will prompt you to trace how the change reverberated throughout the entire relationship and how you responded to the change.

1. How did the change affect interaction routines in the relationship?

2. How did changes in interaction routines affect trust, closeness, and understanding?

3. How did the change affect your relationships with other people? (Did you form or strengthen other friendships when a friend moved away? If your parents divorced, did you become less close to one of them?)

4. How did you try to maintain equilibrium in the face of the change? (Some couples in long-distance relationships try to call daily. Younger children often deny that their parents are divorcing. Older children sometimes regress in an effort to retain their share of attention when a new baby arrives.)

Don't stop with these questions. Go on to identify the ripple effects of the change in your relationship system and the ways in which you both resisted and adapted to the change.

Dynamic equilibrium is a term that captures the contradictory ideas of change and stability. Interactional theory maintains both that systems attempt to maintain a steady state by resisting change and that they are dynamic entities that cannot avoid changing. This helps us understand why we sometimes deny or try to avoid changes that disrupt our habitual ways of acting. At the same time, it explains why we seek novelty and appreciate changes in our lives and the new perspectives they bring.

System is both a theory in its own right (general systems theory founded by von Bertalanffy) and a concept that is used in other theories, including interactional theory.

Levels of Meaning

A second significant contribution of the Palo Alto group was the realization that we are always communicating, or—as the theorists phrased it—one cannot *not* communicate. As we communicate, we are inevitably involved with two levels of meaning. Perhaps you've had the experience of being in a conversation in which you felt the other person was trying to control you. You may have interpreted the other person's statements as ordering or patronizing. Interactional theorists borrowed from the work of Gregory Bateson (1951) to emphasize the idea that all communication includes two levels, or types, of meaning. The first level of meaning is the obvious one: the content of what is said. This is the literal substance of communication. When Cassandra says to her roommate, Glenda, "Clean up this room. It's a mess," the **content meaning** of the communication is that the room looks messy and Cassandra wants Glenda to clean it up.

The second kind of meaning is **relationship meaning**, which carries information about the relationship between people. The relationship-level meaning of Cassandra's statement asserts that she has the right to criticize Glenda and tell her what to do. This expresses her power in the relationship. If Glenda responds by saying "Sorry, I'll clean it up right now," the relationship level of her message is acceptance of Cassandra's power. On the other hand, if Glenda says, "My mess is on my side of the room, and you have no right to complain," on the relationship level she communicates that she doesn't accept Cassandra's effort to control her. In addition to power, affection and responsiveness are also dimensions of relationship meaning (Wood, 2003, 2000).

Relationship-level meanings may be expressed verbally and/or non-verbally. A good deal of research has focused on nonverbal indicators of relationship-level meanings (Brehm, 1992; Dillard, Solomon, & Palmer, 1999; Fletcher & Fitness, 1990; Sallinen-Kuparinen, 1992). If Cassandra smiled while making her statement, it would have a much friendlier relationship meaning than if she scowled. We signal our feelings about others with facial expressions, eye behaviors, distance, touch, and vocal cues. Whatever content we express, we simultaneously communicate how we see ourselves, the other, and our relationship.

The Palo Alto theorists often used the term *metacommunication* to refer to relationship-level meanings. Metacommunication is communication about communication, or commentary on the content level. **Metacommunication** (that is, relationship meanings) says, "This is who I am in relation to you; this is who you are in relation to me; this is who we are together."

Couples counselor Aaron Beck (1988) calls the relationship level of communication "hidden meanings." Hidden meanings are very powerful aspects of relationship systems because they express and sustain the emotional climate between people. It is the relationship level of our communication that says we do or don't pay attention to, respect, and care for another person.

Punctuation

A third contribution of interactional theory is the concept of **punctuation**. In writing, we use periods to define where sentences begin and end. In much the same way, we punctuate interaction by designating when episodes start and stop. Communication tends to go smoothly as long as all parties agree on punctuation (CMM theorists would say there is coordinated management of meanings). But if partners differ in how they punctuate communication, misunderstanding and conflict may arise. José and Maria have an argument and eventually agree to the solution he prefers. José then assumes that episode is closed. Maria, however, resents José for imposing his preference, and she doesn't punctuate the episode as over. The next time she and José disagree, Maria remembers the last argument and feels it is her turn to get her way. She punctuates the two arguments as a single, continuous episode; José punctuates them as two separate episodes. Not only do Maria and José disagree about issues, but they have a more basic disagreement about when episodes of disagreement begin and end.

Relationship counselors have identified a particularly common pattern of disagreement over punctuation (Bergner & Bergner, 1990; Berns, Jacobson, & Gottman, 1999; Christensen & Heavey, 1990; Feldman & Ridley, 2000). Called the demand–withdraw or pursuer–distancer pattern, this occurs when one partner strives to create closeness by talking and the other partner attempts to maintain distance by avoiding interaction. The more the partner who seeks closeness pursues closeness, the more the partner who seeks distance retreats from intimacy; the more the partner wanting distance withdraws, the more the partner seeking closeness pursues.

People tend to punctuate episodes as starting with another's behavior. Thus, the person who wants intimacy thinks, "I pursue because my partner is withdrawing." The person who desires distance, however, thinks, "I withdraw because my partner is pursuing me." Each person perceives the other's actions as the cause, and each sees his or her behaviors as a response. As long as partners don't realize that they are punctuating differently, it's nearly impossible for them to alter the frustrating pattern. CMM theorists might regard this as a strange loop.

Reflection

Identify recurrent patterns in your relationships that involve differences in how you and your partners punctuate communication.

Communication and Power

The final facet of interactional theory we'll consider is the claim that communication establishes and reflects power relationships. Initially, this claim held that all communication is either **symmetrical** (reflects equal power) or **complementary** (reflects different levels of power). At first you might think it odd that a theory of communication emphasizes the issue of power. This focus makes sense when we consider the context in which the theory developed. (Systems theorists would applaud our effort to view the theory in its context.) Remember that the Palo Alto group worked with troubled families. In troubled families, power in many guises (passive-aggression, games, manipulation) is often a central and continuous issue in family interaction.

Watzlawick and his associates (1967) believed that every communication asserts either equality (symmetricality) or inequality (complementarity). In our earlier example, Cassandra's demand "Clean up this room" asserted her power over Glenda. A symmetrical message would have been, "Gee, don't you think this room's messy? Let's clean it up." Of course, systems logic warns us that we can't understand a system by isolating particular parts from the whole. Thus, we can't draw conclusions about the power balance in Cassandra's and Glenda's relationship based on a single statement. Interactional theorists realize that power in relationships is negotiated through sequences of interaction.

To have any insight into the power between the two women, we need to know how Glenda responds to Cassandra's complementary message. We might also want to observe interactions over time to see if there is a consistent power balance between Glenda and Cassandra across various situations and areas of their relationship. Does Cassandra always send complementary messages? Does Glenda always accept them? By observing interaction over time, we can determine whether the overall relationship is one of equality or inequality.

Since the Palo Alto group formulated interactional theory, communication researchers have extended the proposition that all communication is either symmetrical or complementary. Edna Rogers-Millar and Richard Farace (1975) devised a way of coding the power dimension of messages between spouses. Messages that attempt to gain power or control of interaction are coded as one up (▲). Examples would be ordering, interrupting, and threatening. Messages that defer to another are coded as one down (▼). Examples of these are allowing an interruption, obeying an order, asking for advice, and yielding to another's wishes.

Based on the marital interactions they studied, Rogers-Millar and Farace identified a third kind of power message that expresses neither equality nor inequality. They labeled any communication that neutralizes issues of power and control as one across (▶). Examples might include explicitly commenting on power issues ("We've both dug our heels in") or inviting a move away from the struggle for control ("Let's drop this for now"). The Palo Alto theorists might disagree with the idea that some messages can neutralize power. They might argue that "Let's step away from this for now" is a complementary message because it asserts what should be done. Yet many communication scholars think that it's possible to communicate in ways other than the complementary and symmetrical.

Parallel relationships are those in which power is equal overall but distributed so that each individual has primary authority or control in certain realms. For example, Robbie and I have equal amounts of power in our marriage, but each of us has primary control in certain areas. I handle our investments and financial bargaining for major expenses such as cars and homes, and Robbie defers to my authority in the area of family finances. He has primary authority over travel plans and arrangements (though I suggest the overall travel budget), and I defer to his recommendations for trips and don't question the schedules and reservations he makes.

Reflection

Do you think it is possible for communication not to express equality or inequality?

Interactional theory offers an original perspective on communication and its role in sustaining patterns in relationships. Incorporating the insights of general systems theory, interactional theorists proposed that communication and relationships are systems; this is the foundation of their theory. Building on that, they added other propositions, three of which we examined: that all communication has two levels of meaning; that the meaning of communication depends on punctuation; and that communication expresses power relationships. Work done since the Palo Alto group's original theorizing suggests that the third proposition may be modified by the idea that some communication attempts to neutralize power issues in relationships.

Critical Assessment of Interactional Theory

Three criticisms of interactional theory merit our attention.

Theory Is Not Testable   A serious criticism is that the theory resists testing. How could we test the proposition that meaning depends on punctuation? How could we determine that all parts of a system are interrelated and interdependent? How could we measure relational-level meanings, especially since they may depend on hierarchies of meaning that a researcher might not know? As intuitively appealing as these propositions are, they are extremely difficult to verify or disprove through testing. Thus, on the criterion of testability many think the theory is weak.

Theory Overemphasizes Power Between Communicators   Interactional theory also has been criticized for placing too much emphasis on power in describing relationships between people (Owen, 1995). Clearly, power is one dimension of personal relationships, yet it isn't the only one. In stressing equality and inequality so strongly, the Palo Alto clinicians obscured awareness of other, perhaps equally important qualities in many relationships.

We have methods designed to code power (one-up, one-down, one-across messages), but we don't have equivalent methods of coding affection, respect, responsiveness, and so forth. Knowing that interactional theory grew out of therapy with disturbed families may explain why power was so emphasized in the original theorizing. However, the origins of the theory don't provide a satisfactory explanation of why other scholars haven't modified the theory to make it more applicable to a range of human interaction, not all of which is disturbed or governed by power dynamics. If interactional theory is to be a useful theory of communication, scholars need to refine it so that it applies to a greater range of relationship processes.

Theory Ignores Intent   A third criticism concerns the theory's failure to distinguish between intent and effect. Assume Yolanda says, "I can't believe you did that!" to a friend who forgot to do a favor she had promised. The friend hears this as a criticism and feels that the relational meaning of Yolanda's comment is disapproval or judgment. But perhaps Yolanda only felt surprised, not judgmental. Is her intent irrelevant?

Intent and effect are also interwoven in questions about power in a relationship. If Robin agrees to purchase the car Marcus wants instead of the one she prefers, we would code her agreement as a complementary one-down message. Perhaps, though, Robin doesn't care much about models of cars, and she isn't giving up any power that matters by going along with her partner's preference. Is her agreement really expressing her subordinate position in the relationship? In describing and explaining communication, interactional theorists have largely relied on the perspectives and judgments of observers (researchers or clinicians) rather than those of participants. This opens them to criticism from scholars who believe individuals' interpretations are integral to understanding communication and meaning.

These criticisms notwithstanding, interactional theory has been and continues to be influential in the field of communication. It fares well on most criteria for evaluating theory: It offers a good description and explanation of communication patterns; it is fairly simple; it has obvious practical applications and values; and it is quite heuristic. The heuristic strength of the interactional view is evident in the amount of research generated by the provocative insights of this theory. In addition, interactional theory's emphasis on systemic relations propelled new and important lines of thinking about communication as more than a linear, cause–effect sequence.

Interactional theory may be troublesome or seem inadequate to people who require formal testing. The inability to demonstrate interactional premises definitively, however, doesn't concern people who recognize other ways of assessing the value and utility of a theory. One indicator of this theory's significance is that many other communication theories incorporate propositions formulated by interactional theorists.

Dialectical Theory

In your relationships, do you sometimes feel that you can't get enough of intimates, yet at other times you need your own space? Do you seek comfortable routines but also want spontaneity? Do you ever feel conflict between wanting to share your innermost feelings and wanting to maintain a zone of privacy? If you answered yes to any or all of these questions, then **dialectical theory** has a lot to offer you.

In the opinion of many scholars of communication in personal relationships, dialectical theory is perhaps the most exciting theory to emerge in recent years. It provides an especially insightful explanation of particular dynamics in personal relationships. Leslie Baxter has headed the effort to develop and test dialectical theory in the communication field. Over the

Theories About Interpersonal Dynamics

years she and her associates have published many articles and books that explain, refine, and provide empirical support for the theory (Anderson, Baxter, & Cissna, in press; Baxter, 1987, 1988, 1990, 1992, 1993; Baxter & Montgomery, 1996; Baxter & Simon, 1993; Dindia & Baxter, 1987; Wood et al., 1994; Zorn, 1995).

Another communication scholar whose research has contributed to dialectical theory is William Rawlins (1983a,b, 1988, 1989, 1992), who is on the faculty at Purdue University. To appreciate the theory of relational dialectics, we'll consider its root terms, dialectics that have been identified, and empirical evidence of ways partners respond to dialectics.

Root Terms

Stated most simply, this theory asserts that in any relationship there are inherent tensions between contradictory impulses, or **dialectics**. Dialectical tensions and how we respond to them are central dynamics that shed light on how relationships function as well as how they evolve and change over time.

Dialectics   Dialectics are contradictory or opposing tensions. My 12-year-old niece Michelle wants to be grown up and independent, yet she also wants the protection of her parents and extended family. She experiences a dialectical tension between wanting independence and wanting dependence. My close friend Louise is single and cherishes her privacy and freedom from the obligations that come with relationships. Yet Louise also wants the closeness and sharing of intimacy. Louise feels contradictory impulses, to form intimate bonds and to avoid them. I want to tell a new friend named Larry about fears and concerns that trouble me so that he can understand me and we can be closer. At the same time, I don't want to make myself vulnerable by disclosing personal information to someone I don't yet know well. I am caught on the horns of a dialectical tension between wanting openness and wanting to preserve my privacy.

Michelle, Louise, and I are entirely normal in experiencing these tensions between contradictory impulses. Dialectics are natural, normal, even inevitable dynamics in human relationships. The central idea of a dialectic is not the contradictory impulses but rather the tension between them. Thus, dialectical theorists would be less interested in individual desires for independence and dependence than in the friction generated by the contradiction between the two impulses.

Baxter's understanding of dialectics is informed by Mikhail Bakhtin, a Russian philosopher who believed that dialogue infuses human existence. Bakhtin did not adopt the Marxist or Hegelian view of dialectics as oppositions that could ultimately be resolved into some final form. Marx and Hegel saw dialectics as involving a thesis (we are independent) and an antithesis (we are dependent) that are reconciled through a synthesis of the two opposing ideas (we are interdependent). In contrast, Bakhtin and, following him, Baxter believe that tensions between contradictory impulses are continuous and have no ultimate resolution or end point.

Baxter and other dialectical theorists recognize that there can be periods in which the contradictory impulses of dialectics do not generate tension. They do not, however, see these as final resolutions or syntheses that resolve tensions. **Dialectical moments** are temporary periods of equilibrium between opposing dialectics in the larger pattern of continuous change that marks relationships (Baxter & Simon, 1993; Montgomery, 1993). For dialectical theorists, change is the one constant of relationships—they are always in flux and evolving, and any times of stability are but fleeting moments in the larger pattern of ongoing change.

Contradiction Baxter credits Cornforth (1968) with identifying the two root ideas underlying the concept of dialectics. The first root idea is contradiction. The obvious aspect of contradiction is conflict, opposition, contrast, or discrepancy between two things, such as the desire for distance and the desire for intimacy. You want to be close to a friend, yet you also feel the need for your own space. Less obvious but equally important to the notion of contradiction is that the two incongruous impulses are productively interdependent and interactive. Your need to be close is fueled by times when you are separate from your friend; being intimate for a period kindles your desire for time alone. Bakhtin's philosophical position was that tensions between people promote communication, which links them. He believed that the communication prompted by dialectical tensions allows partners to grow individually and together (Baxter, 1994).

According to this perspective, each impulse needs the contradictory one. Independence is meaningful only because there is such a thing as dependence; distance gains its meaning from the opposite notion of intimacy; privacy and openness reciprocally define each other. We couldn't appreciate spontaneous moments and novel experiences if those were all we had. We notice and enjoy novelty because it stands apart from standard routines. Conversely, we value routine as a contrast to too much novelty. If you've ever loved being home after an exciting vacation, you understand how much routine and novelty depend on each other for their meaning and value.

Process The second root idea of dialectics is that of process. Baxter's attention to process reflects Bakhtin's beliefs that change should be desired and celebrated; paradoxically, he viewed it as the only constant in human relationships (Baxter, 1994; Rawlins, 1989).

Viewing dialectics as in process means that we understand they are ongoing, always in motion, forever changing. Dialectics are not static balances between contradictory impulses. Instead, they are fluid relationships that continuously evolve. Emphasizing the processual character of personal relationships, Steve Duck (1990) says they are "unfinished business." By this he means that relationships are never settled, never fixed once and for all. Always, continuously, they are moving to new places and dealing with new issues. Change, then, is a primary dynamic of intimacy—one that is normal and ongoing in relational life.

Viewing dialectics as processes implies that they are moving somewhere. In other words, theorists assume that the tension between contradictory impulses is positive and productive in moving relationships forward. For example, discomfort about their conflicting needs to be together and to be independent leads Derek and Bonita to redefine their routines so that needs for both intimacy and autonomy are satisfied. Because dialectical tensions are seen as productive, contradictory needs have a decidedly complementary relationship with each other.

Dialectical theory's attention to process makes it a highly dynamic theory. As such, it is especially able to consider how relationships change over time, transformations in partners' feelings and behavioral patterns, and varying forms of tensions between contradictory impulses. Rather than viewing changes as departures from the norm or standard of a relationship, dialectical theorists see changes themselves as the norm. Communication scholars Kathryn Dindia and Dan Canary (1993) claim that dialectical theory is distinctive in the extent to which it highlights change as the ongoing character of personal relationships.

Relational Dialectics

You could probably think of many contradictory impulses that you experience in your relationships. Existing research suggests, however, that there are a limited number of basic dialectics. Baxter (1988, 1990, 1993) and other researchers (Dindia & Baxter, 1987; Wood et al., 1994) have identified three dialectics, each of which has both an internal form that concerns tensions within a relationship and an external form that concerns tensions between a relationship and outside systems such as society, family, work, and friends. Table 8.1 summarizes the dialectics.

Table 8.1

Internal and External Forms of Relational Dialectics

	Dialectic of Integration/ Separation	Dialectic of Stability/Change	Dialectic of Expression/ Privacy
Internal Form	Connection/ Autonomy	Predictability/ Novelty	Openness/ Closedness
External Form	Inclusion/ Seclusion	Conventionality/ Uniqueness	Revelation/ Concealment

Integration/Separation   This dialectic involves tension between wanting to integrate ourselves with another person or persons and wanting to be separate from others. Within relationships, partners experience both the desire to be connected to each other and the desire for autonomy. We want to be one with those we love, and we also want to be distinct, independent, our own person. Most counselors believe that the most central friction in personal relationships is between autonomy and connection (Goldsmith, 1990; Scarf, 1987). This dialectic is particularly salient in relationships that endure for some time (Baxter, 1990). Michelle's desire to be both independent of and connected to her parents illustrates this dialectic.

The external form of the integration/separation dialectic involves the tension between wanting a relationship to be included in larger systems and wanting to keep the relationship private. We want to introduce a new romantic interest to members of our family and our social circles. At the same time, couples want time to themselves to nurture their closeness and to be unconstrained by pressures, expectations, and judgments others may impose.

Stability/Change   The second dialectic involves tension between wanting sameness, constancy, or familiarity on one hand and wanting stimulation, novelty, or change on the other hand. Relationships require considerable stability to survive and function; partners have to be able to count on certain routines, roles, and so forth or their lives would be chaotic. Yet too much routine can make relationships rigid or boring. When life is too predictable, we may feel stifled or bored. Consequently, we want the novelty of new experiences, patterns, and surprises. Yet too much novelty can be overwhelming, leaving us feeling unanchored and out of control.

The bottom line with this and the other dialectics is that both needs are natural and both should be satisfied. As you may have already guessed, tension over contradictory needs for novelty and routine tends to be more pronounced in long-term relationships than in ones that are just developing, since novelty is characteristic in the latter.

Mutts

The external form of this dialectic involves tension between wanting to conform to conventional social expectations and patterns in a relationship and wanting to emphasize the relationship's uniqueness (Owen, 1984). To be accepted by others, we have to comply with many prevailing norms, expectations, and patterns of relating. Yet we don't want our relationships to be just like any others. Elaborating this point, Baxter notes that "carbon copy relationships do not provide couples with the sense of uniqueness so central to their intimacy" (1993, p. 143).

Expression/Privacy   The third dialectic pivots on tension between the desire to be open and expressive on the one hand and to be closed and private on the other. Between partners this dialectic is often felt as a struggle between self-disclosing and not sharing personal information.

The romantic ideal of totally open relationships would be undesirable and perhaps unbearable in reality. Partners who shared absolutely everything would soon be intolerably bored by information in which they have no interest. Total openness would also damage a relationship, since some of our private thoughts might hurt our partners.

We want to reveal ourselves to intimates because we feel closer when others understand and accept our innermost selves. Thus, we desire openness. Yet we also know that self-disclosures make us vulnerable, and we want to avoid the potential for personal information to be turned against us. In addition, many people prefer to preserve parts of themselves as completely private: they are just for us and not shared with anyone (Wood, 2000). This dialectic tends to be most prominent in early stages of relationships when individuals are experimenting with how much personal information to reveal (Baxter, 1990).

The external version of this dialectic involves wanting to reveal a relationship to others and wanting to conceal it from public scrutiny. We want to reveal our relationship because that is a standard route to social acceptance and approval. Sometimes we also want to talk with others about particular experiences, problems, and so forth in our relationships. Yet once others know about a relationship or particular issues in it, they can interfere.

Others can offer unsolicited and unwanted advice, make judgments of our partners or patterns in our relationships and otherwise butt into what we regard as a private relationship. In the case of taboo relationships, such as extramarital affairs, partners may have especially strong desires to conceal the relationship from others. We may also be especially motivated to screen a relationship from outsiders when we are ashamed of something, such as an alcoholic partner or abusive behaviors (Klein & Milardo, 1993; Prins, Buunk, & Van Yperon, 1993). Although secrecy about problems is understandable, closing a relationship off from others may actually sustain the problems. Interactional theorists would point out that by sealing the relationship system off from the outside world, the patterns that allow aberrant behavior are kept intact. Unless something is done to disrupt destructive patterns, they will continue and may damage partners and the relationship.

Reflection

Is the frequently extolled ideal of total openness in relationships a dream or a nightmare or both?

Responses to Dialectics

Now that you understand what relational dialectics are, you're probably wondering how people should and do manage them in order to keep relationships healthy. Researchers too have asked this question, and they have begun to find answers at least to how people *do* respond to dialectics. We know less about the effects of different responses and therefore about the advisability of particular ways of managing dialectical tensions. In a recent study, Baxter (1990) interviewed 106 college undergraduates to find out how they dealt with dialectical tensions in romantic relationships. She discovered four basic ways that people respond.

Selection   Some couples manage dialectical tensions by **selection**, which is satisfying one need and ignoring or denying the contradictory one. Gina and Ben give up all of their independent interests and activities and spend all free time with each other. This response selects the need for connection as the one to satisfy and ignores the companion desire for autonomy.

Separation   **Separation** attempts to meet both contradictory needs by satisfying each one in separate situations or spheres of relational life. Some couples are very open about discussing personal and family topics, and they don't share much about issues in their work lives. Other couples meet the need for novelty through vacations and have highly routinized daily patterns.

One indicator of the prevalence of relational dialectics in everyday life is the number of adages or folk sayings that reflect one or the other of contradictory impulses that make up dialectics. Identify the impulse or desire alluded to in each of the following common expressions:

1. A rolling stone gathers no moss.
2. Don't be a stick in the mud.
3. I need some space.
4. We never seem to do anything together anymore.
5. What she/he doesn't know won't hurt her/him.
6. Honesty is the best policy.
7. Don't talk about family problems with outsiders.
8. Keep your own counsel.
9. Absence makes the heart grow fonder.
10. I feel like a fish out of water.

Can you think of other folk sayings or common expressions that reflect one or both contradictory needs in a dialectic?

Friends often affirm their connection through particular shared activities and maintain their autonomy through independent pursuits in other areas.

Neutralization   The third response to dialectics is **neutralization**, which is a compromise that meets both needs somewhat but neither need fully. Friends are somewhat expressive about all topics, but they have no off-limits topics and none which they share in great depth. Mark and Todd make sure their lives intersect on a daily basis, but they don't do a great deal together, and neither of them pursues significant independent activities.

Reframing   **Reframing** is the most difficult and sophisticated response to dialectics, which may explain why it is also the least frequently employed response. According to Baxter, reframing is "a perceptual transformation . . . such that the two contrasts are no longer regarded as opposites" (1990, p. 73). In a study that my students and I conducted, we found an example of reframing (Wood et al., 1994). Several of the romantic couples we interviewed told us that preserving and arguing about differences between them fortified their intimacy by energizing the relationship. In this manner, they reframed the autonomy/connection dialectic so that it wasn't experienced as a contradiction. Another couple marked certain subjects as closed to discussion. However, they have an agreement to respect privacy in these zones, so they are open about the closedness.

Dialectical Theory   **179**

The most common response to all three dialectics is separation. Usually this involves assigning one need to particular topics or spheres of activities and assigning the contradictory need to different topics and spheres. However, in response to the autonomy/connection dialectic, some couples in Baxter's study reported using separation responses that met each need at different times. They cycled between the two needs so that periods of high autonomy were followed by periods of extreme togetherness.

Reflection

Which of these responses to dialectics seem familiar in terms of your own experiences? How has using your preferred responses affected your relationships?

The existence or intensity of dialectics doesn't appear to have a noticeable effect on partners' satisfaction with a relationship. There is evidence, however, that satisfaction is affected by how couples respond to dialectical tensions. The selection strategy is not a satisfying response to the dialectics of stability/change or autonomy/connection. Many couples also aren't satisfied with separation as a response to the openness/closedness dialectic.

There is reason to suspect that reframing could be a very satisfying response, for it reconciles the contradiction between different needs. Yet we have little insight into the effects of reframing, as few people report using this complicated, creative strategy. Baxter (1990) has stated that reframing is a valuable and underused response to dialectical tensions.

In sum, dialectical theory claims that relationships are continuously in flux because of tensions between contradictory needs that are inherent in relationships and in the interaction between relationships and their contexts. The tensions generated by conflicting needs are primary dynamics that explain why and how relationships change over time and circumstances.

Critical Assessment of Dialectical Theory

Response to dialectical theory has been uncommonly positive. As you know from reading Chapters 4 through 7 as well as this chapter's prior discussion of interactional theory, scholars are usually quick to point out flaws in any theory. Why hasn't that been the case with dialectical theory? One answer might be that, because dialectical theory is a relatively new approach, scholars haven't yet had time to render critical judgments. Questions could be raised about how well dialectical theory meets the criterion of testability. How would we measure whether dialectical tensions are continuously present and never fully resolvable in human relationships? Evidence that there are dialectical tensions at particular moments in relationships does not prove that they are either ongoing or irresolvable.

Except for possible problems in meeting the criterion of testability, dialectical theory measures up well on the standards used to evaluate theories. First, does it provide a good description and explanation of what it proposes to study? The answer is yes. The dialectics that Baxter and others have identified substantially enhance our understanding of continuous tensions in relationships and the changes such tensions generate. This theory also fares well on the criterion of simplicity. It has a limited number of concepts, and those are explained in straightforward ways.

Reflection

Can you think of ways to teach people the skill of reframing?

Dialectical theory is especially strong on the criterion of practical value and heuristic power. If you are like most people, learning about dialectical tensions gave you new insights into your feelings and your relationships. You may have felt relief in learning that the contradictory needs you sometimes feel are normal in all relationships. You may have learned new strategies for managing dialectical tensions in your own friendships and romantic bonds. This is sound evidence that the theory has practical merit. Further evidence of the theory's pragmatic strength may come as it becomes better known and more available in training of counselors and teachers.

The heuristic power of dialectical theory is measured by the research it generates and the original lines of thinking it promotes. On both counts, the theory fares well. Since Baxter introduced dialectical theory in the late 1980s, many other researchers have employed it in their own investigations. In addition, a number of current textbooks in communication and personal relationships devote substantial attention to dialectical theory.

Many scholars regard dialectical theory as a remarkably original perspective that ushers in exciting new ways of thinking about communication in relationships. Prior to Baxter's introduction of this approach, interpersonal scholars were restricted to theories that were simplistic, focusing only on narrow aspects of relationships, and/or highly mechanical, describing relational life in terms of "inputs," "outputs," "costs," "rewards," and "exchanges." Dialectical theory offers a broad, dynamic, and humanistic view of interaction in personal relationships.

One question sometimes raised about dialectical theory is whether the three dialectics Baxter and her colleagues have identified are the only dialectics. This question concerns whether the theory has adequately described the phenomena it studies, in this case dialectics. One example of different dialectics comes from the research of Bill Rawlins. In an interview study of adolescents' choices of interaction partners, Rawlins (1988) reported that the dialectic of historical perspective and contemporary experience guided adolescents' choices of whether to talk with parents or friends. He also interpreted the interviews as showing that a dialectic of judgment and acceptance was felt by adolescents and affected their preferences for talking with either parents or peers. Four years later Rawlins

(1992) published another study that reported the judgment/acceptance dialectic in best-friend relationships. When he studied on-the-job friendships, Ted Zorn (1995) found the dialectics Baxter identified, and he found additional ones specific to the work context in which the relationships existed.

Yet other researchers have independently found the dialectics Baxter identified, and they haven't found additional dialectics (Petronio, 1991; Werner, Altman, Brown, & Ginat, 1993; Wood et al., 1994). Limited existing reports by clinicians are also consistent with the description Baxter has advanced (Beck, 1988; Bergner & Bergner, 1990; Goldsmith, 1990; Scarf, 1987). It is clear that the majority of existing work is consistent with dialectical theory as formulated by Baxter.

Rawlins's findings may reflect differences in vocabulary rather than differences in the actual character of dialectics. Tension between judging and accepting a friend might be a particular instance of the larger dialectic of openness/closedness. Would the theory be invalidated if future research were to reveal dialectics beyond the three Baxter has identified? No, because the theory maintains only that tensions between contradictory impulses are inherent in relationships. I know of no dialectical theorists who claim that there are only three relational dialectics, and Baxter herself has never advanced the claim that there are only three dialectics.

Reflection

What would you consider adequate evidence of additional dialectics beyond the three that Baxter and her colleagues have identified?

In the most comprehensive presentation of dialectical theory pertinent to relationships, Leslie Baxter and Barbara Montgomery (1996) state that they have no reason to think there is a finite set of contradictions that operate in personal relationships. Thus, future research may illuminate either other dialectics common to all relationships or certain dialectics in specific relationships. If so, that will refine, not invalidate, dialectical theory.

Summary

This chapter allowed us to explore two distinct theories about the dynamics of communication in relationships. Both are centrally concerned with relationship patterns and processes and the ways in which those affect what happens between people. Yet they differ in terms of which processes and patterns they emphasize. Interactional theory is most concerned with levels of systemic interaction, levels of meaning, power balances, and punctuation. These emphases reflect the theory's genesis in clinical work with dis-

Theories About Interpersonal Dynamics

turbed families. In addition, interactional theory provides some of the most focused attention to pragmatics of communication that has been associated with any theory.

Grounded in different assumptions and focused on different relational processes, dialectical theory emphasizes the continuous, inherent tensions that arise from contradictory impulses for autonomy and connection, openness and closedness, and novelty and routine. Viewing dialectics as natural, ongoing, and productive, this theory provides impressive insight into dynamics that are central, continuous, and never fully resolved parts of relational life. Dialectical theory encourages us to understand and appreciate the contradictions and the continuous changes that saturate, complicate, and enliven our relationships.

Key Terms

complementary	neutralization
content meaning	openness
dialectical moments	parallel relationships
dialectical theory	punctuation
dialectics	reframing
general systems theory	relationship meaning
homeostasis	selection
interactional theory	separation
metacommunication	symmetrical

CHAPTER NINE

Theories About Communication and the Evolution of Relationships

Before reading this chapter, indicate the extent to which you agree or disagree with the following statements, using this scale: 5 = strongly agree; 4 = agree; 3 = no strong feeling; 2 = disagree; 1 = strongly disagree.

1. The more uncertain we are about another person, the less we like that person.

2. People stay in a relationship if the rewards they receive equal or outweigh the costs of being in the relationship.

3. Most romantic relationships follow a standard pattern in their development.

4. People tend to self-disclose more when they are uncertain about each other than when they are more certain of each other.

5. A person who receives greater or lesser rewards from a relationship than her or his partner will be dissatisfied.

6. In most serious relationships, there are turning points that radically change what the relationship is about and where it is headed.

Certain theorists agree strongly with each of these assertions. The only problem is that a theorist who would concur with some of these statements would disagree with others. If you're beginning to suspect that there are different, even conflicting, theories of how and why relationships develop, you're right. There's also no consensus among scholars about which theory is most accurate and useful.

In this chapter we will explore three of the most influential theories of communication and relational development. We'll look first at **uncertainty reduction theory**, which is the simplest, most specific of the three. Next, we'll consider **social exchange theory**, which asserts that people try to maximize rewards and minimize costs in relationships in much the same way they do when buying a car or engaging in other commercial transactions. Finally, we'll study **developmental theory**, which envisions personal relationships as evolving through stages defined by participants' expectations, perceptions, and meanings. Each theory offers an interesting point of view on the evolution of intimacy, and each reflects a particular perspective on human nature. As you study these three theories, see which make sense to you and fit with your experiences in relationships.

Uncertainty Reduction Theory

When two people first meet, there is a high level of uncertainty. They don't know what each other likes, thinks, and believes; how each other responds to certain things; and how each is seen by the other. Neither can predict the other's reactions, and they're unsure what each other expects or wants from interacting. Because uncertainty is very high in initial encounters, reducing it is important if the relationship is to progress. That is the basic premise of uncertainty reduction theory, which was developed primarily by Charles Berger and his associates (Berger, 1979, 1987, 1988; Berger & Bradac, 1982; Berger & Calabrese, 1975).

Laws of Behavior

As its name implies, uncertainty reduction theory spotlights uncertainty as the primary issue in developing relationships. The theory's central goal is to explain how uncertainty (and its counterpart, certainty) affects communication in relationships. Consequently, this theory explains progression in relationships in terms of the communication that uncertainty motivates and the effects of increases and decreases in uncertainty on the development of closeness.

Unlike the other theories we've analyzed, uncertainty reduction theory is a laws approach (Berger, 1977). Because this is the first laws approach we've studied, we'll review what that implies. You'll recall that in Chapter 2 we discussed different types of explanation. Laws explanations assume that human behavior is the result of invariant or probabilistic laws. In Chapter 3 we discussed the different epistemological views that inform theories. Those who believe in covering laws assume that humans respond in predictable (lawlike) ways to external stimuli—in other words, that we react to stimuli predictably rather than in varying ways on the basis of mediation, cognitive processes, rules, meanings, interpretations, and so forth. Because covering laws theories assume that behavior is regulated by laws, the focus of theory building is articulating basic laws that explain why we do what we do.

Theoretical Axioms

An **axiom** is a statement that is presumed to be true on its face and therefore does not require proof or explanation. Examples of axioms are as follows: Life is valuable. The earth revolves around the sun. Abusive relationships are undesirable. We accept these axioms about social and physical life as true. They form the unquestioned foundations of our beliefs and actions.

Theories based on covering laws begin with axioms, which are principles that are presumed to be self-evident. From these axioms, additional principles are deductively derived. Thus, the best way to understand uncertainty reduction theory is by examining the axioms that form its foundations.

Although axioms probably won't make your list of spellbinding reading, they do provide concise descriptions of the building blocks of laws theories. Figure 9.1 summarizes the seven axioms that are the foundation of uncertainty reduction theory. As you read the axioms, imagine you are just starting a relationship with a new person. Ask yourself whether these seven statements accurately describe what you feel and do in initial interaction.

What do these axioms tell us about how people get to know one another and develop relationships? The most basic claim of the theory is that uncertainty is uncomfortable, so we use communication to reduce our uncertainty about others. If you accept this as true, then you would expect people who are getting to know each other to engage in a good deal of communication designed to gain information and reduce uncertainty. In fact, this expectation was confirmed in a study that concluded that uncertainty does tend to promote information gathering in the early stages of a relationship (Berger & Kellerman, 1994). All of the axioms build on and reflect the foundational ideas that uncertainty is discomforting and we seek to reduce it.

Rather than discussing each individual axiom, we'll select two to illustrate what the theory proposes about relationships between communication and uncertainty. Axiom 2 states that nonverbal signs, such as smiles and head nods, reduce our uncertainty about others by giving us clues about what they think and feel and how they view us. As we become more certain about another person, axiom 2 states that we express more friendliness with our own nonverbal behaviors.

Axiom 5 claims that, as two people become more certain of each person, they self-disclose less. The reasoning is that we self-disclose to reduce uncertainty in early stages of a relationship. Once uncertainty is low, there is little need to continue self-disclosing at a high rate. Each of the axioms states a generalization that the theorists think holds true for all or most people who are launching a new relationship.

Theories About Communication and the Evolution of Relationships

Figure 9.1

*Axioms of Uncertainty
Reduction Theory*

1. Given the high level of uncertainty present at the onset of the entry phase [of relationships], as the amount of verbal communication between strangers increases, the level of uncertainty for each person in the relationship decreases. As uncertainty is further reduced, the amount of verbal communication increases.

2. As nonverbal affiliative expressiveness increases, uncertainty levels decrease in an initial interaction situation. In addition, decreases in uncertainty level cause increases in nonverbal affiliative expressiveness.

3. High levels of uncertainty cause increases in information-seeking behavior. As uncertainty levels decline, information-seeking behavior decreases.

4. High levels of uncertainty in a relationship cause decreases in the intimacy level of communication content. Low levels of uncertainty produce higher levels of intimacy.

5. High levels of uncertainty produce high rates of reciprocity [in self-disclosing communication]. Low levels of uncertainty produce low reciprocity rates.

6. Similarities between persons reduce uncertainty; dissimilarities produce increases in uncertainty.

7. Increases in uncertainty level produce decreases in liking. Decreases in uncertainty level produce increases in liking.

Source: Based on Berger, C. R., & Calabrese, R. (1975). Some explorations in initial interaction and beyond: Toward a developmental theory of interpersonal communication, *Human Communication Research, 1*, 99–112.

Reflection

*Can you think of
instances in which
uncertainty was not
uncomfortable and you
didn't act to reduce it?*

Beyond Personal Relationships

Although uncertainty reduction theory was first developed to explain how personal relationships do or don't evolve, it has been extended to other contexts of human communication. One of the more promising extensions of the theory has focused on intercultural communication. Led by William Gudykunst, this program of research asks whether people from different cultures use different strategies for reducing uncertainty in early interaction. Because communication and culture are so closely related, it would make sense that members of different cultures communicate in distinctive ways.

William Gudykunst's interest in intercultural communication began in a very unacademic setting. In his job as an intercultural relations adviser, Gudykunst taught U.S. naval personnel and their families how to adapt effectively to Japanese culture. He realized that, as strangers in Japan, Americans felt uncertain about how to interpret Japanese people and how to act in a new country. The uncertainty led to anxiety, which made the U.S. citizens distinctly uneasy. Gudykunst thought that, if Americans could reduce their uncertainty about Japanese culture, their anxiety would also diminish, and they would feel more comfortable.

Later, in his role as a faculty member at California State University at Fullerton, Gudykunst followed up on his experiences with the navy by conducting research and developing theory, which he has refined over the years. A series of studies conducted by Gudykunst and his colleagues (Gudykunst, 1983; Gudykunst & Nishida, 1984, 1989) showed that there are cross-cultural differences in how people try to reduce uncertainty. Members of more individualistic cultures, such as the United States, tend to use direct verbal strategies to learn about others. For instance, they might ask "Where are you from?" "Are you outgoing?" "Where did you go to school?" In contrast, people in more collectivist cultures, such as Korea, typically rely on indirect strategies to gain information about new acquaintances. For example, they might silently observe new acquaintances to learn if they are outgoing and where their accents suggest they were raised. Members of collectivist cultures might also seek information from third parties to learn about people they have recently met.

Gudykunst and his colleagues (Gudykunst, 1985, 1991, 1993, 1995; Kim & Gudykunst, 1988) extended their early work into a theory that links anxiety and uncertainty reduction in the context of intercultural communication. They advanced a theory called anxiety uncertainty management, which explains how individuals adapt to new cultures. The theory states that individuals who enter unfamiliar cultures often feel uncertainty, which is a cognitive phenomenon. The uncertainty fosters anxiety, which Gudykunst defines as an affective phenomenon. In other words, uncertainty is a thought: What should I do now? What does that mean? Anxiety, on the other hand, is a feeling: I'm uneasy. I'm scared. I'm confused. One of the primary ways to lessen feelings of anxiety is by reducing cognitive uncertainty about how we should act, how others are likely to act, and how to interpret behaviors in the new context.

How do we as strangers (Gudykunst's term for people who enter an unfamiliar culture) reduce our uncertainty so that we develop confidence in our ability to explain and predict the behaviors of natives in the culture? As we learn more about normative behaviors in the new culture, it becomes more familiar and predictable, and we become more confident of our ability to explain and predict others' actions and others' responses to various actions we might take. This reduces our anxiety and allows us to interact with more confidence and more sensitivity to the particular context in which we find ourselves.

Working within the anxiety uncertainty management model of cultural adaptation, Yun Kim (1988, 1995; Kim & Gudykunst, 1988) focuses on the importance of communication. His research shows that communication is a primary means by which we adapt to new cultural contexts. As

Theories About Communication and the Evolution of Relationships

non-natives interact with natives in a culture, the non-natives learn the values and norms of the new context, and they begin to be able to make sense of what happens. With continuing interaction with natives of the culture, the newcomers expand their communication repertoires so that they become progressively more competent in communication that is appropriate to that specific context. The work of Gudykunst, Kim, and others illustrates how a theory originally developed to explain communication in one context (personal relationships) may be extended to shed light on other contexts (intercultural).

Critical Assessment of Uncertainty Reduction Theory

Despite its parsimony and testability, uncertainty reduction theory has not gained widespread support in the field of communication. Considering criticisms of the theory will help you understand why this is so.

Narrow in Scope   The theory has been criticized for being extremely narrow in focusing only on uncertainty, which is surely not the only influence on how relationships or intercultural communication develop. Michael Sunnafrank (1986) faults the theory for claiming that uncertainty is the primary issue in the early stages of relationships. Sunnafrank and others (Duck, 1994a; Wood, 1993d, 1995a) argue that other issues are far greater influences than uncertainty in the developmental course of personal relationships. For instance, attraction, similarity of values and attitudes, and stimulation are influences that we might reasonably think are as important as uncertainty in developing relationships.

Reflection

Do you think uncertainty is the key influence on initial interactions?

Invalid   Far more serious is the accusation that the theory is invalid. This is the most damaging indictment that can be brought against a theory. If a theory is shown to be invalid or false, then it is dismissed by scholars. Critics of uncertainty reduction theory claim that some of its basic axioms (see Figure 9.1) are faulty. If so, then additional laws derived from those axioms also lack credibility. The questions raised about the theory's axioms and the laws deduced from them are too numerous to review comprehensively. We will discuss only two of the specific indictments of claims made by uncertainty reduction theory.

Axiom 3 states that, as our uncertainty about another person decreases, we are less likely to seek information about that person. Axiom 7 claims that our tendency to seek information decreases as our liking for another person increases. Are these claims true? To decide, step back from the theory for a moment and think about relationships in your life. Do you become less interested in learning about another person as you become more certain of what she or he is like and as you develop increasing fondness for her or him?

If these claims were true, then enduring relationships would involve little information seeking. In reality, however, partners continue to seek information about each other throughout relationships that span many years. Robbie and I have been together for 30 years, and information seeking is a continuous and substantial part of our routine interaction: How are you feeling about your new position? How did your writing go today? Are you making good progress on your book? Have you heard from Todd lately? Did you work out the problem with the student who had surgery and missed classes? What's your opinion of today's ruling from the Supreme Court? Do you have any major resolutions for the new year? Is your back still hurting you? How is the new friendship coming along? Is your class going well? Also, like most people, Robbie and I change as individuals. Continuing to communicate and seek information is essential if we are to continue knowing each other in depth.

Communication to learn about each other is continuous in our relationship, as it is in most long-term relationships. Yet, according to uncertainty reduction theory, people are less motivated to seek information as they become more certain of others. It could be that this criticism is less a direct refutation of the theory than an objection to its limited scope.

Originally, uncertainty reduction theory was developed to explain initial interactions, not communication in established relationships. Thus, its dubious applicability to enduring relationships may not invalidate the theory, even though it does raise legitimate questions about whether the theory gives us much insight into communication in personal relationships. Yet Gudykunst and Kim's research provides rather convincing evidence that uncertainty reduction theory is useful in describing, understanding, explaining, and predicting intercultural communication. Perhaps the domains of communication to which this theory is relevant have not been clearly identified.

Related to this criticism is the suggestion that there are other motives for communicating that are more basic and more important than uncertainty. In a stinging indictment of the theory, Kathy Kellerman and Rodney Reynolds (1990, p. 7) stated that "it seems more reasonable to suggest that persons will seek information about and from those they like rather than those they dislike." Although we might initially seek information about people we don't know or don't like, there is no self-evident reason to assume that knowing and/or liking others decreases our interest in learning about them.

Axiom 3 is the most controversial of the seven. It declares that uncertainty motivates information-seeking behavior and that reductions in uncertainty lead to declines in information-seeking behavior. Does this ring true in your experiences? Do you invariably seek information when you are uncertain, or do you seek information only when you care about knowing or understanding someone better? In other words, is uncertainty or interest a more important motive for seeking information?

This is a question raised by Kellerman and Reynolds (1990) in their critical review of uncertainty reduction theory. They point out that often we have no interest in learning about another person. Consequently, even though we are uncertain about the person, we have no motivation to reduce that uncertainty by gathering information. We communicate to gain information not because we are uncertain about people per se but because we care about them, find them interesting, or need to understand them (for example, because they can affect us).

Reflection

In your own relationships, how important are uncertainty, liking, and interest in motivating communication?

What do the proponents of uncertainty reduction theory say in response to these criticisms? To date, they haven't been able to marshal a convincing refutation. In fact, Berger has explicitly acknowledged that the theory includes "some propositions of dubious validity" (1987, p. 40). Yet this admission doesn't lead Berger to abandon uncertainty theory. He still believes it is basically on the right track. He suggests that uncertainty reduction be evaluated as a theory in progress rather than as a fully developed perspective (Berger & Gudykunst, 1991). Berger (1991) argues that, rather than throwing the theory out because of its flaws, communication scholars should work to refine it because it has basic value. Whether uncertainty reduction theory actually has adequate scope and the value that Berger claims remains a matter of controversy.

Social Exchange Theory

It's 7 P.M. and you're starving. You're too tired to fix a meal, and you don't have much money to buy one. Then you remember that the student paper had coupons for several pizza restaurants. Reviewing the paper, you discover that one restaurant offers to deliver a large pizza with five toppings for $10.99. Another pizzeria charges only $8.99 for delivering a large pizza, but only two toppings are included. The third coupon advertises a large, five-topping pizza for $6.99, but you would have to go get it because this restaurant doesn't offer delivery. Which pizza do you order?

If you're tired, you probably don't want to invest the effort to drive to pick up a pizza. Because you're low on money, the $8.99 deal looks good, but you do love lots of toppings. You have to decide whether three additional toppings are worth the investment of an extra $2.00. The choice you make is based on economic principles; you attempt to minimize your costs and maximize your gains.

Reflection

Do you think of your personal relationships in economic terms?

According to social exchange theory, we apply the same economic principles to interpersonal relationships. The basic idea is that people seek to maximize rewards and minimize costs in relationships. Thus, we conduct cost-benefit analyses to make sure we are getting enough out of a relationship given what we're investing in it. We communicate and build relationships to gain rewards, and we stay with relationships that are more rewarding than costly and more rewarding than alternatives.

There is no single exchange theory. Rather, there is a group of related exchange theories that grow out of basic propositions originally formulated by George Casper Homans (1954, 1961) and elaborated by others, including Peter Blau (1967), John Thibaut and Harold Kelley (Kelley & Thibaut, 1978; Thibaut & Kelley, 1959), Michael Roloff (1981), and Caryl Rusbult and Bram Buunk (1993). Our discussion will focus on general concepts and claims common to the group of exchange theories.

Evaluation of Relationships

Exchange theories assume that humans base their behaviors on rational calculations designed to maximize individual profit. In terms of relationships, exchange theorists claim we tally our **costs** and benefits, or rewards, to derive a net outcome. **Rewards** are things that have positive value to an individual. Most of us would positively value acceptance, loyalty, financial support, personal assistance, affection, and companionship. We might also find it rewarding to have a relationship with a person who enhances our social status.

Costs are whatever has negative value for an individual. For example, relationships cost us time, money, and effort. Another cost of relationships is all of the adjustments in personal behaviors we make to coordinate with another person. We may find it costly to stay in a relationship with someone who puts us down, who is insecure and needs a lot of emotional support, or who has health problems that require us to provide assistance. Costs also include forgone opportunities—real and possible benefits we give up by being in a relationship.

The net outcome of a relationship (O) is determined by subtracting costs (C) from rewards (R): $O = R - C$. Positive net outcomes result if relationships provide more rewards than costs; negative net outcomes result if relationships are more costly than rewarding.

Calvin and Hobbes
by Bill Watterson

Standards of Comparison

Calculating rewards and costs tells us whether the net outcome of a relationship is positive or negative. However, outcome alone doesn't tell us what people will do. Some people stay in relationships in which costs outweigh rewards. In other cases, people leave relationships that have positive net outcomes. Thus, the net value doesn't fully explain why we are satisfied or dissatisfied with relationships, and it doesn't explain why we choose to end or continue them.

According to exchange theory, there are two standards against which we compare our relationships (Thibaut & Kelley, 1959). These two standards measure different facets of interpersonal life: one diagnoses individuals' satisfaction; the other predicts relational stability, or how likely people are to stay in relationships.

Comparison Level The **comparison level**, or **CL**, is a subjective standard for what we expect in a particular type of relationship. The CL is based on a person's past and current relationships as well as the person's observations of other relationships and general knowledge derived from books, films, TV, and other sources.

Given all the friendships you've had, you have a general sense of what's involved in friendships and what is average and acceptable for you. Your history of romantic relationships and your observations of others' romantic relationships provide you with a general standard for evaluating the value of a particular romantic relationship in your life. Our CLs reflect the totality of our experiences in relationships, combined with our knowledge of relationships in general.

Comparison levels vary among individuals, since they reflect our personal experiences and knowledge. If you have been blessed by highly rewarding friendships, you will have a high CL for friendships—you will have lofty standards. If your romances have been gratifying, you will have a high CL for those relationships. Conversely, if you have had troubled romantic relationships and consistently disappointing friendships, then you probably will have a lower standard for what is normal and expected in your relationships.

Reflection

How high is your CL for friendships and romantic relationships? Do your present friendships and romances meet your CL?

The CL gauges satisfaction, and it tends to be a fairly stable standard. Because it is an aggregate value based on the totality of our relationship experience and knowledge, the CL tends not to be significantly altered by a single relationship, even one that is dramatically good or bad. According to exchange theory, we are satisfied with a relationship if it meets or exceeds our comparison level. In other words, we feel we're getting a pretty good deal if a relationship is as good as or better than our other relationships of the same type. But does satisfaction lead to commitment? Not necessarily, as we will see.

Comparison Level of Alternatives   Have you ever been in a relationship that you considered very good and then met someone who was more interesting? Have you ever stayed in a relationship that wasn't very satisfying because there weren't any better options? If so, then you understand why satisfaction doesn't always lead to relational continuity and dissatisfaction doesn't necessarily translate into relational demise.

A second standard by which we assess relationships is the **comparison level of alternatives**, or **CL$_{alt}$**. This is a relative measure that evaluates how good a particular relationship is in comparison to real or perceived alternatives to that relationship. Alternatives include both other possible relationships (or that we think are possible) and the choice not to be involved in any relationship. CL$_{alt}$ is the perceived value of alternatives to a given relationship.

Consider a concrete example. Assume that you have been dating Chris for six months and think this is a good relationship. You perceive your romance with Chris as a 7 on a scale of 1 (terrible) to 10 (perfect), and your CL is only a 6. Thus, the relationship with Chris is satisfying. But you think a romance with Kim, whom you just met, would be a 9. Your CL$_{alt}$ is a 9, and it exceeds the net outcome of 7 in the relationship with Chris. Exchange theory predicts that in this case you would leave the relationship with Chris for the one with Kim that you imagine would be better.

Unlike the CL, the CL_{alt} is not particularly stable. It fluctuates according to alternatives that emerge. One day you may have a very low CL_{alt} because you see no options preferable to the relationship you're in. That can change the next day if you meet a new person whom you find really attractive or if you decide you would be happier not being involved with anyone. We should also remember that CL_{alt} isn't necessarily accurate. Many people find out, often when it's too late, that there's a big gap between what they imagine a relationship will be and what it is once they're in it! Kim may not be nearly as lovable or loving as Chris once the novelty and infatuation wear off.

Reflection

Have you ever left a good relationship for one that you thought would be better and then discovered that the new one wasn't better than or even as good as the relationship you left?

The concept of CL_{alt} provides insight into the reasons people sometimes stay in abusive, even dangerous relationships. Many victims of domestic violence perceive that they have no viable alternatives to the abusive relationship. A woman who has young children and few job skills may feel dependent on a man who provides an income, even though he abuses her. Even though her marriage is highly unsatisfying, she may not perceive options for supporting herself and her children. A study I recently conducted (Wood, 2001) shows that another reason some women stay in violent relationships is that they feel they need to be with a man to be complete, and they don't think men other than their current partners would be less abusive.

Equity and Inequity

Homans claimed that people expect a fair exchange in relationships and that, by extension, we are unhappy when we feel an exchange is unfair. Extending this basic idea, exchange theorists have investigated the effects of perceptions of **equity** in personal relationships. Equity moves beyond a focus on immediate exchanges and rigid, cost–benefit analyses of specific interaction. Equity is concerned with whether a relationship is fair to the people in it over the course of time.

Perceived inequity is related to both individual dissatisfaction and relational distress (Sprecher, 2001; Sprecher & Felmlee, 1997; van Yperen & Buunk, 1990). Interestingly, inequity seems uncomfortable regardless of whether it works to our disadvantage or to our advantage. Obviously, people are unhappy when they feel they aren't getting a fair shake. For example, you might be distressed if you felt you consistently invested greater effort in a friendship than your friend did. Likewise, you'd probably be upset if you felt you did a lot more to demonstrate love to a romantic partner than your partner did in return. In a very recent study, Susan Sprecher (2001) reported that feeling underbenefited (getting less than a partner) results in not anger but depression. This was the case for both women and men in Sprecher's study.

According to research, the converse is also true: We are distressed when we feel we get more than our fair share or invest less than our partners in relationships (Brehm, 1992; Sprecher, 2001). People who perceive they are getting more than they are investing in a relationship typically experience guilt. Apparently it's unpleasant to love more and also to be loved more.

Reflection

Is equity a more useful measure of fairness than the immediate calculation of costs and benefits?

What are the sources of perceived inequity in romantic relationships? In-law relations, sex, emotional investments? All these can lead to perceived inequity and the relational dissatisfaction and instability it generates. Yet the most significant elements in perceptions of equity are household chores and child-care (Fowers, 1991; Goldstein, 2000; Risman & Godwin, 2001; Suitor, 1991; van Yperen & Buunk, 1990). Money is the only factor that equals household equity in its importance to overall perceptions of equity in relationships.

Today the majority of marriages in the United States have two bread-winners (Hertz & Marshall, 2001). Spouses' equitable participation in the paid labor force, however, has not been paralleled by equitable divisions in the domestic sphere. In only about 20% of dual-worker families do men assume half of the responsibilities for housework and caregiving (Gold-stein, 2000; Hochschild, 1989; Nussbaum, 1992; Risman & Godwin, 2001).

The cost of inequity in home life is substantial. Women who work one shift in a paid job and then return home to work a second shift at un-paid labor suffer increased stress, fatigue, and vulnerability to illness and disease. In addition, they feel frustrated and resentful at the inequity of the situation (Hochschild, 1989; Risman & Godwin, 2001). When domestic inequity is chronic, it exacts a heavy toll on individuals, and it can sabotage relationships. Research on inequitable home responsibilities suggests that the concept of equity is important in understanding relationships even if we don't accept all the tenets of exchange theory.

In summary, exchange theories suggest that we enter and stay in relationships for what we can get out of them and will leave relationships that are less profitable than alternatives. Although social exchange theories have been used to generate a vast number of specific lawlike propositions, the social exchange view of relationships can be summarized by the five basic claims it advances: (1) Individuals are rational actors who calculate rewards and costs of relationships. (2) Individuals operate to maximize rewards, minimize costs, and optimize outcomes in relationships. (3) Satisfaction with relationships is based on individuals' CLs. (4) Relational stability (and dependence on relationships) is based on individuals' CL_{alt}s. (5) Equity is preferable to inequity; both overbenefiting and underbenefiting are displeasing.

Critical Assessment of Social Exchange Theory

Using the logic of exchange, it seems fair for us to conduct a cost–benefit analysis of this theory. There are four major criticisms of social exchange theory in its many forms.

Little Heuristic Value   Some scholars are sympathetic to the assumptions and claims of exchange theory, yet they fault it for providing little new insight into human behavior and human relationships. Of course people like what is rewarding and dislike what is costly, they say. What does that tell us that we didn't already know? It's obvious that people prefer equity to inequity; where's the news in that finding? Naturally, people are satisfied with relationships that meet or surpass their expectations; why wouldn't they be? What's surprising or even interesting about the idea that people will leave a relationship if a better alternative comes along?

If the claims of exchange theory are self-evident, then they do little to enlarge or extend understanding. The principles and propositions of social exchange theory may tell us what we already know, but do they tell us anything beyond that? If not, then the theory has little heuristic value. A theory that is only self-evident also fares badly on the criteria of providing a satisfying description and explanation and having practical value.

Not Testable   A second criticism made of exchange theories is that they can't be tested. At first glance this doesn't seem valid, for there is a great deal of research that measures exchange concepts, such as stability, satisfaction, and equity, and there is equally substantial research testing propositions, such as that inequity is distressing and that CL_{alt} predicts relational stability. Clearly, much work has been invested in testing the claims of exchange theories.

However, some critics ask what is really being measured in these studies. Their concern centers on the vagueness of definitions of key concepts in the theory. The concept of reward, for instance, is defined as anything that is positively valued. Thus, a person might irrationally value something that shouldn't be valued and consider that something rewarding. The classic example is a masochist who finds pain rewarding. Is the concept of reward so vague that we count pain as rewarding as long as a person says it is? If not, we have to admit that exchange doesn't really offer universal explanations of human behavior, because its laws don't cover some individuals.

Exchange theory states that people seek what they find rewarding. Yet the theory also assumes that humans are rational actors. Thus, a masochist who seeks partners who inflict pain is making an irrational choice, which violates one of the basic assumptions of the theory. But if the masochist makes what would be judged the rational choice and avoids partners who inflict pain, then she or he doesn't experience rewards, which violates a different basic tenet of the theory. If we cannot define basic concepts such as reward adequately, then it is impossible to test the theory and thus to determine its validity and value. One response to this criticism is that exchange theory limits its scope only to psychologically healthy people for whom, presumably, there would be no conflict between acting rationally and seeking rewards.

Reflection

Is it possible to define and quantify rewards and costs in a precise and universal manner for all individuals?

Inappropriate for Humans   Additional questions can be raised about whether exchange theory's focus on individuals is appropriate for a theory of relationships. For example, reward is defined as what an individual values positively. Yet in close relationships, one person's rewards (and costs) are intertwined with those of a partner. Symbolic interaction theorists, for example, assume that intimates internalize each other's perspectives and so don't think about or evaluate relationship issues in a strictly individual manner. In Burke's terminology, intimates become consubstantial and thus identify with each other. When something is costly to Robbie, it is costly to me too. When I value something, Robbie does too. Can a theory that views costs, rewards, net outcome, and satisfaction as separate phenomena really apply to relationships between people?

If relationships are something other than and more than for-profit enterprises, then it may be inappropriate to describe and explain them in terms of economic concepts and capitalistic motives. A number of scholars argue that exchange principles may well apply to commercial transactions but not to personal relationships that are based on feelings, intangible rewards and costs, and subjective experiences. Steve Duck (1993, 1994a) vigorously protests the idea that personal relationships are motivated by crass marketplace calculations. I share his point of view and have published several essays that argue relationships are not governed and cannot be explained by economic principles or cost–benefit considerations (Wood, 1993b, 1995a, 1998a, 2000). Duck and I have joined forces to denounce the idea that close relationships are primarily evaluated in terms of whether we're getting a good deal (Duck & Wood, 1995; Wood & Duck, 1995a). As the most fundamental assumption of exchange theory is that people operate to maximize individual rewards, the entire theory falls if that assumption is faulty.

The criticism that exchange theories are inappropriate for human relationships can't be evaluated by scientific logic, and it can't be proved or disproved by empirical research. Instead, this criticism's strength depends on your values and beliefs. You either do or do not believe that we approach personal relationships with the same orientation we use to buy a car or negotiate a deal. Depending on which ontological and epistemological assumptions (see Chapter 3) you embrace, you will find social exchange theory's view of humans either credible or misguided.

Not Supported by Research   Finally, doubt about the validity of exchange theory is prompted by research that fails to confirm its claims. Investigations (McDonald, 1981; O'Connell, 1984) have found that exchange principles are not evident in close relationships in which trust and commitment exist. Partners routinely tolerate imbalances in net outcomes as long as trust and a desire to sustain the relationships are high. Research by Mary Lund (1985) confirms this by demonstrating that commitment, or relationship stability, is positively related to individuals' investments. This suggests that accepting some costs of being in a relationship may increase our commitment, not decrease it, as exchange theory implies. Finally, one study of different kinds of relationships found that exchange principles do operate in marketplace interactions; in friendships and romantic relationships, however, exchange principles not only did not operate but were disparaged and undesired (Clark, Quellette, Powell, & Milberg, 1987; Wood, 1998a).

Exchange theories assume that people are motivated by the quest to maximize personal rewards. Based on this assumption, the theories attempt to quantify rewards, costs, and comparison levels and to calculate the satisfaction and stability of relationships. Whether relationships and our decisions to abandon or sustain them involve more than the calculus of exchange remains a controversial issue.

Developmental Theories

The final approach to the evolution of relationships that we will consider is developmental theories. As with the social exchange perspective, the developmental viewpoint includes more than one theory. There are theories of how individuals develop cognitively and morally, how groups move through stages of decision making, and how personal relationships evolve over time. To stay with this chapter's focus on relationships, we'll examine developmental theories that are pertinent to personal relationships. We'll focus on ideas and claims that are common to various developmental theories of relationships.

Viewing Relationships Developmentally

Sometimes it may seem that relationships spring to life suddenly or end abruptly. In reality, however, most relationships grow, mature, and decay gradually over the course of time. You see a stranger, talk to her, learn something about her, go out to a few movies and dinners, and pretty soon that person seems naturally woven into your life. When you left for college, you and your friend pledged to remain close even though you'd be separated by many miles. At first you did call and write regularly. Then new people, experiences, and routines filled your life, and your contact lapsed. By now you hardly ever think about the person who was once a close friend.

Like these examples, most of our relationships progress over a more or less lengthy span of days, weeks, months, and years. Because personal relationships wax and wane over time, a number of communication theorists have tried to map the evolutionary course of intimacy. Their work can be classified into two distinct eras of developmental theorizing.

First-Generation Developmental Theories

The first wave of developmental theories emerged in the 1970s. One of the best-known models was developed by Irwin Altman and Dallas Taylor (1973). Choosing the unfortunate label **social penetration model**, Altman and Taylor metaphorically described people as onions that have wedges, or areas, of personality, each of which has multiple layers of progressive depth. Figure 9.2 illustrates the social penetration process using the onion metaphor.

Altman and Taylor proposed that, to develop a personal relationship, people penetrate the outside layers (superficial tastes in books, music, and

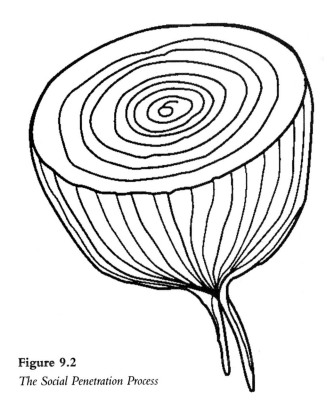

SUPERFICIAL LAYERS
(likes and dislikes in clothes, music, and so on)

MIDDLE LAYERS
(political views, social attitudes, and so on)

INNER LAYERS
(spiritual values, deep fears, hopes, goals, fantasies, secrets, and so on)

CORE PERSONALITY
(most basic self)

Figure 9.2
The Social Penetration Process

food), middle layers (political views and social attitudes), interior layers (spiritual values and beliefs and deeply felt fears, hopes, and goals), and finally reach the inner core of the self-concept.

The social penetration model was a starting point for thinking about how relationships develop. Yet it isn't a very sophisticated explanation of how intimacy evolves. It doesn't even address the question of how relationships deteriorate! The original social penetration model tied relational development to the single process of becoming increasingly open in communication.

Eight years after developing the model, Altman and his colleagues acknowledged that the original model erred in portraying relationships as following an uninterrupted path toward greater openness and intimacy. Influenced by dialectical theory, Altman and his colleagues (Altman, Vinsel, & Brown, 1981; Taylor & Altman, 1987) have amended their ideas to acknowledge that the developmental course of relationships involves a continuous tension between desires for greater openness and intimacy and desires for independence and closedness.

During the mid- and late 1980s and into the 1990s, scholars of personal relationships voiced criticisms of specific developmental models and

Developmental Theories

doubts about the value of a developmental perspective in general. Critics strongly questioned the assumption that relationships develop and deteriorate in linear sequences (Baxter, 1985, 1988; Duck, 1990, 1991; Van Lear, 1992). They argued that many, perhaps most, relationships follow zigzag paths in which moves to increase intimacy are followed by retreats from closeness. Certainly dialectical theory would regard it as natural to vacillate between seeking intimacy and seeking distance.

Another problem with linear models is that they impute an inevitability to relational development: Once you're on the upward spiral, you continue to increase intimacy; once you're headed downhill, there's no turning back. Linear models also suggest there is an ideal of intimacy to be achieved. One model, for example, defines intimate bonding as a public ritual that announces a couple's commitment (Knapp & Vangelisti, 1992). That view of the crux of intimacy excludes gay and lesbian couples as well as heterosexuals who cohabit and do not choose to institutionalize their commitment. Any model that excludes such a substantial portion of relationships is inadequate.

Perhaps the greatest criticism of the first round of models was that they defined stages in terms of events outside the people involved in the relationships. Theorists identified particular kinds of activities, forms of communication, events, and so forth as distinguishing specific stages. Skeptics pointed out that what binds a couple together is more likely to be private understandings and feelings than public rituals (Wood, 1993b, 2000).

Second-Generation Developmental Theories

The second wave of developmental theorizing was launched by James Honeycutt's conceptual breakthrough in 1993. Building on first-generation models, Honeycutt proposed that movement in relationships is both defined and guided by individuals' perceptions. To grasp the importance of this idea, let's consider an example. Tonya and Phyllis have been spending time together for several weeks when Tonya confides that she once had a problem with drugs. Will this disclosure increase the intimacy between the two women?

According to early developmental models, disclosures both indicate and cause increases in intimacy. Honeycutt's reformulation, however, claims that disclosures themselves don't affect intimacy. Instead, it is *how Tonya and Phyllis perceive and assign meaning* to the disclosure that affects their relationship. If Phyllis doesn't perceive Tonya's comment as particularly revealing, it's unlikely to affect how she feels about Tonya. If Tonya tells lots of people about her former drug problem, she may not regard it as an especially disclosive comment. Honeycutt's insight is that behaviors and external events don't affect relationships unless individuals assign them meanings that have

Theories About Communication and the Evolution of Relationships

relational consequences. This view is consistent with the broad trend among communication scholars to emphasize personal interpretations and meanings of behaviors and interactions (Ballard-Reisch & Weigel, 1999; Weigel & Ballard-Reisch, 2002; Yerby, 1995).

Relationship Trajectories

Extending the idea that individuals' meanings are the critical influence on relational evolution, Honeycutt proposed that individuals use their past knowledge and experiences to define movement toward increased or decreased closeness. He suggested that people have "imagined **trajectories**," which are personal understandings of various tracks in relationships (Figure 9.3). If, in your past relationships, arguments have typically presaged deterioration of intimacy, then you may have a trajectory that presumes that conflict leads to decreased closeness and eventually to the end of a relationship.

Honeycutt thought the trajectories were a kind of schema (a concept that originated with constructivist theory) that guides how we think about what's happening between us and others. Perhaps you have a trajectory that defines intimacy as intensifying when a person calls several times during the week to suggest getting together just to hang out. You probably have trajectories that outline how you see the whole range of gradations associated with closeness and distance. You may also have turning points, which are key relational events or feelings that you perceive as marking changes in the direction or intensity of a relationship. According to Baxter and Bullis (1986), most people do perceive definite **turning points** in romantic relationships. Perhaps the best example is saying "I love you." This communication can radically change how people feel about a relationship and its future.

Research supports and elaborates Honeycutt's claim that we develop trajectories that define relational turning points and levels of closeness. Studies have shown that we learn about relationships much as we learn about anything else—from experience, observation, and instruction. Our direct experience in relationships, as well as our reflections on that experience, is a major source of our relationship knowledge (Andersen, 1993; Honeycutt, 1993; Honeycutt & Cantrill, 2001). Because experience is a

Figure 9.3

Relationship Trajectories

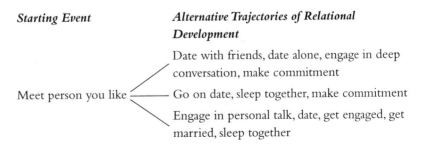

Starting Event

Alternative Trajectories of Relational Development

Meet person you like

Date with friends, date alone, engage in deep conversation, make commitment

Go on date, sleep together, make commitment

Engage in personal talk, date, get engaged, get married, sleep together

TRY IT OUT What are your relationship trajectories? To figure that out, think about what you consider indicators of changes in intimacy. (CMM theorists would ask you to think about your constitutive rules for different stages of intimacy.)

1. How do you know when someone is romantically interested in you?
2. What do you say and do to signal another person that you're interested?
3. What is involved in being infatuated?
4. How do you tell the difference between being infatuated and being in love?
5. What clues you that a relationship is disintegrating?
6. How do you know when a relationship is over?

powerful teacher, individuals who have been involved in serious relationships have more developed expectations and trajectories than people who haven't been seriously involved (Honeycutt & Cantrill, 1991; Martin, R.W., 1991, 1992).

In addition to direct knowledge gained from participating in relationships, our relational trajectories reflect indirect forms of knowledge. We learn about relationships from television and films (although media offer some pretty unrealistic ideas) and from observing others and what happens in their relationships (Andersen, 1993; Honeycutt, Cantrill, & Greene, 1989). We also gain relationship knowledge from conversations in which others give us advice or opinions about relationships and share their perceptions of how relationships do and should operate.

Honeycutt's contribution redirected the course of developmental theory and research. No longer do most scholars focus on behaviors and communication patterns that characterize distinct stages in the rise and fall of intimacy. Instead, current developmental work centers on learning more about how trajectories, or relational schemata, are formed and how they guide communication between people.

Current developmental theories seek to identify stages based on the meanings and perspectives of participants in relationships. The stages, though necessarily presented in a particular order, are not assumed to be in a fixed sequence. Instead, scholars realize that people may skip stages, cycle more than once through some stages, zigzag, and otherwise pursue diverse developmental paths. Figure 9.4 presents one version, or one trajectory, of stages based on the relational schemata of participants. It is the model I use in my teaching (Wood, 2000).

Emerging emphasis on subjective trajectories links developmental theorizing with a number of other theories that concentrate on how individuals interpret experiences to assign meanings. The body of constructivist research, for example, is directly relevant to issues such as the prototypes, scripts, and personal constructs individuals use to define interpersonal in-

Figure 9.4

A Model of One Trajectory of Relational Development

Ongoing Intimacy
(Perceiving routines, rhythms, and patterns in interaction; acting on basis of constitutive and regulative rules worked out between partners; engaging in everyday "small talk"; reflecting on relationship and partner; responding to changes and to dialectical tensions)

Intimate Commitment
(Believing in a shared future of intimacy; deciding to maintain the relationship)

Dyadic Breakdown
(Feeling dissatisfied; experiencing lapses in routines, rhythms, and patterns; transgressing rules)

Intensifying
(Perceiving greater frequency, depth, and value in interaction; gaining a sense of a private world shared with partner; developing personalized communication such as nicknames and private codes; idealizing; publicizing the relationship)

Intrapsychic Phase
(Brooding about relationship problems and partner; feeling negative about relationship; having lessened perception of relationship's good points)

Explorational Communication
(Perceiving increasing breadth and depth in communication; feeling increasingly confident of knowledge about other)

Dyadic Phase
(Discussing tensions and perceived problems in relationship or avoiding confronting problems)

Social Phase
(Experiencing dialectical tension between wanting to conceal problems from outsiders and wanting to talk about problems with friends and family; seeking others' support)

Initial Interaction
(Being attracted/noticing other is attracted; communicating interest/noticing other is interested; forming initial interpretations of the other)

Individuals
(Increasing sense of personal identity, CL, CL_{alt}; growing level of interest in new relationships)

Grave Dressing
(Making sense of the end of a relationship; revising perceptions of the relationship, self, and partner)

Steve Duck (1984) developed the model of relational dissolution featured here. The model of intimacy and relational escalation is based on Wood (2000).

teraction. We have prototypes, or ideals (perfection, in Burke's terms), for relationships, and we have scripts both for dates and for how relationships are supposed to progress.

CMM theory's concept of the hierarchy of meanings provides one way of thinking about how individuals develop coordinated understandings of episodes in relational life. For example, coordination is needed if one partner avoids conflict and thinks it's unhealthy and the other partner views conflict as healthy and as best worked through.

Dialectical theory suggests that trajectories for established intimacy may include both distance and closeness and both openness and closedness. An important contribution of interactional theory is to remind us that we need to consider both content and relationship levels of meaning when thinking about trajectories for intimacy. Narrative theory would encourage us to pay attention to the overall stories people compose to describe the evolution of their relationships.

Symbolic interactionism, too, adds insights to current lines of developmental theorizing. Recall that symbolic interactionism claims that we learn the meanings of our culture through interaction with others who are members of it. This alerts us to the importance of cultural contextualization of trajectories. Your trajectory for falling in love is probably quite different from that of a person from India whose parents have arranged a marriage. What we expect of friends, too, reflects cultural values, and so expectations will vary among diverse cultures.

Even within Western culture there are many distinct social communities, which we will discuss in Chapter 10. Gay and lesbian communities have some patterns for meaning that parallel those of heterosexuals and some that are distinct (Huston & Schwartz, 1996). Some African-American and Hispanic communities have some relationship understandings that diverge from those of European Americans (Gaines, 1995; Houston & Wood, 1996). One of the challenges for developmental theorists is to integrate cultural influences into their thinking about the evolution of personal relationships (Wood & Duck, 1995a; Wood, 1995c).

Critical Assessment of Developmental Theories

Most criticism of developmental views of relationships was leveled at the first generation of theories. Critics legitimately reproached the early models for deterministic, linear depictions of relational evolution and for reliance on external phenomena to define stages in intimacy. As we have seen, recent work has addressed those criticisms by advancing more dynamic theories of relational growth that rely on individuals' perceptions and meanings to define movement toward greater and lesser intimacy. The

Theories About Communication and the Evolution of Relationships

refinements in the second generation of theorizing illustrate that dialogue among scholars is critical to the development of sound theories.

Theories or Perspectives?   One question that has been raised is whether developmental views are theories or merely perspectives. To answer this question, we can ask whether developmental research meets the goals of theory that we discussed in Chapter 2. Does the work describe relational evolution? Yes, current models of relational development offer useful descriptions of phases in relational life and recognize that stages may be skipped, revisited, and experienced in various orders. A second goal of theories is to explain phenomena. By tying relational development to individual cognitions and meanings, second-generation theories provide satisfying explanations of why relationships move toward greater and lesser degrees of intimacy.

The third goal of theory is to allow prediction and control or to enhance understanding. Most developmental scholars are less interested in prediction and control than in understanding, so we want to assess the understanding generated by developmental work. What is your judgment? Does what you've read about developmental theories enhance your insight into the developmental paths in your own relationships? Most people respond affirmatively to the question of whether developmental research adds to understanding of relationships.

Reflection

How does knowing about developmental theory alter your understanding of relationships in your life?

A final observation we might make about developmental theories is that they seem especially capable of synthesizing and integrating a number of other theories into a holistic view of communication and relationships. The ability of developmental theory to integrate other theories gives it unusual power to describe, explain, and enhance understanding of developmental dynamics of relationships.

Summary

The three theories we've studied in this chapter offer distinct perspectives on communication and relationships. The most narrow and controversial theory is uncertainty reduction, which focuses on how uncertainty influences interpersonal communication and relational development.

A far broader yet also controversial theory is social exchange, which explains relational activities and evolution in terms of costs, rewards, and standards of evaluation. Although research generated by exchange theory has produced some interesting information about relational issues such as equity, the value of the theory itself is questioned by scholars who don't share the theory's assumption that humans are primarily rational, calculating animals whose primary goal in relationships is to maximize individual profit.

Developmental theories offer a third way of thinking about relationships. Emphasizing change and process, the developmental view aims to describe, explain, and increase understanding about alternative evolutionary paths that relationships follow. Although the first generation of developmental theorizing suffered from assuming that relational development is strictly linear and that stages are defined by external phenomena, these flaws in the theory have been corrected in the second generation of research.

Most current developmental theorists assume there are multiple possible paths of relational development. Further, most current theorists focus on subjective perceptions, schemata, and meanings to define moments in relational life. By drawing from other theories with compatible assumptions, developmental theory offers an unusually broad and rich view of the role of communication in the growth, maintenance, and deterioration of personal relationships.

Key Terms

axiom

comparison level (CL)

comparison level of alternatives (CL_{alt})

cost

developmental theory

equity

reward

social exchange theory

social penetration model

trajectory

turning point

uncertainty reduction theory

CHAPTER TEN

Theories About Communication Communities

In her 1990 novel, *Lucy*, Jamaica Kincaid tells the story of a young woman who is transplanted to urban America from the Caribbean island where she grew up. Lucy assumes the position of a nanny in the home of Mariah and Lewis, a white upper-class couple. In her role Lucy is privy to the intimate details and contexts of upper-class family life. At the same time, she is outside of them as "the girl." She is what's called an **outsider within**, a person who is inside a particular social group through daily interactions and activities but is also excluded from that group because she is defined as not "one of them."

From her position as an outsider within, Lucy notices luxuries that infuse the family's lifestyle. She observes not just material luxuries but luxuries born of always having known privilege. About Lewis, she sees that "everything was done for him" (p. 119). Of Mariah, she notes, "Things must have always gone her way . . . she has never had to doubt . . . the right thing always happens to her. . . . How does a person get to be that way?" (p. 26). Lucy notices that Mariah is one of those "people who knew the correct way to do things such as hold a teacup, put food on a fork and bring it to their mouth without making a mess on the front of their dress—they were the people responsible for the most misery" (pp. 98–99).

Mariah claims to be an environmentalist, and she belongs to an organization that is committed to preserving the countryside within which her country home is nestled. Lucy notices what Mariah and others in the land preservation organization do not: "connection between their comforts and the decline of the world that lay before them" (p. 72). Lucy also sees that Mariah carelessly and unthinkingly regards Lucy as a black servant girl, an identity that Lucy does not embrace for herself. Lucy recognizes and objects to Mariah's unquestioned acceptance of a history of cultural imperialism that has erased Lucy's own culture and given it to the colonizer to use. From her position as outsider within, Lucy sees and comes to criticize the thoughtlessness of privilege and the ease with which privileged people categorize her as Other.

At least since the time of George Herbert Mead (1934), whose symbolic interaction theory we discussed in Chapter 5, communication scholars have recognized the intricate connections between communication and culture. The relationships between the two are reciprocal and interactive: on the one hand, communication creates and sustains culture; on the other hand, communication reflects, or expresses, culture. In an ongoing cycle, communication creates, expresses, reproduces, and sometimes alters cultural life.

In recent years communication scholars, as well as scholars from other fields, have extended the notion of culture to include distinct groups within a single society. For instance, some Native Americans preserve their cultural traditions and practices even as they live within the broader American society. The fictional character Lucy gives us an introduction to theories that seek to describe, explain, and sometimes critique the ways in which communication is used to construct communities and to define the rights and opportunities of each community.

In this chapter we encounter three theories that focus on the ways in which communication both reflects and perpetuates particular cultures. The theories we will discuss concentrate on cultures within the United States, yet the basic perspectives they offer can be applied to communication in cultures around the world.

Communication and Culture

Before we discuss specific theories, let's consider the relationships between communication and culture. Communication creates, expresses, sustains, and alters cultural life. Your culture directly shapes how you communicate, teaching you whether it's polite to interrupt, how much eye contact is appropriate, whether individuality is desirable, and whether conflict is healthy.

Patterns of communication reflect cultural values and perspectives. Consider, for example, that many Asian languages include numerous words to describe particular relationships: my grandmother's brother, my father's uncle, my youngest son, my oldest daughter. This linguistic focus reflects the cultural emphasis on family relationships (Ferrante, 1995). The fact that there are fewer and less specific English words to describe kinship bonds reflects the lesser salience of familial relationships in Western culture.

Some Asian cultures also revere the elderly, and this too is reflected in language. "I will be 60 tomorrow" is a Korean saying that means "I have enough years to deserve respect." The Korean language makes fine distinctions among different ages, and any remark to another person must acknowledge the other's age (Ferrante, 1995). To say "I am going to school" in Korean, a teenager would say "hakkyo-eh gahndah" to a peer of the same age, "hakkyo-eh gah" to a parent, and "hakkyo-eh gahneh" to a grandparent (Park, 1979). In contrast, Western cultures tend to prize youth and to have positive words for youthfulness (*young in spirit, fresh*) and negative words for seniority (*has-been, over the hill, outdated, old-fashioned*).

Language also reflects cultural views of identity. Western cultures tend to emphasize individuals, whereas many Eastern cultures place greater emphasis on family and community. If I were a Korean, I would introduce myself as Wood Julia to communicate the greater value placed on familial identity than on personal identity. In the United States and many other Western societies, a person is regarded as an independent being who has an individual self that is separate from those of others. Thus, terms such as *individualism, autonomy*, and *independence* have positive connotations (Gaines, 1995; Wood & Duck, 1995a) in Western societies.

In contrast, the Korean word for individual, *kaein*, connotes selfishness and interest only in one's own concerns (Ferrante, 1995), which are strongly disapproved of in Korean society. Korean and American children learn their cultures' distinct attitudes toward individualism through a variety of communication practices. For instance, most Western parents provide a separate bed for each child. Korean babies often sleep with parents for several years, a practice that communicates that children are inseparable from their families.

The intimate relationship between communication and culture has inspired a number of theories. Of these, we will consider three. The broadest of the three is **standpoint theory**, which traces how distinct social groups within a society shape members' experiences, knowledge, and ways of interacting. **Speech community theory** offers a more specific analysis of how interaction with particular social groups shapes styles of communication that differ for women, men, and members of different ethnicities. Finally, we'll consider **organizational culture theory**, which illuminates the role of communication in creating and sustaining distinct cultures in organizational life. All three of these theories echo ideas we've explored in earlier chapters. In particular, you'll notice the influence of symbolic interactionism and narrative theory, both of which examine how communication creates meaning and coherence in social life.

Dating back to the early 1800s, standpoint theory claims that the social groups to which we belong powerfully shape what we experience and know as well as how we communicate. At the outset, it's important to note that standpoint theory focuses on the conditions that shape the lives of *social groups*. The theory does not focus on individuals' perceptions, values, and experiences. Instead, standpoint theory emphasizes the conditions that shape the lives—and therefore, the knowledge—of groups. We'll examine five central ideas in standpoint theory.

Locations in Cultural Life

Recall that symbolic interactionism claims that we are socialized into cultural meanings and values that predate any individual. Mead's quest was to understand how society "gets into individuals" so that members of a culture share common understandings, patterns, and values. Mead noted that there is a common social world, and his theory emphasizes the ways in which individuals come to understand and participate in that common world. Yet Mead also hinted that we are affected by membership in more specific social communities and groups. Standpoint theory extends Mead's ideas by highlighting multiple social groups within an overall society.

According to standpoint theorists (Collins, 1986, 1998; Haraway, 1988; Harding, 1991, 1998; Hartsock, 1983), a culture is not experienced identically by all of its members. Instead, cultures are hierarchically ordered so that different groups within them offer dissimilar power, opportunities, and experiences to members. Thus, this theory claims that the social, material, and symbolic circumstances of a social group shape the standpoints of members of that group.

Writing in 1807, the German philosopher Georg Wilhelm Friedrich Hegel provided an insightful analysis of how different positions in a society result in different perspectives on self, others, and social life. Hegel focused on the master–slave relationship to demonstrate the disparate standpoints that different social groups have regarding the "same" phenomena. Although slaves and masters participate in a common society, wrote Hegel, they do so from vastly different positions that affect what each group can and cannot see.

Hegel concluded that, because societies involve unequal power relationships, there can be no single perspective on social life. People perceive and understand society primarily as it is experienced from the perspectives of their social groups, and those perspectives are shaped by groups' locations in the culture as a whole. Thus all perspectives are partial in what they notice and emphasize as well as in the meanings they assign to social activities and identities.

Most societies have ways of defining groups and assigning disparate power to them. The universality of social hierarchies lends credence to Burke's claim that we are goaded by the hierarchy, or the need to create ranks. Among Native Americans and many Asian cultures, age is a primary factor in determining an individual's status. In the United States, social groups are organized along lines of race-ethnicity, socioeconomic class, gender, sexual orientation. Societies define distinct groups not only as different but as differentially worthy, valuable, or capable. Thus, arbitrarily created social groups are granted dissimilar rights, roles, and opportunities.

Standpoint

Standpoint arises out of the material, social, and symbolic conditions that shape a group's experiences. However, standpoint is not a birthright that comes automatically with being born into a particular group such as Hispanics or women. Instead, standpoint is an achievement—something that is accomplished only if someone who is born into a group engages in political struggle to understand and critically question the conditions that shape the group's life.

To achieve a standpoint, a person must become aware of and reflect on the conditions that define and shape a group's experiences. Consider a few examples. People who learn about cultural practices and ideology that devalue women and limit their opportunities may develop a feminist standpoint; people who do not become aware of discriminatory practices and ideology will not develop a feminist standpoint. African Americans who become conscious of America's history of racial discrimination and devaluation of blacks can develop a black standpoint; African Americans who are unaware of racism will not develop a black standpoint. If Lucy had simply accepted her position as "the girl who takes care of the children," she would not have developed a standpoint. To do so, she had to become aware of how others defined and categorized her, and she had to reflect critically on the awareness she had.

In recent years **critical race theory** has emerged as a significant extension of standpoint thinking (Crenshaw, Gotanda, Peller, & Thomas, 1996; West, 2001; Williams, 1992). Critical race theory examines how laws and legal institutions have constructed race. For instance, in the United States Irish immigrants and Jewish people once were not classified as

Standpoint Theory

"white." Today they are. At one point, blackness was defined by the "one drop rule," which specified that a person with a single drop of black blood was black. Both of those definitions have changed, which gives credence to critical race theorists' claim that race is socially constructed.

Critical race theorists use the idea that race is constructed to turn race into a critical perspective through which to examine and challenge cultural views of justice and fairness. For example, the practice of racial profiling is based on the unspoken assumption that people who are not white are more likely to break the law. Thus, some law enforcement officers are inclined to stop black or Hispanic drivers doing nothing different from white drivers.

Accompanying the emergence of critical race theory is **white studies**. It didn't take critical race theorists long to realize that whiteness is largely unquestioned in America. To be white is to be "without race" because the culture defines whiteness as the norm. When asked to describe themselves, most Hispanics, African Americans, and Asian Americans mention their race; most whites do not (Delgado & Stefancic, 1997). White studies invites us to engage in the same kind of critical, political struggle about the meaning of whiteness that we do about other races. People who do this may achieve a critical standpoint; people who do not will not.

Situated Knowledges

Donna Haraway (1988) coined the term **situated knowledges** to emphasize that knowledge is situated in social circumstances. For Haraway and other standpoint theorists, knowledge is not singular but plural. It refers to the overall ways of perceiving, experiencing, and knowing that are shaped by our social locations. Elaborating this idea, Susan Hekman (2000) says, "If there are multiple feminist standpoints, then there must be multiple truths and multiple realities" (p. 19).

A useful illustration of situated knowledge comes from the work of Sara Ruddick (1989). Concentrating on the activities of mothers, Ruddick argued that the practices of mothering cultivate "maternal thinking." Ruddick asserted that mothers develop values, priorities, understandings of others, and skills at nurturing that are specifically required to fulfill the role of mother. Ruddick distinguished between *maternal instinct* and *maternal thinking*. Maternal instinct is an innate capacity to mother. Departing from this viewpoint, Ruddick argued that maternal thinking is a learned capacity and that more women than men learn it because they tend to occupy different locations from men. If this claim is true, then we would expect that men in domestic situations and caregiving roles would also develop skill in maternal thinking.

In fact, research bears out this claim. In her study of men who are primary parents of young children, Barbara Risman (1989) found that men who are primary caregivers are more nurturing, attentive to others' needs, patient, and emotionally responsive than men in general and as much so as women in general. A separate investigation of men who care for elderly people also concluded that men in these caregiving roles become more nurturing, attentive, and interpersonally sensitive than men in general (Kaye & Applegate, 1990).

TRY IT OUT How has your social location shaped your thinking, skills, and orientations toward others? Which of the following statements describe you?

1. I am good at caring for others.
2. I like to argue for my ideas.
3. I would be unhappy if I couldn't afford my own home, car, and yearly vacations.
4. I am more comfortable eating at McDonalds than at fancy, expensive restaurants.
5. I think it's very important to sustain close ties with family throughout life. Living near family and getting together regularly are what I expect.

Now ask how your sex, ethnicity, and socioeconomic class have shaped your attitudes about the above activities and involvements. How do you think your attitudes would be different if you were of another race, ethnicity, and/or socioeconomic class?

The Accuracy of Different Standpoints

We've already noted that standpoint theory claims that a group's location in the social order shapes the standpoint of members. Consequently, there are multiple, sometimes contradictory perspectives on social life. Yet the theory doesn't regard different standpoints neutrally. Instead, it argues that some standpoints are more complete and thus more accurate than others.

Standpoint theorists maintain that groups in positions of lesser power in a society have more comprehensive, more accurate views of social life than groups that occupy higher positions in the social hierarchy. Sandra Harding (1991, p. 59) explains that there are two reasons for this. First, people with subordinate status have greater motivation to understand the perspectives of more powerful groups than vice versa. Economic security and survival, material comforts, and so forth depend on developing insight into the motives, expectations, values, and behavioral patterns of those who hold power (Puka, 1990; Wood, 1994d).

A second reason why members of subjugated groups may have fuller insight into the social order is that they have no personal investment in maintaining, much less justifying, the status quo. Groups that are advantaged by the prevailing system have a vested interest in not perceiving social inequities that benefit them at the expense of others.

Reflection

If all standpoints are incomplete, can some standpoints be less incomplete than others?

To understand why subordinated standpoints might be more complete and accurate, let's return to Hegel's analysis of the master–slave relationship. Because slaves have subordinate positions of power, their comfort and well-being and perhaps their survival depend on understanding the views, values, and even the moods of masters. No reciprocal understanding of slaves is required of masters who occupy dominant positions of power in the social order.

For the same reason, members of other subordinated groups are likely to develop keen skill in interpreting members of dominant groups. For example, children, prisoners, and women demonstrate greater skill in decoding and deciphering parents, guards, and men than vice versa (Janeway, 1971; Puka, 1990; Wood, 1994a,d). Muted group theory, which we consider in Chapter 12, elaborates this point by exploring how dominant groups control language and meanings.

The second reason for suspecting that members of dominant groups have less complete, more limited perspectives than members of subordinate groups is that the former are likely to want to preserve a system of power relations that benefits them. It is easier to sustain and justify an inequitable system if we don't recognize the harms it imposes on groups that aren't privileged.

Standpoint logic suggests that whites are less likely than people of color to recognize the continuing legacy of racism and discrimination and to support programs to equalize opportunities in education and the workplace. Because minorities have suffered historical injustices and the persisting consequences of these, they are more likely to perceive and denounce inequities and to see the need for and the justice of programs designed to reduce or eliminate inequality.

The Outsider Within

Within standpoint theory, the richest epistemological position is that of the outsider within. As the story of *Lucy* shows, someone who is both part of and removed from a particular group can see that group in ways that the insiders in the group cannot or will not. Speaking of her own life as a Caribbean black woman in America, Jamaica Kincaid said, "It's true that I noticed things that no one else seemed to notice. And I think only people who are outsiders can do this" (Perry, 1993, p. 130). But Kincaid is not only an outsider; she is also an insider. It is this double location that gives her fuller knowledge than is possible for someone who is only an outsider or only an insider. People who are outsiders within can understand the logic of a group from both that group's perspective and a perspective removed from the group. This enables double consciousness, which standpoint theorists think is more accurate than any single consciousness.

Standpoint's Relation to Communication

Standpoint theorists posit a reciprocal relationship between communication and standpoints. Consistent with Mead's analysis of socialization, standpoint theorists assume that we develop standpoints by communicating with others in our groups and by participating in society as a whole. Through communication with members of our groups, we learn the values, meanings, and ways of interpreting the world that are common to our groups. Through interaction in the broader society, we learn how it views our groups, and we can reflect critically on its views.

At the same time, standpoints influence how we communicate and how we interpret the communication of others. How we talk and the nonverbal behaviors in which we engage reflect the norms, meanings, and patterns of our social groups. Thus, some African Americans engage in braggadocio, which is bragging that isn't perceived as arrogant in their communities (Houston & Wood, 1996; Smitherman, 1977). For example, as Fred gets ready for a date with a new woman named Geneva, he might say to his roommate, "Man, am I a hunk. Geneva is one lucky woman to have the pleasure of stepping out with a dude as cool as I am." This form of verbal artistry is cultivated, practiced, and admired in some African-American communities. It is often misinterpreted as egotism by people outside those communities because they don't share the understandings of that group. Thus, standpoints also shape communication.

In sum, standpoint theory highlights social location as a primary influence on the experiences, opportunities, and understandings of group members. Further, standpoint theory maintains that the perspectives of subordinate groups are more complete and thus better than those of privileged groups in a society. Although standpoint logic doesn't deny individuality, it focuses on social groups as powerful influences on how we perceive and act in the world.

TONY AUTH, *The Philadelphia Inquirer.* Reprinted with permission of Universal Press Syndicate. All rights reserved.

Critical Assessment of Standpoint Theory

Two important reservations about standpoint theory have been voiced.

Theory Unjustifiably Privileges Marginalized Standpoints   The first reservation centers on the claim that some perspectives are better than others. Some critics ask whether it is reasonable to assert that any particular standpoint is superior to or more accurate than any other. Because the theory itself claims that all standpoints are necessarily incomplete, is there any justifiable basis for privileging one vision over another?

In response to this question, proponents of standpoint insist that there are degrees of incompleteness, and thus some standpoints are more limited and more incomplete than others (Harding, 1991). They insist that inequities are unlikely to be seen or corrected by those who benefit from them. Consequently, marginalized standpoints have the greatest potential to provide insight into how societies maintain unequal power relations between social groups.

Reflection

Does Lucy have a better understanding of Mariah's world than Mariah does, or are the two understandings only different?

Theory Obscures Human Diversity   A second criticism is that standpoint theory runs the risk of obscuring diversity within groups. Terms such as *African Americans, gays, European Americans, working class, men, women,* and so forth suggest a homogeneity among members of those groups. Yet we know that there are differences as well as commonalities among members of all groups. I have much in common with women who, like me, are European American, professional, heterosexual, and middle class. Yet I also differ from some of them. For instance, I am less socially conservative than some women in these groups, and I am more involved in my career than a number of them. I have more in common with several gay, lesbian, and African-American friends than I do with some individuals who share my own race and sexual orientation.

Does standpoint's emphasis on social groups obscure differences among members of groups? Todd Gitlin (1995) worries that it does. He says that standpoint insists on the universality of identities such as "women" or "Hispanics." Extending this criticism, Gitlin cautions that universalizing group identities can reinforce them rigidly, which encourages people to form enclaves with others like themselves and not to embrace what is common to all members of a society.

Emphasizing group identity also invites stereotyping that erases the distinctiveness of each member of a group. Emphasizing this point, Jamaica Kincaid resists labeling herself by her race or sex. She says, "Whatever I may say about being black, and Caribbean, and female when I'm sitting down at the typewriter, I am not that. So I think it's sort of limited and stupid to call anyone by these names. . . . My life is not a quota or an action to affirm an idea of equality. My life is my life" (Vorda, 1993, p. 83). Kincaid, then, is resisting group labels that could be used to erase any of the parts of her complex personal identity.

Standpoint theorists have responded to this criticism in three ways. First, they argue that the concept of social groups is politically and pragmatically useful (Blum & Press, 2002; Wood, 1993a). Most of the major reforms of discriminatory practices would not have been achieved had we been unable to speak about "women's issues" and "racial oppression." If we treat each person as an absolute individual unaffected by membership in any group, then we jeopardize the ability to prod legal and social changes that result in greater overall equality for all people in our society.

A second response to the criticism is that recognizing a range of social groups is a move away from viewing individuals in terms of membership in one particular group. The concept of *women*, for instance, lumps all women together regardless of differences in race, sexual orientation, socioeconomic status, and so forth. Yet the problems, opportunities, concerns, and experiences of poor women are not the same as those of upper-class women. Similarly, African-American and European-American men as groups have distinct pressures and prospects. Standpoint theory's attention to our participation in multiple social groups attenuates its tendencies to obscure differences among people within any specific group.

The third response made by standpoint theorists is that an emphasis on groups is not incompatible with recognition of diversity within groups (Blum & Press, 2002; Collins, 2000; Hallstein, 2000). It would be inaccurate to argue that people are defined only by what is common to their social groups, yet it would be equally inaccurate to suggest that our social groups don't shape who we are in important ways. Like other dialectical tensions, the contradiction between acknowledging differences among members of groups and also recognizing what is common to most members of particular social groups may generate new ways of thinking and organizing cultural life (Spelman, 1988; Wood, 1993c). For example, we might sustain the tension by remembering that all men are men and no man is only a man, all Native Americans are Native Americans and no Native American is only a Native American.

Reflection

Where would the idea of social locations fit within CMM's hierarchy of meanings?

In highlighting different and unequal social locations, standpoint theory usefully augments symbolic interactionism and other theories that imply that all of us participate in society in similar ways. Although scholars need to refine analysis of the dialectical tension between commonality and diversity, this theory has exciting potential to shed light on general differences in the values, understandings, and communication styles of different social groups.

Speech Communities

If you've ever felt that everyone but you understood what was going on in a conversation, then you understand the basis of speech community theory. This theory, which shares much of standpoint's logic, focuses specifically on how different social groups teach members distinct styles of communicating and interpreting the communication of others. This line of thinking, which is implicit in standpoint theory, emerges as the center of speech community theory.

Speech Community Theory

Nearly 60 years ago, philosopher Suzanne Langer introduced the idea of *discourse communities*. Like Mead, Langer saw language as the key to shared cultural life. She wrote that collective life is possible only when a group of people shares a symbol system and the meanings associated with it. Langer's early interest in the power of discourse to both create and sustain community recurred throughout her writings over the years (1953, 1979).

Building on Langer's ideas, scholars began to study the distinct communication patterns that reflect the circumstances of different groups and the values, understandings, experiences, and ways of perceiving that those circumstances invite and preclude. In 1962 Dell Hymes offered a first definition of **speech community**, based on his ethnographic studies. He defined a speech community as a group of people who share not only a common language but also understandings of rules and norms that guide how members of the group practice and interpret speech activities. Just a few years later William Labov (1972) offered a similar definition. He wrote that a speech community exists when a group of people understands goals and styles of communication in ways not shared by people outside of the group.

Hymes's (1974) anthropological studies led him to conclude that communication is understandable only within the cultural contexts that define the rules, meanings, and uses of communication. According to Gerry Philipsen (1997), a speech *code* is "a system of socially constructed symbols and meanings, premises, and rules pertaining to communicative conduct" (p. 126). In other words, members of a particular community have a speech code that they understand and people outside of their community don't.

If you recognize an echo of CMM theory here, you're thinking like a theorist. CMM claims that communication occurs within a hierarchy of meanings, the highest of which is cultural patterns. That's very similar to speech community theory's premise that the context of a social group shapes how members communicate and interpret others' communication.

Speech communities are not defined simply by language or membership in a distinct culture. It's easy to recognize dissimilar communication practices among Nepalese, Indian, and Western cultures. Distinct speech communities are less apparent when people in them rely on a common language yet use it in disparate ways and to achieve varying goals. Yet theorists maintain that speech communities are not defined by geography per se. Instead, as Labov and Hymes originally noted, they exist when members of a social group use language in ways and to achieve goals not shared by people outside of the group.

Larry Samovar and Richard Porter (2000) recognize a number of different speech communities within the United States. They analyze the distinctive communication rules and practices characteristic of gays, Native Americans, African Americans, Hispanics, people with disabilities, and women and men. To determine whether a speech community exists, we ask, "Are there communication patterns, practices, and understandings used by members of this group that are not understood and/or employed by people outside the group?"

Gerry Philipsen (1975, 1992) provides an interesting example of a speech community and an excellent ethnographic study. He spent three years doing an ethnographic study of blue-collar workers in Teamsterville, a name he gave to a multiethnic Chicago community. Within the Teamsterville community, speech is used to establish and display manhood and allegiance to the group. Thus, rules for talk in Teamsterville include using it to establish communal bonds with other members of the group and to assert loyalty to the group. Another rule in Teamsterville is not to engage in "sissy talk," which is the way the members believe you talk to women and children. The speech community in Teamsterville has distinctive rules for communication, and those rules create an identity for the men in the group. Philipsen's study highlights the importance of rules in identifying speech communities, and we turn now to that concept.

Rules of Communication

Theorists of speech communities seek to discover the genesis of distinct **communication rules** of different groups. Communication rules are regular patterns in the use and interpretation of communication within particular groups. Rules are socially constructed rather than determined by forces outside of humans. To identify communication rules, scholars study interaction in particular groups, especially among new members of the groups. This emphasis allows researchers to learn how children and newcomers to communities learn communication rules of specific groups.

A great deal of recent research has investigated masculine and feminine speech communities, so we'll use this line of study to illustrate how members of different communities learn and employ distinct communication rules. The classic study in this area was conducted by Daniel Maltz and Ruth Borker in 1982. Studying young children at play, Maltz and Borker first noticed that children usually play in sex-segregated groups. They also realized that the two sexes tend to prefer different sorts of games; many young girls favor games such as house, school, and jump rope, whereas boys typically play games such as war, football, and baseball.

If we look at the games typically favored by boys and girls, we can identify differences in their structures. Boys' games require large groups (nine players for baseball teams, eleven for football teams). Games such as house and school, however, require fewer players—two or three are sufficient for the game to work. Boys' games also tend to be competitive; the goal is to beat the other team. In contrast, girls' games typically tend to be cooperative, since all players have to get along and work out differences or the game can't continue.

A third difference in patterns of the games for the sexes is that boys' games typically have clear rules and goals. Definitions of legal and illegal

Theories About Communication Communities

passes, fouls, touchdowns, and so forth are stipulated by rules that are external to any particular players. There are not such clear-cut and external rules to structure typical girls' games. There's no touchdown in playing school, and there's no predefined rule for a foul in playing house. Rather than pursuing an instrumental end such as gaining points, girls seem to perceive the process of interaction and the development of relationships among players as primary goals. Thus, interaction is an end in itself, not a means to some other instrumental objective. The lack of external structure typical of girls' games explains why girls talk among themselves to organize their games and their relationships, whereas boys have less need to work out rules of their games through interpersonal communication.

Reflection

Think back on the games you played as a child. Can you identify the structure, goals, and degree of communication emphasized by these games?

Maltz and Borker's initial findings have been confirmed and extended by many other scholars (Aries, 1987; Beck, 1988; Clark, 1998; Inman, 1996; Johnson, F., 1996; Tannen, 1990; Wood & Inman, 1993). Figure 10.1 summarizes research, on gendered speech communities.

Misunderstandings

Speech community theory is particularly helpful in explaining misunderstandings that recurrently surface in communication between people of different social groups. For example, a common misunderstanding between women and men concerns what Tannen (1990) calls "troubles talk." Denise is upset because she just got back an exam on which her grade is a 65. When she gets together with her boyfriend, Glenn, she tells him that she feels stupid. Glenn responds by saying, "You just need to study harder for the next exam." Denise shrugs and says, "That's not the point. I really don't understand why I did so poorly. I thought I understood the material. Maybe I'm so stupid I don't even know what I do and don't understand." Glenn replies, "You should talk with your professor." In exasperation, Denise explodes, "I don't know why I even try to talk with you. You never care how I feel." Glenn is astonished by her comment because he thought he was being caring and supportive by offering solutions to her problem.

Speech community theory sheds light on the reasons that underlie the misunderstanding between Denise and Glenn. Operating from a feminine speech community, Denise uses communication to build a connection with Glenn and to express her feelings to him. By the rules of her community, Glenn should show support by inviting her to talk about her feelings and by caring that she feels stupid. Glenn, however, is following the

Figure 10.1

Rules of Gendered Speech Communities

Feminine Communication Rules	*Masculine Communication Rules*
Use communication to maintain relationships.	Use communication to assert yourself and your ideas.
Use talk to cooperate with others.	Use talk to compete with others.
Avoid criticizing or outdoing others.	Aim to outdo others in interaction.
Create equalities with others.	It's important to excel as an individual.
Support others by using talk to build connections and to show you understand how others feel.	Support others by using talk to accomplish instrumental goals—give advice, solve problems, and so on.
Include others in interaction; invite them to participate, and support their ideas and feelings.	Try to get and maintain the talk stage. Reroute topics to keep attention on yourself.
Speak tentatively so that others feel they can offer different points of view and ask questions about your ideas.	Speak with authority and confidence so that you appear in control and so that others don't question you.

rules of a masculine speech community, which tell him to do something concrete—to solve Denise's problem. Denise and Glenn, like many women and men, have different understandings of how to show support. They can improve their relationship by learning and adapting to each other's communication rules.

You've probably realized that speech community theory includes ideas we've encountered before. For example, CMM theorists would analyze the interaction between Denise and Glenn in terms of the different speech acts, episodes, autobiographies, and so forth in their respective hierarchies of meaning. Interactional theorists would focus on the relational level of meanings to point out that Glenn is not responding only to the content level meaning of Denise's communication; he is dealing with the specific problem of the bad grade on an exam. What he is not addressing is Denise's relational message ("I feel stupid") and her tacit request for reassurance from him ("Please tell me you don't think I'm stupid").

Troubles talk is just one example of situations in which communication between women and men is laced with misunderstandings that arise because of their socialization in distinct speech communities. Scholars have identified a number of communicative tensions between women and men in personal relationships (Beck, 1988; Hendrick & Hendrick, 1996; Tannen, 1990; Wood, 1994b,c, 1996b, 2000), as well as in professional interaction (Murphy & Zorn, 1996; Natalle, 1996; Tannen, 1994; Taylor & Conrad, 1992).

TRY IT OUT Observe interactions between women and men. You may focus on your own interactions and/or those of others you can observe. Can you identify tensions and misunderstandings that reflect the gendered speech communities into which many women and men are socialized?

1. How competitive are women and men in conversations? (Which group interrupts most often, invites others into interaction, shows interest in what others say, asserts their own ideas and personalities?)

2. How much do women and men emphasize individuals, and how much do they emphasize relationships? (Observe the frequency of terms such as *I, my, you, our,* and *we.*)

3. Are women and men similar in their focus on instrumental goals in communication? (Observe how much each sex proposes solutions, gives advice, and so on, and how much each focuses on feelings in conversations.)

From your observations, is speech community theory a useful way to understand and explain generalizable differences in women's and men's communication styles?

Critical Assessment of Speech Community Theory

Because speech community theory builds on and is consistent with the assumptions and claims of standpoint theory, it's not surprising that one criticism of it parallels a criticism leveled at standpoint theory. In addition, two other criticisms have been voiced.

Theory Obscures Human Diversity   Some scholars think that speech community theory focuses too much on differences between groups and too little on differences within groups. Concepts such as "women's speech communities" and "men's speech communities" may foster gender stereotypes and the misimpression that all women are alike and all men are alike.

This is less a criticism of academic scholarship than of popular works such as those by Deborah Tannen (1990) and John Gray (1992). Tannen's writing—unlike Gray's—is based on some research. Yet both Tannen and Gray portray all women as alike, all men as alike, and men and women as fundamentally different. Communication scholars have criticized both Tannen and Gray (Goldsmith & Fulfs, 1999; Wood, 2002) for stereotyping the sexes and glossing over differences among women and differences among men. In contrast to popular writers, scholars attempt to recognize both commonalities and differences among members of groups.

Theory Fosters Divisions Among Social Groups   An extension of this criticism is that emphasizing differences between social groups fuels

Speech Communities   225

divisions that harm individuals and collective society (Gilroy, 2001). Once we identify differences between women's and men's or blacks' and whites' styles of communicating, it's tempting to make comparative judgments about which style is better. Thus, we hear competing pronouncements about the quality and superiority of men's and women's communication and black and white speaking styles. Such claims and counterclaims do little to encourage respect for differences among people.

Scholars who endorse speech community theory respond to this criticism by pointing out that they have encouraged respect for and understanding of diverse styles of interaction (Tannen, 1990, 1994; Wood & Inman, 1993). If others use findings of difference to justify judgments of better and worse, say speech community theorists, that is not the fault of the theory. How adequate you consider that response to be depends on whether you hold a theory responsible for consequences—including consequences not intended or supported by the originators.

Reflection

Do you think a theory should be evaluated according to others' use and interpretation of findings, if others' uses are inconsistent with the theory itself?

Theory Is Insufficiently Critical   Ironically, a final criticism of speech community theory is that it isn't as evaluative as it should be. Some feminist critics charge that it is both wrong and politically naive to claim that the communication of different groups is equal. Such a claim, the critics argue, totally ignores marked and enduring inequalities between social groups. Senta Troemel-Ploetz (1991), a German communication scholar, argues that the difficulties women and men experience in conversations don't result from simple misunderstandings. She asserts that men know perfectly well what women want—understanding, for instance—but men don't choose to give it to women and don't have to because they hold greater power than women in society.

Responding to this criticism, some speech community theorists assert that assuming equality and urging equal respect for different communication styles are more likely to promote actual equality than belaboring inequalities between groups.

Organizational Culture

A third theory concerned with relationships between communication and culture focuses on the specific setting of the workplace. Studying professions, companies, labor groups, and institutional life, organizational cultural scholars describe and explain how communication creates, sustains, and expresses the values and ideology of particular work environments. As with standpoint and speech community theories, organizational culture theories assume a reciprocal relationship between cultures and communication in which each shapes and is shaped by the other.

Organizations as Cultures

Traditionally, studies of organizations have explored lines of authority, channels of communication, productivity, and so forth toward the goal of making organizations work better. That emphasis, although still alive and well in some arenas, has been largely replaced in the field of communication by a focus on organizational cultures in which the objective is to understand how organizational life is constituted through communication (Pacanowsky & O'Donnell-Trujillo, 1982, 1983).

The study of organizational culture was strongly influenced by the work of anthropologist Clifford Geertz (1973). At first glance the ideas of an anthropologist who studies Moroccan and Indonesian cultures don't seem relevant to organizations. As we shall see, however, Geertz's insights have opened up rich understandings of organizations as cultures.

Geertz perceived culture as systems of shared, or common, meaning. Like standpoint and speech community theorists, Geertz realized that cultures aren't homogeneous but honeycombed with different social groups. He claimed that cultures are ways of life that are sustained through stories, rituals, and other symbolic activities that continuously vitalize and uphold shared meanings among members.

Communication and Organizational Culture

Drawing on Geertz's general observations about cultural life, some communication scholars have developed a theory that views organizations as cultures that are produced and reproduced through communication activities among members of organizations (Anderson, 1988; Pacanowsky, 1989; Van Maanen & Barley, 1985). This perspective directs scholars' attention to how interactions define members of organizations and organize, coordinate, and normalize collective values, policies, practices, and goals. Theorists have identified a number of symbolic activities, or performances, that create and uphold organizational life. Of these, we will discuss vocabulary, stories, and rites and rituals, which are particularly important symbolic processes.

Vocabulary One symbolic dimension of organizations is **vocabulary**. Just as the language of an ethnic culture reflects and expresses its members' experiences and values, so does the language of an organization reflect and express the norms and ideology of the organization.

The military, for example, relies on verbal and nonverbal communication that continuously acknowledges rank ("Yes, sir," "salute," "chain of command"), which reflects the fact that status, respect, and privilege are tied to official rank. In a study of police, researchers noted the pervasiveness of derogatory descriptions of civilians. The officers routinely called them "creeps," "dirtbags," and "maggots" to emphasize the undesirable element with which police often deal (Pacanowsky & O'Donnell-Trujillo, 1983).

In some organizations there is a great deal of language that emphasizes interests and experiences more typical of men than women. Consider the number of phrases in the working world that are taken from sports (*home run, ballpark estimate, touchdown, develop a game plan, team player, starting lineup*), military life (*battle plan, mount a campaign, plan of attack, under fire, get the big guns, offensive strike*), and sexual activities (*hit on a person, screw someone, stick it to them, so-and-so has real balls*). Whether intentional or not, such language reflects men's experiences more than women's and serves to bind men together into a community in which many women may feel unwelcome and/or uncomfortable (Wood, 1994b).

Language in the workplace may also normalize sexist practices, including sexual harassment. From behaviors such as calling women "hon" and "sweetheart" to more egregiously sexualized comments about women's appearances, these language activities spotlight women's sexuality and obscure their professional abilities and status. Writing in 1992, Mary Strine analyzed the ways in which academic institutions define and describe sexual harassment in terms that make it seem normal and acceptable. Shereen Bingham (1994, 1996) and others (Taylor & Conrad, 1992; Wood, 1994c) have added to Strine's insights by documenting additional ways in which the idea of sexual harassment is normalized or resisted in the workplace. In related work, Carol Blair, Julie Brown, and Leslie Baxter (1994) demonstrated that norms of thought and speech in academic communities are used to marginalize women scholars and feminist research.

Stories   Organizational culture theory follows narrative theory's lead in assuming that humans are inveterate storytellers. Further, both groups of theorists assume that stories are coherent narratives that create meaning. Within the organizational context, Michael Pacanowsky and Nick O'Donnell-Trujillo (1983) identified three kinds of stories.

Corporate Stories   **Corporate stories** convey the values, style, and history of an organization. Just as families have favorite stories that are retold often, organizations have favorite stories that reflect their collective vision of themselves. Stories serve to socialize new members into the culture of an organization. When retold among veteran members of an organization, stories foster feelings of ties among members and vitalize organizational ideology. For example, both Levi Strauss and Microsoft pride themselves on their informal style of operation. New employees are regaled with narratives that emphasize the laid-back character of the companies—stories about casual dress, relaxed meetings, and nonbureaucratic methods of getting things done. These stories socialize new employees into the informal ideology of the firm.

Reflection

What stories does your school tell about itself? What did you hear from school leaders during orientation? What is highlighted in recruiting materials and catalogs?

Personal Stories   Members of organizations also tell stories about themselves. **Personal stories** are accounts that announce how people see themselves and how they wish to be seen by others. For example, if Sabra perceives herself as a supportive team player, she could simply tell new employees this by saying, "I am a supportive person who believes in teamwork." On the other hand, she could define her image by telling a story: "When I first came here, most folks were operating in isolation, and I thought a lot more could be accomplished if we learned to collaborate. After I'd been on staff for three months, I was assigned to work up a plan for downsizing our manufacturing department. Instead of just developing a plan on my own, I talked with several other managers, and then I met with people who worked in manufacturing to get their ideas. The plan we came up with reflected all of our insights and proposals." This narrative performance gives a concrete, coherent example of the personal image Sabra wishes to project.

Reflection

How important are content and relationship levels of meaning in personal stories?

Collegial Stories   **Collegial stories** offer an account of other members of the organization. "If you need help getting around the CEO, Jane's the one to see. Once when I couldn't finish a report by the deadline, Jane rearranged the CEO's calendar so that he thought the report wasn't due for another week." "Roberts is a real stickler for rules. Once when I took an extra 20 minutes on my lunch break, he reamed me out." "Pat trades on politics, not performance. Once Pat took several of the higher-ups out for lunch and golfed with them for the month before bonuses were decided." Whether positive or negative, collegial stories assert identities for others in an organization. They are an informal network, or rumor mill, that teaches new members of an organization how to get along with various other members of the culture.

Rites and Rituals   **Rites** and **rituals** are also symbolic practices that express and reproduce organizational cultures. Rites are dramatic, planned sets of activities that bring together aspects of cultural ideology into a single event. Harrison Trice and Janice Beyer (1984) identified six kinds of organizational rites (see Table 10.1).

Rites of passage are used to mark entry into different levels of organizations. Fraternity hazing, although recently under attack, was long used to initiate new pledges into the brotherhood. Engagement parties and baby showers are rites that acknowledge changes in individuals' identities and lives. Rites of integration serve to affirm and enhance the sense of community in an organization; examples are holiday parties, annual picnics, and graduation ceremonies at campuses.

Organizational cultures also include rites that perform the speech acts of blaming and praising. Rites of degradation are used to punish members of organizations and thus to proclaim the organization's disapproval of certain identities or activities. Firings and demotions are common degradation rites. The counterparts of degradation rites are enhancement rites, which shower praise and glory on individuals or teams who represent the organization's self-image. Campuses that value teaching, for instance, bestow awards on faculty who are inspirational teachers. Many sales companies give awards for productivity—most sales of the month, quarter, year. In my department, faculty meetings always open with announcements of the honors and achievements of individual faculty. This recognition rite gives each of us moments in the limelight.

Organizations also develop rites for managing change. Renewal rites aim to revitalize organizations. Training workshops and periodic retreats allow organizations to retool and revise their self-images. Organizations also develop ritualized ways of managing conflict between members. Conflict resolution rites are regularized methods of dealing with differences and discord. Examples are arbitration, collective bargaining, media-

Table 10.1

Examples of Organizational Rites

- Rites of Passage: Engagement party, retirement dinner
- Rites of Integration: Annual company picnic, department soccer games
- Rites of Degradation: Public censure, dishonorable discharge
- Rites of Enhancement: Promotion announcement, MVP award
- Renewal Rites: Annual retreat, retooling seminars
- Conflict Resolution Rites: Collective bargaining, secret ballot voting

tion, executive fiat, voting, and ignoring or denying problems. The conflict resolution rite that typifies an organization reflects the values of its overall culture.

Reflection

What different organizational values do you see reflected in the alternative methods of conflict resolution?

Rituals are forms of communication that occur regularly and that members of an organization perceive as familiar and routine parts of organizational life. Rites differ from rituals in that the latter don't necessarily bring together a number of aspects of organizational ideology into a single event; rather, rituals are repeated communication performances that express a particular value or role definition. Within organizations there are personal, task, and social rituals. Personal rituals are performances that individuals routinely engage in to define themselves. In their study of organizational cultures, Pacanowsky and O'Donnell-Trujillo (1983) noted that Lou Polito, the owner of a car company, opened all of the company's mail himself each day. Whenever possible, Mr. Polito hand-delivered mail to the divisions of his company to communicate his openness and his involvement with the day-to-day business.

Social rituals are standardized performances that affirm relationships among members of organizations. Graduate students in my department, for instance, routinely get together for beer each Friday afternoon. Tamar Katriel (1990) identified a social ritual of griping among Israelis. (Some of us who aren't Israelis might be familiar with this ritual!) *Kiturim*, the name Israelis give to their griping, most often occurs during Friday night social events called *mesibot kiturim*, which is translated as "gripe sessions." Unlike much Western griping, *kiturim* focuses on national issues, concerns, and problems rather than on personal complaints. Many Jewish families engage in ritualized *kvetching*, which is personal griping that aims to air personal frustrations but not necessarily to resolve them. The point of the ritual is to complain, not to feel better.

Task rituals are repeated activities that help members of an organization perform their jobs. For example, most organizations have forms and procedures that employees must follow to do various things. These forms and procedures regularize task performance in a manner consistent with the organization's view of itself and how it operates. In their study of a police unit, Pacanowsky and O'Donnell-Trujillo (1983) identified the routine that officers are trained to follow when they stop drivers for violations. The set of questions officers are taught to ask ("May I see your license, please? Do you know why I stopped you? Do you know how fast you were going?") allows them to size up traffic violators and decide whether to give them any breaks.

Thick Description

You will recall that we discussed ethnography in Chapter 6 when we examined performance ethnography. Ethnography as a method of learning about communication, however, is not confined to the realm of performance. It also informs research and theorizing in many other spheres of communication. Organizational culture theory has been built largely on ethnographic research that helps scholars extensively observe communication in organizations to discern what it means and what speech acts it performs within particular organizations.

Like ethnographers in other areas of study, organizational culture scholars rely on *thick description* (Denzin, 2001; Geertz, 1973), a term that calls attention to the method's emphasis on interpreting the intricately entwined layers of meaning that constitute organizational life. For Geertz and other cultural researchers, it isn't sufficient to gather data such as memos, statements of company policy, and statistics on who does what. Instead, the goal of research is to analyze and interpret the surface information (what Searle would call brute facts) in order to develop a coherent account of an organization's culture.

Because engaging in thick description requires learning about the details of daily rituals, rites, and other activities, it is extremely time consuming. Organizational culture researchers often spend months or even years observing, recording, and interpreting the raw data of organizational life in order to clarify central ideology and the communication activities that sustain it. Only by immersing themselves in an organization's day-to-day activities can researchers discover centrally important meanings embedded in cultural practices that create, uphold, and express the values and ideology of the organization.

The ideal role for the researcher is that of true participant, who can observe and understand an organization from the inside (Philipsen, 1992). To learn how police trainees are socialized into their profession,

John Van Maanen (1973) joined the rookie class at a police training academy. After that, he spent months riding in a police car with a novice and a veteran officer.

Reflection

How is participant observation similar to the outsider-within epistemological position advocated by standpoint theory?

Critical Assessment of Organizational Culture Theory

Response to organizational culture theory has been more positive than the response to many theories. Only one major reservation has been voiced. In addition, there is a debate about the appropriate uses of the theory. We'll discuss both.

Theory Has Limited Generalizability   Although few scholars question the validity of viewing organizations as cultures, some doubt the theoretical power of this viewpoint.

You'll recall from Chapter 2 that a traditional goal of research is to derive generalizations that describe, explain, and predict events. A major criticism of organizational culture theory is that it is incapable of doing this. Critics charge that this theory's commitment to thick description of individual organizations prevents it from generating findings that tell us much about organizations in general. This criticism extends beyond studies of organizational communication to call into question all inquiry that focuses on situated activity. Writing in 1994, Kristine Fitch warned that "approaching meaning as something that is radically localized, the product of individuals in single times and places, . . . seems to close off any possibility of understanding a *social* world" (p. 35).

At first glance, this criticism seems to pinpoint a weakness of the theory. Before we jump to this conclusion, however, let's inspect the charge more carefully. The claim is that case studies of individual organizations do not and cannot produce knowledge about organizations in general. That charge may be justified if we define knowledge as information about concrete aspects of organizations' cultures. Existing studies of many organizations don't identify generalizable task rituals, enhancement rites, or stories that are performed in most organizations.

On the other hand, studies of particular organizations do give us the generalizable knowledge that in most or all organizations members engage in rituals, rites, and storytelling. We have a generalization about forms of communication that seem common, if not universal, to organizational life. By analogy, we don't know the content of constructs that are salient in any individual's cognitive interpretations, but we do know with reasonable certainty that all individuals rely on constructs to interpret experiences.

Similarly, we don't know the constitutive and regulative rules any person uses to guide her or his communication, but we are relatively sure that all of us have constitutive and regulative rules. If you believe that generalizable knowledge about forms of communication is valuable, then you will probably not agree with this criticism of organizational culture theory.

Reflection

Is it sufficient for a theory to identify, describe, and explain forms of communication, or should it provide knowledge about the content of communication?

How Should Findings Be Used?   Finally, we want to consider a debate about the uses of research about organizational cultures. Organizational culture theory has been strongly influenced by anthropology, which has the goal of understanding various cultures. Anthropologists generally do not seek to control or change cultures, and few approve of efforts to use their research to alter cultural life.

Yet those who regard organizations as cultures often *do* wish to induce change—sometimes to benefit management's objectives, sometimes to improve work life for employees. The goal of changing organizational cultures obviously deviates from the purist anthropological posture. Whether that is appropriate, ethical, or valuable is a matter of current controversy.

Reflection

Do scholars have the right to prescribe and/or attempt to implement changes in organizations?

Whatever you think of this debate, it is clear that organizational culture theory offers a particularly powerful way of understanding the meanings at work in organizations and the ways in which those are affirmed, sustained, and sometimes altered through communication.

Summary

In this chapter we've focused on theories that emphasize reciprocal relationships between communication and culture. The broadest of these is standpoint theory, which extends symbolic interactionism by noting that a society is experienced not identically by everyone but differently by members of different social groups within it. Standpoint theory highlights how cultural definitions of social groups shape members' experiences, knowledge, identity, and opportunities.

Speech community theory is compatible with standpoint yet offers more particular attention to specific social groups. The central claim of this theory is that communication is a primary socializing process that teaches us how to see ourselves and others; it shapes our understandings of communication and how to use it in our relationships with others. Knowledge about disparate speech communities expands our awareness of human diversity and has the potential to improve our skills in communicating with people who differ from us.

In the third section of the chapter, we discussed organizational culture theory, which draws on the fundamental knowledge and methods of anthropology to gain insight into the ways in which communication activities produce, reproduce, and express meanings of particular organizations. Studies of organizational cultures have opened scholars' eyes to the importance of daily performances such as rituals and storytelling in upholding a coherent set of meanings and activities for people involved in collective enterprises.

Taken together, these three theories enlarge our understanding of the formative power of communication in constituting individual identity, social life, and organizational activities. In addition, these theories help us understand the communicative genesis of diversity in communication, meaning, identity, and social interaction.

Key Terms

collegial story

communication rules

corporate story

critical race theory

organizational culture theory

outsider within

personal story

rite

ritual

situated knowledges

speech community

speech community theory

standpoint

standpoint theory

vocabulary

white studies

CHAPTER ELEVEN

Theories of Mass Communication

_____1. What do you think is the chance that you will be involved in some form of violence during an average week?

A. 1 in 100

B. 10 in 100

C. 25 in 100

D. 1 in 200

_____2. On an annual basis, what percentage of crimes in the United States are violent crimes such as murder, rape, robbery, and assault?

A. 75%

B. 50%

C. 25%

D. 10%

_____3. On an average day, how much television do you watch?

A. none

B. 2 hours or less

C. 3–4 hours

D. more than 4 hours

The correct answer for questions 1 and 2 is D. The more television you watch, the more likely it is that you overestimated both the amount of violent crime in the United States and the probability that you personally will be a victim of violent crime. The theories we'll consider in this chapter should help you understand the relationships among media, our views of the world, and our attitudes, beliefs, opinions, and actions.

In this chapter we turn our attention to theories of **mass communication**. In our technological world, mass communication is a major source of information, companionship, and entertainment. Along with the news and the story line, mass media present views of human beings, cultural events, and social life. Mass communication is aimed at large audiences. Mass media include books, film, television, radio, computer programs and games, magazines, and other forms of visual and print communication. Mass communication does not include personal kinds of mediated interaction, such as communication with others on the Internet or participation in electronic bulletin boards and discussion groups.

In this chapter we'll consider two prominent theories of mass communication. We'll explore what they say about media's effects on our thinking and behavior and on our understanding of social life. Later, in Chapter 13, we'll discuss postmodern perspectives, which also have much to say about mass communication's impact on individual and collective life.

Technological Determinism

A Canadian academic trained in literary criticism seems an unlikely candidate to be a popular cultural guru. Marshall McLuhan, however, defied the odds to become a celebrity in the 1960s. Dubbed the "Oracle of the Electronic Age" and the "Prophet of the Media," McLuhan attracted a sizable following of laypeople and professionals in media industries. The causes of his popularity were both his bold proclamations about the media and his dynamic style of presenting ideas. No doubt McLuhan would be pleased that both style and substance gave rise to his stardom, since he coined the phrase "The medium is the message."

The theory Marshall McLuhan advanced has been called **technological determinism**. As with any deterministic theory, the basic claim is that some single cause or phenomenon determines other aspects of life. Biological determinism states that biology controls human life (remember Freud's dictum "Anatomy is destiny"), and Marxist theory asserts that economics is the central social dynamic that determines all aspects of life.

McLuhan saw media as the critical force that determined other things. The theory of technological determinism states that technology—

Figure 11.1
Media Epochs in Human History

Tribal Epoch		Literate Epoch		Print Epoch		Electronic Epoch
	2000 B.C.		A.D. 1450		A.D. 1850	

specifically, media—decisively shapes how individuals think, feel, and act and how societies organize themselves and operate.

Reflection

To what extent do you think deterministic theories are compatible with systems theories such as interactional theory?

Media History of Human Civilization

McLuhan claimed that the dominant media at any given time in a society determine the basis of social organization and collective life. To explain his ideas, McLuhan traced the history of human societies by identifying media that have emerged and dominated in particular eras. According to McLuhan (1962, 1964; McLuhan & Fiori, 1967), history can be divided into four distinct media epochs (see Figure 11.1).

The Tribal Epoch During the **tribal epoch**, the oral tradition reigned. Communication consisted of face-to-face interactions. Oral cultures were knitted together by stories that passed along the history and traditions of a culture, by the oral communication of information, and by oral rituals, performances, and forms of entertainment. Reliance on the spoken word for information and recreation made oral cultures highly cohesive communities. The tribal epoch's emphasis on morality made hearing a dominant sense (McLuhan, 1969).

Although most societies have moved beyond the tribal epoch, some largely preliterate groups remain. For example, the oral tradition thrives among the Hmong of Laos. Without books, the Hmong rely on face-to-face interaction. Within their culture, storytelling predominates, even in interpersonal interaction (Shuter, 1994). As McLuhan's theory states, the Hmong's reliance on the oral tradition makes them a highly interdependent and cohesive community.

The Literate Epoch Invention of the phonetic alphabet ushered in the **literate epoch**, in which common symbols allowed people to communicate without face-to-face interaction. The emergence of writing made it possible for individuals to gain information privately, isolated from others in their communities. Because written communication can be reread, this medium requires less memory than oral communication.

The alphabet also fostered ascendance of sight as a primary sense. For those who could read and write, sight replaced hearing as a dominant sense. Written forms of communication also established a linear form for communication. In writing, letter follows letter, word follows word, sentence follows sentence. According to McLuhan, the continuous, sequential order of written communication cultivated linear thinking and with that the development of disciplines such as mathematics that are based on linear logic. Diminished in prominence was the more fluid, weblike communication form typical of storytelling.

The Print Epoch Although invention of the alphabet made written communication possible, print did not immediately gain prominence as the preferred medium of communication in society. When the alphabet was first developed, monks and scribes laboriously copied individual books and other written materials. There was no way to mass-produce the written word. Thus, both reading and access to print media were restricted to the elite classes of society. The **print epoch** began when Johann Gutenberg invented the printing press. The printing press made it possible to print thousands of copies of a single book at a moderate cost. Thus, the printed word was no longer restricted to people with status and money; instead, it was increasingly accessible to all types and socioeconomic classes, making print a mainstream medium.

As with other evolutions in media, the printing press changed human life. Reliance on the visual sense was no longer restricted to the elite who had access to individually copied books and print matter. The capability to mass-produce printed material made visual perception dominant. In addition, mass-produced writing cultivated a homogeneity among people, as the same message could be delivered to many people. At the same time, widely available printed material further fostered fragmentation of communities, as people no longer needed to be together to share information and tell stories. Each woman and man could read a book, newspaper, or magazine in isolation from others. No longer was face-to-face contact necessary for gaining information (McLuhan & Fiori, 1967).

Reflection

What are the personal and social implications of media that allow people to separate from one another?

The Electronic Epoch The dominance of print as a medium and the eye as a primary sense organ diminished with the invention of the telegraph, which was the forerunner of the **electronic epoch** in human history. According to McLuhan (1969), electronic media revived the oral tradition and the preeminence of hearing and touch. The telegraph made it possible for people to communicate in individual, personal ways across great distances.

Technological Determinism

Do you agree with McLuhan's contention that electronic media bring people together into a "global village," or do you think electronic communication isolates people from each other?

The telegraph was only the first of a long line of electronic media that McLuhan believed resurrected community among people. We watch television and gain insight into what is happening in Rwanda or Afghanistan; we see a newscast and know what our president said and how he looked; we use modems to "talk" with people in other places, sometimes thousands of miles away. No longer are people separated from one another by distance. Instead, claimed McLuhan, the electronic epoch creates a "global village" (McLuhan & Fiori, 1967). McLuhan's media history of human civilization was the basis of his theory that the dominant media of an era determine the dominant human senses and the ways that humans organize their societies.

The Medium Is the Message/Massage

McLuhan's best-known idea is that "the medium is the message" (McLuhan & Fiori, 1967). For him, this phrase had multiple meanings. It implied, first, that the medium, or channel of communication, determines the substance of communication. In other words, although the content of communication is not irrelevant, it is less important than the form, or medium, of communication. For example, McLuhan argued that the act of watching television shapes how we think, regardless of what we watch on television (McLuhan & Fiori, 1967).

"The medium is the message" also had other meanings for McLuhan. By changing only one letter, the phrase is transformed into "The medium is the massage." This metaphor implies that media manipulate how we perceive ourselves, others, society, and the world. The media massage our consciousness and transform our perceptions. Finally, McLuhan sometimes made a play on the phrase by saying, "The medium is the mass-age," by which he meant that the dominant medium has become mass communication in our age.

To understand McLuhan's point, reflect on the changes brought about with the emergence of new media in each of the epochs we've just discussed. Humans adapt to their environments by developing sensory abilities that enhance their ability to survive and function. When listening and speaking were the only ways to convey information and survive, we developed keen oral and aural senses and prodigious memories. Once people could rely on printed matter for information and entertainment, sight supplanted hearing and speaking as the dominant sense, and memory became less important.

McLuhan died in 1980. Yet others (Levinson, 1999) have followed McLuhan's theory in thinking about how new technologies of communication are changing our ways of interacting and thinking. Jack Lule (1998), who teaches in the Department of Journalism and Communication at Lehigh University, predicts that "hypertext will encourage nonlinear narrative—blocks of text that readers pursue in the order they choose" (p. B8). Thus, the linear thinking that the print epoch introduced may not be the rule in an epoch of new technologies.

Lule is particularly wary of the expectation of immediacy that new technologies encourage. He notes that users of online news expect immediate, up-to-the-minute reporting, which jeopardizes the careful checking of facts and background information that affect accuracy. A dramatic example of exactly the danger that concerns Lule occurred on June 7, 1998, when CNN reported that the U.S. military had used a lethal nerve gas in Laos. *Time* magazine quickly repeated the report both in print and online. Shortly thereafter both *Time* and CNN had to retract the story because, when they had the time to check evidence, they found no support for the story. When reporters face deadlines every minute instead of every day, the probability of getting the facts right—of even getting them at all—is at risk.

TRY IT OUT Call to mind a recent experience in your life. Describe that experience using a pen and a sheet of paper. Next, share the experience with another person by talking face-to-face. Third, recount the experience to an acquaintance in an electronic mail message. How does the message change as you change the medium of conveying it? How does your sense of the message vary with the different media of transmission?

New technologies also promote **multitasking,** which is engaging in multiple tasks simultaneously or in overlapping and interactive ways. The Windows-based technology was designed to enable a user to do multiple tasks at once. As I type this chapter, the Office Assistant pops up occasionally to offer me formatting options; my email program lets me know when new messages have arrived; and my program alerts me when a diskette is full and asks me to stop what I'm doing and put in a new diskette or remove files from the present one. Joseph Urgo argues that, in the information-saturated, technological environment of today, human consciousness "becomes multicentered, chronically distracted to the point that distraction is its chief characteristic" (2000, p. 49).

Research on the impact of computer use on children's minds suggests that one effect is diminished capacity for sustained attention to any single topic or activity (Healy, 1990). It appears that the continuously shifting images and messages on computer games and other programs shape neural

Technological Determinism

maps so that we expect new images or stimulation frequently—so we learn to pay attention for only short spans of time.

A second way that computer use affects attention is through unequal stimulation of the two brain lobes. The right lobe of the brain is specialized in artistic activity, parallel processing, and visual and spatial tasks. The left lobe is specialized in sequential thought, abstraction, and analytic thinking. Because computers, especially computer games, are highly visual, they stimulate the right side of the brain (so does television). Highly visual and spatially oriented media such as computers powerfully stimulate the right side of the brain, encouraging it to develop. Conversely, because computers do not particularly simulate the left side of the brain, its development is not encouraged. Because the left side of the brain is specialized in sequential activities such as reading and math, children who use computers heavily may have difficulty with some academic subjects (Gross, 1996; Healy, 1990).

Multitasking extends beyond computers. People interrupt conversations or other activities to answer cell phones and check pagers. Drivers talk while navigating traffic. Students bring laptops to class, and, when not taking notes, they check email or work on other tasks. Families watch television during mealtimes. The buzz of call waiting prompts a person to suspend the present telephone conversation. Multitasking and interruptability seem to be emblematic of our era.

Hot and Cool Media

McLuhan drew a basic distinction between "hot" and "cool" media. **Hot media** are those that include relatively complete sensory data. Thus, a person doesn't need to fill in a lot of information to understand the message. For example, radio, printed material, photographs, and films are hot media because they require limited effort to interpret.

Cool media, on the other hand, demand involvement from individuals. A telephone conversation requires our participation, as do interactive computer games and face-to-face interactions. Lectures are hot, class discussions are cool; pop music is hot, rapping is cool; newspapers are hot, crossword puzzles are cool.

Hot and *cool* not only describe qualities of media but also correspond to different kinds of thinking. McLuhan believed that hot media encourage individuals to be passive. By supplying everything necessary for understanding, hot media allow us to be uninvolved in learning and thinking. Cool media, in contrast, require participation, involvement, and mental activity on our part. Cool media require imagination, effort, and emotional involvement, all of which McLuhan thought are healthy for individuals and society.

Critical Assessment of Technological Determinism

McLuhan was a highly controversial thinker, and his ideas continue to be debated vigorously today. Media industries applauded McLuhan's ideas, which isn't surprising, as he glamorized and popularized media. In academic circles, however, McLuhan has been less well received.

Lack of Empirical Support   One of the most common and most serious criticisms of McLuhan's theory is that convincing research has not been produced in support of his claims. A number of scholars think McLuhan promulgated fantastic claims and coined catchy phrases but didn't systematically test his ideas. When academics did test some of his ideas, they didn't find support for his claims (Baran & Davis, 1995). In a sharp denunciation of McLuhan's work, communication professor George Gordon (1982, p. 42) stated flatly, "Not one bit of *sustained and replicated* scientific evidence, inductive or deductive, has to date justified any one of McLuhan's most famous slogans, metaphors, or dicta." The lack of evidence to support McLuhan's theory led Gordon to brand his work "McLuhanacy" (Gordon, 1982).

Hyperbolic Speculation   McLuhan's ideas are frequently criticized for being wildly exaggerated and unproven (Baran & Davis, 1995). It is hyperbolic, assert critics, to proclaim the death of literacy when reading is still a major activity in developed countries. Likewise, it seems foolhardy to dismiss linear logic as inferior when it has given rise to many of the most important capabilities in the world.

Overly Deterministic   Another criticism is that McLuhan's theory is highly deterministic in asserting that human consciousness is determined by media. The idea that humans are passive victims of mass media is problematic for two reasons. First, believing that we are powerless to control media and its effects on us can become a self-fulfilling prophecy. If we believe our fate is determined by technology, we're unlikely to attempt to control technology and its consequences. Thus, we might yield the degree of control we could have.

Second, the claim that media determine both human consciousness and social life obscures the multiple complex variables that influence how we think as individuals and how we organize social life (Boulding, 1967). This objection to technological determinism has spurred the development of theories that assume audiences actively participate in constructing the meanings of mass communication (DeFleur & Ball-Rokeach, 1989; Kellner, 1995).

How did Marshall McLuhan respond to his critics? As you might suspect, he dismissed them with vintage McLuhan flamboyancy. Those critics, he sneered, are pedantic, left-brained academics who are able to conduct only detached, linear analyses of life. They can't appreciate imaginative, creative thinking about the "big picture." Contrasting those pedantic, left-brained academics with himself, McLuhan rather immodestly claimed that he was able to transcend linear, literary thinking and engage in more inventive, artistic, right-brained thought.

Although overstated and sloganistic, McLuhan's theory was valuable in stimulating interest in how media influence individual and collective life. Despite the excesses of his ideas and style, McLuhan contributed to both scholarly and popular awareness of the impact of media on cultural life. If he was mistaken in many details, he still may have been insightful about the big picture. Economist Kenneth Boulding (1967, p. 57) suggested that McLuhan might be like other creative thinkers in his tendency to "hit very large nails not quite on the head." Perhaps we shouldn't dismiss McLuhan's overall views just because his aim was a little off.

Cultivation Theory

In contrast to McLuhan's speculative, colorful ideas, a second theory of media has been built on a long-term program of empirical research. **Cultivation theory** claims that television cultivates, or promotes, a view of social reality that is inaccurate but that viewers nonetheless assume reflects real life. Beginning in 1967, George Gerbner and his colleagues at the Annenberg School of Communication in Pennsylvania systematically developed, tested, and refined cultivation theory (Gerbner, 1990; Gerbner, Gross, Morgan, & Signorielli, 1986; Signorielli & Morgan, 1990). By now there is a solid base of research for the claims made by scholars in this school, although there are also challenges to this research and the inferences drawn from it.

Cultivation theory emerged when Gerbner lent his scientific expertise to two national efforts to understand media's effects: the National Commission on the Causes and Prevention of Violence, which met in 1967 and 1968, and the Surgeon General's Scientific Advisory Committee on Television and Social Behavior, which conferred during the course of 1972. Both these councils were concerned with possible connections between televised violence and increases in actual violence and tolerance of it.

The genesis of cultivation theory in national studies of violence explains why the theory concentrates on the ways in which television cultivates attitudes and beliefs about violence and views of the world as a dangerous place.

Cultivation

Cultivation is the cumulative process by which television fosters beliefs about social reality. According to the theory, television portrays the world as more violent and dangerous than it really is. Thus, goes the reasoning, watching television promotes distorted views of life.

Reflection

To what extent do you think people assume television represents real life?

The word *cumulative* is important to understanding cultivation. Theorists in this school don't argue that a particular program has significant effects on what viewers believe. They do, however, claim that watching television over a long period of time has effects on viewers' beliefs and world views. By extension, the more television a person watches, the more distorted her or his ideas of life are likely to be. Simply put, the theory claims that television cumulatively cultivates a synthetic world view that heavy viewers are likely to assume represents reality.

To begin this chapter, I asked you to answer questions based on surveys used by cultivation theorists. Heavy television viewers are more likely to accept the world view portrayed by television, which is not equivalent to a world view based on empirical data. In television entertainment programming, 57% of all programs include some violence, and about two-thirds of characters engage in violence. In the real world, however, roughly 10% of reported crimes are violent, and the average person has a 1 in 200 chance of being involved in a violent crime during any given week (Choi, Massey, & Baran, 1988; Colvard, 1997; National Television Violence Study, 1996).

The world of television teems with violence. The Annenberg Public Policy center reports that 28% of children's shows include four or more acts of violence, and fully 75% of these programs do not carry the FV (fantasy violence) rating ("Value of Children's Shows," 1999). By age 6 the average child in the United States has watched 5,000 hours of television; by age 18 the average person has watched fully 19,000 hours of television. Most of those children watch television without parents present and without any rules for what they may view (Rideout, Foehr, Roberts, & Brodie, 1999). According to the *Statistical Abstract of the United* States (2000), each year the average person in America spends 3,297 hours engaged with media, and approximately half of that time is spent watching television—about 68 24-hour days each year. What happens during all the hours in

"*Would you mind talking to me for a while? I forgot my cell phone.*"

front of the television set? According to one researcher (Zuckerman, 1993), the average 18-year-old in the United States has viewed 200,000 separate acts of violence on television, including 40,000 murders. Given the prevalence of violence on television, it's no wonder many heavy viewers may think the world is more violent than it really is.

Why is violence so much greater on television than in real life? The answer varies with different kinds of programs. Violence in prime-time shows and cartoons may be used to increase interest and stimulation. Although most people in real life aren't shooting or mugging each other, many people find it dull to watch shows in which there is little action.

The high incidence of violence in news programming reflects, in part, the fact that the abnormal is more newsworthy than the normal. It's not exciting when people do not riot, but news shows gave extensive coverage to the Watts riots in August of 1991 and to the tumult that filled the streets following the jury's 1992 acquittal of the man accused of beating Rodney King (Mander, 1999). It isn't news that 99.9% of couples are either getting along or working out their problems in nonviolent ways; it *is* news when Nicole Brown Simpson is murdered. It isn't news that most immigrants and foreign nationals living in the United States support America; it *is* news when a few living in this country bomb the World Trade Center. Simply put, violence is news.

Theories of Mass Communication

Another reason for the inordinate violence shown on news programs is the breadth of coverage. Approximately 15 news items are presented in a 30-minute news program. When we subtract the time for the 25 to 30 different commercials in a half-hour news program, the total time for presenting news is closer to 23 minutes. Because so much information is presented so quickly, there is little analysis, depth, or reflection (Fallows, 1996; Kellner, 1995; Schiller, 1996).

In his book *Amusing Ourselves to Death*, cultural critic Neil Postman (1985) argued that the fast-and-furious format of news programming creates the overall impression that the world is unmanageable, beyond our control, and filled with danger and violence. Consequently, reports on crime and violence may do less to enhance understanding and informed response than to agitate, scare, and intimidate us.

Furthermore, we may not watch news critically or even attentively. In a study of college students' news-viewing habits, communication scholars Kevin Barnhurst and Ellen Wartella (1998) found that most students turned news programs on regularly but did not engage the programs actively. For the most part, students in this study treated news programs more as daily rituals and background experience than as foci of attention.

Reflection

Should news programs aim to represent real life accurately, or to selectively present what is news and thus, by definition, not typical of real life?

The Power of Synthetic Reality

Perhaps you think that few people confuse television with real life. Research, however, indicates that this may not be the case. Children's sex-role stereotypes seem directly related to the amount of commercial television (but not educational television) that they watch. Gerbner (2001) agrees. He claims that by age 6 a child's world view has been established by television.

In a comparison of communities that did not have television with ones that did, one researcher (Kimball, 1986) found that children who watched commercial television had notably more sex-stereotypical views of women and men than children who didn't watch commercial television. Further, when television was introduced into the communities that had not had it, children's sex-stereotypical attitudes increased. Research also shows that nonstereotypical portrayals of the sexes on television actually decrease viewers' sex stereotypes (Rosenwasser, Lingenfelter, & Harrington, 1989).

Media cultivate unrealistic ideas of what a normal relationship is. MTV programming strongly emphasizes eroticism and sublime sex, and people who watch a lot of MTV have been shown to have expectations for sexual perfectionism in their real-life relationships (Shapiro & Kroeger, 1991). Mass communication researchers Jeanne Steele and Jane Brown

T R Y   I T   O U T   Make a list of all of the news events (not sports reports or weather information) you recall from last night's news program (or the most recent news program you watched). How many specific news events do you recall? If you're like most people, you don't remember many of the events presented on television news, because they are presented so quickly and superficially that viewers seldom absorb or reflect on them.

What does this experience suggest to you about the newsworthiness of news programming?

(1995) reported that most of the young girls they interviewed "held an abiding faith in finding true love [and they] looked for and found reinforcement for a romantic myth in media" (p. 570). Steele and Brown concluded that "the romantic myth over time begins to seem real" (p. 570). Relatedly, people who read a lot of self-help books tend to have less realistic views of relationships than people who read few or no self-help guides.

Investigations have also shown that people who watch sexually violent MTV are more likely to regard sexual violence as normal in relationships, and this is true of female as well as male viewers (Dieter, 1989). (Notice that this is a finding of correlation, not causation.) If we believe that all relationship problems can be fixed, that sex can always be sublime, and that couples live happily ever after, then we're likely to be dissatisfied with real relationships that can't consistently live up to these synthesized images. If we believe violence is normal in intimate relationships, we may accept it— and its sometimes lethal consequences—in our own lives. Further, if we believe that the images broadcast by media are accurate, then we're likely to reject normal relationships in a futile quest for ones as perfect as those that exist on television but not in real life.

What accounts for television's ability to cultivate world views? Cultivation theorists identify two mechanisms to explain the cultivation process: **mainstreaming** and **resonance**.

Mainstreaming   Mainstreaming is television's ability to stabilize and homogenize views within a society. If television programs from Saturday morning cartoons to prime-time dramas feature extensive violence, then viewers may come to believe that violence is common. It's important to realize that heavy viewers are not necessarily the only people affected by televised versions of reality. As they interact with others, heavy viewers communicate their attitudes and thus affect the attitudes of others. In this way televised versions of life permeate the mainstream.

Describing the power of television to insinuate its views into the mainstream of cultural life, Gerbner and his colleagues (Gerbner et al., 1986, p. 18) stated that "television is a centralized system of storytelling. . . .

Television cultivates from infancy the very predispositions and preferences that used to be acquired from other primary sources. . . . [T]elevision has become the primary common source of socialization and everyday information (mostly in the form of entertainment) of an otherwise heterogeneous population."

Reflection

What connections do you perceive between the idea of mainstreaming and McLuhan's claim that electronic media are making us into a "global village"?

Resonance   The second explanation for television's capacity to cultivate world views is resonance, which is the extent to which something is congruent with personal experience. For instance, a person who has been robbed, assaulted, or raped is likely to identify with televised violence. In so doing, the viewer heightens the impact of the televised message by fortifying it with her or his own real experience. In other words, we participate in creating the drama and its impact on our own thoughts, feelings, attitudes, and actions.

Reflection

How is resonance related to narrative theory's concept of fidelity?

We should note that resonance and mainstreaming are explanations that Gerbner and his colleagues developed *after* discovering that heavy television viewers believe the world is more violent than do light viewers. Because these explanations were generated after data were gathered, they haven't been directly tested. Consequently, although research documents a relationship between heavy television viewing and beliefs about violence, we can't be sure that mainstreaming and resonance cause or explain the correlation. Other explanations are possible.

Reflection

Can you generate alternative explanations for the finding that heavy television viewers believe the world is more violent than light television viewers do?

Assumptions of Cultivation Theory

Now that we have a basic grasp of cultivation theory, we're ready to examine its assumptions. After more than two decades of research, Gerbner (1990) summarized cultivation theory by stating six key assumptions, or claims, that guide research and development of cultivation theory.

Television Is Unique   Perhaps you've been wondering why cultivation theory focuses exclusively on television in an age when there are many, many media. The reason is found in the theory's first assumption, which is that television is a unique medium of communication. Cultivation theorists believe that television is fundamentally different from other media in several ways. First, it is pervasive. In 1950, only 9% of households in the United States owned televisions. By 1991, 98.3% of Americans had at least one television in their home, and fully two-thirds of households had more than one set (Television Bureau of Advertising, 1991, p. 2). In 2001, over 99% of American households had at least one television (Potter, 2001). In the average home, a television set is on seven hours each day, making its potential influence pervasive.

Second, television is more available and affordable than many forms of mass communication. It doesn't require particular skills, such as literacy for reading or computer knowledge for touring the Internet and playing computer games. Television is also inexpensive. Other than the initial cost of the appliance and the minimal cost of electricity, television is free. Even with moderate fees for cable or satellite, television is affordable. The same cannot be said for going out to movies.

Third, television is uniquely accessible to all types of people at all stages of life. Individuals with mobility impairments can view television without the exertion required to go to a library or a theater. Children who are too young to go out on their own can be entertained by television, as can people whose health problems keep them homebound. Because no other medium of communication has all of these qualities, television is unique.

Television Forms the Cultural Mainstream   Cultivation theorists claim that television is the "central cultural arm" of U.S. society (Gerbner, 2001; Gerbner, Gross, Jackson-Beeck, Jeffries-Fox, & Signorielli, 1978, p. 178). Because it is uniquely accessible to most people, television is able to construct the **cultural mainstream**, or the general view of life in the society. In heavy viewers, this cultivates (mis)understandings based more on the synthetic images of television than on real life. Joshua Meyrowitz (1995) worries that, in presenting a synthetic vision of mainstream America that does not match the real lives of significant segments of society, "television has raised expectations without providing many new opportunities" (pp. 52–53).

To describe the process by which television achieves this, theorists identify "the three Bs": blurring, blending, and bending reality in ways that normalize a synthetic yet coherent world view. Explaining these, Gerbner (1990) noted that television blurs traditional distinctions in world views; blends diverse realities into a single, homogeneous mainstream view; and bends that mainstream view to serve the institutional interests of television's sponsors.

Television Cultivates Broad Assumptions About Life Rather Than Specific Attitudes and Opinions   This premise asserts that television is less influential in fostering specific beliefs and opinions than in shaping viewers' underlying assumptions about life and how it works (Gerbner, Gross, Morgan, & Signorielli, 1986). Obviously, the coherent, synthetic system of life portrayed on television may lead to specific attitudes about groups of people, levels of violence, and so forth. The focus of cultivation theory, however, is not specific opinions and attitudes but rather more general underlying ideas about the world.

The basic world view studied by cultivation theorists is exemplified in research on the **mean world syndrome**, which is the belief that the world is a dangerous place full of people who cannot be trusted and who are likely to harm us. Television represents the world as a mean and dangerous place in which everyone is at risk. In a study of over 2,000 children's programs aired between 1967 and 1985, Nancy Signorielli (1990) found that 71% of prime-time and 94% of weekend programs included acts of violence. On average, there were more than five acts of violence per hour of prime-time programming and six per hour of weekend programming.

Signorielli then surveyed people at five different times to discover their views of the world. Her findings indicate that heavy viewers are more likely than lighter viewers to see the world as a mean place and people as untrustworthy. This study is consistent with cultivation theory's claims. However, because Signorielli's finding is one of correlation, it doesn't directly support cultivation theory's causal claims about the effects of television on world views.

TRY IT OUT Following are statements adapted from the mean world index used in research. Ask 10 people whether they basically agree or disagree with each statement. Then ask respondents how much television they watch on an average day. Do your results seem to support the claim that television cultivates a mean world syndrome?

1. Most public officials are not interested in the plight of the average person.
2. Most people usually look out for themselves rather than trying to help others.
3. Most people will try to take advantage of you if they have a chance.
4. You can't be too careful in dealing with people.

Television Is a Medium of Conservative Socialization This fourth assumption is a logical extension of the first three. Here, as when we discussed criticisms of narrative theory, conservative doesn't refer to political positions or social values. Instead, it refers to the tendency to support and normalize established cultural practices and values.

Because television reaches so many people, it is a major socializing agent for members of a culture. Further, claim cultivation theorists, television is conservative because it reinforces existing social patterns and promotes resistance to change. In other words, television serves to normalize and preserve the status quo. One reason that television stabilizes social patterns is that the medium itself is highly repetitive, a quality that cultivates comfort with familiar, standard patterns (Gerbner et al., 1978). In this sense, television is ritualistic, relying on generic formulas to tell stories in news, drama, and comedy programs as well as in advertising. A second reason for television's conservative bias is that programming is controlled by a few large corporations that benefit from existing power relations in society (Fallows, 1996; Kellner, 1995; Potter, 2001).

The Observable Effects of Television on Culture Are Relatively Small

At first you might be surprised by this assumption, since cultivation theorists insist that television profoundly affects individuals and social life. To understand this proposition, consider the ice age metaphor (Gerbner, Gross, Morgan, & Signorielli, 1980, p. 14) used to explain it: "Just as an average temperature shift of a few degrees can lead to an ice age or the outcomes of elections can be determined by slight margins, so too can a relatively small but pervasive influence make a cultural difference. The 'size' of an 'effect' is far less critical than the direction of its steady contribution." Cultivation theorists assert that television's cumulative effect on cultural consciousness is significant, although specific effects may be small.

New Technologies Extend Television's Influence

The final proposition—one that was added to the theory in 1990—addresses the emergence of newer technologies. Gerbner (1990) believes that additional technologies will not diminish the impact of television as a medium but will actually reinforce and magnify it. Why might this be so?

To understand this claim, let's recall the first assumption made by cultivation theorists: that television is a unique medium. The same may be said of any new technologies that offer the same kind of accessibility, economy, and range of content to appeal to various groups of people. Videos that can be viewed in the home meet these criteria; thus, they extend the mainstreaming of the television medium. Interactive and convergent computer technologies are also becoming more accessible as computers become less expensive and competition among online companies drives down the cost of those services.

These six propositions sum up cultivation theory. In concert, they argue that television is a uniquely accessible medium that creates and mainstreams a synthetic view of the world that heavy viewers may come to accept as representing real life.

Critical Assessment of Cultivation Theory

Debate over cultivation theory has been intense and sometimes antagonistic. We'll consider four major criticisms of cultivation theory and discuss responses made by Gerbner and his colleagues.

Weak Support for the Theory One major criticism is that research has shown only a very weak relationship between television viewing, viewers' fear of violence, and belief that the world is a mean, dangerous place. Some critics assert that the demonstrated relationship is so slight that the theory should be dismissed. In a fiery assault, Paul Hirsch (1980) contended that cultivation theorists have selectively reported only results that support their claims and have obscured findings that are inconsistent with the theory. For example, Hirsch claimed that his own reanalysis of the data collected by Gerbner and his colleagues indicated that many nonviewers too believed the world was a dangerous, mean place and were fearful of violence.

Cultivation theorists dismissed Hirsch's charges, calling his reanalysis highly selective and certainly no basis for disregarding the cumulative results of a decade of careful research (Gerbner, 1981, p. 39). The validity of Hirsch's claims may become clearer if other researchers reanalyze data gathered by Gerbner and his colleagues.

Incompatibilities in the Theory A second criticism is that cultivation theory mixes incompatible frameworks, relying on the traditional tools of social science to explore decisively humanistic questions. Many conventional social scientists are uncomfortable with the fifth assumption of cultivation theory, which holds that the observable, measurable effects of television are relatively small. Traditional social science is built on the idea that the effects of phenomena can be observed and measured. Traditional social scientists are also disturbed by the lack of control in much cultivation research. Instead of observing viewers in carefully controlled laboratory settings, Gerbner and his colleagues have relied primarily on self-reports of viewing habits. People might deliberately or inadvertently misestimate how much they watch television.

We should also note that cultivation researchers haven't observed people watching television, so they haven't checked for influences of situational factors that might affect both viewing (for example, whether television is the focus or the background) and motivations (for example, whether fearful people watch more television). Thus, some social scientists think that cultivation theory is built on a shaky foundation of nonrigorous research.

Humanists, on the other hand, have a different complaint. From a staunch humanistic perspective, phenomena such as meaning, values, and beliefs resist precise scientific measurement. Ien Ang (1995, p. 211) explains that a focus on the amount of television viewing does not "give us insight into the more qualitative and more 'subjective' aspects of media consumption." Knowing that a person watches two, four, or six hours of television a day doesn't tell us what the programs *mean* to the person. Is the viewer equally engaged with each show? Does the viewer admire some characters, despise others, identify with still others? Does the viewer regard some characters as models for her or his own life?

A more serious concern for humanists is that cultivation theory presumes humans are powerless puppets of the media. Horace Newcomb (1978) argued that individuals have the capacity to defy the mainstreaming effect of television. They can, he insisted, resist, challenge, and redefine the intended messages of television. To assume that all viewers are taken in by the synthetic world view depicted on the tube is to reduce humans to non-human status. Other scholars (Ang, 1995; DeFleur & Ball-Rokeach, 1989; Kellner, 1995; Potter, 2001) also insist that it is naive to assume television is the singular cause of viewers' attitudes. They assert that there are very complex interactions among television, viewers, and society. If this is so, then a theory that concentrates only on a linear relationship between television viewing and attitudes is suspect.

People actively choose which television programs to watch. In addition, the characters and plots of entertainment shows and the reports on news programs interact with viewers' experiences, hopes, dreams, and fears. If this is true, then audiences are not consumers who submit mindlessly to media. Instead, they are actively involved in producing the meaning of what they watch. Supporting this view, Ang (1995, p. 214) argues that audiences "decode or interpret media texts in ways that are related to their social and cultural circumstances."

Reflection

Do viewers apply the criteria for narrative rationality to television? What does your answer imply about the active or passive nature of audiences?

Neglects Individual Variation   Newcomb's humanistic arguments are the basis for a third criticism. Cultivation theorists conceive "viewers" as a homogeneous group. Yet some critics of cultivation theory insist that people are diverse in their motives and world views as well as their specific attitudes and opinions. By extension, individuals apply their particular and highly diverse meanings to interpret television programming.

Cultivation theorists rely on very crude measures of both television (pure viewing time) and effects of television (mean world and violence indexes). These rough measures assume that all television is the same (and all violence presented on television is alike) and that all people interpret and respond to research questions in like manner. Critics argue that glossing over the range of meanings people attribute to the diverse communication transmitted by television reflects an inaccurate and inappropriate view of human nature.

Correlation Versus Cause; Cause Versus Effect   A final important challenge to cultivation theory is that it may be guilty of confusing correlation and cause on the one hand and cause and effect on the other hand.

Theories of Mass Communication

In Chapter 2 we distinguished between causation (one thing brings about another thing) and correlation (two things go together). Some scholars believe that cultivation theorists have confused cause with correlation in suggesting that television cultivates (causes) views of violence and a mean world. The two may go together (be correlated), argue critics, but this doesn't necessarily mean one strictly causes the other.

Cultivation research suggests that heavy viewing and fearful views of the world go together. Cultivation theorists have interpreted this finding as indicating that television causes fearfulness. However, the results could equally well be interpreted to indicate that people who are fearful are more likely to be heavy viewers of television. According to the alternative interpretation, belief that the world is mean, dangerous, and violent is a direct cause of heavy viewing. Which explanation is more accurate or more plausible? We don't know, and that's the point of this criticism: The research demonstrates only correlation, not causation. Claims for the mainstreaming, homogenizing power of television cannot be supported by correlational data.

A related criticism is that television viewing may be an effect of other causes rather than a primary cause in its own right. Even if research were to demonstrate that fearful views of the world follow television viewing (rather than vice versa), we could not be sure that television is the cause of those views. It's entirely possible that there is another factor or factors that cause both television watching and fearful views of the world. For example, perhaps physically frail and homebound people watch more television than more able-bodied people. Physical limitations may cause both feelings of fear (because they are more vulnerable than physically stronger individuals) and heavier television viewing (because that medium is most accessible to them).

Support for the idea of more basic causes of fearful attitudes was produced in a study by Anthony Doob and Glen Macdonald (1979). Studying four Toronto cities with distinct rates of crime, these researchers found that the empirical danger of neighborhoods accounted for nearly all of the variation in residents' fearfulness. In other words, the effect of television viewing was nil.

As you might suspect, Gerbner and his colleagues have responses to their critics. Rather than seeing cultivation theory as entailing incompatible assumptions, its proponents believe that their work marks a critical nexus of two formerly separate scholarly paradigms. It is a strength of the theory, they claim, that it can bring together heretofore disparate research traditions.

In response to the humanistic criticism that cultivation theory ignores humans' ability to produce meanings and to interpret images presented to them, Gerbner and his colleagues (1986) asserted that humans

Cultivation Theory

learn their meanings from the culture, of which television is a major part. They went on to claim that television is the mainstream that cultivates stable images for heavy viewers. If you accept the idea that television is a primary socializing agent of the culture (the second assumption of cultivation theory), then it is reasonable to assume that we learn meanings and patterns of interpretation from television.

Yet Gerbner's research group doesn't assume people are necessarily passive puppets of the media. In fact, Gerbner has led efforts to invigorate critical responses to media. In 1996 Gerbner founded the Cultural Environmental Movement, which is a coalition of more than 150 individuals and organizations from 15 countries who are committed to making media accountable to the public's voice. In an interview with Sara Kelly (1997), Gerbner spoke about the founding convention in March of 1996. He was particularly pleased by two concrete outcomes of the meeting: Delegates drafted "A Viewer's Declaration of Independence," which reclaims television viewers' rights to influence media, and "The People's Communication Charter," which is a program of 25 actions related to publishing, networking, and advertising. Gerbner's founding of the Cultural Environmental Movement is testimony to his belief that people can be active in responding to and shaping media and its influence on them.

In a further effort to democratize media and involve people actively in shaping it, Gerbner has made three videotapes that present his ideas and show why the findings of his research compel all of us to become active participants both in our individual responses to media and our collective efforts to chart its directions and impact (Media Education Foundation, 1994, 1997a,b).

Cultivation theorists have been less effective in refuting charges that they conflate correlation with causation and cause with effect. Gerbner's response to the study by Doob and Macdonald is that it supports cultivation theory by illustrating the resonance principle: People in dangerous neighborhoods find violence on television congruent with their personal experiences. This response, however, doesn't address the central finding that the effects of television were minimal once real-life circumstances were taken into account.

Cultivation theory has been badly battered by critics and research that challenge its basic claims. Even so, many people find it intuitively sensible that there are links between television viewing and world views, especially views of violence, meanness, and danger. We should also note that, even if cultivation theory is not completely correct in all of its claims, there is some evidence that television viewing is related to world views. Regardless of whether the relationship is causal or correlational, the connection is important. Whether cultivation theory is the best, or even an adequate, way of conceiving and studying those links is an open question.

Summary

In this chapter we've examined two theories of mass communication. In some respects the theories are distinct. Technological determinism claims that the dominant media of an epoch shape how we think, process information, and communicate. In contrast, cultivation theory focuses on ways in which the specific medium of television cultivates basic world views.

Another distinction between the theories is scope. Technological determinism is broadly concerned with any and all media that affect individual and collective sensory adaptation. McLuhan and those who accept his ideas want to understand the effects of various media on individual and social behavior. Cultivation theory, on the other hand, concentrates on television, a medium it regards as a uniquely influential socializing agent of the culture.

A third area of divergence is the impact the theories assume media have. For cultivation theorists, violence and beliefs in a mean world are key concerns. These theorists have focused exclusively on investigating relationships between television viewing and views of violence and the dangerousness of the world. Technological determinism, however, considers a broader range of consequences of media. Theorists in this school look at "the big picture" and advance sweeping claims about the power of media in many dimensions of cultural life.

These differences notwithstanding, there are also important similarities between cultivation theory and technological determinism. A key commonality is that both theories assume that media (or, in the case of cultivation theory, one particular medium) profoundly affect us as individuals and as a society. Thus, both theories assume that media are extremely powerful.

A second similarity between the theories is that both place greater emphasis on media, or channels, than on the content of communication. McLuhan concentrated on the ways in which particular media advance or foster development of different human senses, such as sight and hearing, and various forms of human thought, such as right- and left-brain specialization. Gerbner and his colleagues pursue similar lines of inquiry with their attention to the ways in which television shapes human consciousness and fundamental views of the social world.

A final similarity between the two theories is that both focus primarily on description and explanation. McLuhan described media epochs and explained how different media shape human sensory development. Cultivation theorists describe the mainstreaming effects of television and explain how television cultivates world views that, though inaccurate, are believed by heavy viewers. Thus, both of these theories are efforts to describe and explain how media operate.

Neither theory is centrally concerned with critical analysis of media and their effects. In different ways both theories emphasize the goals of explanation and prediction. For example, McLuhan and other technological determinists note the evolution of media and human sensory skills, but they offer no critical appraisal of the developments they find. Originally, research by Gerbner and his colleagues focused on describing and explaining television's influence on world views. As we saw, however, in recent years Gerbner has adopted a notably more critical perspective on media. As we noted in Chapter 2, not all theories pursue all goals. In examining a range of theories, we've seen examples of ones that focus on description and explanation (symbolic interactionism) and others that aim for social reform (standpoint theory). Whether or not you think mass communication theories should promote social reform reflects your own values and the theoretical priorities you endorse, as much as it does the character of cultivation theory or technological determinism.

If you are dissatisfied with theories that describe the status quo but fail to assess it critically, then you'll be interested in the next chapter. In it we will explore critical theories that seek to transform society from a brutal hierarchy in which some groups are oppressed into a more egalitarian world that respects a diversity of needs, heritages, experiences, and voices.

Key Terms

cool media

cultivation

cultivation theory

cultural mainstream

electronic epoch

hot media

literate epoch

mainstreaming

mass communication

mean world syndrome

multitasking

print epoch

resonance

technological determinism

tribal epoch

CHAPTER TWELVE

Critical Communication Theories

In the opening chapters of this book, we considered the goals of theory and noted that many **theories** share the goals of describing, explaining, and understanding or predicting phenomena. Only some theories, however, embrace the goal of reforming social life. **Critical theories** critique prevailing social practices that create or uphold disadvantage, inequity, and/or oppression.

Scholars are divided on the question of whether it is appropriate for theories to have strong and explicit motives of social reform. Many other conventional scholars insist that theories should be value free and that any ideological biases in theories inevitably compromise the search to discover constant truths and pure knowledge.

On the other side of the debate are critical scholars who proclaim that inevitably all theories and all theorists have values. For this group of scholars, the question is not whether a theory should have value commitments but whether theorists admit the values that inhere in and guide theories. Learning about theories that openly profess values and seek specific social changes should help you decide whether you think theories can be and should be value free. We've already encountered one example of critical theorizing. Performance as political action, which we discussed in Chapter 6, assumes that performances can and should do political work, including critique inequities and instigate social change.

In this chapter we will examine three other critical theories. The first, **feminist theories**, is a group of theories that focus on gender and its derivative, power. Second, we'll examine **muted group theory**, which claims that certain groups, such as women, have been silenced because

259

white men as a group have had the power to name the world. Finally, we'll look at **cultural studies theories**, another group of theories that aim to unmask the techniques by which privileged groups maintain their positions of power and control cultural ideologies. Although these three theories differ in notable respects, they are alike in their common focus on criticizing and resisting existing power relations that create inequities among social groups.

Feminist Theories

There are many definitions of feminism. The meanings assigned to the word range from stereotypes of man-hating, bra-burning radicals to men and women who recognize the equal value of all human beings and seek to diminish discrimination and oppression based on sex.

Reflection

How do you define feminism?

However you define feminism, you would probably agree that it is concerned with gender and gender inequities. That broad agreement would be shared by most who identify themselves as feminist scholars, although they do widely different kinds of research (Wood, 1995a). Feminist theories have roots in Western society at least as far back as the early 1800s, when some women first challenged prevailing social definitions of women. At that time, the central issues were the rights to vote, to own property, to participate in university education, and to engage in gainful employment (Davis, 1991).

Contemporary feminists address different issues. They are concerned that women don't yet have equal representation in the lawmaking institutions of society, equal respect and equal treatment in the classroom, equal opportunities for professional advancement, and equal pay for work. Most women in heterosexual relationships also don't have equal participation from their male partners in homemaking and child care (Godwin & Risman, 2001; Wood, 1994d). The continuing inequities between women and men in private and public life are the focus of feminist critical theories. To understand feminist theories, we'll examine their key concepts.

Gender

Many people who have not studied feminist scholarship mistakenly believe it concentrates on women and men. Although the sexes do receive attention from feminist scholars, they are not the focus of inquiry. Instead, **gender** is the primary concept in feminist work. Gender is a socially created system of values, identities, and activities that are prescribed for women and men. Unlike **sex**, which is biologically determined, gender is socially constructed. Unlike sex, which defines an individual characteristic, gender refers to socially produced meanings that are imposed on individuals but are not an innate property of individuals. Unlike sex, which is absolute and permanent (unless radical surgery is undergone), gender is fluid, variable across cultures and eras in a single culture, and subject to continual change (Wood, 2003).

Reflection

In the years since your parents were your age, how has gender (social views of and prescriptions for men and women) changed?

Feminist theorists note that gender refers to deeply ensconced social relations that define women and men and structure relationships between them. For example, the overall society expects men to be assertive and women to be deferential, men to be independent and women to be relationship oriented, men to be physically strong and women to be physically attractive, men to be sexually knowledgeable and active and women to be sexually innocent and discriminating, men to be emotionally controlled and women to be emotionally expressive. These broad social expectations exemplify the cultural character of gender.

Patriarchy

A second key concept in feminist theorizing is **patriarchy**. Literally, the term means "rule by the fathers." This denotative definition highlights the central idea that patriarchy is not about individual men and what they do and don't do. Instead, the concept is concerned with values, institutions, and practices that reflect the experiences, values, and interests of men as a group and protect their privileges while simultaneously denying, dismissing, and/or devaluing the experiences, values, and interests of women as a group. Patriarchy is an overall system of structures and practices that sustain inequities between the experiences, responsibilities, status, and opportunities of different social groups, especially women and men.

Contrary to popular belief, patriarchy does not refer to the views, values, or behaviors of individual men. Patriarchy, like gender, is a social system, not individuals or their behaviors, beliefs, and status. Thus, feminist criticisms of patriarchy and patriarchal values are not attacks against individual men; instead, they are indictments of a system that reflects the views and interests of men as a group. It is a system that was originally created by men who once dominated public life in Western culture. Whether men today would create the same social system that their forefathers did is an open question.

"I'm tired of this full-time job. I want a part-time job."

A Patriarchal Universe of Discourse

Patriarchal systems are sustained in large measure by a patriarchal universe of discourse. Stephen Littlejohn (1992, p. 243) explains that a universe of discourse is "a set of language conventions that reflect a particular definition of reality." Symbolic interaction theory (Chapter 5) claims that language is a key to meaning, because we learn a society's meanings and values in the course of interacting with others. Thus, the universe of discourse that prevails at any moment in the life of a culture shapes the understandings of all who participate in that universe of discourse.

Historically and today, Western culture has been dominated by a masculine universe of discourse that accords priority to masculine experiences, values, and interests. For example, the prevailing universe of discourse reflects the assumption that women should assume primary care for homes and children, regardless of whether women work in the paid labor force as much as men. We're all familiar with terms such as *housewife*, *mothering*, and *maternal instinct*. But we have few parallel words to describe men's participation in family life: words like *househusband*, *fathering*, and *paternal instinct* are not part of social vocabulary. We hear about the "mommy track" in businesses, but there is no equivalent "daddy track," as it is not generally assumed that fathers will be primary caregivers of their children.

Feminist theorists, like many other communication theorists we've studied, believe that language powerfully shapes our views of the world.

Consequently, a patriarchal universe of discourse encourages us to perceive the world from a decidedly masculine point of view.

TRY IT OUT Is our language biased toward masculine perspectives and interests? Consider the following common terms and sayings, and decide for yourself whether women's experiences and identities are equally captured in the prevailing universe of discourse.

1. Man and wife
2. She kept her name.
3. I have a female lawyer.
4. Successful professionals have a competitive instinct.
5. Man-on-the-street interview
6. Freshman
7. Headline: "Feisty blonde wins election."
8. Mankind
9. Everyone should cast his vote this November.
10. Mrs. Aaron Berkfield

Multiple Ways of Knowing

Most feminist theorists believe there are multiple ways of perceiving the world and that no one way is absolutely true or best. This is consistent with standpoint theory's emphasis on situated knowledges, which are the diverse ways of knowing that people develop in response to the particular circumstances of their lives. A good deal of research in recent years has focused on identifying feminine ways of knowing, experiencing, and acting.

The emphasis on feminine ways without equal attention to masculine ways reflects the fact that masculine ways are already well codified into the prevailing universe of discourse and the perceptions of reality it invites. Drawing on standpoint theory, which we discussed in Chapter 10, feminist theorists point out that women and men are typically socialized in sex-segregated groups that shape how they communicate and experience life. Existing research suggests that women generally are interdependent, concerned with relationships, cooperative, egalitarian, and at least as interested in process as in outcomes. Masculine orientations, in comparison, emphasize independence, competition, control, and outcome over process (Foss, Foss, & Trapp, 2001; Gilligan, 1982; Wood, 1986, 1993a,c, 1995a, 1996a,b, 1998b,c, 2000, 2003).

Here's where the critical impulse shows up in feminist theory: Although both feminine and masculine perspectives exist, the masculine are more valued. "Women's work" is routinely devalued in Western culture, and homemaking and child care have lower status than jobs in the public sphere. Within a patriarchal universe of discourse, women's interdependence and concern for relationships are viewed as a lack of independence, not a choice for relatedness; women's willingness to nurture children and others who need help is admired less than is earning a high income; women's cooperativeness and efforts to achieve equality are recast as fear of success and lack of competitive instinct. In each case, women's ways are judged against a masculine standard rather than recognized and evaluated on their own terms.

If we operated within a matriarchal universe of discourse, we'd be more likely to disparage men who focused on jobs to the neglect of family life, and we'd criticize men for lacking a cooperative instinct and for being too insecure to enter into interdependence with others. The oddity of phrases such as "He lacks a cooperative instinct" and "He's too independent" is good evidence that a patriarchal universe of discourse prevails in our society.

Most feminists don't want to eliminate masculine meanings and values. Nor do they aim to invert the existing hierarchy so that masculine experiences and interests are subordinated to feminine ones. Instead, most feminist scholarship aims to diminish the gendered inequities in cultural life. It's not sufficient to document inequities, for that alone doesn't change them. It's not even enough to criticize practices and structures that marginalize women and their experiences. Description and critique are only starting points in the larger attempt to restructure the social world so that it recognizes and accords equal value to all who participate in it.

Sonja Foss, Karen Foss, and Robert Trapp (2001) state that feminist theorizing proceeds in two stages. First, there is an **inclusion stage**, in which scholars attempt to increase awareness of women's contributions, experiences, values, and modes of communication and to raise awareness of inequality between women and men. For example, one line of feminist inquiry documented differences in how women and men tend to learn and participate in classrooms (Hall, with Sandler, 1982; Sadker & Sadker, 1986; Treichler & Kramarae, 1983). Over time, feminist scholars showed that feminine styles of communication are devalued in many classrooms and that women students are taken less seriously than their male peers. Increasing awareness of inequities is a necessary foundation for the second stage of feminist theorizing.

In the second stage, feminists work to revise the prevailing universe of discourse so that it includes women's meanings, experiences, and interests alongside those of other social groups. Feminist scholars interested in education have proposed specific teaching strategies and styles to render education equally hospitable to women and men (Wood, 1993a; Wood &

Critical Communication Theories

Lenze, 1991a,b). During the **revisionist stage** of theorizing, feminist scholars might attempt to broaden views of significant communication beyond public speaking to include the kinds of communication activities in which women have traditionally participated, to enlarge perspectives on professional communication to incorporate cooperation and attention to relationships, and to confer value on homemaking and nurturing that is equivalent to the value accorded to earning money.

Reflection

How would you go about revising the prevailing universe of discourse? Would you focus on language in private settings, the public arena, or both?

Ideas developed in the revisionist stage have theoretical importance. By identifying existing theories' failure to account for the full range of human communication (that of women as well as men), revisionist research reveals that the theories are incomplete. In turn, this paves the way for developing theories that describe, explain, and shed light on a more complete scope of human communication. Including women's communication styles and contexts in theories also serves the heuristic value of enlarging awareness of communication goals and practices that are not visible within theories that are limited to contexts and forms more typical of men than women.

In sum, feminist theory is actually a group of related theories concerned with gender, power, and inequities. Feminist communication theorists focus especially on language as a means by which masculine perspectives, experiences, and interests are privileged while feminine perspectives, experiences, and interests are marginalized. A long-term goal of feminist theorizing is to impel changes that will yield a more equitable society for everyone.

Critical Assessment of Feminist Theories

Feminist theories are indisputably gaining stature and influence in the academic and social world. Despite the ascension of feminist thought, the theories have received some criticism.

Fosters Divisions Between Women and Men
One criticism of feminist theory is that its focus on binary oppositions between the sexes has the potential to reify and reinforce differences between women and men. Linda Putnam (1982), who supports feminist goals, questions the value of concentrating on masculine/feminine, male/female dichotomies. Putnam points out that such a focus oversimplifies human life by emphasizing gender to the virtual exclusion of many other influences on how people think, act, and communicate. Further, it is possible that intense attention to general differences between men and women obscures both similarities among the sexes and diversity within each sex (Wood, 1993c).

To this criticism, some feminist scholars respond that it is necessary to emphasize gender differences in the short term to get beyond them in the long term. Until we fully recognize gendered disparities in social life, we cannot possibly reach a point where gender isn't an issue. Further, note some feminist scholars, a key criterion for evaluating a theory is whether it accurately and adequately describes phenomena. In pointing out gender inequities in social life in general and in communication in particular, feminist theorists assert that they are accurately describing existing inequities between women and men.

It's also worthwhile to note that the third wave of the feminist movement directly resists and works against divisions between women and men. The third wave of feminism affirms relationships between women and men and seeks to improve them by involving both sexes in creating changes that enrich life in both the private and public realms (Heywood & Drake, 1997; Howry & Wood, 2001; Stoller & Karp, 1999). The third wave is also committed to escaping other binary divisions, such as those between white women and women of color, straight and lesbian women, and so forth (Bailey, 1997).

Overstates and Distorts Gender Differences   A second and more serious criticism of feminist work is that it has exaggerated differences between the sexes. Daniel Canary and Kimberly Hause (1993) and Kathryn Dindia (Wood & Dindia, 1998), for example, claim that sex differences in social action are actually very small and not consistent across contexts. Other communication scholars maintain that women and men differ very little in self-disclosure (Dindia & Allen, 1992), tendency to help others (Eagly & Crowley, 1986), and leadership (Eagly & Karau, 1991). If these claims are true—if women and men really do differ very little—then feminist theory is inaccurate in its claims and misdirected in its goals.

Not all scholars, however, agree that gender differences are as minor as critics of feminist work suggest. Sharon Brehm (1992), who has devoted a long career to studying intimate relationships, maintains that gender is probably the single greatest influence on personal relationships. Supporting Brehm's claim are numerous studies that report definite differences in how women and men view conflict and aggression (Campbell, 1993), relationship crises (Wood, 1986, 1994c), demonstrations of love (Wood, 1996b, 1998b; Wood & Inman, 1993), and appropriate styles of interacting in work contexts (Murphy & Zorn, 1996).

Counselors agree that gendered dynamics operate in relationships and that relationships cannot be understood without recognizing differences in how women and men think, feel, and communicate (Beck, 1988; Gottman & Carrère, 1994; Walsh, 1993). Thus, at present scholars disagree about whether gender differences are real and important. To decide for yourself, you might review your own experiences and read some of the studies that have been conducted.

A Monolithic View of Women   A final criticism of feminist theory is that it has treated women as a monolithic category, which means it has treated them as all alike. To be more specific, critics charge that feminist theories have centered women who are white, middle-class, heterosexual, and able bodied and thus have marginalized and neglected women who do not fit this description.

This criticism had legitimacy 20, perhaps even 10 years ago. The second wave of U.S. feminism certainly focused its political, social, and intellectual energies on fairly privileged white, heterosexual women (Allen, 1999). This focus was the subject of much debate within mainstream feminism and even more criticism from those not in the mainstream of the movement. Yet second-wave feminists heeded the criticism that the movement focused too much on white, middle-class women. As a result, contemporary feminism recognizes that gender does not have a universal meaning. What gender means is shaped by diverse cultures, economic circumstances, sexual orientations, and so forth (Anzaldúa, 1999; Collins, 1998).

Before leaving this discussion of feminist theory, we should note that feminist theorizing is not isolated from other intellectual currents. In fact, feminist work increasingly intersects with other lines of research and theory in the humanities and social sciences (Wood, 1995a). This allows feminist scholars both to draw from and to contribute to the larger body of knowledge that makes up understandings of the world.

Muted Group Theory

Muted group theory is often classified as a feminist theory because it shares many of the concerns of feminist theories in general. Yet this theory deserves separate attention because of two of its distinctive features: (1) a focus on how language names experiences and therefore determines what is socially recognized; and (2) close attention to the way that a dominant discourse silences, or mutes, groups that are not in a society's mainstream.

Muted group theory claims that the masculine bias of Western society has silenced and marginalized women's experiences. Let's consider the concepts and research that have shaped this theory.

Masculine Bias

Anthropologists Edwin Ardener and Shirley Ardener first advanced the theory that women's experiences have been muted by masculine bias—a set of biases that favor masculine perspectives and experiences. After reviewing a large number of studies of cultures, Edwin Ardener (1975) observed that anthropologists tend to be biased toward men's perspectives. He observed that many anthropological investigations relied entirely on interviews with males to describe and understand how a culture works. Other anthropologists didn't dispute the charge that they relied on males to understand a culture. They did, however, justify this bias by explaining that women are more difficult to interview because they focus a good deal on emotions, relationships, and other topics that were not of great interest to anthropologists looking for the objective facts of a culture.

Ardener agreed that women do provide perspectives and information beyond the "scientific data" anthropologists typically seek. However, he noted, women's perceptions and perspectives are as rooted in their culture as are those of men. Ardener cautioned that we should be skeptical of any description of a culture that is based on the views of only half of its members (E. Ardener, 1975).

As Edwin Ardener continued to examine this issue, he concluded that the masculine bias in anthropological research was deeper than he had first realized. Not only are men the ones consulted about cultural life, but also the very language of cultures has a masculine bias. Ardener reasoned that this is because males generally dominate public life and consequently create the language and meanings of a culture.

Muted Language/Muted Experience

Working with her colleague and husband, Shirley Ardener (1978) extended the original insights about discrimination in anthropological research by tracing the implications of a masculine bias in language. She pointed out that when words and their meanings do not reflect the experiences of some groups, members of those groups are constrained in their ability to express themselves. How can people describe or fully know an experience for which there is no name?

Shirley Ardener noted that women are not always silent, but they tend to be less comfortable expressing themselves in certain contexts. Because the public sphere has been predominantly populated by men, many women hesitate to participate in public discourse.

Reflection

In your experience, how articulate are women and men in private settings and public ones?

Adding to muted group theory is Cheris Kramarae's (1981) observation that Western society remains divided into public and private spheres that are occupied, respectively, by men and women. Because women and men have participated primarily in different spheres of social life, they have distinct experiences. Yet, men's experiences and priorities prevail because they have created language, and they have done so from the perspective of their experiences—ones that in some ways are distinct from those of

Critical Communication Theories

women as a group. If language reflects masculine experiences and interests, then it gives only partial insight into a culture.

It's important to understand that not all muted group theorists assume that men have deliberately conspired to silence women. A majority of scholars don't assert that men have intentionally named the world from their perspectives and deliberately obscured women's experiences and perspectives (for an exception, see Spender, 1984a,b).

What the theory argues is that we all tend to see the world in terms of our own perspectives, experiences, and interests. Consequently, we are inclined to develop a vocabulary to represent what we know and consider significant and to be unaware of all that we don't name because it is unfamiliar and unimportant to us. Although the masculine bias in language may not be an intentional effort to mute feminine experiences, that is nevertheless the effect when one half of a society creates a language to describe the life of all members of the society.

The Power to Name

Dale Spender (1984a,b), an Australian communication scholar, added to muted group theory by highlighting the power of naming. To illustrate the ways in which language can mute experience, Spender used the example of childbirth. Giving birth, she pointed out, is described from a male point of view that emphasizes the joy and beauty of the experience. Although Spender agreed that childbirth is a miraculous and joyous experience, she observed that it also can be an intensely painful one. Because men have not undergone the physical pain of giving birth, the painfulness of childbirth is not encoded into the language used to describe the experience.

Reflection

Have you had experiences, feelings, or ideas for which there is no name in our language?

For the Ardeners and for Spender, the power to name experiences is equivalent to the power to construct reality. Those who name the world have the privilege of highlighting their experiences and what they consider important by naming them, and the privilege of erasing experiences they do not know or consider important by not naming those. Consequently, groups that have marginal status in cultural life are denied a vocabulary to define and express their experiences.

A clear example of the power of naming is recent recognition of sexual harassment. Prior to the 1970s, the term *sexual harassment* was not used. Thousands of women, perhaps more, endured unwelcome and inappropriate conduct of a sexual nature in the workplace and in educational institutions, but our language included no term to describe what happened to them. Without words to highlight the abuse, degradation, humiliation, and

TRY IT OUT If you are fluent in more than one language, identify words in the non-English language that are not found in English (for example, the French language has no word for *teenager*). How is the ability to think about ideas, feelings, and experiences limited by the lack of certain words in English?

If you speak only one language, talk with someone who is bilingual or multilingual to discover absences in the English language and to explore how these absences affect communication.

fear brought on by unwanted sexual impositions, victims had no socially recognized way to name or condemn what happened. Coining the term *sexual harassment* conferred social reality on their experiences and gave them language to capture the meaning of and protest against unwelcome sexual conduct.

A number of communication researchers argue that sexual harassment is made to seem normal by the dominant discourses in institutions. Mary Strine (1992), a critical scholar, showed how the universe of discourse in academia perpetuates the perception that unwanted sexual conduct is acceptable and natural. Robin Clair (1993) identified discursive strategies used in organizations to trivialize, minimize, or redefine complaints of sexual harassment so that the victim, not the perpetrator, was defined as being at fault.

The same universe of discourse dismisses victims' protests as hysteria, excessive sensitivity, troublemaking, and so forth. Other communication scholars have emphasized the ways in which discourse throughout society encourages men to be sexually aggressive and women to be deferential—a pattern that supports sexual harassment (Bingham, 1994, 1996; Taylor & Conrad, 1992; Wood, 1992, 1994b). By extension, terms such as *date rape* and *marital rape* name experiences that have previously not been recognized.

Resistance to Dominant Discourses

Because muted group theory is a critical theory, it aims to produce social change. In the case of this theory, one desired change is for women to assume the power to name their experiences in ways that reflect their meanings. Women cannot rely on a language invented by men to represent their experiences. Thus, they must create words to reflect the rhythms and facets of their lives.

At first, the idea of creating a new and more inclusive language may seem implausible. However, Julia Penelope (1990), an influential critical theorist, insists that language is a dynamic, changing system of words and meanings. With other muted group theorists, Penelope believes the dominant discourse in most societies is decidedly masculine. She does not, however, think this has to remain the case. She argues that creating a more equitable society requires revising the universe of discourse to fully include and value women's experiences, interests, knowledge, values, and perspectives.

Karen Foss (1991) asked women students to create words to describe experiences they had that were not represented in existing language. *Soul rinse* was a term coined by the women to express the feeling after a big cry. *Solo wholo* was a term invented to describe a person who isn't in a romantic relationship at the moment and who is neither actively searching for a partner nor uninterested in meeting a partner; the person is whole as a solo. Women students in my classes came up with the word *noman* to describe a man who is uncomfortable with an assertive or powerful woman. Mary Catherine Bateson (1990) coined the term *placemaking* to describe the care and skill women invest in creating homes.

Reflection

What names can you create for experiences you have had that are not represented in the English language?

There are several systematic efforts to develop and record language for women's experiences that are not yet reflected in "standard" English. Suzette Elgin (1988) invented an entire language, which she calls Laadan, to capture women's experiences and interests. Cheris Kramarae and Paula Treichler (1985) published *A Feminist Dictionary*. Included in the dictionary are the terms *birthing*, defined as an "archetypal experience exclusive to women," and *foremother*, defined as "an ancestor." Feminist critical theorists use the fluidity and change characteristic of language to introduce new words that resonate with women's lives.

TRY IT OUT What experiences have you had that are not represented in the English language? Think about the examples provided in the foregoing text. What can you add in terms of feelings, experiences, thoughts, and so forth that are part of your life but not part of the common language?

Feeling: Describe one feeling that is familiar to you but has no name. Give it a name: _____

Experience: Describe an experience you have had for which there is no term. Give it a name: _____

Identity: Describe an aspect of your identity that's important to you but is not captured in any existing words. (*Ms.* was a term coined to describe a woman who chose not to be identified by her marital status with the terms *Miss* or *Mrs.*) Name your identity: _____

Others: Describe a kind of person or a pattern of attitudes and actions by persons for which there is no word. Give it a name: _____

Let's summarize our discussion of muted group theory. Beginning with the observation that language has a masculine bias, scholars have traced the genesis and implications of language that highlights men's experiences and interests while obscuring those of women. Current thinking is that men's experiences and perceptions are privileged because men have dominated the public life of most societies and thus have named the world from their perspective. One effect of this is that women are muted by a linguistic system that doesn't adequately reflect or recognize many of their experiences. Consequently, they are at a disadvantage when it comes to participating in cultural discourses.

Because language shapes meanings and cultural consciousness, a masculine bias has the potential to obscure or distort the experiences of women and girls. Muted group theorists believe that the need for both women's expression and a language that accurately reflects an entire society demands the remaking of our present language so that it fully recognizes and values women and their lives. Encoding women's interests and experiences in language not only would increase women's voices but also would give men a more complete vision of cultural life.

Critical Assessment of Muted Group Theory

Three criticisms of muted group theory merit our attention.

Women's Oppression Exaggerated   First, this theory, like the more general feminist theories we considered earlier in the chapter, is criticized for overstating women's oppression. Because we considered this indictment in closing our discussion of feminist theories, there's no need to reiterate it here.

Inappropriately Political   A second criticism, also familiar, is that muted group theory is political in its goals. Critics charge that muted group theory is being used to advance a political agenda to empower women. Muted group theorists (and other critical theorists as well) would agree that they are committed to a political agenda—constructive change in society by reducing the inequities between women and men.

Muted group theorists, however, do not see a problem with the presence of values in a theory. In their opinion, values inhere in all theories, although conventional theorists deny the values that inform their work. Further, argue critical scholars, theories about social life *should* be based on values and *should* attempt to improve society.

Unrealistic   The final criticism of muted group theory is that it is utopian. Not unique to muted group theory, this criticism has been leveled at critical theories in general (Blumler, 1983; Real, 1984). Critics claim that critical theorists in general, and muted group theorists in particular, are too idealistic in believing that the changes they desire can be realized. According to some who have misgivings about critical theories, sweeping changes—for instance, remaking language—are not possible because of existing inequities that must be recognized and accommodated.

Perhaps it is utopian to imagine remaking language to include women's experiences and perspectives. Then again, perhaps that isn't such a far-fetched idea. Think about the changes that have occurred since the 1970s, when scholars began calling attention to sexist language:

- *Ms.* is now widely accepted as a title for women.
- Male generic terms (*he, chairman*) have been replaced by nonsexist alternatives (*he or she, chair*).
- Many women who marry choose to keep their birth names or to hyphenate their birth names and their husbands' birth names.
- Most book and journal publishers have an explicit policy prohibiting sexist language.
- The newest conventional dictionaries—*Webster's*, for instance—reflect a conscious effort to reduce the sexism and male bias in language.
- Terms such as *sexual harassment*, *date rape*, and *marital rape* that describe experiences nearly exclusive to women have entered into general vocabulary in society.

Maybe the goal of changing language and thus its effects on social relationships isn't so utopian after all. The goal of revising language to include women and men equally is an ongoing experiment whose success and impact we'll be unable to judge for many years.

Cultural Studies Theories

A few years ago, an African-American community in the South noticed that its residents were suffering an unusually high incidence of cancer. A decade earlier, a major chemical company had buried drums of toxic waste in this neighborhood; the drums had eventually leaked into the soil and from there into the land and water of citizens living in the area. Members of the community asked local officials and health agencies to help them find the source of their cancer and other health problems. They were told that their medical conditions came from poor diet and various other influences that they controlled. Nobody would listen to their questions about the drums; nobody would comment on why the skin that came in contact with the drums was eaten away.

My partner, Robbie, visited with members of the community and then used his voice as president of the Sierra Club to capture media attention. The bad publicity in turn came to the attention of the president of the chemical company that had dumped the waste. After months of negotiations and meetings, the grassroots leaders of the community and the president of the chemical company came to an agreement that required the company to remove all buried toxins and to compensate citizens who had been harmed or killed by the lethal chemicals. The fact that the African Americans had difficulty getting a hearing suggests they were a muted group—one denied a public voice. If another agent who had a voice in the dominant universe of discourse hadn't intervened, members of this community might never have secured any justice.

The situation I've recounted is precisely the kind that interests cultural studies theorists. They examine the ways a culture is actually produced, reproduced, and changed through struggles among differing **ideologies**. Within cultural studies, much attention is devoted to analyzing the means by which dominant groups in society privilege their interests and impose their ideology on less powerful groups.

Reflection

What, if any, pragmatic value is there in analyzing how dominant groups sustain their dominance?

Cultural studies does not have a single, unvarying focus. Because cultural studies is interested in historical and political conditions that affect life in societies, it must change to respond to the issues and conditions that arise in particular moments of cultural life. Larry Grossberg (1996), a preeminent cultural studies scholar, explains that cultural studies is "driven by its attempt to respond to history, to what matters in the world of political struggle" (p. 18).

Because history, our understandings of it, and political struggles are continuously changing, so must cultural studies if it is to maintain its commitment to responding to historical conditions. John Storey (1996) points out that cultural studies' central concern with issues of class was disrupted in the 1970s by feminism's assertion that gender matters and by civil rights' insistence that race must be given serious attention. In response, cultural studies scholars began to theorize about the nature and impact of race and gender as well as class.

For Grossberg and other cultural studies theorists, popular culture is an important site in which oppressed groups may empower themselves and resist subordination. The task of the cultural studies scholar is "analysis and identification of the agents and agencies (economic, cultural, and political) which construct the configuration of everyday life, specific positions within it, and the relation between these and the larger formation" (Grossberg, 1996, p. 378). In other words, a primary goal is to bring a critical perspective to bear on the dominant structures of a society and on how those structures affect political and material lives of members of a culture, especially those who are not in the mainstream.

Like feminist scholars and muted group theorists, scholars of cultural studies embrace a reformist agenda. Ted Striphas (1998) explains that cultural studies does not aim "simply to criticize, but more pointedly to intervene actively to make, remake, and unmake social, political, and historical contexts" (p. 455). They differ from the other two schools of thought in that they do not regard gender or any other single factor as sufficient to explain why some groups are able to dominate and impose their views on others in a society. To understand cultural studies, we'll consider the ideas that inform theorizing in this area.

Culture

Not surprisingly, a central concept in cultural studies theorizing is **culture**. For theorists in this area, culture does not refer to aesthetics or to intellectual or spiritual development. Instead, "'culture' in cultural studies is defined politically . . . as the texts and practices of everyday life" (Storey, 1996, p. 2). This means that cultural studies scholars are interested not just in elite spheres of social life but also and especially in popular culture.

Reflection

What connections can you identify between the interests of cultural studies and those of performance theories?

Culture has two facets or meanings (Littlejohn, 1992, p. 252). First, a culture consists of ideology, which includes ideas, values, beliefs, and understandings that are common to members of a society and that guide the activities and customs of that society. Second, culture refers to the actual, concrete practices characteristic of a society. Concrete practices include cultural rituals that stand out, such as holidays, marriage ceremonies, and funerals. In addition, cultural practices encompass the routinized activities of individuals who embody and create culture through their daily ways of living. For example, Westerners typically drive cars, shop in malls, listen to music, and watch television—these are aspects of day-to-day living that express and sustain some of the meanings of our culture.

Cultural studies scholars see these two dimensions of culture as interlinked and inseparable. They believe that practices—both occasional and daily ones—reflect and uphold (and sometimes challenge) the ideology of a culture, and conversely, the ideology of a culture reflects and guides what most individual members think, feel, believe, and do. The democratic ideology of the United States explains the concrete practice of voting in elections. At the same time, the concrete practice of voting reflects and reinforces the democratic ideology. The capitalistic ideology so prominent in

Western culture undergirds specific practices such as a competitive market-place, individuals working to outdo one another, and the awarding of money in lawsuits for personal damage or loss—money is the measure of how much something matters in a capitalistic society. At the same time, competition for raises, prizes, athletic victories, and status involves specific practices that simultaneously express and sustain capitalistic values.

TRY IT OUT Consider your school as a miniculture. Identify the dominant code of meanings, or ideology, that is promoted by your school. For example, it might be portrayed as an "institution of higher learning," "a place for personal and intellectual growth," or "a school devoted to the liberal arts." Can you identify specific documents, school rituals, and so forth that express the dominant ideology of your school?

Now identify specific practices that you and other students engage in that reflect and sustain the dominant ideology of your school. Going to classes, making notes, studying, taking exams, and so forth are all particular activities that support a view of your school as a place in which learning is the preeminent goal and value.

Ideological Domination

The concept of **ideological domination** is also central to cultural studies. Stuart Hall, a British scholar who is especially prominent in cultural studies, defines *ideology* as a set of ideas that organize a group's, or society's, understandings of reality. He also refers to ideology as a code of meanings that shapes how a group of people sees and acts in the world (Hall, 1986a, 1989a).

Hall and other cultural studies scholars believe that in any culture there are competing ideologies, or ways of understanding reality. Like standpoint theory, cultural studies theory recognizes that a culture is not homogeneous but includes different groups whose distinct experiences, circumstances, and social identities shape understanding of the overall culture.

The dominant ideology of a culture is the one that has the greatest power and the adherence of the greatest number of people at a given moment in the life of a culture. The dominant ideology maintains its domination by virtue of the support of social institutions, such as churches and temples, schools, legislatures, and media. These institutions function both individually and in interaction with one another to legitimize the prevailing ideology and to suppress, marginalize, or silence competing ideologies.

Let's consider an example of how ideological determination works. The perspectives and interests of white, middle-class, heterosexual, able-bodied men are made to seem normal and distinctly important by a host of social institutions and practices. Leaders in churches and temples are usually male; top executives in business and industry are virtually all white men; the majority of educational institutions are run by white men; media feature far more white men and fewer women and people of color than is representative of population statistics; and the curricular content in schools emphasizes the achievements and concerns of white, heterosexual, able-bodied men who are economically comfortable. Because prevailing interests are privileged and normalized by cultural institutions, it is difficult for groups outside of the mainstream to gain a fair hearing.

Reflection

If nonprivileged groups don't have access to institutions that produce and reproduce culture, how can their voices ever be heard and their interests ever served?

In the case of the African-American community that suffered the effects of toxic waste, the dominant ideology privileged corporate interests over those of poor, marginalized citizens of color. Institutions ignored community members' questions and criticisms of the chemical company. Until someone in a position of respect and power within the mainstream spoke out for the citizens' rights, their ideology was resisted, denied, and demeaned by cultural institutions that supported the interests and ideology of the dominant group.

The media are unusually potent tools of the dominant ideology. Although many, if not most, cultural institutions support the dominant ideology, the media are particularly powerful in representing the ideology of privileged groups as normal, right, and natural (Hall, 1986a,b, 1988, 1989b; McChesney, 1999; Potter, 2001; Urgo, 2000). Television programs, from children's shows to prime-time news, represent white, heterosexual, able-bodied males as the norm in the United States, although they are actually not the majority.

Despite critiques of bias in television programming, minorities continue to be portrayed most often as criminals, victims, subordinates, or otherwise less than respectable people (James, 2000; *Media Studies Journal*, 1994). Although there are exceptions, most women in popular media continue to be shown as dependent, primarily decorative, and related to men through roles such as girlfriend, homemaker, and mother, although the majority of women in the United States now work outside the home. In these and other respects, television presents a world view that is out of sync with "the facts" but that squarely supports the dominant white male ideology of the culture.

Because of their influence in fortifying dominant ideologies, media receive extensive attention in cultural studies. However, media are not the only concern of scholars in this area, nor are media themselves the primary concern. Rather, cultural studies scholars are most keenly interested in how dominant ideologies secure and sustain their domination and how they can be contested and changed. Thus, media are seen as a particular site of ideological struggle, but it is the struggle, not media per se, that is of greatest interest.

The "Theatre of Struggle"

Cultural studies theorists view culture and ideology as highly fluid—always in flux and subject to change. Culture in general and a dominant ideology in particular are not fixed but are in continuous process. Stuart Hall (1986a,b, 1989a) refers to the ongoing battle for ideological control as a **"theatre of struggle"** or *"theatre of conflict."*

Hall insists that we should not think of cultures or power relations as absolute. Instead, he argues that they must be understood as situated in particular historical circumstances (1986a,b, 1989a). Thus, racial oppression has a different character in the United States in the 1990s than it did in the United States in the 1890s. Racial oppression refers to something different still from either of those meanings when considered in the context of South Africa now, much less 15 years ago. This suggests that the struggle among ideologies is continuously shifting as different groups gain hearings and secure the support of cultural institutions.

Resistance to the dominant ideology and efforts to legitimize alternate world views are particularly evident in music, especially new forms of music. Lawrence Grossberg (1986) has studied rock music, including punk and rock 'n' roll, as a practice that opposes the dominant ideology. According to Grossberg, rock music addresses an expansive set of issues, including the identity of young people and their place in society. Grossberg argues that rock 'n' roll "energizes new possibilities" and makes these possibilities central in everyday life (1986, p. 57). More recently, punk and gangsta rap have challenged rock 'n' roll and offered possibilities of meaning radically opposed to those supported by the dominant ideology.

An interesting example of challenge to the prevailing music is Riot Grrrls. In 1990 in Olympia, Washington, two new bands began to attract a following. Bikini Kill and Bratmobile, the two bands, are unusual in that the band members and fans are mostly female (D. Hall, 1995). Rather than following the conventional route of successful bands, Bikini Kill and Bratmobile and other women's bands created a support network for women musicians and their fans. The collective movement that resulted is Riot Grrrls, in which fans and members of the bands are equally considered to be "riot grrrls." This radically egalitarian structure opposes the practice of hierarchy that is a central part of the dominant ideology in Western culture.

Critical Communication Theories

Specializing in hardcore punk music, these bands insistently challenge prevailing practices. According to one of the bands (Bikini Kill, 1991, p. 1), "Riot Grrrl is . . . because us girls crave records and books and fanzines that speak to us, that we feel included in and can understand in our own ways . . . because we are angry at a society that tells us girl = dumb, girl = bad, girl = weak, because we see fostering and supporting girl scenes and girl artists of all kinds as integral." Shunning conventional prescriptions for femininity, Riot Grrrls bands embody anger, dogmatism, resistance, and assertion. They speak openly about sex and sexual experience, and they resist conventional devaluation of feminine experiences and qualities.

Reflection

To what extent do you think oppositional music forms instigate changes in Western culture's views of women and minorities?

Overdetermination

An especially noteworthy facet of cultural studies is the assumption that no single cause determines ideological domination. Hall and others in this intellectual tradition believe that there are numerous, interlinked causes of any cultural ideology or practice (Hall, 1986a). They use the term **overdetermination** to indicate that aspects of social life, including ideological domination, are determined by multiple causes rather than any single cause.

For example, there is no single cause of the privilege that white, able-bodied, heterosexual men have in Western culture. The prevailing view that white men are superior to others in the society is supported by a language that reflects and supports their interests, as well as by the preponderance of white men who make and apply the laws of our land. In addition, the normativeness of white men is supported by their prominence as anchors of newscasts, as stars in movies and television programs, and as high-ranking executives in professions. Thus, a range of cultural structures and practices sustain ideological domination. From the perspective of cultural studies, it is naive and mistaken to believe that any single cause accounts for ideology or how it is reproduced and embodied in the thought and action of individuals.

Most cultural studies scholars have been strongly influenced by Marxism, so economic class is viewed as a major influence on what individuals believe and how they act. According to Marxist theory, economic systems and structures determine all other aspects of life, including politics, religion, social status, and the overall social system of a society. The fundamental economic character of a society creates what Marx called the *superstructure*, which is composed of social institutions and practices that assist in reproducing and normalizing the underlying economic system that is at the base of a society (Becker, 1984).

Although cultural studies theorists have been deeply influenced by Marxist theory, they do not accept the Marxist notion that economics *determine* individual action. As we've already seen, cultural studies theorists believe that social life is overdetermined, which means there are multiple, often overlapping and interacting determinants of individual and collective behavior. Economics is one factor; gender is another; race is a third; age is a fourth; affectional orientation is a fifth; religion is a sixth; and so forth. And each of these factors is also determined by multiple influences ranging from language to education. Careful analysis of complex and interrelated forces is required to understand how cultures operate so as to legitimize and reproduce dominant ideologies or to overturn them in the ceaseless "theatre of struggle."

Response to Dominant Ideologies

What are we to do when confronted with television images that tell us European Americans, heterosexuals, men, and affluent classes are better than other races, gays and lesbians, women, and poor people? Are women powerless in the face of relentless advertising that urges them to be unrealistically thin and to spend large sums of money on shoes that damage their feet and clothes that restrict their comfort? Are men helpless to argue against the unremitting social messages that their worth depends on how much status and money they earn? Are we all defenseless pawns of cultural institutions such as media?

Cultural studies scholars are not so pessimistic as to believe we are totally susceptible to efforts at ideological control. They have identified three different ways individuals may respond to communication that reflects and attempts to perpetuate the dominant ideology (Fiske, 1987; Hall, 1982, 1989b). First, we may uncritically consume messages and their ideological underpinnings. This response is one in which we accept the view of reality that supports the interests of the privileged and is expressed by tools of the culture. A second response is to qualify our acceptance of dominant ideology as reflected in cultural institutions and practices. For example, you might agree that competition is generally good (thereby accepting the basic dominant ideology) but decide it is not appropriate in romantic relationships or friendships (thereby refusing to give unconditioned assent to the ideology).

A third response is to oppose the dominant ideology. Engaging in this response requires us first to see through the false claims of the dominant ideology: we must recognize that it is not unvarnished truth but instead is partial and serves the interests of the "haves" while oppressing the "have nots" in society. Second, we must rely on an alternative ideology supplied by others, or we may invent one of our own as a substitute for the dominant ideology that we are resisting. Feminists, for example, have offered oppositional readings of television advertising that encourages women to be passive, deferential, and obsessed with weight and appearance (Rakow, 1992). Feminist scholars have also offered oppositional meanings for previously accepted practices of imposing unwanted sexual conduct on others (Bingham, 1994, 1996; Strine, 1992; Taylor & Conrad, 1992; Wood, 1994b). Riot Grrrls have invented a novel universe of discourse that privileges women and their experiences and resists a strong hierarchy between performers (stars) and fans (followers).

Most scholars working in the area of cultural studies believe that human beings can exercise considerable control over efforts to persuade them to accept dominant ideologies. They also assume that people are more likely to exercise critical control over media and other cultural institutions if they are informed about how those institutions work to sustain and normalize particular world views that serve the interests of only some groups. Thus, the goal of this program of inquiry is to increase individuals' ability to identify and respond critically to prevailing ideologies and the means by which their domination is sustained.

Critical Assessment of Cultural Studies Theories

There are four primary criticisms of cultural studies theories.

Inaccessible   Academics in general and theorists in particular are often ridiculed for using obscure language that makes it difficult for most people to understand ideas. Cultural studies theorists, say critics, have taken this tendency to new levels with language that is virtually inaccessible to anyone without substantial training in cultural studies. This is an important criticism, not only because it maintains that cultural studies is even more obscure than most theories, but also because it strikes at the heart of what cultural studies declares as its mission—helping those who are not privileged in cultural life.

Too Broad in Scope   A second frequently voiced criticism of cultural studies is that it is excessively broad in scope. To understand why this might be considered a problem, consider Elin Diamond's (1996, p. 6) statement that cultural studies "ranges from early study of working-class culture and popular traditions, through work on subcultures and media studies, to work on racism, hegemony, and feminist revisioning." That's a huge expanse of territory to study and theorize about! If this is the domain of cultural studies, one might ask, then what is *not* cultural studies?

Theorists in the area do not disagree that their focus is broad. Grossberg (1996, p. 16) explicitly and unapologetically recognizes the "open-endedness of cultural studies." He goes on to say, "there never was an orthodoxy of cultural studies . . . there never was a singular and homogeneous, pure and unsoiled center" (p. 17). Yet to cultural studies scholars, this is not a problem. Rather, the breadth of their work is inherent in the nature of what they study—popular culture as a site of both reproduction and contestation of dominant ideology. Political struggles, claim cultural studies theorists, are deeply embedded in particular historical settings and times and are influenced by multiple conditions and factors. If this is true, then cultural studies theories must be broad to do the job they are intended to do.

Insufficient Attention to Gender   It is ironic that one criticism of cultural studies comes from feminists, who share many of the critical impulses and values of their colleagues in cultural studies. Where cultural studies and some feminist scholars part ways is in the emphasis placed on gender as a, or the, primary basis of ideological struggle and oppression. For many feminists, gender structures personal and cultural relations. Although other factors may also create, sustain, and normalize oppression, feminist scholars see socially constructed gender as uniquely influential. Thus, some feminists think gender is too powerful an influence on identity, opportunities, and experiences to be lumped indiscriminately with a host of other influences.

For cultural studies scholars, on the other hand, gender is one of many factors that influence the workings of culture (remember the idea of overdetermination). Further, cultural studies theorists assume that gender, like other social constructions, is fluid and subject to change across time and place. Cultural studies' unwillingness to emphasize gender (or any other single basis of oppressed identity) does not reflect lack of concern about the discrimination many women experience. Instead, it reflects cultural studies' distrust of the political utility of identity politics, which focuses on particular social identities defined by factors such as race, sex, class, and sexual orientation. According to Grossberg (1996, pp. 377–382), identity politics are politically ineffective because they refuse to transcend the very identities and subordination that they contest. For example, because feminists do not transcend the identity of women, they are unable to change cultural structures and practices that define women. Furthermore, the focus on any single site of oppression, such as race or sex, undermines awareness and political action based on recognition of how power and oppression subordinate multiple groups in cultural life.

Reflection

To what extent is it appropriate to view gender as one of many relatively equal influences on individual identity and life?

Too Ideological   By far the strongest and most frequent criticism of cultural studies is that it generates flawed theories because it is mired in ideology. Cultural studies theory is attacked on the same grounds as feminist theory and muted group theory—they are indicted by some for their explicit and unapologetic commitment to values. The value-laden nature of cultural studies, charge critics, necessarily compromises the search for truth. In response to this criticism, Hall and his associates would probably shrug and ask, "Whose truth is compromised?" The point, of course, is that scholars of cultural studies do not accept the idea that there is a single, absolute, capital-T Truth. Instead, they insist that all aspects of cultural life are subject to multiple readings that lead inevitably to quite different views of what is and is not true (Weedon, 1987). That is why the "theatre of struggle" never closes its doors.

Summary

In this chapter we examined three critical theories of communication. Although they differ in some respects, they share a commitment to understanding and altering inequities in cultural life. All three are centrally concerned with the role of communication in creating, sustaining, and changing power relationships in society.

Feminist theories—and there are many of these—focus on gender as a, if not the, primary source of oppression in modern societies. This group of theories attempts to identify the ways in which communication structures and practices marginalize women and their experiences. The same focus energizes muted group theory, which concentrates more specifically on the power of dominant masculine discourses to silence women and to exclude their experiences from the so-called "common language" of the culture.

Many feminist theorists and the specific subgroup of scholars who endorse muted group theory believe that historical and still-present inequalities between women and men are neither inevitable nor unchangeable. Consequently, these theorists generate practical recommendations for enlarging women's presence and voice in the life of society.

The third set of theories that we explored in this chapter is cultural studies, which shares the reformist impulses of feminist and muted group theories. It differs from the other two in not claiming that gender deserves special status in explaining oppression. Cultural studies scholars believe that race, class, age, economic resources, and other factors—along with gender—overdetermine the oppression of particular groups in society. They also believe that power relations in society are never fixed but always under negotiation in the "theatre of struggle" that includes competing voices and rival views of reality.

The goal of scholars in the critical tradition is to unmask the apparatuses that uphold and perpetuate ideological domination by those who have privileged positions in society. Because of their influence in modern life, media receive extensive attention from scholars of cultural studies. Media, however, are not viewed in isolation. Instead, they are seen as interacting with other institutions and practices that work together to sustain and legitimize a particular and partial view of social life that defines the roles of specific groups within an overall culture.

All three of these theories have gained increasing respect and influence in recent years, perhaps because there is widespread awareness and concern about the injustice and unevenness of social life. Even though critical theories have earned considerable regard in the scholarly community, two reservations about them are often expressed. First, there is disagreement about whether theories that have explicit value commitments can provide worthwhile knowledge. Although some traditional researchers believe that theories must be neutral to engage in a search for truth, an increasing number of scholars think that values inhere in all theories and are unavoidable. Further, critical scholars see value commitments and efforts to foment social change as important pragmatic contributions of theories.

A second criticism of critical theories is that they are unrealistic in assuming that long-standing inequities in society can be changed. Some people think it's futile to attempt to alter historical inequalities between women and men, European Americans and minorities, and economically comfortable and poor groups. Critical theorists don't share this pessimistic view. Without falling prey to utopian thinking, critical theorists believe that cultural life is an ongoing process that has changed many times and will change more in the future. What they hope to do is to direct that change in ways that result in a society that is fairer, more just, and more inclusive for all who participate in it. Understanding how cultures and power relations are made and sustained is the first step in remaking a culture and the power relations it authorizes.

Key Terms

critical theories

cultural studies theories

culture

feminist theories

gender

ideological domination

ideologies

inclusion stage

masculine bias

muted group theory

overdetermination

patriarchy

revisionist stage

sex

superstructure

"theatre of struggle"

CHAPTER THIRTEEN

Postmodern Theorizing

Professor D. Soyini Madison spent two and one half years doing ethnographic fieldwork in Ghana, West Africa. Her goal was to understand a traditional religious practice called *trikose*, in which young females are consigned to monasteries where they serve priests for a period ranging from a few years to a lifetime. In recent years, the practice of trikose has become highly controversial. In areas where it is still practiced, residents are split between believing it is a religious tradition that should be upheld and believing it is a violation of the young girls' human rights. After extensive fieldwork, Madison (in press) returned to the United States and devoted a year to scripting and staging a performance entitled *Is It a Human Being or a Girl?*

In creating this performance, Madison resisted an easy answer or resolution, of the debate. As a Western woman she was appalled by the practice of removing young girls from their families and lives and forcing them into nonvoluntary service. Yet as someone who had immersed herself deeply in Ghana's culture, she came to understand the other side of the debate—the strong feeling among some people that trikose upholds important traditional religious and cultural values. She crafted the performance to complicate the debate by giving voice to both sides. She wanted those who attended the performance to struggle, as she had, with the multiple, conflicting views of trikose.

In choosing to enter into different perspectives and give voice to each, Madison drew upon the tradition of performance as political action, which we discussed in Chapter 6. Madison's project also was informed by postmodern theories, which are the focus of this chapter. By giving voice and legitimacy to different points of view, Madison embodied the postmodern conviction that there are multiple truths on most matters and that no one point of view can be declared right in an absolute or ultimate sense. In the fieldwork on which her performance was based, Madison followed Norman Denzin's (2001) advice to learn about multiple truths by paying attention to "the stories people tell one another about the things that matter to them" (p. 12).

Madison's study of trikose fits within the scholarly tradition of active engagement with "real-world" issues. Like people in other walks of life, scholars care about concerns such as discrimination, disadvantage, and injustice. Yet scholars cannot fully respond to these issues within traditional scientific frameworks that emphasize detachment, in which researchers separate themselves from what they study. Many critical scholars believe that responding adequately demands passionate engagement, which can inform and fuel efforts to identify and alter communication structures and practices that sustain disparities in social life. In Norman Denzin's (2001) words, "there is a pressing demand to show how the practices of critical, interpretive qualitative research can help change the world in positive ways" (p. xi). Madison's work and that of many postmodern scholars exemplify active scholarly engagement that aims to identify and redress inequities in cultural life.

In this chapter we consider the character and impact of postmodern theories. Beginning in the middle of the 20th century, postmodern and poststructural philosophies began to shape theorizing and, more broadly, understanding of cultural life. There are differences between poststructuralism and postmodernism. However, as Madan Sarup (1989) notes, the similarities between poststructuralist and postmodernist points of view are so great that it is artificial and misleading to separate the two. In this chapter we'll use the term *postmodern* to discuss theories that are informed by both postmodern and poststructural thought.

Postmodernism cannot be reduced to a single theory; instead it is best understood as a broad perspective on, or way of thinking about, both social life and research. As in other chapters, we'll explore postmodernism by identifying and discussing its key concepts. First, however, we'll need to discuss **modernity** and modernist thought, since postmodernity and postmodernist thought are defined in relation to them.

Modernity

Modernity, or the modern period, followed three other periods in history: the Renaissance, which began in Italy in the middle of the 14th century; the Reformation, which began in 1517 and continued through the mid 1550s; and the Enlightenment, which roughly spanned the 18th century. The Enlightenment is also known as the Age of Reason, and it paved the way for the modern era, during which science and reason ascended as ways of knowing about the world. Historians generally mark the modern period as beginning near the end of the 19th century and ending around the start of World War I. Modernist ways of thinking first arose in Europe, particularly the North Atlantic. In both Europe and, later, America, modernist worldviews emphasized order, rationality, and reason and attempted to reconcile reason with faith. Given these emphases, it's not surprising that modernism propelled efforts to predict and control phenomena and to tame or remove disorder from cultural life.

The Rise of Science and Reason

Historically, Western societies revered religion as the source of ultimate truth. With the enlightenment and modernity, however, came skepticism about religion as the only or best source of knowledge. The exclusive authority of religion was challenged by belief in science as a primary means to valid knowledge about the world (Becker, 1992; Cassirer, 1968; Habermas, 1990; Popkin & Stroll, 2002). Perceiving science as orderly, rational, and objective, modernists believed that science would allow us to discover and use the laws that order the world and everything in it. By extension, science was seen as the key means of progress: once we discovered the scientific laws that order phenomena, we could manipulate them to achieve great things (Becker, 1992). Scientific knowledge would lead to cures for dreaded diseases, to interplanetary travel, to technologies to improve efficiency and quality of life, to understanding of the human psyche, and to ever-increasing economic productivity. The ascendance of belief in science paralleled the rise of deterministic views of human nature (see Chapter 3) and scientific accounts of human evolution. Consistent with the modernist love of reason, science was perceived as neutral and objective. Because science was believed to be neutral and objective, its discoveries were not subject to question—they were considered accurate and indisputable.

Consistent with the general mindset of the era, modernists regarded language as rational and descriptive of the "real world." In other words, language was perceived as an objective, neutral, and value-free means of representing reality. Language was not regarded as laden with values. For this reason, language wasn't perceived as capable of creating, or constituting, reality. Theories about language that were developed during the modernist period sought to discover the inherent order, logic, coherence, and stability of the phenomena they studied.

Reflection

How would muted group theorists assess the modernist view that language is objective and value free?

The Coherent, Autonomous Self

The modernist view of individuals was consistent with the modernist view of science. If science is rational and coherent, then ideally individuals should also be rational and coherent. Thus, the modernist conception of individuals was as rational beings who are capable of using reason and science to arrive at reliable knowledge of the objective, true character of the world and everything in it. The human mind was elevated above feelings and soul. Therefore, knowledge gained through the mind was considered superior to knowledge gained through intuition, divine insight, or other means.

During the modernist era, evolutionary theory challenged religious accounts of human existence because the former offered a more scientific, logical, and coherent explanation of the origins of the human species. Since modernists esteemed order and coherence, it isn't surprising that they considered the self to be relatively constant and fixed. In other words, once an individual developed a self, this self was assumed to endure throughout life and to account for unity, or coherence, in an individual's behaviors, values, and so forth. Modernists saw the self not only as stable and coherent but also as autonomous. Instead of regarding individuals as controlled by supernatural forces, modernists conceived them as rugged, self-made beings who could use reason to arrive at truth and knowledge and make free choices accordingly.

The Stable, Coherent Society

Modernists assumed that society, like individuals, had a continuing, relatively fixed character. Beliefs in a stable self and society were reflected in theories that emphasized order, logic, and continuity. Among theories we've studied, uncertainty theory and exchange theory are consistent with modernist worldviews because both claim there are predictable, durable patterns in how relationships develop.

The enduring character of a society was embodied in **grand narratives**, which are coherent stories that cultures tell about themselves, their practices, and their values (Lyotard, 1984). One grand narrative that was widely endorsed during modernity was that science was a key to progress in combating problems and advancing the dominance of Western culture. Scientific advances led to creation of the atom bomb, travel to the moon, and cures for polio and other dreaded diseases. Another grand narrative in the United States was that America is the "land of opportunity," where rights and opportunity are equal for everyone and where any person can succeed through individual effort. Broadly embraced cultural stories about equality invite all members of a society to see themselves as able to succeed on their own merits. This grand narrative also encourages people who don't succeed to view their failures as personal rather than the result of structural forces that constrained their opportunities.

Postmodernity

Postmodernism is an intellectual and political movement that does its work through critical analysis (Best & Kellner, 1991). From the start, postmodernist thought has challenged modernist notions of order, particularly the notion that a particular social order is natural and right. In contrast to modernist thought, postmodernists maintain that reality is unordered and unorderly. It follows that postmodernists believe that reality cannot be known or understood in a single, absolute way (Best & Kellner, 1991). All efforts to define and order society and people within it are contingent and therefore arguable. Any particular social order can be challenged; any particular social order is open to change or reordering.

Most theorists and historians place the beginning of postmodernity sometime after World War II. John Storey (1999) and Susan Sontag (1966) more specifically designate the 1950s and 1960s as the time when postmodern ideas began to flourish. Although Sontag did not use the term *postmodern*, she described the change in thinking that came to be known as postmodern when in 1966 she wrote that "the distinction between 'high' and 'low' culture seems less and less meaningful" (p. 302).

Why might an intellectual revolution first announce itself by blurring long-established lines between high and low culture? The answer is that postmodern thinking takes popular culture seriously. In other words, postmodernists pay attention to what average people in a society enjoy in music, art, and so forth. Brahms may be a great composer, opera may be highly sophisticated, and Rembrandt may be a superb artist; yet rock music, fiddlers' conventions, and folk art also matter to people. The focus on popular culture is not simply or even primarily an aesthetic choice. It is also a deeply political statement: The elite is not all that counts. The masses matter.

Carrying popular politics further, postmodernists criticize cultural practices and structures that privilege some groups and what they value and devalue and disadvantage other groups and what they value. Postmodernists are "defiantly pluralistic" (Sontag, 1966, p. 304), refusing to define some kinds of art or ways of life as "better" and other forms of art as "lesser." This refusal is based on postmodernists' rejection of the idea that anyone can determine in an absolute sense what is important, good, and so forth (Frith and Horne, 1987). Who, they ask, has a right to decide for everyone what is "good art," "good music," "beautiful architecture," and so forth? As this question implies, most postmodernists reject universal standards for determining what is good or important in cultural life. They recognize that people in diverse circumstances and with diverse experiences will have different views of what matters—what is good, important, beautiful, and so forth.

Postmodernism was first noticeable in architecture and art. During the modern era, art and architecture reflected the order, coherence, and unity that modernists so valued. Although there was some improvisational art, it did not celebrate disorder. Instead, improvisational art bemoaned the loss of coherence and expressed a yearning for a return to order.

Marking entry into the postmodern era were artistic forms that resisted unity and conventional order and emphasized incoherence and discontinuity. Postmodern architecture rejected traditional structures, designs, and spaces in favor of forms such as collage and montage and eclectic, deliberately disjointed art forms. Postmodern design may feature elegant antique furniture in a stark, angular contemporary building. Paintings by Picasso and Monet may hang side by side, each calling into question the authority of the other. Also typical of postmodern art is a movement away from an aesthetic that celebrates only "high art" or "high culture." Pop art, such as paintings by Warhol in the mid 1900s, blurred the boundaries between high and low art and the boundaries between art and commerce. Continuing to blur the lines, postmodern art salutes folk art, aesthetic treatments of the mundane, and other kinds of popular art. Postmodernists see art as one way of symbolizing and celebrating life—in all of its pluralistic forms, not just those that members of the elite class designate as the "most cultured." This is one of many ways in which postmodernist thinking challenges the traditional social order, which allows the most privileged members of a society to declare absolutely what and who is normal, good, beautiful, and right.

Art and architecture were perhaps the harbingers of postmodernity, but they are not its only implications. The celebration of disjointed, pluralist art presaged new ways of thinking about identity and cultural life. In stark contrast to modernist views of self, postmodern thinkers regard the self as decisively unfixed, unstable, incoherent. The same is true of society—it is always in flux, wavering, open to change. Postmodern thinking also rejects science as the only legitimate route to knowledge. Postmodern thinking also questions the authority of grand narratives to represent or unify societies. We'll explore these aspects of postmodern theories in the following pages.

The Fall of Grand Narratives

As we noted above, modernists believed in grand narratives that unified a society and led all of its members to share a coherent view of society. One of the grand narratives in America was that this country provides equal rights and opportunities to all citizens so anyone can succeed and prosper if she or he is willing to work hard. Postmodern thinking challenges the accuracy of this grand narrative with questions such as these:

- Why should a woman in a factory who earns 74 cents an hour believe this narrative when the man working beside her makes $1.00 an hour?
- Why should a gay man believe this narrative when he is denied the right to adopt a child but heterosexual men are not?
- Why should a person with disabilities believe this narrative when she can't enter classroom buildings on a campus?
- Can we believe that America offers equality of educational opportunity when traditionally black schools often receive less generous financial support than do predominantly white schools?
- Can we think the sexes truly have equality when, each day, four women in the United States are beaten to death by intimates?
- Can we believe claims that discrimination is a thing of the past when the Ku Klux Klan still gathers, when hate sites proliferate on the Internet, and when toxic waste dumps are routinely located in poor communities populated primarily by people of color, but middle- and upper-class white communities enjoy healthier environments?

The narrative that America is equal for all, that anyone can succeed through hard work, is built on the story of Horatio Alger, who pulled himself up "by his own bootstraps" to become very successful. But Horatio Alger was white. And male. And able-bodied. And heterosexual. And he had boots whose straps he could use to pull himself up. Can someone born to homeless parents who doesn't have enough to eat and isn't enrolled in school pull herself up by her bootstraps? Do Hispanics and whites get the same respect and wages for the work they do? Do women and men who have equal skills and experience get equal opportunities for career advancement?

Reflection

Can you think of other grand narratives that historically were embraced in the United States? Have they been challenged?

If grand narratives are not to be trusted, then perhaps the society that declares them to be true is not to be trusted either. Michel Foucault (1994, 1995) raises this question in his analysis of how society uses social institutions to uphold a particular social order that privileges some at the cost of others. According to Foucault, society regards crime as a sin against the social order. Discipline must be exerted to maintain the existing social order and the comforts it affords to those who are privileged by it. Foucault also argues that there are important similarities among social institutions such as prisons, factories, barracks, and schools. He asserts that all of them are coercive institutions that seek to uphold the existing social order and socialize people into regarding it as normal and right.

Skepticism about grand narratives cultivated skepticism toward universalizing claims about society. During the 1950s and 1960s social movements such as the Civil Rights Movement and the second wave of American feminism convinced many people that some of America's grand narratives were not true for all people. These and other social movements called attention to what—and who—is left out of America's grand narratives.

In turn, this fueled a number of theories that sought to make sense of more limited spheres of social life. In previous chapters we've discussed some of these: standpoint theory, speech communities theory, organizational culture theory, muted group theory, and feminist theories. Rejecting the modernist ideas of universal truths and objective knowledge, postmodern theories aim to understand the specific "truths" that structure life in particular social communities and contexts.

Localized Action

Because postmodernists are skeptical of grand narratives, they tend to distrust efforts to study "society" as a whole. In fact, a term such as "society" implies a kind of coherence and stability that postmodernists doubt. Postmodern scholars regard social life as fragmented and fluid. Words such as *society* and *culture* are abandoned as fictional representations of a homogeneous social order that doesn't really exist. One of postmodernist theory's strongest claims, in fact, is that grand narratives and societies are full of contradictions, inconsistencies, omissions, and incoherence. The rejection of grand narratives and universal views of power has two implications.

First, many postmodernists claim that power is not centralized in any one location (Baudrillard, 1987; Foucault, 1980). For example, a central kind of power in the United States is capitalism. But where would you locate capitalism—in Washington, D.C., or on Wall Street, or in the office of a particular CEO? Although capitalism is practiced in each of these places, it is not fully located in any one of them. Instead, capitalist power is diffused throughout society.

Because power itself is decentered, many postmodernists assert that resistance to power must also be decentered. Decentered resistance may take the form of **micropolitics**, which involves resistance at local levels. Thus, if you wanted to oppose capitalism, you might boycott a local grocery store that sells products made by underpaid workers, refuse to buy stock in companies that pay managers 500 times more than they pay workers, and take jobs in the nonprofit sector. All of these are examples of micropolitics—resistance at the local, sometimes personal level.

Second, postmodernists view society as a collage of many different communities, each with its own experiences, understandings, and ways of living, and each in dynamic flux. Given this, postmodern scholars question the possibility of studying "power," "resistance," and so forth as absolute, universal things. Instead, postmodernists favor focusing on local narratives that explain practices, beliefs, and identities in particular contexts. By extension, through study of local narratives, postmodernists think they can gain insight into what counts as power or resistance to power in particular contexts. To return to the example that opened this chapter, people in Ghana who wish to resist trikose would do so in ways quite different from those that Westerners might use to challenge sexist practices.

Reflection

College students may not think and act like middle-aged professionals or like college students of the 1970s; Korean Americans may not endorse the values commonly held by European Americans; lesbians don't necessarily adopt the same patterns of relating that heterosexual women do; and members of the working class may have values, attitudes, and customs that do not necessarily parallel those of middle- and upper-class citizens. When people differ so greatly in experiences, values, and communication goals and rules, it makes little sense to speak about *the* culture or *the* society. It may make more sense to develop political goals and strategies that fit specific groups of people and their particular contexts and histories.

Fragmented, Multiple, Relational Selves

Postmodernist thinkers reject the modernist idea of a stable, coherent, autonomous self. Instead, postmodernists proclaim that each person is fragmented and continuously changing in both large and small ways. Each of us has multiple selves, all of which are shaped—though not wholly determined—by complex conditions of our lives. We are subject to change and endless opportunities to remake ourselves.

Postmodern theorists often use the term **subject** to refer to persons. This is a deliberate effort to move away from modernist connotations associated with the term *individual*. For postmodernists, a subject is a way of being, not a fixed essence (Weedon, 1987). Subjects are always in the process of constructing and reconstructing themselves (Hall, 1996). For example, in different moments a person might be a parent, child, spouse, worker, and friend. Each of these subjects, or subject positions, is constructed in specific social interactions and in relation to particular times and goals. The parent subject is most likely to emerge in relationships with a child, whereas the friend subject may arise in interactions with close peers. Each subject is a position that is formed within particular relationships and cultural conditions and may fade when those relationships and conditions are no longer present.

Because subjects are multiple and fluid, contradictions are likely to arise. Sometimes we experience incongruity between two or more of our multiple subject positions. Consider a few examples of contradictions in self that students of mine have expressed:

- Jana is a black woman who is drawn to feminism, but she feels it is in tension with her loyalty to her race.

- Matthew always thought he was unprejudiced until he began interviewing for jobs. He says he believes in affirmative action, but he also wants to get the best job for himself.

- Maria was born in New York to a father who is Venezuelan and a mother who is Puerto Rican. She identifies as an American, but many people view her as a Latina. She feels she should celebrate her Latin heritage, but she doesn't speak Spanish and has never traveled outside of the United States.

- Rebecca is a single mother and a student. When her son developed a serious ear infection, she had to rush him to the emergency room, where she felt torn between concern for him and resentment that his illness was preventing her from studying for an exam.

Reflection

Can you identify contradictions in yourself? Which subject positions that you occupy or consider occupying are in tension with other subject positions?

Rather than presuming that identity is a constant that we carry with us wherever we go, postmodern theorists believe that our identities (always plural) are fluid and flexible; they emerge and continuously re-form as we enter specific situations and relationships. In this sense, subjectivity can be seen as a performance, a production—something that is crafted and presented in a particular time and context but which may not be the same (or even exist at all) at another time and place. Consequently, we are not one constant self but a kaleidoscope of always forming and re-forming selves. Kenneth Gergen (1991) refers to this as a **relational self** because identity comes into being as we participate in particular relationships. Thus, identity is emergent and variable, not established and unvarying.

Nor is identity something we fashion outside of cultural contexts. We are positioned within social processes and institutions that define status, rights, power, roles, and appropriate codes of conduct. In other words, social life is structured by institutions and practices that constrain how we think, feel, and act. Yet postmodern theory is not rigidly deterministic, for it sees both social life and subjects as ever changing and ever changeable. Therefore, subjectivity is paradoxical: To some extent, we are free subjects who choose our actions; at the same time, we and our choices of action are inevitably shaped by cultural conditions in general and power relations in particular (Althusser, 1971). Within postmodernist worldviews, subjective consciousness is linked to social structures, and both are open to change, change, and more change (Sarup, 1989; Weedon, 1987).

The photographer Cindy Sherman exemplifies postmodern notions of the instability of subjects. One of her exhibits features photographs of very different-looking women who represent a range of social classes and personal qualities. Only upon reading the catalogue for the exhibition do most viewers realize that all the women in the photographs are actually one woman—the artist Cindy Sherman. Through her photographs, Sherman embodies and comments on the plasticity of identity and—equally important—the possibility of masking. Another example of postmodern posturing is Madonna, who has embodied many identities (or masks), including traditional woman, vamp, and dominatrix. Which is the "real" Cindy Sherman? Which is the "real" Madonna? Which is mask? For postmodernists those questions are misdirected, because there is no "real" self but only masks—multiple masks, or subject positions, that we create, wear, and change as we find useful and possible in the ever-shifting contexts of cultural constraints, contexts, goals, and moods.

Reflection

Describe the self you are in relationships with friends, girlfriends or boyfriends, parents, and employers. Are you different selves in these different relationships, or are you different versions of a stable, single self?

Media and new technologies spur fragmentation by producing changes in how we experience space and time. For example, a few years ago if one of my students had a question, she or he would either drop by my office or call me, and we would talk. Today, it's at least as likely that a student with a question will email me; at some later time I will open the email and respond to it, and at a still-later time the student will read my response and perhaps reply. No longer does interaction occur in continuous, sequenced time. Instead, it is fragmented, with the question and answer separated by space and time and all that occurs within them.

Television programs occur in episodes, so we may have to wait a week to find out how various characters deal with problems in their lives. In presenting characters and their activities in discrete units separated by time, television teaches us to expect time and life to be discontinuous. Technologies also change our sense of time by making speed the norm. You understand the new sense of time and speed if you have ever been frustrated because a Web site's page took more than a second to load.

Media and new technologies also make it possible for us to have new modes of experience. We enter chat rooms and talk with people we've never met and may never meet face-to-face. We join and desert virtual communities that are often focused on a single topic or interest area. These virtual communities mock traditional notions of community as enduring, face-to-face groups in which people accommodate to each other and work out differences in order to persist (Urgo, 2000). You can visit the Web sites of people who broadcast their lives using an online digital camera that records everything that happens in the people's environments.

New technologies teach us to think in parallel ways that differ from the sequential ways of thinking that characterized the modernist period. While I am writing this chapter, the email program running behind my word processing program alerts me to incoming mail. I stop writing, check the message, decide whether to answer it now or later, and then return to my writing. You go to Amazon.com to order a book and encounter six pop-up ads and suggestions for further reading or products related to the book you want to order. You note these interruptions, perhaps explore some of them, perhaps check out related links, and then order your book.

Because the cultural institutions and practices that structure our lives are inconsistent, it's not surprising that we sometimes simultaneously experience competing social structures and practices that invite us to assume contradictory subject positions (Weedon, 1987). Recently, Rebecca, a student of mine, came to talk with me about her upcoming marriage. "I think I want to keep my name," she began, "but my fiancé says that a wife should take her husband's name." I nodded, and she continued, "But a lot of my girlfriends tell me that I should keep my name so that I have an identity independent of his." Rebecca was struggling with competing efforts to define her subject position—should she define herself as a wife—an identity that exists in relation to a husband—or as an independent person?

Are there other options for Rebecca's subject position that do not force a choice between an identity based on relationship and one based on autonomy? When she completes college, Rebecca will meet coworkers who define her as a woman or wife or mother and who invite her to assume a subject position based on her gender. She will also meet others who signify that she is a professional, colleague, or boss and who invite her to assume a subject position reflective of her professional abilities. Like most of us, Rebecca is continuously immersed in different, often contradictory efforts to construct herself as a subject in the social world.

Reflection

How have you reconciled contradictory possibilities for defining your subject position in particular moments?

Commodification

A particularly important postmodern claim is that all phenomena, including people, are increasingly commodified, or made into commodities. **Commodification** is the process by which phenomena are treated as products to be acquired and used. Commodification grows out of several trends in the contemporary era. One is the fragmentation of society and selves, which we have already discussed. Once society and self are no longer viewed as stable, enduring phenomena, it is possible to regard and treat them as parts, as pieces unconnected to one another. By extension, this invites us to deal with pieces of people or social phenomena rather than an illusory whole. We may learn to see and treat people as commodities that are useful to us in particular ways.

Also propelling comodification are industrialization and its successor, technology. With the advent of the Industrial Revolution, workers were seen and treated as commodities. They were valued not for who they were, but for what they could produce—how much, how fast. Further, as workers engaged in selling their labor as a commodity to employers, workers came to see themselves and each other as commodities. As Marx (1887) pointed out in his classic work, *Capital*, industries don't care about a worker's dreams, needs, family situation, and so forth. They care only whether a person is a good worker. Any worker who doesn't produce enough goods at a fast-enough pace can be dismissed and replaced by another worker. Within the factory system, workers become only commodities—valued for what they produce, not who they are (Althusser, 1971; Tucker, 1999).

The Industrial Revolution made mass production possible. Before factories existed, if you wanted a pair of shoes, you had to go to a shoemaker, who would spend hours or days crafting a pair of shoes specifically for you. With factories, however, great numbers of shoes can be mass produced and sold to consumers. The cost of a pair of factory-made shoes is less because it takes relatively little time and a minimum of human labor to produce shoes en masse. The same is true for other products that used to be made by hand and individually—shirts, books, furniture, even homes. With mass production, most items can be made quickly and relatively cheaply. As products cost less, more people can afford them.

Commodification of labor and mass production paved the way for workers to become alienated from their work and each other (Marx, 1887). Previously many people had lived and worked on their own land. Their lives were intimately connected to the work they invested in tilling soil, planting and harvesting crops, and raising livestock. In this agrarian life, people depended personally on one another—everyone in a farm family had to contribute, many members of a community pitched in to build barns and houses for each other. Within this way of living, the work one did was directly connected to the quality of one's life. The Industrial Revolution severed the direct connection between a person's work and how she or he lived. With the spread of factories and a paid labor market, selling one's labor for money was the link between labor and living.

A third trend spurring commodification is the increasing affluence of Western culture. As John Storey (1999) notes, the late 1950s and 1960s in Europe and North America was the first time in which working people could afford to buy things beyond the basic necessities. Storey observes that average people began to consume "on the basis of 'desire' rather than 'need'" (p. 134). People's feeling that they "could afford" things slipped easily into the sense that they "must have" various products. Fanning the desire to have and use more was mass advertising, also a fairly new phenomenon in the 1950s, that encouraged people to have the latest-model car, the newest appliances, and the "coolest" clothes.

How many shirts or blouses do you own? How many would you own if you or someone else had to make each one individually and by hand?

As hinted at above, media are a fourth important trend that fuels commodification. Television programs and especially advertising encourage us to think of people as commodities by offering images of only parts of people. Obvious examples are ads and MTV shows in which the camera focuses on only one part of women's bodies, usually breasts, legs, or buttocks. As viewers, we're invited to forget the subjective consciousness of the women on the screen and regard them only as body parts. Another example is television programs that feature Hispanic or black characters but do not make the characters whole people by presenting them in the context of their racial-ethnic heritage and communities (Holtzman, 2000; Merritt, 2000).

Media also contribute to commodification by manufacturing needs and desires. As primary players in the capitalist economy, media aim to make profits. Many advertisements do not simply inform us of products and services that we already want or need. They often cultivate needs in us by convincing us that we need things we never thought we needed. If advertisers can convince us we need a product, we will buy it and enrich the company that makes it.

A good historical example of advertising's power to create new needs is the campaign to get women to shave their underarms. Until the early 1900s women in the United States didn't shave their underarms. Beginning in 1915, U.S. marketers mounted a campaign to persuade women that underarm hair was unsightly, unfeminine, and socially incorrect (Adams, 1991). By 1922—just seven years after ads encouraging women to remove underarm hair were launched—there was a strong market for women's razors and depilatories. Many ads are designed to create needs in us so that we buy more products to solve problems we didn't know we had.

Review your checkbook stubs or charge card statements for the last year. Have you purchased things you didn't think you needed before you saw or heard them advertised?

Should we resist the commodification of people, including ourselves? Should we fight to regain our control as autonomous beings who cannot be reduced to mere objects, much less parts of objects? Certainly some people encourage us to identify and fight against efforts to objectify us and shrink or colonize our subjective consciousness.

Quite another answer comes from Jean Baudrillard (1990), a premier postmodern theorist. Instead of resisting efforts to objectify us, Baudrillard suggests that we go with these forces. Baudrillard encourages us to adopt what he calls "fatal strategies," which pursue a course of action to its extreme in the hope of surpassing its limits. For example, many people resist and argue against pornography because they believe it objectifies humans. Baudrillard might advise us instead to let pornography proliferate to such an extreme that it is no longer interesting, no longer effective in objectifying humans. When taken to excess, pornography might become banal and boring. Let it appear not only in X-rated films and specialized magazines, but on billboards, posters in classrooms, juice cartons, and home and garden shops—everywhere! At that point, pornography might mean something quite different from what it means today, or it might be replaced by something else.

Language

Postmodern theories consider language to be perhaps the most important means by which subjects and the social order are constituted, normalized, reproduced, challenged, and changed. Along with many of the theories we have studied in previous chapters, this one assumes that communication constructs our sense of reality. Many European philosophers who have developed postmodern perspectives draw heavily on poststructuralist theory (Derrida, 1973, 1974; Foucault, 1967, 1977, 1980; Habermas, 1971, 1984; Lacan, 1977, 1981), which insists that knowledge of the world, ourselves, and others is determined by language. Language shapes what we can and do perceive as well as the meanings we assign to our perceptions.

Within a postmodern perspective, the self arises in language and is possible only because of language (Lacan, 1977; Sarup, 1989). This is because humans are continuously immersed in language and can never escape from a realm that is inevitably symbolically mediated. In other words, it's impossible to think about ourselves, others, or situations without language. Further, the language that we use reflects and reproduces the values, social relations, and subject positions endorsed by our culture. In many Asian cultures, terms to describe individuals include references to their places within their families. Thus, the language they use to name themselves includes relationships to family members. This is not necessarily true for Westerners, as the English language uses highly individualistic terms to describe persons.

Reflection

Would George Herbert Mead, the "father of symbolic interactionism," agree with the postmodern claim that the self arises in language?

Although postmodernists insist that we exist as subjects only in and through language, they do not assume that any term or terms can completely describe a person. Instead, they claim that we can neither escape linguistic definition nor be completely represented by it (Sarup, 1989, p. 15). For example, the term *African American* describes ethnicity, but it does not define gender, socioeconomic class, sexual preference, religious beliefs, or many other aspects of a subject. Further, the term *African American* replaced other, previous terms such as *colored* and *Negro*. And the term *African American* is currently not the only one preferred by people of African descent: *Afro American* and *Black* are also in common usage. Each term may be both accurate and incomplete.

Postmodern theorists also note that many facets of identity are fluid. For instance, a person may define himself as straight at one time, gay at another, and bisexual at a third time. A person may be raised Catholic, declare herself to be a Buddhist at age 20, a Taoist at 25, and an atheist at 36. A person who is born able-bodied may become disabled, and a person who has a disability may become nondisabled. Sex change operations make it possible for people to change their biological (if not chromosomal) sex, which has long been viewed as an absolutely fixed aspect of identity. This insight beckons communication theorists to explore the ways in which language both highlights and obscures facets of subjects.

Reflection

What terms do you use to describe yourself? Which aspects of who you are does each term highlight and obscure?

Meaning

Jacques Derrida (1973, 1974) was particularly interested in the precarious character of meanings that are constituted by language. He argued that no meaning can ever be adequately represented by a single word, even though we do depend on single words in our daily interaction. (Remember the general semanticists' advice to use *etc.*?) To emphasize both the inadequacy of words and the necessity of them, Derrida coined the term ***sous rature***, a term that means "under erasure." He sometimes places an X through a word (lonely, friend, angry) to indicate that the term is both necessary and inadequate to describe its referent. For Derrida, meaning is scattered throughout extensive chains of symbols in which each symbol bears the traces of other symbols that precede and follow it. Thus, a word can point to or indicate meanings, but it can never fully capture them.

TRY IT OUT To gain an initial understanding of Derrida's argument that meaning is scattered throughout symbolic chains, read the words below by looking at only one line at a time.

> I am
> going
> to the bank
> to withdraw everything from our account
> before I leave you for good.

The two words on the first line make sense all alone, yet to understand what they mean we have to grasp all of the other words in the entire sentence. The I that is cleaning out a bank account and then leaving someone is not the same as an abstract I without a specified purpose. Likewise, "going to the bank" is a phrase with meaning, but what it means changes when we read the words that follow it.

Neither single words nor even whole chains of words can explain the meanings we create. Instead, meaning arises from interaction between a person (*subject* in postmodern terminology) and language in their contexts, and people, language, and contexts are all fluid, in flux. In other words, the experiences that we have and the subject positioning we accept in any particular moment shape how we interpret communication. Consider an example. The word *rainbow* once referred only to a lovely array of colors produced when rain and sun are simultaneous. Today *rainbow* is also a symbol of gay rights and support of gay rights. *Rainbow* and *Rainbow Coalition* are also terms used by the Reverend Jesse Jackson to refer to celebration of America's pluralistic culture, which includes people of many ethnicities and colors. The meanings of *rainbow* are continuously rearticulated in American culture. Each new articulation at once is distinct and bears the traces of prior meanings.

If a man says to a woman, "Let's run away for the weekend," how will she interpret his meaning and respond to it? That depends on how the woman constitutes her subjectivity and that of the man in the particular situation. If the man is a romantic partner, she may interpret the words as an invitation for romance and respond affirmatively. If such invitations have resulted in good experiences in the past, she may accept; if they have resulted in negative experiences in the past, she may decline. On the other hand, if a colleague at her workplace makes the statement, she may take offense at the "same" words. She may consider the words to be an act of sexual harassment. She defines herself and her romantic partner as subjects between whom romantic talk is welcome; at her workplace she defines herself and her colleague as professionals between whom comments of a romantic nature are unwelcome and inappropriate.

Social Relations

Postmodern theorists assume that social relations, like subjects and meaning, are constructed by social institutions and practices, including language. Michel Foucault (1967, 1972, 1977, 1980) has been particularly influential in advancing the idea that the world view of a society is determined by what he calls "the predominant discursive structures of the era." For Foucault, **discursive structures** are deeply ensconced ways of thinking about and expressing identity and conducting social life. For example, in Western societies, gender is a primary discursive structure that shapes both individual and cultural identities and activities. Likewise, European Americans are deeply wedded to individualism and notions of independence, whereas many African Americans, Hispanics, Hispanic Americans, Asians, and Asian Americans tend to embrace more communal and collective identities.

If discursive structures influence human behavior, it follows that what we notice and think in any era and social location is shaped by the discursive structures that organize and direct knowledge. This claim, like others in postmodern theory, is not deterministic, because it resists the idea of any constancy in social life. Instead, discursive structures are presumed to be fluid, continuously shaped and reshaped by the prevailing world view, which in turn is sculpted by discursive formations.

Reflection

How are the rules that interest Foucault similar to and different from those in CMM theory?

Foucault (1994, 1995) and other postmodern theorists contend that discourses are controlled by rules that specify who may talk and who may not, define which topics can and cannot be discussed, and designate when (in which circumstances) particular kinds of talk are appropriate and inappropriate. If you remember muted group theory's claim that women have been silenced in Western culture, then you'll appreciate Foucault's point. This connection also explains why power is an issue of central concern to postmodernists. They seek to understand the origin and operation of discursive rules that allow and prohibit voices of different social groups. In this respect they share many of the impulses of critical theories.

Criticisms of Postmodern Perspectives

Postmodernist perspectives are not accepted or endorsed by all scholars. We'll discuss three particularly significant criticisms of postmodern perspectives.

Unacceptable Epistemic Relativism

One of the severest criticisms is that postmodern perspectives are foolishly dismissive of facts, evidence, and science. This criticism takes aim at the postmodernist claim that truth is relative and reality is socially constructed.

This criticism surfaced dramatically in 1996 in a remarkable incident in the academic world. Alan Sokal, a physicist at New York University, was distressed by what he considered sloppy thinking by many postmodernist scholars. In Sokal's view, postmodernists erred in confusing truth with assertions of fact. Sokal agreed that "truth" may be subjective and may be shaped by diverse social locations. However, Sokal did not agree that facts are subjective and irrelevant. He wanted to expose what he considered the sloppy thinking of postmodernists.

Sokal chose a dramatic way to achieve his goal. He submitted a paper to *Social Text*, a premiere journal in cultural studies and postmodern scholarship. His paper, "Transgressing the Boundaries: Toward a Transformative Hermeneutics of Quantum Gravity" (Sokal, 1996c), was accepted and published in *Social Text* in 1996. In this paper Sokal argued that laws of quantum gravity are socially constructed and that physics has been repressed by modernist notions of truth and scientific authority.

The only problem was that the entire article was a parody, a spoof. Sokal didn't believe that laws of physics were socially constructed, and he didn't produce any credible evidence to support the claims in his article. After the article was published, Sokal revealed his "experiment." He said he submitted the bogus article to "expose and challenge nonsense and sloppy thinking" among postmodernists (Sokal, 1996a, p. 62). Sokal went on to scold postmodernists, for excessive claims about the social construction of reality. He said that insisting reality is socially constructed won't help us develop treatments for AIDS or devise strategies to prevent global warming. Instead, Sokal argued, we need scientific facts to help us address these problems. And, he insisted, facts do exist—they are not mere social constructions (Sokal, 1996b, 1998; Sokal & Briemont, 1998). Sokal maintained that science is a progressive force for combating serious problems in cultural life.

Sokal further indicted postmodernist work for being guided more by politics than by evidence. He claimed that the editors accepted his essay because they agreed with its political stance and conclusions and didn't care whether he had evidence to support his position. The editors, however, insist that they did ask Sokal to temper some of his speculative claims about physical science and to revise his questionable footnotes (Robbins & Ross, 1996).

TRY IT OUT Decide for yourself what you think of the Sokal affair. To read his original paper and the comments by him and the editors of *Social Text* that followed, go to: http://www.physics.nyu.edu/faculty/sokal/. Don't worry—you don't have to understand quantum physics to follow the arguments. As you read the article and subsequent commentaries, consider these questions:

1. Should Sokal have submitted a bogus paper to an academic journal? Was this unprofessional, as the editors of *Social Text* claim?

2. Did the editors of *Social Text* have a responsibility to check Sokal's evidence before publishing the article?

3. Do you think Sokal is correct in accusing postmodern scholars of confusing claims of truth with assertions of fact?

Clearly there were some excesses in early postmodern theorizing. At the same time, there are excesses in Sokal's criticisms and claims about

Criticisms of Postmodern Perspectives

postmodern theorizing. Skepticism about science, which postmodernists have, is not the same as wholesale dismissal of it, which Sokal attributes to postmodernists. By extension, postmodernists don't necessarily reject the findings of science. They simply don't accept the idea that facts and science (particularly as science is currently practiced) are the only route to useful knowledge. Similarly, defenders of postmodernist theory point out that asserting that there are multiple ways of knowing and experiencing social life is not the same as saying we can know nothing about the social world and is certainly not the same thing as saying we cannot hold some politics better than others.

Ted Striphas (2000) incisively points out that Sokal mistakes "a respectful politics seeking to meet people 'where they are' for a lack of political engagement" (p. 29). In other words, efforts to recognize and understand different points of view and the circumstances that inform them is not the same as saying all points of view and all political stances are equally good. Striphas (2000) elaborates:

> Meeting people where they are means acknowledging the beliefs (investments, values, etc.) to which they hold in their everyday lives. But meeting people where they are by no means implies ending up with people where they are political speaking. . . . To meet people "where they are" . . . by no means constitutes an end in its own right. Rather, it is something to start a conversation. . . ." (pp. 38–39)

Nihilistic

Related to the criticism that it is excessively subjective, postmodern theories have also been criticized for being nihilistic (Becker, 1992). **Nihilism** is denial of any absolute basis of meaning in life. Identities, values, guides for conduct, ethical standards—all are so subjective that there can be no clear or stable basis for judging some beliefs, codes of ethics, social practices, and ways of being as better than others.

Postmodernists agree with the charge that they reject universal, indisputable sources of judgment and meaning. After all, postmodern theory began with a repudiation of the kind of absolute, universal foundations for knowledge and judgment that had been endorsed by previous intellectual frameworks. Does this mean, as some critics claim, that postmodern theory has no way to make distinctions among disparate values, social practices, actions, and so forth?

Postmodernists have two responses to the charge of nihilism. Some agree that postmodern theory is nihilistic but argue that this isn't necessarily a problem. These postmodernists might say that, in an absolute sense, life is meaningless, but so what? It always was; we just didn't realize it. The task for

"Scientists confirmed today that everything we know about the
structure of the universe is wrongedy-wrong-wrong."

us as particular subjects and as collective societies is to generate provisional meanings for our lives. In letting go of the belief that our lives have a single enduring meaning, we are empowered to cultivate meanings that work in particular times and places, even knowing that meanings that suffice at one moment may be replaced by other meanings in different moments and contexts. Within this perspective the lack of absolute and stable meanings liberates us to create and recreate ourselves and our world endlessly.

Other postmodernists have responded to the charge of nihilism with serious reflection on problems in postmodernist theory. They acknowledge that postmodern theory, as so far developed, is vulnerable to the charge of radical subjectivity, in which there can be no basis for judging some actions, values, and practices as better than any others. These theorists admit that this creates a serious bind for postmodernism. On the one hand, postmodernism rejects universal, abstract bases of judgment and meaning. On the other hand, it doesn't want to lapse into utter subjectivity and a kind of radical relativism that allows no means of adjudicating between competing social structures and practices. The question is how to get out of the bind.

One way out of this bind is to draw upon rhetorical theory. At least since Aristotle's time, rhetorical theorists have concerned themselves with

Criticisms of Postmodern Perspectives

finding ways to make practical judgments in the contingent social world. Such judgments are not guided by a priori, absolute values or criteria. Instead, judgments are made with sensitivity to specific circumstances, people, and activities. Like postmodern theorists, rhetorical theorists eschew universal standards of judgment that are imposed on all phenomena. Yet rhetorical theorists do not let the rejection of absolute standards propel them into a totally subjective, relativistic morass. Instead, they ask what is good (or better), effective (or more effective), or possible, in any particular case.

Sound judgments are possible, yet they cannot be made in the abstract, and they are not immune to questioning. Because judgments are made with reference to specific circumstances, the bases of judgment in one situation may not be useful or appropriate in different situations. Every judgment is contingent—that is, it depends on particular situations and their constraints. A judgment can be made and justified, but it is not beyond question. Rather, any judgment—any evaluation—is open to further argument and rethinking.

Destructive of Human Identity

Related to the criticism of nihilism, some critics indict postmodern worldviews for being at least hyperbolic and perhaps inaccurate in claiming that there is no stable, core self. Many people, scholars and laypeople alike, don't accept the claim that there is no core to the human self but only various performances of identity that emerge and dissolve in response to particular relationships and contexts.

Certainly, many of the theories we have studied assume that there is something relatively stable and enduring about the self. Symbolic interactionism, for example, shares with postmodern theory the idea that selves are acquired. However, symbolic interactionists do not think the self that is acquired through interaction with others is only a superficial role or roles that a person casually slips on and off in various situations.

In response to this, postmodernists might shake their heads at what they would call "old-school world views." The idea of coherent selves was an illusion of modernity, they would assert. We need to move beyond that to live in the postmodern era. Postmodernists do not see it as necessarily tragic that we are fragmented and commodified. For postmodernists, this invites us to engage in ironic, playful performances, secure that we can easily abandon any that don't work out or cease to suit us.

Summary

Postmodern theories chart new territory and new ways of thinking. At the same time, they decisively challenge many of the claims, and even the fundamental assumptions, of some existing theories. In the new millennium, postmodern perspectives are significantly shaping multiple theories of communication. Postmodern theories arise out of a strong commitment to critical scholarship and an explicit embrace of certain values, including respect for multiple truths and the people who hold them and dedication to helping make cultural life more equitable and more humane for everyone.

Before leaving our discussion of postmodern thinking, we should note that it is continuing to evolve. Postmodernists regard their own world view as contingent and subject to change, just like everything else. In other words, postmodernist ideas and the theories they generate are not frozen, not set in stone.

Key Terms

commodification

discursive structures

grand narrative

micropolitics

modernity

nihilism

postmodernism

relational self

sous rateur

subject

CHAPTER FOURTEEN

Communication Theories in Action: A Final Look

Our journey through the world of communication theories has allowed us to consider a broad range of ideas and issues. At this point you may be wondering how all the pieces fit together into the "big picture." In this closing chapter we want to place discussions of specific theories in a larger perspective on research and social life. In the pages that follow, we'll reflect on what we've learned and what it means for scholarship and practical life. First, we'll reconsider the nature and goals of theorizing in

Reflection

What are the most useful understandings of communication that you have gained from studying theories?

light of the knowledge we now have of specific theories. Then we'll highlight themes that weave through *Communication Theories in Action* and trace their implications for our ongoing efforts to make sense of human interactions.

An Integrating Perspective on Communication Theories

We launched our study of theory by asking what theories are and what they attempt to do. In Chapters 2 and 3, we outlined the goals of theories and how they are built, tested, and evaluated. As you'll recall, the traditional goals of theory have been to describe, explain, predict, and control phenomena. Endorsing these goals, communication researchers attempt to describe what is involved in communication, to explain relationships among those phenomena, and to predict and control communication. These tradi-

"By God, for a minute there it suddenly all made sense!"

tional purposes of describing and explaining have generated substantial insight into how communication works (or doesn't work) and how we can influence particular communication encounters.

Controversy Over Theoretical Goals

No longer do all scholars limit themselves to the orthodox goals of theory. Although description and explanation are consensually endorsed objectives of theories, many current scholars are more enthusiastic about understanding as a goal, as opposed to prediction and control. Rather than trying to predict or control how people will communicate, these theorists accord priority to understanding the dynamics of interaction.

Reflection

Now that you've considered theories that seek prediction and control and theories that highlight understanding, how do you evaluate these different goals?

In addition to emphasizing understanding, some theorists advocate a fourth aim of theory: positive social change. The aim of instigating social reform is not necessarily at odds with traditional theoretical objectives such as prediction and control. It is, however, inconsistent with conventional epistemologies that view science as a value-free enterprise. The debate over the role of values in research is one of the most controversial issues in communication theory today.

Historically, theories have been regarded as objective descriptions of reality. Within this perspective, theorists are supposed to observe and record what exists without imposing their own values on the process or outcomes of inquiry. It is presumed that detached, dispassionate research is feasible and that it is capable of producing objective knowledge of reality.

Beginning in the 1970s, some scholars began to question both the possibility and the desirability of value-free inquiry. Philip Wander (1983) argued that values infuse the entire research process, from the choice of a topic of study (and the accompanying choice not to pursue other topics) to methods of gathering and analyzing data to inferences drawn from data. Scholars always unavoidably operate from values, said Wander. The only question is whether they recognize and explicate the values that inform their work.

Since Wander's pivotal article was published, many researchers in communication and other fields have echoed and extended the opinion that scholarship is necessarily entwined with values (Blair et al., 1994; Conquergood, 1991, 1992; Denzin, 2001; Keller, 1985; Wander, 1984; West, 1993, 1995; Wood & Cox, 1993; Wood & Duck, 1995a). These critics of objectivity insist that only by recognizing the presence and influence of human values on research can scholars become accountable for the ways in which their values enter into the process of inquiry. Awareness of biases and values enables scholars to monitor their impact on research.

Critical theorists are particularly vocal in promoting the use of research for social reform. They believe that theories should increase insight into the ways that communication legitimizes unequal power relations. Increasing awareness of dominant ideologies and the ways that they are sustained empowers individuals to resist the influence of dominant ideology in their own lives and to work toward remaking society so that it is more inclusive, progressive, and humane.

In the foregoing chapters we've encountered theories that exemplify both schools of thought on the goals of theory, specifically the appropriateness of theoretical value commitments. Based on what you've learned, you should now be able to decide where you personally stand in relation to this controversy.

Reflection

Can the process of inquiry be free of human values? Should it be?

Evaluating Theories

Chapter 2 identified five standards for evaluating theories: scope, testability, parsimony, practical value (or utility), and heuristic strength. Now that you've studied a number of communication theories, you know that each

Communication Theories in Action: A Final Look

theory meets some evaluative standards better than others. It is possible for a theory to offer very rich description and explanation (scope) and to generate substantial new ideas (heurism) but to be difficult to test and confirm. CMM and dramatism are examples of exceptionally broad accounts of how humans create meanings, yet it's hard to find incontrovertible evidence that we use communication rules or are always motivated by guilt. On the other hand, some theories can be easily tested but lack explanatory scope and practical value. Uncertainty reduction theory's axioms and hypotheses are easy to test empirically, yet this theory has limited heuristic power.

There is no agreed-upon hierarchy for ranking the importance of different standards used to evaluate theories. Some people think that scope and testability are the most significant criteria, whereas others regard practical value in making a difference in the real world as the most important measure of a theory's worth. Because scholars differ in the significance they attach to various evaluative standards, they naturally disagree in their assessments of specific theories. This suggests that our judgments of theories are influenced by the values we consider most important. Thus, evaluation of theories, perhaps like theories themselves, reflects subjective interests, commitments, and values.

TRY IT OUT Review the theories you've studied in preceding chapters. You may wish to use the table of contents to make sure that you recall each theory. Decide which theories rank highest on each evaluative standard.

- *Scope:* Which theories provide the fullest description and explanation of human communication?

- *Testability:* Which theories are most easily tested to determine their validity?

- *Parsimony:* Which theories are the most appropriately simple and understandable?

- *Practical Value:* Which theories have the greatest pragmatic value? Explain what kind of practical impact each theory has (for example, controlling organizational communication, promoting social reform, improving family relations).

- *Heuristic Power:* Which theories generate the most important new insights into communication and/or the most valuable new ways of thinking about what communication is and how it functions?

Based on your judgments about which theories most fully satisfy each criterion, can you identify a single theory that you consider the best overall?

Among scholars there is ongoing debate about what theories are and should be and, by extension, how we can best assess their merits. These disagreements are constructive because they stimulate thinking, reflection, and openness to new ideas about communication and the functions it serves.

Communication Theories in Review

Chapters 4 through 13 presented a sample of existing communication theories. The theories we've discussed differ in their philosophical foundations and views of communication.

Philosophical Foundations

The theories we've studied vary in ontological and epistemological assumptions. We examined a few theories that view human behavior as relatively determined by universal, or at least very general, laws of behavior. Uncertainty reduction theory, for example, claims that individuals react in predictable and generalizable ways to greater and lesser degrees of uncertainty about others. Exchange theory posits that relationships are determined by people's efforts to maximize their profits and minimize their costs in interaction. Technological determinism and, to a lesser extent, cultivation theory suggest that human meaning is at least strongly influenced, if not completely determined, by media.

A larger number of theories endorse ontological and epistemological positions that presume that humans are active, interpreting agents who act on the basis of meanings that they create and assign to phenomena, including themselves, others, behaviors, and situations. This philosophical stance moves theorizing away from an emphasis on external stimuli as causes of behavior and toward a focus on the processes by which we develop and share meanings that guide what we think, feel, and do.

Both symbolic interactionism and dramatism assume that humans are interpretive agents who rely on symbols to know and represent the world. CMM explains communication as a rule-guided process in which we create and follow regular, but not externally determined, patterns of interaction. Constructivism argues that humans construct meaning by using cognitive schemata to make sense of experiences. Performance theories view humans as constructing meanings through performances—both those they observe and those in which they participate.

Another theory that views humans as interpretive agents is standpoint theory, which asserts that different social groups develop distinct ways of understanding the world as a function of their social locations and the experiences those locations and experiences allow and preclude. Narrative theory portrays all communication as a matter of telling and hearing stories that aim to create coherent accounts of human experience.

If you believe that human behavior is determined by external stimuli that operate in lawlike ways, then you'll be unimpressed by theories that assume individuals actively work to create meanings for the world and its happenings. On the other hand, if you think humans are proactive beings who interpret their experiences, then it's unlikely you'll place much store in theories that rely on laws to explain human reactions to external stimuli.

Reflection

How do ontological and epistemological beliefs affect tendencies to hold individuals accountable for their actions in everyday life?

As is true of other theoretical issues, ontology and epistemology are arguable. There is no way to prove conclusively that humans do or do not have a degree of free will; there is no definitive evidence that external stimuli do or do not strictly determine our behaviors. The nature of humans and the process by which we acquire knowledge, then, are ultimately matters that cannot be scientifically tested and proved or disproved.

It is less important that scholars and laypeople agree about ontology and epistemology than that we understand different philosophical positions and their implications for theory and its applications. What you've learned about the process of theorizing and the insight you've gained into specific theories should allow you to discern the ontological and epistemological foundations that underlie different theoretical positions. In turn this will enable you to decide whether a given theory is consistent with your own philosophical assumptions.

Reflection

Thinking back on the theories that you found most and least useful, what can you infer about your own ontological and epistemological assumptions?

Views of Communication

Another difference among the theories we've studied is the views of communication that they advance. The Try It Out exercise on the next page gives you an opportunity to match views of communication with different theories that we've discussed.

Identify the theory reflected in each of the following statements:

1. Communication is a bartering of profits and costs.
2. Communication reflects continuous tension between contradictory human impulses.
3. Communication is storytelling.
4. Communication is a primary way in which people create and sustain cultures.
5. Communication creates and reflects positions within a given social order.
6. Symbols move us farther and farther from "raw reality."
7. Communication is a process by which people try to coordinate their meanings.
8. Communication is a tool that upholds and justifies the status quo.
9. Communication is how society gets into individuals so that members of a society can participate in a common social order with consensual meanings.
10. Communication relies on rites, rituals, and routines to sustain a common view of reality.
11. Communication is a means of reducing of uncertainty.
12. Communication is an exclusionary apparatus that mutes nondominant social groups.
13. Communication punctuates interaction to construct meaning.
14. Communication is a reflection of varying degrees of intimacy.
15. Communication is a symbolic dance on the stage of life.
16. Communication rituals allow people to understand and sustain the values and traditions of their communities.
17. Communication is the primary means by which subjects and the social order are constructed, yet words can only indicate meanings, never fully capture them.
18. Communication is a means of cultivating world views.
19. Communication is the tool that shapes human sensory abilities and civilized life.

Each view of communication in the Try It Out is advanced by one of the theories we've studied. Each of these views of communication makes sense in its own way, yet not all are compatible with one another. That raises an important question: Which view of communication and which theory of communication should we believe?

The Value of Theoretical Plurality

As you learned about different communication theories, you may have found yourself thinking, "That makes sense," again and again. Perhaps you agreed with CMM theory's claim that rules of communicating explain many of the regularities in human interaction. Yet it also seems true that communication is an interplay between contradictory impulses or dialectics. And who would argue with the idea that communication includes both content and relationship levels of meaning?

Reflection

What are the values and limitations of adopting a single theoretical lens through which to view communication?

Studying a range of communication theories gives you a rich reservoir of ways to think about communication. This empowers you to think about interaction from a variety of perspectives instead of being limited to a single viewpoint or only a few viewpoints. You may find, as many scholars do, that you don't want to pledge exclusive allegiance to any one theory but prefer to draw on multiple theories to understand your own experiences as well as interactional dynamics in the many contexts of your life.

Every theory we've studied offers a particular way of thinking about communication. Each one is a specific set of lenses that clarifies certain aspects of what we observe but that may not allow us to see other aspects. What a theory helps us see and what it keeps invisible reflect, in part, the philosophical assumptions of those who develop the theory.

Because underlying assumptions of theories are not always compatible, only some theories fit well together (such as dramatism and narrative, symbolic interactionism and constructivism). Other theories are less compatible (such as technological determinism and CMM, dialectics and uncertainty reduction), and we must choose between them if we wish to create a coherent view of communication. Because partiality and incompatibilities are inevitable, a plurality of theories provides us with the richest reservoir for understanding the multifaceted process of communication in its many forms. That's why we may want to use—or, at least, be *able* to use—more than one set of lenses to make sense of interaction.

Putting Theories Into Practice

To realize the value of multiple theoretical perspectives, let's consider a concrete case study to which we can apply communication theories.

> Police receive an anonymous call telling them that a domestic dispute is in progress. When two officers arrive on the scene, they separately ques-

tion the man and the woman about what has been happening. The man explains that he got home tired after a hard day's work and his wife provoked him until he finally beat her up to teach her a lesson. He shakes his head and mutters, "Damn it, she drives me to it. I go to work every day and earn a good income for her and the kids. If she can't appreciate that and let me have peace in my own home, then maybe she needs to be straightened out. Anyway, what happens all the time on TV is a lot worse than anything I do to her."

The woman tells the officer who questions her that she doesn't know why her husband beat her up and that she usually doesn't have any warning before a violent episode. From her perspective, his outbursts are random and beyond her control. The officer asks if she wants to press charges and go to a shelter for abused women. Without hesitation, the woman shakes her head, explaining, "Sure, he hits me sometimes, but he's a good provider, and I can't support myself and the kids. Once the babies started coming, I quit work. What could I do now after ten years being outside of the job market?" After a moment she adds, "Besides, I guess he's got a right to blow off steam every so often, as hard as he works. And he's always sorry after he hits me, and then he's very loving for a while. Judging by what I see every day on TV, I haven't got it so bad after all."

Can communication theories help us understand this couple? Can theories diminish violence between intimates?

Theories Cultivate Understanding

One of the first insights we might have is that the spouses tell different stories about episodes of violence. The husband's narrative portrays him as an unwilling victim of her provocations—he is only responding to what she does. In contrast, the wife's narrative is a mystery story in which she sees herself as a helpless victim of random and unpredictable bouts of abuse.

Reflection

How would symbolic interactionists explain the finding that watching violence leads to increased tolerance of violence?

CMM theorists would also point out that this couple is involved in a recurring episode in which they have coordinated rules that allow him to hit her, encourage her to tolerate abuse, and provide justifications for his violence. To this analysis, interactional theorists would add that the wife and the husband don't agree on how to punctuate interaction. He sees his abuse as a response to her "provocation," whereas she sees the abuse as initiated by him independent of anything she says or does. We can also see a clear example of exchange premises in the wife's statement that the abuse (a cost of the relationship) is outweighed by the value of the economic security the marriage provides (a benefit of the relationship).

Moving beyond a focus on the interpersonal dynamics between the wife and the husband, communication theories help us see how this specific relationship is embedded in and shaped by larger cultural patterns. James West (1993, 1995), a critical scholar, identified cultural structures and practices that sustain violence between intimates. He pointed out, for example, that many battered women seek help from clergy, only to be told that a good Christian woman should keep the family together. In addition, West reports that some law enforcement officers try to avoid domestic disputes because of the cultural view that family life is in the private sphere, which should be relatively immune to intervention from outsiders.

We should also realize that social prescriptions that specify that women should be primary caregivers in families can restrict women's economic freedom and thus their alternatives to remaining in dangerous relationships (Wood, 1994d, 2001). Because the woman in our example is a full-time homemaker and mother, she has no independent source of support for herself and her children. Thus, her options are constrained by economic realities that arise partially from cultural views of gender and the social standpoint into which those views place the wife.

Performance theorists might point out that the woman's performance of her role depends on repeated cultural definitions of what it means to be a good woman. Extending that insight, postmodern thinkers might argue that the police officers', man's, and woman's identities are constituted by their social locations and all make a kind of sense, but none is the absolute "truth" of what is happening. Cultivation theorists would note that both spouses see the husband's abuse as relatively minor in comparison to the "mean world" outside of their relationship. Judged relative to this synthetic reality, the husband's violence is perceived as insignificant.

Critical theories help us see that this woman's experiences, as well as her ability to express them, are muted by a dominant ideology to which both she and her husband subscribe. The story that each of them tells indicates that the husband's role as breadwinner entitles him to certain prerogatives, including "blowing off steam" by beating his wife. Cultural studies scholars might call our attention to the role of media, including pornographic* films and magazines, in legitimizing violence against women. Pornographic films outnumber nonpornographic films by three to one, and pornographic films gross $365 million a year in the United States. Over 80% of X-rated films include scenes of domination, 75% of X-rated

---

*Pornography is not the same as erotica. Pornography favorably portrays subordination and degradation of individuals and represents sadistic actions as pleasurable. Erotica, in contrast, portrays consensual sexual activities that are pleasurable to all involved parties.

Putting Theories Into Practice

films show physical violence, and fully 50% of X-rated films include explicit rape scenes (Cowan, Lee, Levy, & Snyder, 1988; Wolf, 1991).

Research documents connections between pornographic media and violence in real relationships. Several studies have found that women who view sexually violent material have greater tolerance, or even approval, of violence in their own relationships (Dieter, 1989; Russell, 1993). Other investigations indicate that men who read or view sexually violent media are more likely to believe rape myths (she really wants sex; men have uncontrollable sexual urges; rape occurs only between strangers), to be less sensitive to rape, and even to believe that forced sex is acceptable in their relationships (Demare, Briere, & Lips, 1988; Donnerstein, Linz, & Penrod, 1987). The links between media's positive portrayals of sexual aggression and violence and individuals' acceptance of sexual violence in their relationships are convincing evidence of the claim that media are powerful instruments of ideological control.

Reflection

What individual and institutional actions could alter media portrayals of sexual violence?

This case study demonstrates that multiple theories maximize our insight into human communication. Narrative, exchange, CMM, cultivation, and interactional theories all contribute to our understanding of the abuse in this relationship. Critical and interpretive theories enhance our insight by contextualizing the dynamics of this specific marriage within broader horizons of cultural meaning. It's unwise to limit ourselves to any single theory. The more theories we can understand and use, the more fully we can analyze the complexities of human communication.

Multiple Theories Promote Social Progress

But does understanding facilitate positive social change? Can it reduce or eliminate domestic violence? A number of counselors make use of theories we've discussed to understand how communication dynamics sustain abusive relationships. Clinicians use insight into the interactional patterns that allow abuse to teach clients to recognize how their communication sustains destructive patterns and how they might alter their communication to change what happens (Goldner, Penn, Scheinberg, & Walker, 1990). For example, the wife in our case might resist violence by engaging in a different kind of performance than she currently enacts.

Both cultural studies theorists and theorists of performance as political action would see the interaction between these spouses as a site for resistance and change both in this marriage and in broader social attitudes about marriage and what is and is not acceptable in them.

In addition, identifying cultural practices that allow or even support violence against intimates guides our thinking about changes that might diminish domestic brutality. For example, research we've discussed suggests that violence would be decreased if there were less sexually violent pornographic media. Violence between intimates could be further redressed if law enforcement agencies designed training programs to reduce officers' reluctance to enter domestic battlefields and to teach officers how to intervene safely and effectively.

It seems reasonable to conclude that understanding the role of communication in sustaining or changing unjust and unhealthy relations is a necessary foundation for instigating positive change. By extension, the greater the number of theories from which we can draw, the greater resources we have for addressing social problems.

TRY IT OUT Identify an issue or problem that you consider especially important and that has both social and personal dimensions. Possibilities include the AIDS/HIV crisis, the drug problem, prejudice and hate crimes, the breakdown of families, and increasing violence in all spheres of life.

Apply at least four of the theories we've studied to the social issue you selected. What does each theory contribute to your overall understanding of the issue or problem? Which aspects of the issue are highlighted by each theory? Which facets of the issue are obscured or neglected by each theory?

Because no single theory is comprehensive, integrating several philosophically compatible theories allows rich and useful insights into communication. The more ways we have of thinking about communication, the greater the understanding we can achieve.

Communication Theories in Social Contexts

By now you should realize that theorizing is not a process that has a fixed end or finite resolution. Instead, theorizing is and should be an ongoing activity that evolves and changes in response to personal and social circumstances. In other words, theories arise within—not outside of—social life. Thus, they reflect the urgencies and issues of particular eras (Epstein, 1988; Keller, 1985; Wood & Duck, 1995a).

Consider a few examples of the interaction between social life and academic theories. In the 1940s, theorists were concerned with understanding obedience, conformity, and prejudice, topics that were salient in the aftermath of the world wars. Scientists in the 1940s didn't study HIV and forms of communication that promote safer sex, either because HIV didn't exist or because it wasn't identified at that time. Both natural scientists and social scientists in the 1990s do study HIV. From their research, they have generated useful theories about the effects of different communication strategies on partners' willingness to practice safer sex (Bowen & Michal-Johnson, 1995, 1996).

The majority of theories about communication in personal relationships are based on and pertain to the romantic relationships of college-age, European-American, middle-class, able-bodied heterosexuals who live close to or with one another. Only in recent years has growing awareness of cultural diversity prompted scholars to study and develop theories about gay and lesbian commitments (Huston & Schwartz, 1996), relationships between members of cultural minorities (Gaines, 1995), enduring marriages between mature individuals (Dickson, 1995), relationships conducted over electronic communication systems (Lea & Spears, 1995), and long-distance relationships (Rohlfing, 1995). As we create and participate in new kinds of relationships, scholars develop theories that describe and explain the emergent relational forms.

Another example of cultural influences on theory building is the emphasis on individuality, individualism, and individual rights that characterizes most Western theories of communication. In some societies, notably many Asian ones, collective or communal values are esteemed more highly than individualism. Thus, theories that reflect Eastern cultures are more likely to focus on the collective than on individuals (Chang & Holt, 1991; Wenzhong & Grove, 1991). By extension, dominant ideologies in collectivist cultures emphasize harmony, conformity to the group, humility, and deference, in contrast to individualist cultures' emphasis on assertion, self-confidence, autonomy, and conflict (Berg & Jaya, 1993; Klopf, 1991).

In contrast to Western communication theorists' substantial attention to self-disclosure, Eastern theorists have shown little interest in personal revelations and displays of emotions, which are frowned upon in many Eastern societies (Ishii & Bruneau, 1991; Johnson & Nakanishi, 1993; Ting-Toomey, 1991). These examples highlight the extent to which cultural ideologies and concerns shape the character of theories at any given moment in the life of a society.

Summary

Throughout this book we've seen that theorizing is both a specialized scholarly endeavor and a routine activity in which all of us engage. Perhaps the introduction to communication theory that you've gained from this book and the course it accompanies has whetted your appetite for further study. If so, you can look forward to an exciting time learning about theories and theoretical controversies whose surface we have only scratched in this introductory book. Perhaps you will choose an academic career in which you work with theories, both ones generated by others and ones you develop to explain the aspects of communication of greatest interest to you.

Even if you don't pursue further academic study of theory, theorizing will be an ongoing process in your life. You will enter situations, decide what they mean and how they operate, and analyze the probable consequences of various communication strategies you might choose to advance the goals or social change you favor. You'll then select a particular course of action, put it in practice, evaluate what happens and why, and then move forward in the ongoing process of human communication. Each of these familiar daily activities involves theoretical thinking. What you have learned in this book and the course it accompanies should allow you to be more informed, rigorous, and effective in your everyday theorizing.

Whether as scholars engaged in theorizing as a vocation or as nonacademics using theories to understand our own lives and our environments, all of us are theorists. This is why theories are eminently practical. They are the best tools we have for creating order and meaning in our lives and for improving the human condition.

Each of us is a theorist, forever engaged in trying to make sense of what happens in our personal lives and our social world, each of us trying to communicate in ways that foster personal identities and relationships that nourish us and that promote a society that is humane and just.

And that is why theories matter.

Glossary

abstraction   One of three measures of cognitive complexity; the extent to which an individual interprets others in terms of internal motives, personality traits, and character as opposed to more concrete factors such as actions, physical appearance, and so forth.

act   One element in the dramatistic pentad; that which is done.

agency   One element in the dramatistic pentad; the means or channel through which an act is performed.

agent   One element in the dramatistic pentad; the one who performs an act.

attitude   In the dramatistic hexad, incipient action based on how an actor positions herself or himself relative to others and the contexts in which she or he acts; the sixth element that Kenneth Burke added to the original dramatistic pentad, making it a hexad.

autobiography   One of six levels in the hierarchy of meanings; an individual's view of himself or herself that both shapes communication and is shaped by communication.

axiom   A statement that is presumed to be true on its face and therefore does not require proof or explanation.

back stage   In dramaturgy, behaviors and appearances that are not visible to audiences (or others in an interactional situation).

behaviorism   A form of science that focuses on observable behaviors and that assumes human motives, meanings, feelings, and other subjective phenomena either don't exist or are irrelevant to behavior.

brute fact   An objective, concrete phenomenon unadorned by interpretations of meaning.

causal   A form of explanation that asserts that one phenomenon directly determines another.

cognitive complexity   In constructivist theory, the degree to which an individual's interpretive processes are differentiated, abstract, and organized.

cognitive schema (pl. *schemata*)   A knowledge structure on which individuals rely to interpret experience and construct meanings. There are four types of cognitive schemata: prototypes, personal constructs, stereotypes, and scripts.

coherence   In narrative theory, a standard for judging the quality of a story according to whether it is internally consistent, complete, and believable.

collegial story   An account about one member of an organization told by a different member of the organization.

commodification   In postmodernist theory, the process by which phenomena, including people, are treated as products to be acquired and used.

communication   A systemic process in which individuals interact with and through symbols to create and interpret meanings.

communication rules   Regular patterns in the use and interpretation of verbal and nonverbal behaviors and their functions within a particular group.

comparison level (CL)   In social exchange theory, a subjective standard of what we expect in a particular type of relationship such as friendship or romance.

comparison level of alternatives (CL_{alt})   In social exchange theory, a relative measure that evaluates how good a particular relationship is in comparison to real or perceived alternatives to that relationship.

complementary   In interactional theory, of or petaining to a form of communication and a type of relationship in which power is unequal between individuals.

constitutive rule   In CMM theory, a rule that defines what counts as what in communication (for example, what counts as support, meanness, joking, praise).

constructivism   The point of view that humans create meanings by relying on four basic cognitive schemata, or knowledge structures.

consubstantiality   In dramatism, identifying with another or becoming common in substance.

content   One of six levels in the hierarchy of meanings; the denotative or literal meanings of words in communication.

content meaning   One of two levels of meaning identified by interactional theorists; the literal significance, or denotative meaning, of communication.

control   The use of explanations and predictions to govern what a phenomenon actually does.

cool media   McLuhan's term for media that include incomplete sensory data and thus require human involvement and participation.

coordinated management of meanings (CMM)   See *rules theory*.

corporate story   A narrative that serves to convey the values, style, and history of an organization. Told to newcomers, stories perform socialization; told among veteran members of an organization, stories serve to bind members together and vitalize the organization's ideology.

correlational A form of explanation that asserts that two things go together but not that one causes the other.

cost In social exchange theory, anything that has negative value to an individual.

critical analysis Research that goes beyond description and explanation to argue for changes in communicative practices that are judged to be oppressive, wrong, or otherwise undesirable.

critical race theory A theory that examines how laws and legal institutions construct race and uses race as a critical perspective for questioning cultural views of justice and fairness.

critical theories A group of theories that seek to produce change in oppressive or otherwise undesirable practices and structures in society.

cultivation In cultivation theory, the cumulative process by which television fosters beliefs about social reality, including the belief that the world is more dangerous and violent than it actually is.

cultivation theory The point of view that television promotes a view of social reality that may be inaccurate but that viewers nonetheless assume reflects real life.

cultural mainstream In cultivation theory, the general view of social life that television constructs.

cultural pattern One of six levels in the hierarchy of meanings; understandings of speech acts, episodes, relationships, and autobiographies that are shared by some groups and some societies.

cultural studies theories A group of related theories that seek to unmask and challenge the techniques by which privileged groups maintain their privilege and power in society.

culture Both the ideology of a society and the actual, concrete practices that occur in that society.

description One goal of theory; the use of symbols to represent something and to identify its parts.

descriptive statistics Numerical representations of human behavior that describe populations, proportions, and frequencies.

determinism The belief that human behavior is governed by forces beyond individual control, usually biology, environment, or a combination of the two.

developmental theory The point of view that relationships evolve through stages defined by participants' expectations, perceptions, and meanings.

dialectical moments In dialectical theory, momentary periods of equilibrium between opposing dialectics in the larger pattern of continuous change that marks relationships.

dialectical theory The point of view that certain tensions between contradictory desires are inherent in personal relationships.

dialectics In dialectical theory, points of contradiction that cause tension and impel change in relationships. Three relational dialectics have been identified: autonomy–connection, openness–closedness, and novelty–routine.

differentiation   One of three measures of cognitive complexity; the number of distinct interpretations (constructs) an individual uses to perceive and describe others. More cognitively complex individuals use more constructs to interpret others than do less cognitively complex individuals.

discursive structures   Michel Foucault's term for deeply ensconced ways of thinking about and expressing identity and conducting social life. Gender, race–ethnicity, and socioeconomic class are examples of discursive structures that reflect and embody cultural ideologies.

dramatism   The point of view that life is a drama that can be understood in dramatic terms such as act, agent, scene, agency, and purpose. Identification is viewed as the primary goal of symbolic interaction, and guilt is viewed as the ultimate motive for communication.

dramatistic pentad (hexad)   The method of conducting dramatistic analysis of communication in terms of act, scene, agent, agency, and purpose. Later, attitude was added as a sixth element of the method, making it a hexad.

dramaturgical model   The view of everyday life in which social interaction is performance, settings of interaction are stages, people are actors, and viewers are audiences.

dramaturgy   In communication theory, a theory that describes, explains, and predicts human behavior in terms of dramatic actions and settings. Also called *dramaturgical theory*.

electronic epoch   The fourth era in McLuhan's media history of civilization, ushered in by the invention of the telegraph, which made it possible for people to communicate personally across distance.

episode   One of six levels in the hierarchy of meaning; a recurring routine of interaction that is structured by rules and has boundaries.

epistemology   The branch of philosophy that deals with the nature of knowledge, or how we know what we know.

equity   In social exchange theory, the fairness of a relationship to individuals over time.

ethnography   A qualitative method of research that interprets actions so as to generate understanding consistent with the frameworks of those who perform the actions.

experiment   A controlled study that systematically manipulates one thing (called the *independent variable*) to determine how it affects another thing (called the *dependent variable* because what it does depends on the independent variable).

explanation   One goal of theorizing; an effort to account for why and/or how something works.

extensional orientation   A view of meaning and communication that is based on objective particulars of phenomena.

external validity   The generalizability of a theory across contexts, especially those beyond the confines of experimental situations.

fantasy theme   An idea that spins out in a group and captures its social and task foci.

feedforward   In general semantics theory, the process of anticipating the effects of communication and adapting it in advance of actually engaging in communication.

feminist theories   A group of theories related by their focus on gender and its derivative, power.

fidelity   In narrative theory, one standard for judging a story's quality according to whether it "rings true."

frame   In dramaturgy, the ways people define situations for themselves and others.

front stage   In dramaturgy, behaviors and appearances that are visible to audiences (or others in an interactional situation).

gender   A socially created system of values, identities, and behaviors that are prescribed for women and men. Unlike sex, which is biologically determined, gender is socially constructed.

general systems theory   Theory originated by Ludwig von Bertalanffy, which claims that all living organisms are dynamic wholes that function as a result of organized interaction among parts.

generalized other   In symbolic interaction theory, the organized perspectives of a social group, community, or society.

grand narrative   A coherent story that a culture tells about itself, its practices, and its values.

guilt   In dramatism, any tension, discomfort, sense of shame, or other unpleasant feeling that humans experience; the motive of all human action.

hermeneutic circle   A process that consists of (1) meanings of behaviors and practices that reflect the understandings of those who are behaving, (2) meanings that are removed from the actors but represent the understandings of someone studying or viewing actors, and (3) translating the former into terms understandable in the vocabularies and experiences of the latter. Ethnographers move within the hermeneutic circle as they try to understand and represent practices that initially are unfamiliar to them.

heurism   A criterion for evaluating theories; the capacity of a theory to provoke new insights, thoughts, and understandings.

hierarchy   In dramatism, a social ordering in which phenomena, including people, are classified into groups with different value, status, or rank.

hierarchy of meanings   In rules theory (coordinated management of meaning), the multiple levels of meaning, each contextualized by higher levels. We rely on the hierarchy of meanings to interpret communication.

homeostasis   A steady state; equilibrium; balance. General systems theory claims that living systems (relationships, for example) strive for, but never fully sustain, homeostasis. Dialectical theory, on the other hand, claims that continuous change is the very nature of relationships.

hot media   McLuhan's term for media that include relatively complete sensory data and hence do not require significant human participation.

humanism   A form of science that focuses on human choices, motives, and meanings and assumes that the reasons or causes of human behavior lie within humans, not outside of them.

hypothesis   A carefully stated, testable prediction of a theoretical relationship or outcome.

I   In symbolic interaction theory, the phase or part of self that is impulsive, creative, and unconstrained by social norms and knowledge.

ideological domination   In cultural studies, the set of meanings, values, and concrete practices that has the greatest power and the adherence of the greatest number of people at a given moment in the life of a culture.

ideology   The ideas, values, beliefs, and understandings that are common to members of a social group and that guide the practices and customs of the society.

impression management   In Goffman's dramaturgical theory, the process of managing settings, words, nonverbal communication, dress, and appearance in an effort to give others a specific view of oneself.

inclusion stage   The first stage in feminist theorizing; the work of this stage is to raise consciousness of gendered inequities.

indexing   Associating referents (such as names) with specific dates, situations, and so forth to remind ourselves that meanings change; advocated by general semanticists as a remedy for misunderstanding.

institutional fact   The meaning of an act, event, or other phenomenon; interpretations of brute facts.

intensional orientation   A view of meaning and communication that is based on factors inside individuals (biases, experiences, etc.).

interactional theory   A theory built on the premise that communication and relationships are systems in which meaning is established through contexts, punctuation, and content and relationship levels of meaning.

intercultural communication   The branch of communication field that studies communication among people from different cultures, including distinct cultures within a single country.

internal validity   The degree to which the design and methods used to test a theory actually measure what they claim to measure.

interpersonal communication   Communication between people. Interpersonal communication exists on a continuum ranging from impersonal (between social roles) to highly personal.

intrapersonal communication   Communication with oneself, including self-talk, planning, and reflections.

law   An inviolate, unalterable fact that holds true across time and space. Also called *universal law* and *covering law*.

laws-based explanation   A theoretical explanation of the form, "Anytime *x* happens, *y* will invariably or probably follow,"or "*x* and *y* always or almost always go together."

literate epoch   The second era in McLuhan's media history of civilization, in-augurated by invention of the phonetic alphabet and during which common symbols allowed people to communicate in writing.

logical force   In CMM theory, the degree to which a person feels he or she must act or cannot act in a situation.

looking glass self   In symbolic interaction theory, the image of oneself that one gains by seeing the self mirrored in others' eyes.

mainstreaming   In cultivation theory, the effect of television in stabilizing and homogenizing views within a society; one of two processes used to explain television's cultivation of synthetic world views.

masculine bias   Giving primary or exclusive attention to men's behaviors, be-liefs, and contexts and using these phenomena to describe and explain social life. Bias exists because roughly half of the social world (that is, women) is not studied and is therefore not represented in theories that are developed.

mass communication   Collective term for forms of communication aimed at large audiences.

ME   In symbolic interaction theory, the phase or part of self that is socially aware, analytical, and evaluative.

meaning   The significance conferred on experiences and phenomena; meaning is constructed, not intrinsic to communication. In general systems theory, commu-nication has two levels of meaning: the content level, which concerns the infor-mation in a message; and the relationship level, which concerns what the message implies about the power, liking, and responsiveness between the communicators.

mean world syndrome   In cultivation theory, the belief that the world is a dangerous place full of selfish, mean people who cannot be trusted and who are likely to harm others. Cultivation theorists assert that the mean world syndrome is fostered by heavy viewing of television.

metacommunication   Communication about communication.

micropolitics   Resistance to existing structures and practices of power at local, sometimes personal levels. This decentered type of resistance to existing power struc-tures is associated with postmodernist assumption that power itself is often not lo-cated in one central place but diffused throughout society.

mind   In symbolic interaction theory, the ability to use significant symbols. Mind is acquired through symbolic interaction with others.

modernity   Roughly from the end of the 19th century to the start of World War I; the period in which society was believed to be coherent and absolute truth was thought to be knowable through the methods of science. Order was highly val-ued, "high" and "low" culture were distinguished in nature and value, and individ-uals were assumed to be rational, autonomous, and stable.

monitoring   Observing and managing our own thoughts, feelings, and actions. Monitoring is possible because humans are symbol users.

mortification   In dramatism, a method of purging guilt by blaming ourselves, confessing failings, and seeking forgiveness.

multitasking   Engaging in two or more activities at once or in interacting, overlapping ways.

muted group theory   A feminist theory that claims that women (and other groups) have been silenced because (white, heterosexual, middle-class) men have had the power to name the world and thus to constitute experience and meaning.

narrative   Telling a story about experience, identity, and so forth. Narratives are not necessarily objective representations or re-creations of experiences and identities.

narrative paradigm/narrative theory   The point of view that humans are natural storytellers and that most, if not all, communication is storytelling.

narrative rationality   In narrative theory, the judgment of the quality of narratives, or stories, according to their coherence and fidelity.

negative   In dramatism, the capacity to say no; the basis of moral conduct and thought.

neutralization   In dialectical theory, the method of responding to the tension of relational dialectics by means of a compromise that meets both dialectical needs to a degree but satisfies neither need fully.

nihilism   The denial of any absolute basis for making meaningful distinctions among values, moral codes, social practices, and forms of social organization.

objectivism   The belief that reality is material, external to the human mind, and the same for everyone.

objectivity   The quality of being uninfluenced by values, biases, personal feelings, and other subjective factors.

ontology   The branch of philosophy that deals with the nature of humans.

openness   In general systems theory, the extent to which a system affects and is affected by factors and processes outside of it. Living systems may be more or less open to outside influence and more or less influential on their contexts.

operational definition   A precise description that specifies how to observe the phenomena of interest. Operational definitions provide clarity and precision to research hypotheses and research questions used to test theory.

organization   One of three dimensions of cognitive complexity; the extent to which a person notices and is able to make sense of contradictory behaviors.

organizational culture   Understandings about identity and codes of thought and action that are shared by members of an organization.

organizational culture theory   A point of view that focuses on the ways in which communication creates and sustains distinct customs, understandings, and perspectives within particular organizations.

outsider within A person who is both inside a particular social group through regular interactions with members of the group and outside of the group because he or she is defined as not "one of them."

overdetermination The idea that aspects of social life, including ideological domination, are determined by multiple, often overlapping and interacting causes rather than by any single cause.

parallel relationships In interactional theory, relationships in which individuals have equal power overall but power is distributed so that each person has greater power in particular spheres of activity.

parsimony One criterion for evaluating theories; the appropriate simplicity of a theory.

participant-observation A method often used in ethnographic research, in which the researcher-observer is also a participant in the situation being studied.

particular other In symbolic interaction theory, an individual who is significant to another person.

patriarchy Literally, "rule by the fathers"; in feminist theory, the cultural values, institutions, and practices that reflect and normalize the experiences of men as a group while denying, dismissing, and/or devaluing the experiences, values, and interests of women as a group. Patriarchy does *not* refer to individual men but to a cultural system established by and reflective of men as a group.

perfection In dramatism, our imagined ideal or perfect form of things and ourselves. The inability to achieve perfection is a source of guilt.

performance ethnography A presentation that is based on intimate acquaintance with and understanding of people and experiences in a specific culture or social community and that seeks to make those people and experiences knowable to audiences who are not part of the indigenous groups.

performativity The extent to which performance realizes (or makes real) identities and experiences. It is both the doing (the act of performing) and what is done (the reiteration or challenging of social norms in performance).

personal construct One of four cognitive schemata used to interpret experience; a bipolar scale of description (for example, happy–unhappy).

personal story An account that announces how people see themselves and how they wish to be seen by others in an organization.

person-centeredness The ability to tailor communication to particular individuals with whom we interact. Individuals who are highly complex cognitively seem capable of more person-centered communication than do less cognitively complex individuals.

postmodern The post–World War II era of social life that emerged after modernism. Postmodern society is described as fragmented, uncertain, and continuously in flux; the individual is described not as a core self but as a range of selves brought forth by and embodied in particular contexts.

postmodernism   An intellectual and political movement that began after World War II and flourished in the 1950s and 1960s. Postmodernism challenges the modernist views that life is orderly, the self is coherent, and a particular social order is natural and right.

prediction   Projecting what will happen to a phenomenon under specified conditions or exposure to particular stimuli.

print epoch   The third era in McLuhan's media history of civilization, in which invention of the printing press made it possible to mass-produce written materials so that reading was no longer restricted to elite members of society.

process   The quality of being ongoing, in flux, ever changing. Communication is a process.

prototype   One of four cognitive schemata; an ideal or optimal example of a category of person, situation, object, and so on.

punctuation   In interactional theory, subjective designations of the start and stop of particular communication episodes.

purpose   One element in the dramatistic pentad; the reason for an act.

qualitative methods   Forms of research that involve probing and interpreting the subjective meanings of experience.

quantitative methods   Forms of research that involve gathering quantifiable data.

ratio   In dramatism, the proportion of different elements in the dramatistic pentad.

reform   One goal of theorizing; the use of theory to instigate change in pragmatic life. Also called "producing positive social change."

reframing   In dialectical theory, a method of managing relational dialectics that involves transforming the perception of dialectical needs as opposing, and reframing them as unified, complementary, or otherwise allied.

regulative rule   In CMM theory, a rule that tells us when it's appropriate to do a certain thing and what we should do next in an interaction.

relational self   In postmodern theory, a self that has no stable core but is formed in particular relationships and changes as it enters and leaves relationships.

relationship   In rules theory, one of six levels in the hierarchy of meanings; a scripted form of interaction that we engage in with a particular other.

relationship meaning   In interactional theory, one of two levels of meaning in communication; what communication reflects about feelings and relationships between people. Relationship-level meanings may express liking, power, and/or responsiveness.

reliability   A criterion for evaluating theoretical research that concerns the consistency of particular behaviors, patterns, or relationships.

research question   A question that specifies the phenomena of interest to a scholar but does not predict relationships between phenomena. Research questions are less formal than hypotheses.

resonance   In cultivation theory, the extent to which something (specifically, phenomena on television) is congruent with personal experience; one of two mechanisms used to explain television's ability to cultivate synthetic world views.

revisionist stage   The second stage in feminist theorizing, during which the goal is to re-vision (or revise) cultural practices, structures, and modes of interpreting experiences in ways that do not marginalize women and their activities.

reward   In social exchange theory, anything that has positive value for an individual.

rite   A dramatic, planned set of activities that brings together aspects of cultural ideology into a single event.

ritual   Communicative performance that is regularly repeated in an organization and that members of an organization come to regard as familiar and routine.

role taking   In symbolic interaction theory, an individual's internalization and perception of experiences from the perspective of another person or persons.

rule   Regularity in behavior that is consistent within a particular situation or situations but is not assumed to be universal. Rules are guides for behavior, not determinants of it.

rules-based explanation   A form of theoretical explanation that articulates regularities, or patterns, in human behavior that are routinely followed in particular types of communication situations and relationships.

rules theory   The point of view that socially constructed and learned rules guide communication. Also called coordinated management of meaning (CMM) theory.

scapegoating   In dramatism, displacing sins into a sacrificial vessel whose destruction serves to cleanse an individual or group of its sins.

scene   In the dramatistic pentad, the context in which an act is performed.

scope   One criterion for evaluating theories; the range of phenomena a theory describes and explains.

script   One of four cognitive schemata; a routine, or action sequence, that reflects our understanding of how a particular interaction is supposed to proceed.

selection   In dialectical theory, one means of managing relational dialectics that involves satisfying one need in a dialectic and ignoring or denying the contradictory one.

self   In symbolic interaction theory, the ability to reflect on oneself from the perspective of others. Self is not present at birth but is acquired through symbolic interactions with others.

self-fulfilling prophecy   Behaving and seeing ourselves in ways that are consistent with how others label us.

separation   In dialectical theory, one means of managing relational dialectics that attempts to meet both contradictory needs in a dialectic by satisfying each one in separate situations or spheres of relational life.

sex   The biological and genetic quality of maleness or femaleness; not the same as gender.

significance   The conceptual or pragmatic importance of a theory.

situated knowledges   In standpoint theory, the idea that any individual's knowledge is situated within her or his particular circumstances and that there are thus multiple knowledges, not a singular one.

social desirability bias   A tendency for research participants to give responses that they perceive as socially acceptable, which may not be honest.

social exchange theory   The point of view that in relationships people try to minimize costs, maximize rewards, and ensure equity.

social penetration model   One of the first-generation theories of relational development; likens the development of personal relationships to peeling the layers of an onion to move progressively toward the center or core self.

sous rature   Literally, "under erasure." Term coined by Jacques Derrida, a postmodernist, to call attention to the necessity of words to refer to phenomena and simultaneously the inability of words to fully represent them.

speech act   In rules theory, one of six levels in the hierarchy of meaning; an action that is performed by speaking (for example, pleading, joking, apologizing, inviting).

speech community   A group of people who share understandings of communication that are not shared by people outside of the group.

speech community theory   The point of view that explains the communication styles of particular social groups with reference to the cultures in which members of the groups are socialized.

standpoint   The viewpoint and knowledge that grow out of political awareness of and struggle with material, symbolic, and social circumstances that shape the lives of a particular group.

standpoint theory   The view that the material, social, and symbolic circumstances of a social group shape what members of that group experience, as well as how they think, act, and feel.

stereotype   One of four cognitive schemata; a predictive generalization about a person's behavior that is based on general knowledge about the group to which we classify the person as belonging.

strange loop   In CMM theory, an internal conversation (intrapersonal communication) by means of which the individual is trapped in a destructive pattern of thinking and/or acting.

subject   Term used by postmodern–poststructural theorists to distinguish persons as individuals and to call attention to subjectivity as a way of being— a process, not a fixed essence.

substance   In dramatism, the general nature or essence of some thing or person.

superstructure   In Marxist theory, the social institutions and practices that assist in reproducing and normalizing the underlying economic system of a society.

survey   A quantitative method of research that relies on instruments, questionnaires, or interviews to find out about feelings, experiences, and so forth.

symbolic interactionism/symbolic interaction theory   The point of view that claims society predates individuals, who acquire minds and selves in the process of interacting symbolically with other members of a culture. Symbols are also necessary to the functioning and continuation of collective life.

symbol   An arbitrary, ambiguous, and abstract representation of other phenomena. Symbols are the basis of language, much nonverbal behavior, and human thought.

symmetrical   In interactional theory, of or pertaining to a form of communication and relationships in which power is equal between partners.

systemic   Related to systems, which are organized and interacting wholes in which all parts interrelate. Communication is systemic.

technological determinism   The point of view that media decisively influence how individuals think, feel, and act, as well as how they view collective life.

testability   The extent to which a theory's claims can be appraised. Testability is one criterion for evaluating a theory.

testimony   A statement based on personal experience about some action, experience, person, event, or other phenomenon.

text   All symbolic activities, written, oral, or nonverbal; a form of data useful in qualitative research.

theatre of struggle   A term used by cultural studies theorists to describe the ongoing battle for ideological control of cultures.

theory   An account of what something is, how it works, what it produces or causes to happen, and what can change how it operates. Theories are points of view, human constructions.

thick description   An ethnographic method that describes cultural practices from the point of view of people who are members of the particular culture or social community being studied.

thrownness   The arbitrary conditions of the particular time and place of an individual's life.

trajectory   A personal understanding of various tracks in relationships. Trajectories define relational courses based on past experiences and observations.

tribal epoch   The first era in McLuhan's media history of civilization, during which the oral tradition reigned and face-to-face talking and listening were primary forms of communication.

turning point   A critical event, process, or feeling that individuals perceive as marking a new direction or intensity in a personal relationship.

uncertainty reduction theory   The point of view that uncertainty motivates communication and that certainty reduces the motivation to communicate.

understanding   One goal of theorizing; gaining insight into a process, situation, or phenomenon, not necessarily with the goal of predicting or controlling it.

Glossary   **335**

unobtrusive methods   Means of gathering data that intrude minimally on naturally occurring interaction.

utility   A criterion for evaluating theories; practical merit or applied value of a theory.

validity   A criterion for evaluating a theory. Validity has both internal (the theory measures what it claims to measure) and external (the theory applies to real life beyond the laboratory) dimensions.

victimage   In dramatism, a method of purging guilt by identifying an external source (a scapegoat) for some apparent failing or sin.

vocabulary   Language used by members of a culture, social group, or institution. The languages of particular groups reflect their experiences, values, norms, and ideology.

white studies   An emerging discipline that focuses critical attention on what whiteness means (and has meant) and how whiteness is and has been constructed as "normal" in Western cultures.

References

Abbott, H. (2002). *The Cambridge introduction to narrative*. Cambridge University Press.

Acitelli, L. (1988). When spouses talk to each other about their relationship. *Journal of Social and Personal Relationships, 5*, pp. 185–199.

Adams, C. (1991, April). The straight dope. *Triangle Comic Review*, p. 26.

Allan, G. (1989). *Friendship: Developing a sociological perspective*. London: Harvester Wheatsheaf.

Allan, G. (1993). Social structure and relationships. In S. W. Duck (Ed.), *Understanding relationship processes, 3: Social context and relationships* (pp. 1–25). Newbury Park, CA: Sage.

Allen, K. (1999, May 24). Third wave versus second wave. http://www. io.com/~wwwave/

Althusser, L. (1971). *Lenin and philosophy and other essays*. (Trans., Ben Brewster). London: New Left Books.

Altman, I., & Taylor, D. (1973). *Social penetration: The development of interpersonal relationships*. New York: Holt, Rinehart & Winston.

Altman, I., Vinsel, A., & Brown, B. (1981). Dialectical conceptions in social psychology: An application to social penetration and privacy regulation. In L. Berkowitz (Ed.), *Advances in experimental social psychology, 14* (pp. 135–180). New York: Academic Press.

Andersen, P. (1993). Cognitive schemata in personal relationships. In S. W. Duck (Ed.), *Understanding relationship processes, 1: Individuals in relationships* (pp. 1–29). Newbury Park, CA: Sage.

Anderson, J. A. (Ed.). (1988). *Communication yearbook, 11* (pp. 310–405). Newbury Park, CA: Sage.

Anderson, R., Baxter, L., & Cissna, K. (Eds.). (In press). *Dialogue: Theorizing difference in communication studies*. Thousand Oaks, CA: Sage.

Ang, I. (1995). The nature of the audience. In J. Downing, A. Mohammadi, & A. Sreberney-Mohammadi (Eds.), *Questioning the media: A critical introduction* (pp. 207–220). Thousand Oaks, CA: Sage.

Anzaldúa, G. (1999). *Borderlands/la frontera: The new mestiza*. San Francisco: Spinsters/Aunt Lute.

Applegate, J. (1990). Constructs and communication: A pragmatic integration. In R. Neimeyer & G. Neimeyer (Eds.), *Advances in personal construct psychology, 1* (pp. 203–230). Greenwich, CT: JAI Press.

Ardener, E. (1975). Belief and the problem of women: The problem revisited. In S. Ardener (Ed.), *Perceiving women* (pp. 1–27). London: Malaby Press.

Ardener, S. (1978). *Defining females: The nature of women in society.* New York: Wiley.

Aries, E. (1987). Gender and communication. In P. Shaver (Ed.), *Sex and gender* (pp. 149–176). Newbury Park, CA: Sage.

Baesler, J. (1995). Construction of an empirical measure for narrative coherence and fidelity. *Communication Reports, 8,* pp. 97–101.

Bailey, A. C. (1997). Making waves and drawing lines: The politics of defining the vicissitudes of feminism. *Hypatia, 12,* pp. 27–29.

Baird, J. E. (1976). Sex differences in group communication: A review of relevant research. *Quarterly Journal of Speech, 62,* pp. 179–192.

Ballard-Reisch, D., & Weigel, D. (1999). Communication processes in marital commitment: An integrative approach. In J. Adams & W. Jones (Eds.), *Handbook of interpersonal commitment and relationship stability* (pp. 407–424). New York: Kluwer Academic/Plenum.

Baran, S., & Davis, D. (1995). *Mass communication theory: Foundations, ferment, and future.* Belmont, CA: Wadsworth.

Barge, J. (1985). *Effective leadership and forms of conversation: A field descriptive study.* Unpublished master's thesis, University of Kansas, Lawrence, KS.

Barnhurst, K., & Wartella, E. (1998). Young citizens, American TV newscasts, and the collective memory. *Critical Studies in Mass Communication, 15,* pp. 279–305.

Basow, S. (1992). *Gender: Stereotypes and roles* (3rd ed.). Belmont, CA: Brooks-Cole/Wadsworth.

Bateson, G. (1951). Information and codification. In J. Reusch & G. Bateson (Eds.), *Communication.* New York: W. W. Norton.

Bateson, M. C. (1990). *Composing a life.* New York: Penguin/Plume.

Baudrillard, J. (1984, Spring). Games with vestiges. *On the Beach, 6,* pp. 19–25.

Baudrillard, J. (1987). *Forget Foucault.* New York: Semiotext(e).

Baudrillard, J. (1990). *Seduction.* New York and London: St. Martin's Press and Macmillan.

Baxter, L. A. (1985). Accomplishing relationship disengagement. In S. W. Duck & D. Perlman (Eds.), *Understanding personal relationships: An interdisciplinary approach* (pp. 243–265). Beverly Hills, CA: Sage.

Baxter, L. A. (1987). Symbols of relationship identity in relationship cultures. *Journal of Social and Personal Relationships, 4,* pp. 261–279.

Baxter, L. A. (1988). A dialectical perspective on communication strategies in relationship development. In S. W. Duck, D. F. Hay, S. E. Hobfoll, W. Iches, & B. Montgomery (Eds.), *Handbook of personal relationships* (pp. 257–273). London: Wiley.

Baxter, L. A. (1990). Dialectical contradictions in relationship development. *Journal of Social and Personal Relationships, 7,* pp. 69–88.

Baxter, L. A. (1992). Forms and functions of intimate play in personal relationships. *Human Communication Research, 18,* pp. 336–363.

Baxter, L. A. (1993). The social side of personal relationships: A dialectical perspective. In S. W. Duck (Ed.), *Understanding relationship processes, 3: Social context and relationships* (pp. 139–165). Newbury Park, CA: Sage.

Baxter, L.A. (1994). Thinking dialogically about communication in personal relationships. In R. Conville (Ed.), *Structure in human communication*. Westport, CT: Greenwood.

Baxter, L. A., & Bullis, C. (1986). Turning points in developing romantic relationships. *Human Communication Research, 12*, pp. 469–493.

Baxter, L. A., & Montgomery, B. (1996). *Relating: Dialogues and dialectics*. New York: Guilford Press.

Baxter, L. A., & Simon, E. P. (1993). Relationship maintenance strategies and dialectical contradictions in personal relationships. *Journal of Social and Personal Relationships, 10*, pp. 225–242.

Beck, A. (1988). *Love is never enough*. New York: Harper & Row.

Becker, S. (1984). Marxist approaches to media studies: The British experience. *Critical Studies in Mass Communication, 1*, pp. 66–80.

Becker, C. (1992). *The heavenly city of the eighteenth century philosopher*. New Haven, CT: Yale University Press.

Berg, I., & Jaya, A. (1993). Different and same: Family therapy with Asian-American families. *Journal of Marital and Family Therapy, 19*, pp. 31–38.

Berger, C. R. (1977). The covering law perspective as a theoretical basis for the study of human communication. *Communication Quarterly, 25*, pp. 7–18.

Berger, C. R. (1979). Beyond initial interaction: Uncertainty, understanding, and the development of interpersonal relationships. In H. Giles & R. St. Clair (Eds.), *Language and social psychology* (pp. 122–144). Oxford, UK: Basil Blackwell.

Berger, C. R. (1987). Communicating under uncertainty. In M. Roloff & G. R. Miller (Eds.), *Interpersonal processes: New directions in communication research* (pp. 39–62). Newbury Park, CA: Sage.

Berger, C. R. (1988). Uncertainty and information exchange in developing relationships. In S. Duck (Ed.), *A handbook of personal relationships* (pp. 239–255). New York: Wiley.

Berger, C. R. (1991). Communication theories and other curios. *Communication Monographs, 58*, pp. 101–113.

Berger, C. R., & Bradac, J. (1982). *Language and social knowledge: Uncertainty in interpersonal relations*. London: Arnold.

Berger, C. R., & Calabrese, R. (1975). Some explorations in initial interaction and beyond: Toward a developmental theory of interpersonal communication. *Human Communication Research, 1*, pp. 99–112.

Berger, C. R., & Gudykunst, W. B. (1991). Uncertainty and communication. In B. Dervin & M. Voigt (Eds.), *Progress in communication sciences, 10* (pp. 21–66). Norwood, NJ: Ablex.

Berger, C. R., & Kellerman, K. (1994). Acquiring social information. In J. Daly & I. Wiemann (Eds.), *Strategic interpersonal communication* (pp. 1–31). Hillsdale, NJ: Erlbaum.

Berger, P., & Kellner, H. (1964). Marriage and the construction of reality: An exercise in the microsociology of knowledge. *Diogenes, 46*, pp. 1–24.

Bergner, R., & Bergner, L. (1990). Sexual misunderstanding: A descriptive and pragmatic formulation. *Psychotherapy, 27*, pp. 464–467.

Berns, S., Jacobson, N., & Gottman, J. (1999). Demand/withdraw interaction in couples with a violent husband. *Journal of Consulting and Clinical Psychology, 67*, pp. 666–674.

Best, S., & Kellner, D. (1991). *Postmodern theory: Critical interrogations*. New York: Guilford Press.

Bikini Kill. (1991). *Bikini Kill 1*, n.p.

Billig, M. (1987). *Arguing and thinking: A rhetorical approach to social psychology.* New York: Cambridge University Press.

Bingham, S. (Ed.). (1994). *The discursive construction of sexual harassment.* Westport, CT: Praeger.

Bingham, S. (1996). Sexual harassment: On the job, on the campus. In J. T. Wood (Ed.), *Gendered relationships* (pp. 233–252). Mountain View, CA: Mayfield.

Blair, C., Brown, J., & Baxter, L. (1994). Disciplining the feminine. *Quarterly Journal of Speech, 80,* pp. 383–409.

Blau, P. (1967). *Exchange and power in social life.* New York: Wiley.

Blum, L., & Press. A. (2002). What can we hear after postmodernism? Doing feminist field research in the age of cultural studies. In C. Warren & M. Vavrus (Eds.), *American cultural studies* (pp. 94–114). Urbana: University of Illinois Press.

Blumer, H. (1969). *Symbolic interactionism: Perspective and method.* Englewood Cliffs, NJ: Prentice-Hall.

Blumler, J. (1983). Communication and democracy: The crisis beyond and the ferment within. *Journal of Communication, 33,* pp. 166–173.

Boal, A. (1974). *Theatre of the oppressed.* (Trans. 1985, Charles and Maria-Odilia McBride). New York: Theatre Communications Group.

Bolger, N., & Eckenrode, J. (1991). Social relationships, personality, and anxiety during a major stressful event. *Journal of Personality and Social Psychology, 61,* pp. 440–449.

Bolger, N., & Kelleher, S. (1993). Daily life in relationships. In S. Duck (Ed.), *Understanding relationship processes, 3: Social context and relationships* (pp. 100–109). Newbury Park, CA: Sage.

Bormann, E. G. (1975). *Discussion and group methods: Theory and practice.* New York: Harper & Row.

Bormann, E. G., Putnam, L. L., & Pratt, J. M. (1978). Power, authority and sex: Male response to female dominance. *Communication Monographs, 45,* pp. 119–155.

Boulding, K. (1967). The medium is the massage. In G. E. Stearn (Ed.), *Hot and cool* (pp. 56–64). New York: Dial Press.

Bowen, S., & Michal-Johnson, P. (1995). HIV/AIDS: A crucible for understanding the dark side of sexual interactions. In S. Duck & J. T. Wood (Eds.), *Understanding relationship processes, 5: Confronting relationship challenges* (pp. 150–180). Thousand Oaks, CA: Sage.

Bowen, S., & Michal-Johnson, P. (1996). Being sexual in the shadow of AIDS. In J. T. Wood (Ed.), *Gendered relationships* (pp. 177–196). Mountain View, CA: Mayfield.

Bradbury, T. N., & Fincham, F. D. (1990). Attributions in marriage: Review and critique. *Psychological Bulletin, 107,* pp. 3–33.

Brandt, D. R. (1980). A systematic approach to the measurement of dominance in human face-to-face interaction. *Communication Quarterly, 28,* pp. 21–43.

Branham, R., & Pearce, B. (1985). Between text and context: Toward a rhetoric of contextual reconstruction. *Quarterly Journal of Speech, 71,* pp. 19–36.

Brecht, B. (1961). *Poems on the theatre.* (Trans., J. Berger & Anna Bostock). Lowestoft, Suffolk: Scorpion Press.

Brecht, B. (1964). *Brecht on theatre.* (Ed. & Trans., John Willett). New York: Hill and Wang.

Brehm, S. (1992). *Intimate relationships* (2nd ed.). New York: McGraw-Hill.

Brenders, D. (1987). Fallacies in the coordinated management of meaning: A philosophy of language critique of the hierarchical organization of coherent conversation and related theory. *Quarterly Journal of Speech, 73,* pp. 329–348.

Bruner, J. (2002). *Making stories: Law, literature, life*. New York: Farrar, Straus & Giroux.

Burke, K. (1945). *A grammar of motives*. Englewood Cliffs, NJ: Prentice-Hall.

Burke, K. (1950). *A rhetoric of motives*. Englewood Cliffs, NJ: Prentice-Hall.

Burke, K. (1965). *Permanence and change*. Indianapolis: Bobbs-Merrill.

Burke, K. (1966). *Language as symbolic action*. Berkeley: University of California at Berkeley Press.

Burke, K. (1968). Dramatism. In D. L. Sills (Ed.), *The international encyclopedia of the social sciences, 7* (pp. 445–452). New York: Collier Macmillan.

Burleson, B. (1984). Comforting communication. In H. E. Sypher & J. L. Applegate (Eds.), *Communication by children and adults: Social cognitive and strategic processes* (pp. 63–104). Beverly Hills, CA: Sage.

Burleson, B. (1986). Communication skills and childhood peer relationships: An overview. In M. L. McLaughlin (Ed.), *Communication yearbook, 9* (pp. 143–180). Beverly Hills, CA: Sage.

Burleson, B. (1987). Cognitive complexity. In J. C. McCroskey & J. A. Daly (Eds.), *Personality and interpersonal communication* (pp. 305–349). Newbury Park, CA: Sage.

Burleson, B. (1989). The constructivist approach to person-centered communication: Analysis of a research exemplar. In B. Dervin, L. Grossberg, B. O'Keefe, & E. Wartella (Eds.), *Rethinking communication, 2* (pp. 29–46). Newbury Park, CA: Sage.

Burleson, B. (1991, November). *Communication skills that promote the maintenance of friendships: Contributions of comforting and conflict management*. Paper presented at the Speech Communication Association Convention, Atlanta, GA.

Burleson, B., Albrecht, T., & Sarason, I. (1994). *Communication of social support*. Thousand Oaks, CA: Sage.

Burleson, B., & Waltman, M. (Eds.). (1988). Cognitive complexity: Using the role category questionnaire measure. In C. Tardy (Ed.), *A handbook for the study of human communication* (pp. 1–35). Norwood, NJ: Ablex.

Butler, J. (1990). *Gender trouble*. London: Routledge.

Butler, J. (1993). *Bodies that matter: On the discursive limits of sex*. London: Routledge.

Campbell, A. (1993). *Men, women and aggression*. New York: Basic Books.

Campbell, K. (1995). In silence we oppress. In J. T. Wood & R. B. Gregg (Eds.), *Toward the 21st century* (pp. 137–149). Cresskill, NJ: Hampton Press.

Canary, D., & Hause, K. (1993). Is there any reason to research sex differences in communication? *Communication Quarterly, 41*, pp. 129–144.

Canary, D., & Stafford, L. (Eds.). (1994). *Communication and relational maintenance*. New York: Academic Press.

Cassirer, E. (1968). *The philosophy of the enlightenment*. (Trans., F. Koelin; Ed. J. Pettigrove). Princeton, NJ: Princeton University Press.

Chang, H., & Holt, R. (1991). *The challenge of facework: Cross-cultural interpersonal issues*. Albany: State University of New York Press.

Charon, R., & Montello, M. (Eds.). (2002). *The role of narrative in medical ethics*. London: Routledge.

Chesebro, J. W. (1992). Extensions of the Burkean system. *Quarterly Journal of Speech, 78*, pp. 356–368.

Chesebro, J. W. (1995a). Communication technologies as cognitive systems. In J. T. Wood & R. B. Gregg (Eds.), *Toward the 21st century* (pp. 15–46). Cresskill, NJ: Hampton Press.

References

Chesebro, J. W. (1995b, May). Personal communication.

Choi, Y. S., Massey, K. K., & Baran, S. J. (1988). *The beginnings of political communication research in the United States: Origins of the "limited effects" model.* Paper presented at the Annual Convention of the International Communication Association, San Francisco, CA.

Christensen, A., & Heavey, C. (1990). Gender and social structure in the demand/withdraw pattern in marital conflict. *Journal of Personality and Social Psychology, 59,* pp. 73–81.

Clair, R. P. (1993). The use of framing devices to sequester organizational narratives: Hegemony and harassment. *Communication Monographs, 60,* pp. 113–136.

Clark, M. S., Quellette, R., Powell, M., & Milberg, S. (1987). Recipient's mood, relationship type, and helping. *Journal of Personality and Social Psychology, 53,* pp. 93–103.

Clark, R. A. (1998). A comparison of topics and objectives in a cross section of young men's and women's everyday conversations. In D. Canary & K. Dindia (Eds.), *Sex differences and similarities in communication: Critical essays and empirical investigations of sex and gender interaction* (pp. 303–319). Mahwah, NJ: Erlbaum.

Clark, R. A., & Delia, J. (1977). Cognitive complexity, social perspective-taking, and functional persuasive skills in second- to ninth-grade students. *Human Communication Research, 3,* pp. 128–134.

Clemetson, L. (1999, February 8). The slur that wasn't. *Newsweek,* p. 39.

Cohen, S. (1988). Psychosocial models of the role of social support in the etiology of physical disease. *Health Psychology, 7,* pp. 269–297.

Cohen-Cruz, J. (1998). General introduction. In J. Cohen-Cruz (Ed.), *Radical street performance: An international anthology* (pp. 1–6). New York: Routledge.

Collins, P. (1998). *Fighting words: Black women and the search for justice.* Minneapolis: University of Minnesota Press.

Collins, P. H. (1986). Learning from the outsider within. *Social Problems, 23,* pp. 514–532.

Collins, P. H. (2000). Comment on Hekman's 'Truth and method: Feminist standpoint theory revisited.' Where's the power? In C. Allen & J. Howard (Eds.), *Provoking feminisms* (pp. 43–49). Chicago: University of Chicago Press.

Colvard, K. (1997). Crime is down: Don't confuse us with the facts. *Harry Frank Guggenheim Review, 14,* pp. 19–26.

Combs, J., & Mansfield, M. (Eds.). (1976). *Drama in life: The uses of communication in society.* New York: Hastings House.

Condit, C. (1992). Post-Burke: Transcending the substance of dramatism. *Quarterly Journal of Speech, 78,* pp. 349–355.

Conquergood, D. (1985). Performing as a moral act: Ethical dimensions of the ethnography of performance. *Literature in Performance, 5,* pp. 1–13.

Conquergood, D. (1986a). Performing cultures: Ethnography, epistemology, and ethics. In E. Iembeck (Ed.), *Miteinander sprechen und bandeln: Fetschrift für Hellmut Geissner* (pp. 55–66). Frankfurt: Scriptor.

Conquergood, D. (1986b). Performance and dialogical understanding: In quest of the other. In J. Palmer (Ed.), *Communication as performance* (pp. 30–37). Tempe: Arizona State University.

Conquergood, D. (1988). Health theatre in Hmong refugee camp: Performance, communication, and culture. *The Drama Review, 32,* pp. 174–208.

Conquergood, D. (1991). Rethinking ethnography: Toward a critical cultural studies politics. *Communication Monographs, 58,* pp. 179–194.

Conquergood, D. (1992). Ethnography, rhetoric, and performance. *Quarterly Journal of Speech, 78,* pp. 80–97.

Conquergood, D. (1998). Beyond the text: Toward a performative cultural politics. In S. Dailey (Ed.), *The future of performance studies: Visions and revisions* (pp. 25–36). Annandale, VA: National Communication Association.

Conquergood, D., Friesema, P., Hunter, A., & Mansbridge, J. (1990). *Dispersed ethnicity and community integration: Newcomers and established residents in the Albany Park area of Chicago.* Evanston, IL: Center for Urban Affairs and Policy Research, Northwestern University.

Conrad, C. (1995). Was Pogo right? In J. T. Wood & R. B. Gregg (Eds.), *Toward the 21st century* (pp. 185–208). Cresskill, NJ: Hampton Press.

Conrad, C., & Poole, M. (2002). *Strategic organizational communication* (5th ed.). New York: Harcourt.

Contarello, A., & Volpato, C. (1991). Images of friendship: Literary depictions through the ages. *Journal of Social and Personal Relationships, 8,* pp. 49–75.

Cornforth, M. (1968). *Materialism and the dialectical method.* New York: International Publishers.

Cowan, G., Lee, C., Levy, D., & Snyder, D. (1988). Dominance and inequality in X-rated videocassettes. *Psychology of Women Quarterly, 12,* pp. 299–311.

Crenshaw, K., Gotanda, N., Peller, G., & Thomas, K. (Eds.). (1996). *Critical race theory: The key writings that formed the movement.* New York: The New Press.

Crockett, W. H. (1965). Cognitive complexity and impression formation. In B. A. Maher (Ed.), *Progress in experimental personality research, 2* (pp. 47–90). New York: Academic Press.

Cronen, V. (1991). Coordinated management of meaning theory and postenlightenment ethics. In K. Greenberg (Ed.), *Conversation on communication ethics* (pp. 21–53). Norwood, NJ: Ablex.

Cronen, V., Chen, V., & Pearce, B. (1988). Coordinated management of meaning: A critical theory. In Y. Kim & W. Gudykunst (Eds.), *Theories in intercultural communication* (pp. 66–98). Newbury Park, CA: Sage.

Cronen, V., & Pearce, B. (1981). Logical force in interpersonal communication: A new concept of the "necessity" in social behavior. *Communication, 6,* pp. 5–67.

Cronen, V., & Pearce, B. (1982). The coordinated management of meaning: A theory of communication. In F. E. X. Dance (Ed.), *Human communication theory* (pp. 61–89). New York: Harper & Row.

Crow, B. (1988). Conversational performance and the performance of conversation. *The Drama Review, 32,* pp. 23–54.

Dance, F. (1970). The concept of communication. *Journal of Communication, 20,* pp. 201–210.

Davis, F. (1991). *Moving the mountain: The women's movement in America since 1960.* New York: Simon & Schuster.

DeFleur, M. L., & Ball-Rokeach, S. (1989). *Theories of mass communication* (5th ed.). White Plains, NY: Longman.

DeFrancisco, V. (1991). The sounds of silence: How men silence women in marital relations. *Discourse and Society, 2,* pp. 413–423.

Delgado, R., & Stefancic, J. (Eds.). (1997). *Critical white studies: Looking behind the mirror.* Philadelphia: Temple University Press.

Delia, J., O'Keefe, B., & O'Keefe, D. (1982). The constructivist approach to communication. In F. E. X. Dance (Ed.), *Human communication theory* (pp. 147–191). New York: Harper & Row.

Demare, D., Briere, J., & Lips, H. M. (1988). Violent pornography and self-reported likelihood of sexual aggression. *Journal of Research in Personality, 22,* pp. 140–153.

Denzin, N. (2001). *Interpretive interactionism* (2nd ed.). Thousand Oaks, CA: Sage.

Derrida, J. (1973). *Speech and phenomena, and other essays on Husserl's theory of signs.* Evanston, IL: Northwestern University Press.

Derrida, J. (1974). *Of grammatology.* (Trans., G. Spivak). Baltimore: Johns Hopkins University Press.

Derrida, J. (1978). *Writing and difference.* London: Routledge & Kegan Paul.

Diamond, E. (Ed.). (1996). *Performances and cultural politics.* New York: Routledge.

Dickson, F. (1995). Mature relationships. In J. T. Wood & S. Duck (Eds.), *Understanding relationship processes, 6: Understudied relationships: Off the beaten track* (pp. 22–50). Thousand Oaks, CA: Sage.

Dieter, P. (1989, March). *Shooting her with video, drugs, bullets, and promises.* Paper presented at the meeting of the Association of Women in Psychology, Newport, RI.

Dillard, J., Solomon, D., & Palmer, M. (1999). Structuring the concept of relational communication. *Communication Monographs, 66,* pp. 49–65.

Dindia, K., & Allen, M. (1992). Sex differences in self-disclosure: A meta-analysis. *Psychological Bulletin, 12,* pp. 106–124.

Dindia, K., & Baxter, L. A. (1987). Strategies for maintaining and repairing marital relationships. *Journal of Social and Personal Relationships, 4,* pp. 143–158.

Dindia, K., & Canary, D. (1993). Definitions and theoretical perspectives on maintaining relationships. *Journal of Social and Personal Relationships, 10,* pp. 163–174.

Dixson, M., & Duck, S. W. (1993). Understanding relationship processes: Uncovering the human search for meaning. In S. W. Duck (Ed.), *Understanding relationship processes, 1: Individuals in relationships* (pp. 175–206). Newbury Park, CA: Sage.

Donnerstein, E., Linz, D., & Penrod, S. (1987). *The question of pornography: Research findings and policy implications.* New York: Free Press.

Doob, A., & Macdonald, G. (1979). Television viewing and fear of victimization: Is the relationship causal? *Journal of Personality and Social Psychology, 37,* pp. 170–179.

Duck, S. W. (1984). A perspective on the repair of personal relationships: Repair of what? When? In S. W. Duck (Ed.), *Personal relationships, 5: Repairing personal relationships.* London: Academic Press.

Duck, S. W. (1990). Relationships as unfinished business: Out of the frying pan and into the 1990s. *Journal of Social and Personal Relationships, 7,* pp. 5–24.

Duck, S. W. (1991). *Friends for life.* Hemel Hemstead, UK: Harvester Wheatsheaf.

Duck, S. W. (1992). *Human relationships* (2nd ed.). Newbury Park, CA: Sage.

Duck, S. W. (Ed.). (1993). *Understanding relationship processes, 1: Individuals in relationships.* Newbury Park, CA: Sage.

Duck, S. W. (1994a). *Meaningful relationships.* Thousand Oaks, CA: Sage.

Duck, S. W. (1994b). Steady as (s)he goes: Relational maintenance as a shared meaning system. In D. Canary & L. Stafford (Eds.), *Communication and relational maintenance* (pp. 45–60). New York: Academic Press.

Duck, S. W., & Pond, K. (1989). Friends, Romans, countrymen, lend me your retrospections: Rhetoric and reality in personal relationships. In C. Hendrick (Ed.), *Close relationships* (pp. 17–38). Newbury Park, CA: Sage.

Duck, S. W., & Wood, J. T. (Eds.). (1995). *Understanding relationship processes, 5: Confronting relationship challenges.* Thousand Oaks, CA: Sage.

Duck, S. W., & Wright, P. (1993). Reexamining gender differences in same-gender friendships: A close look at two kinds of data. *Sex Roles, 28,* pp. 709–727.

Eagly, A., & Crowley, M. (1986). Gender and helping behavior: A meta-analytic review of social psychological literature. *Psychological Bulletin, 100,* pp. 283–308.

Eagly, A., & Karau, S. (1991). Gender and the emergence of leadership: A meta-analysis. *Journal of Personality and Social Psychology, 60,* pp. 685–710.

Eakins, B. W., & Eakins, R. G. (1976). Verbal turn-taking and exchanges in faculty dialogue. In B. L. DuBois & I. Crouch (Eds.), *Papers in southwest English, IV: Proceedings of the conference on the sociology of languages of American women* (pp. 53–62). San Antonio, TX: Trinity University Press.

Elgin, S. (1988). *A first dictionary and grammar of Laadan* (2nd ed.). Madison, WI: Society for the Furtherance and Study of Fantasy and Science Fiction.

Ellis, A., & Harper, R. (1977). *A new guide to rational living.* North Hollywood, CA: Wilshire Books.

Entman, R. M. (1994). Representation and reality in the portrayal of blacks on network television news. *Journalism Quarterly, 71,* pp. 509–520.

Epstein, C. F. (1988). *Deceptive distinctions: Sex, gender and the social order.* New Haven, CT: Yale University Press.

Evans, D. (1993, March 1). The wrong examples. *Newsweek,* p. 10.

Fallows, J. (1996). *Breaking the news: How the media undermine democracy.* New York: Pantheon.

Fehr, B. (1993). How do I love thee? Let me consult my prototype. In S. W. Duck (Ed.), *Understanding relationship processes, 1: Individuals in relationships* (pp. 87–122). Newbury Park, CA: Sage.

Feldman, C., & Ridley, C. (2000). The role of conflict-based communication responses and outcomes in male domestic violence toward female partners. *Journal of Social and Personal Relationships, 17,* pp. 552–573.

Felsenthal, E. (1996, January 3). Lawyers learn how to walk the walk, talk the talk. *Wall Street Journal,* pp. B1, B2.

Ferrante, J. (1995). *Sociology: A global perspective* (2nd ed.). Belmont, CA: Wadsworth.

Fine, E., & Speer, J. (Eds.). (1992). *Performance, culture and identity.* Westport, CT: Praeger.

Fisher, B. A. (1982). The pragmatic perspective of human communication: A view from system theory. In F. E. X. Dance (Ed.), *Human communication theory* (pp. 192–219). New York: Harper & Row.

Fisher, W. R. (1978). Toward a logic of good reasons. *Quarterly Journal of Speech, 64,* pp. 376–387.

Fisher, W. R. (1984). Narration as a human communication paradigm: The case of public moral argument. *Communication Monographs, 51,* pp. 1–22.

Fisher, W. R. (1987). *Human communication as narration: Toward a philosophy of reason, value, and action.* Columbia: University of South Carolina Press.

Fishman, P. (1978). Interaction: The work women do. *Social Problems, 25,* pp. 397–406.

Fiske, J. (1987). *Television culture.* London: Methuen.

Fitch, K. (1994). Criteria for evidence in qualitative research. *Western Journal of Communication, 58,* pp. 32–38.

Fletcher, G. J., & Fincham, F. D. (1991). Attribution in close relationships. In G. J. Fletcher & F. D. Fincham (Eds.), *Cognition in close relationships* (pp. 7–35). Hillsdale, NJ: Lawrence Erlbaum.

Fletcher, G. J., & Fitness, J. (1990). Occurrent social cognition in close relationship interaction: The role of proximal and distal variables. *Journal of Personality and Social Psychology, 59,* pp. 464–474.

Fletcher, G. J., & Fitness, J. (1993). Knowledge structures and explanations in intimate relationships. In S. Duck (Ed.), *Understanding relationship processes, 2: Learning about relationships* (pp. 121–142). Newbury Park, CA: Sage.

Fletcher, G. J., Rosanowski, J., & Fitness, J. (1992). *Automatic processing in intimate settings: The role of relationship beliefs.* Unpublished manuscript.

Flundernik, M. (1996). *Towards a natural narratology.* London: Routledge.

Foss, K. (1991). Personal communication cited in S. Littlejohn (1992). *Theories of human communication* (4th ed., p. 241). Belmont, CA: Wadsworth.

Foss, K., & Foss, S. (1991). *Women speak: The eloquence of women's lives.* Prospect Heights, IL: Waveland.

Foss, S., Foss, K., & Trapp, R. (2001). *Contemporary perspectives on rhetoric.* Prospect Heights, IL: Waveland.

Foucault, M. (1967). *Madness and civilization.* London: Tavistock.

Foucault, M. (1972). *The order of things.* London: Tavistock.

Foucault, M. (1977). *Discipline and punish.* London: Penguin.

Foucault, M. (1980). *Power/knowledge: Selected interviews and other writings: 1972–1977.* Edited by C. Gordon. Brighton, UK: Harvester.

Foucault, M. (1994). *The order of things: An archeology of the human sciences.* New York: Vintage Books.

Foucault, M. (1995). *Discipline and punish: The birth of the prison.* (Trans., A. Sheridan). New York: Vintage Books.

Fowers, B. J. (1991). His and her marriage: A multivariate study of gender and marital satisfaction. *Sex Roles, 24,* pp. 209–221.

Frank, A. (1995). *The wounded storyteller: Body, illness, and ethics.* Chicago: University of Chicago Press.

Frith, S., & Horne, H. (1987). *Art into pop.* London: Methuen.

Gaines, S., Jr. (1995). Relationships between members of cultural minorities. In J. T. Wood & S. W. Duck (Eds.), *Understanding relationship processes, 6: Off the beaten track: Understudied relationships* (pp. 51–88). Thousand Oaks, CA: Sage.

Garfinkel, H. (1967). *Studies in ethnomethodology.* Englewood Cliffs, NJ: Prentice-Hall.

Gates, H. L., Jr. (1987). The blackness of blackness: A critique of the sign and the signifying monkey. In H. L. Gates, Jr. (Ed.), *Figures in black* (pp. 235–276). New York: Oxford University Press.

Geertz, C. (1973). *The interpretation of cultures.* New York: Basic Books.

Geertz, C. (1983). *Local knowledge: Further essays in interpretive anthropology.* New York: Basic Books.

Gerbner, G. (1981). A curious journey into the scary world of Paul Hirsch. *Communication Research, 8,* pp. 259–280.

Gerbner, G. (1990). Epilogue: Advancing on the path of righteousness (maybe). In N. Signorielli & M. Morgan (Eds.), *Cultivation analysis: New directions in media effects research* (pp. 250–261). Newbury Park, CA: Sage.

Gerbner, G. (2001). *Telling all the stories*. New York: Peter Lang Publishing.

Gerbner, G., Gross, L., Jackson-Beeck, M., Jeffries-Fox, S., & Signorielli, N. (1978). Cultural indicators:Violence profile No. 9. *Journal of Communication, 28,* pp. 176–207.

Gerbner, G., Gross, L., Morgan, M., & Signorielli, N. (1980). The "mainstreaming" of America:Violence profile No. 11. *Journal of Communication, 30,* pp. 10–29.

Gerbner, G., Gross, L., Morgan, M., & Signorielli, N. (1986). Living with television: The dynamics of the cultivation process. In J. Bryant & D. Zillmann (Eds.), *Perspectives on media effects* (pp. 17–40). Hillsdale, NJ: Lawrence Erlbaum.

Gergen, K. (1991). *The saturated self: Dilemmas of identity in contemporary life*. New York: Basic Books.

Gerstel, N., & Gross, H. (1985). *Commuter marriage*. New York: Guilford Press.

Gilligan, C. (1982). *In a different voice: Psychological theory and women's development*. Cambridge, MA: Harvard University Press.

Gilroy, P. (2001). *Against race: Imagining politics beyond the color line*. Cambridge, MA: Harvard University Press.

Gitlin, T. (1995). *The twilight of common dreams*. New York: Metropolitan.

Glassie, H. (1982). *Passing time in the Balleymenone: Culture and history of an Ulster community*. Philadelphia: University of Pennsylvania Press.

Godwin, G., & Risman, B. (2001). Twentieth-century changes in work and family. In D. Vannoy (Ed.), *Gender mosaics* (pp. 134-144). Los Angeles: Roxbury.

Goffman, E. (1959). *The presentation of self in everyday life*. Garden City, NY: Doubleday.

Goffman, E. (1967). *Interaction ritual: Essays on face-to-face interaction*. New York: Doubleday.

Goffman, E. (1974). *Frame analysis: An essay on the organization of experience*. Cambridge, MA: Harvard University Press.

Goffman, E. (1983). The interaction order. *American Sociological Review, 83,* pp. 1–17.

Goldner, V., Penn, P., Scheinberg, M., & Walker, G. (1990). Love and violence: Gender paradoxes in volatile attachments. *Family Process, 19,* pp. 343–364.

Goldsmith, D. (1990). A dialectic perspective on the expression of autonomy and connection in romantic relationships. *Western Journal of Speech Communication, 54,* pp. 537–556.

Goldsmith, D., & Fulfs, P. (1999). "You just don't have the evidence": An analysis of claims and evidence in Deborah Tannen's *You Just Don't Understand*. In M. Roloff (Ed.), *Communication yearbook, 22,* pp. 1–49, Thousand Oaks, CA: Sage.

Goldstein, A. (2000, February 27). Breadwinning wives alter marital equation. *Washington Post*, p. A1.

Goleman, D., Mckee, A., & Boyatzis, R. (2002). *Primal leadership: Realizing the power of emotional intelligence*. Cambridge, MA: Harvard University Press.

Gordon, G. (1982, January). An end to McLuhanacy. *Educational Technology*, pp. 39–45.

Gottman, J. M., & Carrère, S. (1994). Why can't men and women get along? Developmental roots and marital inequities. In D. Canary & L. Stafford (Eds.), *Communication and relational maintenance* (pp. 203–229). New York: Academic Press.

Gouran, D. S. (1990). *Making decisions in groups: Choices and consequences*. Glenview, IL: Scott, Foresman.

Gray, J. (1992). *Men Are From Mars, Women Are From Venus*. New York: HarperCollins.

Gray, P., & VanOsting, J. (1996). *Performance in Life and Literature*. Needham Heights, MA: Allyn & Bacon.

Griffin, E. (1994). *Communication: A first look at communication theory*. New York: McGraw-Hill.

Gronbeck, B. (1980). Dramaturgical theory and criticism: The state of the art (or science?). *Western Journal of Speech Communication, 44*, pp. 315–330.

Gross, N. (1996, December 23). Zap! Splat! Smarts! *Newsweek*, pp. 64–71.

Grossberg, L. (1986). Is there rock after punk? *Critical Studies in Mass Communication, 3*, pp. 50–73.

Grossberg, L. (1996). *We gotta get out of this place*. London: Routledge.

Gudykunst, W. (1983). Uncertainty reduction and predictability of behavior in low and high context cultures. *Communication Quarterly, 31*, pp. 49–55.

Gudykunst, W. (1985). The influence of cultural similarity, type of relationship and self-monitoring on uncertainty reduction processes. *Communication Monographs, 52*, pp. 203–217.

Gudykunst, W. (1991). *Bridging differences: Effective intergroup communication*. Newbury Park, CA: Sage.

Gudykunst, W. (1993). Toward a theory of effective interpersonal and intergroup communication: An anxiety/uncertainty management (AUM) perspective. In R. Wiseman & J. Koester (Eds.), *Intercultural communication competence* (pp. 33–71). Newbury Park, CA: Sage.

Gudykunst, W. (1995). Anxiety uncertainty management (AUM) theory: Current status. In R. Wiseman (Ed.), *Intercultural communication theory* (pp. 8–58). Newbury Park, CA: Sage.

Gudykunst, W., & Nishida, T. (1984). Individual and cultural influences on uncertainty reduction. *Communication Monographs, 51*, pp. 23–36.

Gudykunst, W., & Nishida, T. (1989). Theoretical perspectives for studying intercultural communication. In M. Asante & W. Gudykunst (Eds.), *Handbook of international and intercultural communication* (pp. 17–46). Newbury Park, CA: Sage.

Gusfield, J. R. (Ed.). (1989). Introduction. *On symbols and society*. Chicago: University of Chicago Press.

Habermas, J. (1971). *Knowledge and human interests*. (Trans., J. J. Shapiro). Boston: Beacon Press.

Habermas, J. (1984). *The theory of communicative action, I: Reason and the rationalization of society*. (Trans., T. McCarthy). Boston: Beacon Press.

Habermas, J. (1990) *The philosophical discourse of modernity: Twelve lectures*. (Trans., F. Lawrence). Boston: MIT Press.

Hall, A. D., & Fagen, R. (1956). Definition of a system. *General Systems, 1*, pp. 18–28.

Hall, D. (1995). *Revolution grrrl style now! The rhetoric and subcultural practices of Riot Grrrls*. Unpublished master's thesis in the Department of Communication Studies at the University of North Carolina at Chapel Hill.

Hall, J., Leloudis, J., Korstad, R., Murphy, M., Jones, L., & Daly, C. (1987). *Like a family: The making of a cotton mill world*. Chapel Hill: University of North Carolina Press.

Hall, R. M., with Sandler, B. R. (1982). *The classroom climate: A chilly one for women?* Washington, DC: Association of American Colleges, Project on the Status and Education of Women.

Hall, S. (1982). The rediscovery of "ideology": Return of the repressed in media studies. In M. Gurevitch, T. Bennett, J. Curran, & J. Woollacott (Eds.), *Culture, society, and the media* (pp. 56–90). London: Methuen.

Hall, S. (1986a). Cultural studies: Two paradigms. In R. Collins (Ed.), *Media, culture, and society: A critical reader*. London: Sage.

Hall, S. (1986b). The problem of ideology—Marxism without guarantees. *Journal of Communication Inquiry, 10,* pp. 28–44.

Hall, S. (1996). Introduction: Who needs identity? In S. Hall & P. du Gay (Eds.), *Questions of cultural identity*. London: Sage.

Hall, S. (1988). *The hard road to renewal: Thatcherism and the crisis on the left*. London: Verso.

Hall, S. (1989a). Ideology. In E. Barnouw et al. (Eds.), *International encyclopedia of communication* (Vol. 2, pp. 307–311). New York: Oxford University Press.

Hall, S. (1989b). Ideology and communication theory. In B. Dervin, L. Grossberg, B. O'Keefe, & E. Wartella (Eds.), *Rethinking communication theory* (Vol. 1, pp. 40–52). Newbury Park, CA: Sage.

Hallstein, L. (2000). Where standpoint stands now: An introduction and commentary. *Women's Studies in Communication, 23,* pp. 1–15.

Hampden-Turner, C. (1982). *Maps of the mind: Charts and concepts of the mind and its labyrinths*. New York: Macmillan/Collier.

Hansen, C. H., & Hansen, R. D. (1988). How rock music videos can change what is seen when boy meets girl: Priming stereotypic appraisal of social interactions. *Sex Roles, 19,* pp. 287–316.

Haraway, D. (1988). Situated knowledges: The science question in feminism and the privilege of partial perspective. *Signs, 14,* pp. 575–599.

Harding, S. (1991). *Whose science? Whose knowledge? Thinking from women's lives*. Ithaca, NY: Cornell University Press.

Harding, S. (1998). *Is science multicultural?* Indianapolis: University of Indiana Press.

Harris, L. (1979). *Communication competence: Empirical tests of a systemic model*. Unpublished doctoral dissertation. University of Massachusetts, Amherst, MA.

Hartsock, N. (1983). The feminist standpoint: Developing the ground for a specifically feminist historical materialism. In S. Harding & M. B. Hintikka (Eds.), *Discovering reality* (pp. 283–310). Boston: Ridel.

Harvey, D. (1989). *The condition of postmodernity*. London: Basil Blackwell.

Harvey, J., Weber, A., & Orbuch, T. (1990). *Interpersonal accounts: A social psychological perspective*. Oxford, UK: Basil Blackwell.

Hayakawa, S. I. (1978). *Language in thought and action*. Orlando, FL: Harcourt Brace Jovanovich.

Healy, J. (1990). *Endangered minds: Why children don't think and what we can do about it*. New York: Simon & Schuster.

Hegel, G. W. F. (1807). *The phenomenology of mind*. (Trans., J. B. Braillie). Germany: Wurtzburg & Bamberg.

Heidegger, M. (1927, original publication). *Being and time*. (Trans., J. Macquarrie & E. S. Robinson, 1962). New York: Harper & Row.

Hekman, S. (2000). Truth and method: Feminist standpoint theory revisited. In C. Allen & J. Howard (Eds.), *Provoking feminisms* (pp. 9–34). Chicago: University of Chicago Press.

Hendrick, C., & Hendrick, S. (1996). Gender and the experience of heterosexual love. In J. T. Wood (Ed.), *Gendered relationships* (pp. 131–148). Mountain View, CA: Mayfield.

Hertz, R., & Marshall, N. (Eds.). (2001). *Working families: The transformation of the American home*. Berkeley: University of California Press.

Heywood, L., & Drake, J. (Eds.). (1997). *Third wave agenda: Being feminist, doing feminism*. Minneapolis: University of Minnesota Press.

Hirokawa, R., & Poole, M. (Eds.). (1996). *Communication and group decision-making* (2nd ed.) Thousand Oaks, CA: Sage.

Hirsch, P. (1980). The "scary world" of nonviewer and other anomalies. *Communication Research, 7*, pp. 403–456.

Hochschild, A., with Machung, A. (1989). *The second shift*. New York: Viking.

Hojat, M. (1982). Loneliness as a function of selected personality variables. *Journal of Clinical Psychology, 38*, pp. 136–141.

Holtzman, L. (2000). *Media messages: What film, television, and popular music teach us about race, class, gender, and sexual orientation*. New York: M. E. Sharpe.

Homans, G. C. (1954). Social behavior as exchange. *American Journal of Sociology, 62*, pp. 594–617.

Homans, G. C. (1961). *Social behavior: Its elementary forms*. New York: Harcourt, Brace, & World.

Honeycutt, J. M. (1993). Memory structures for the rise and fall of personal relationships. In S. W. Duck (Ed.), *Understanding relationship processes, 1: Individuals in relationships* (pp. 30–59). Newbury Park, CA: Sage.

Honeycutt, J., & Cantrill, J. (1991). Using expectations of relational actions to predict number of intimate relationships: Don Juan and Romeo unmasked. *Communication Reports, 4*, pp. 14–21.

Honeycutt, J., & Cantrill, J. (2001). *Cognition, communication, and romantic relationships*. Mahwah, NJ: Erlbaum.

Honeycutt, J., Cantrill, J., & Greene, R. (1989). Memory structures for relational escalation: A cognitive test of the sequencing of relational actions and stages. *Human Communication Research, 16*, pp. 62–90.

HopKins, M. (1995). The performance turn-and-toss. *Quarterly Journal of Speech, 81*, pp. 228–236.

Hopper, R. (1993). Conversational dramatism and everyday life performance. *Text and Performance Quarterly, 13*, pp. 181–183.

House, J., Umberson, D., & Landis, K. (1988). Structures and processes of social support. *Annual Review of Sociology, 14*, pp. 293–318.

Houston, M. (1994). When black women talk with white women: Why dialogues are difficult. In A. González, M. Houston, & V. Chen (Eds.), *Our voices: Essays in culture, ethnicity, and communication* (pp. 133–139). Los Angeles: Roxbury.

Houston, M., & Wood, J. T. (1996). Difficult dialogues, enlarged horizons: Friendships among members of different social groups. In J. T. Wood (Ed.), *Gendered relationships* (pp. 39–56). Mountain View, CA: Mayfield.

Howry, A., & Wood, J. T. (2001). Something old, something new, something borrowed: Themes in the voices of a new generation of feminists. *Southern Journal of Communication, 66*, pp. 323–336.

Huston, M., & Schwartz, P. (1996). Relationships of lesbians and gay men. In J. T. Wood & S. W. Duck (Eds.), *Understanding relationship processes, 6: Off the beaten track: Understudied relationships* (pp. 89–121). Thousand Oaks, CA: Sage.

Hyde, M. J. (1995). Human being and the call of technology. In J. T. Wood & R. B. Gregg (Eds.), *Toward the 21st century* (pp. 47–49). Cresskill, NJ: Hampton Press.

Hymes, D. (1962). The ethnography of speaking. In T. Gladwin & W. Sturtevant (Eds.), *Anthropology and human behavior* (pp. 13–53). Washington, DC: Anthropological Society of Washington.

Hymes, D. (1974). *Foundations in sociolinguistics: An ethnographic approach.* Philadelphia: University of Pennsylvania Press.

Inman, C. (1996). Friendships among men: Closeness in the doing. In J. T. Wood (Ed.), *Gendered relationships* (pp. 95–110). Mountain View, CA: Mayfield.

Ishii, S., & Bruneau, T. (1991). Silence and silences in cross-cultural perspective: Japan and the United States. In L. Samovar & R. Porter (Eds.), *Intercultural communication: A reader* (6th ed., pp. 314–319). Belmont, CA: Wadsworth.

James, N. (2000). When Miss America was always white. In A. González, M. Houston, & V. Chen (Eds.), *Our voices: Essays in culture, ethnicity, and communication* (pp. 42–46). Los Angeles: Roxbury.

Janeway, E. (1971). *Man's world, woman's place.* New York: Dell.

Jarmon, L. (1996). Performance as a resource in the practice of conversational analysis. *Text and Performance Quarterly, 16,* pp. 336–355.

Johnson, F. (1996). Friendships among women: Closeness in dialogue. In J. T. Wood (Ed.), *Gendered relationships* (pp. 79–94). Mountain View, CA: Mayfield.

Johnson, K., & Nakanishi, M. (1993). Implications of self-disclosure on conversational logics, perceived communication, competence, and social attraction: A comparison of Japanese and American cultures. *International and intercultural communication annual* (Vol. 17, pp. 204–221). Newbury Park, CA: Sage.

Jones, W. H., & Moore, T. L. (1989). Loneliness and social support. In M. Hojat & R. Crandall (Eds.), *Loneliness: Theory, research, and applications* (pp. 145–156). Newbury Park, CA: Sage.

Judicial Council of California. (1986). *1986 Annual report to the governor and legislature.* San Francisco, CA.

Katriel, T. (1990). "Griping" as a verbal ritual in some Israeli discourse. In D. Carbaugh (Ed.), *Cultural communication and intercultural contact* (pp. 99–114). Hillsdale, NJ: Lawrence Erlbaum.

Kaye, L. W., & Applegate, J. S. (1990). Men as elder caregivers: A response to changing families. *American Journal of Orthopsychiatry, 60,* pp. 86–95.

Keller, E. F. (1985). *Reflections on gender and science.* New Haven, CT: Yale University Press.

Kellerman, K., & Reynolds, R. (1990). When ignorance is bliss: The role of motivation to reduce uncertainty in uncertainty reduction theory. *Human Communication Research, 17,* pp. 5–75.

Kelley, H. H., & Thibaut, J. (1978). *The social psychology of groups.* New York: Wiley.

Kellner, D. (1995). *Media culture: Cultural studies, identity & politics between the modern and postmodern.* London: Routledge.

Kelly, G. A. (1955). *The psychology of personal constructs.* New York: W. W. Norton.

Kelly, S. (1997, January–February). To free the world. *Utne Reader,* pp. 80–81.

Kim, Y. (1988). *Communication and cross cultural adaptation.* Philadelphia: Multilingual Matters.

Kim, Y. (1995). Cross cultural adaptation: An integrated theory. In R. Wiseman (Ed.), *Intercultural communication theory* (pp. 170–193) Newbury Park, CA: Sage.

References

Kim, Y., & Gudykunst, W. (Eds.). (1988). *Cross cultural adaptation: Current approaches*. Newbury Park, CA: Sage.

Kimball, M. (1986). Television and sex-role attitudes. In T. M. Williams (Ed.), *The impact of television: A natural experiment in three communities* (pp. 265–301). Orlando, FL: Academic Press.

Kincaid, J. (1990). *Lucy*. New York: Plume

Kirkwood, W. (1992). Narrative and the rhetoric of possibility. *Communication Monographs, 59*, pp. 30–47.

Klein, R., & Milardo, R. M. (1993). Third-party influence on the management of personal relationships. In S. Duck (Ed.), *Understanding relationship processes, 3: Social context and relationships* (pp. 55–77). Newbury Park, CA: Sage.

Klopf, D. (1991). Japanese communication practices: Recent comparative research. *Communication Quarterly, 39*, pp. 130–139.

Knapp, M. L., & Vangelisti, A. (1992). *Interpersonal communication and human relationships* (2nd ed.). Boston: Allyn & Bacon.

Korzybski, A. (1958). *Science and sanity: An introduction to non-Aristotelian systems and general semantics*. Lakeville, CT: Institute of General Semantics.

Kramarae, C. (1981). *Women and men speaking*. Rowley, MA: Newbury House.

Kramarae, C., & Treichler, P. (1985). *A feminist dictionary*. Boston: Pandora.

Kuhn, T. (1970). *The structure of scientific revolutions* (2nd ed.). Chicago: University of Chicago Press.

Labov, W. (1972). *Sociolinguistic patterns*. Philadelphia: University of Pennsylvania Press.

Lacan, J. (1977). *Ecrits: A selection*. London: Tavistock.

Lacan, J. (1981). *The four fundamental concepts of psycho-analysis*. London: Penguin.

Landa, J., & Onega, S. (1996). *Narratology*. New York: Addison-Wesley.

Langer, S. (1953). *Feeling and form: A theory of art*. New York: Scribner's.

Langer, S. (1979). *Philosophy in a new key: A study in the symbolism of reason, rite and art* (3rd ed.). Cambridge, MA: Harvard University Press.

Lea, M., & Spears, R. (1995). Love at first byte? Building personal relationships over computer networks. In J. T. Wood & S. W. Duck (Eds.), *Under-studied relationships: Off the beaten track* (pp. 197–233). Thousand Oaks, CA: Sage.

Lee, W. S. (1993). Social scientists as ideological critics. *Western Journal of Communication, 57*, pp. 221–232.

Levinson, P. (1999). *Digital McLuhan: A guide to the information millennium*. New York: Routledge.

Lichter, S. R., Lichter, L. S., Rothman, S., & Amundson, D. (1987, July/August). Primetime prejudice: TV's images of blacks and Hispanics. *Public Opinion*, pp. 13–16.

Ling, D. A. (1970). A pentadic analysis of Senator Edward Kennedy's address to the people of Massachusetts, July 25, 1969. *Central States Speech Journal, 21*, pp. 81–86.

Littlejohn, S. (1992). *Theories of human communication* (4th ed.). Belmont, CA: Wadsworth.

Lule, J. (1998, August 7). The power and pitfalls of journalism in the hypertext era. *Chronicle of Higher Education*, pp. B7, B8.

Lund, M. (1985). The development of investment and commitment scales for predicting continuity of personal relationships. *Journal of Social and Personal Relationships, 2*, pp. 3–23.

Lyotard, J. (1984). *The postmodern condition*. Minneapolis: University of Minnesota Press.

Madison, D. S. (1991). "That was my occupation": Oral narrative, performance, and black feminist thought. *Text and Performance Quarterly, 13,* pp. 213–232.

Madison, D. S. (In press). Critical ethnography: Performance, protest, and the meaning of home. In N. Denzin & Y. Lincoln (Eds), *Handbook of qualitative research* (3rd ed.). Thousand Oaks, CA: Sage.

Madison, S. (1999). Performing theory/embodied writing. *Text and Performance Quarterly, 19,* pp. 107–124.

Maltz, D., & Borker, R. (1982). A cultural approach to male–female miscommunication. In J. J. Gumpertz (Ed.), *Language and social identity* (pp. 196–216). Cambridge, UK: Cambridge University Press.

Mander, M. (Ed.). (1999). *Framing friction: Media and social conflict.* Urbana: University of Illinois Press.

Mangan, K. (2002, July 5). Horse sense of nonsense? *Chronicle of Higher Education,* pp. A8–A10.

Martin, A. (Adapter and Director). (1988). *Things fall apart: Literature that speaks to AIDS.* Presented at the annual meeting of the Speech Communication Association, New Orleans, LA

Martin, C. (1993). Anna Deavere Smith: The word becomes you. *The Drama Review, 37,* pp. 45–62.

Martin, R. W. (1991). Examining personal relationship thinking: The relational cognition complexity instrument. *Journal of Social and Personal Relationships, 8,* pp. 467–480.

Martin, R. W. (1992). Relational cognition complexity and relational communication. *Communication Monographs, 59,* pp. 150–163.

Marx, C. (1887). *Capital.* (Trans., S. Moore & E. Aveling; Ed., F. Engels). Moscow, USSR: Progress Publishers.

McBath, J. H., & Burhans, D. T., Jr. (1975). *Communication education and careers.* Falls Church, VA: Speech Communication Association.

McChesney, R. (1999). *Rich media, poor democracy: Communication politics in dubious times.* IL: University of Illinois Press.

McDonald, G. (1981). Structural exchange and marital interaction. *Journal of Marriage and the Family, 43,* pp. 825–839.

McLuhan, M. (1962). *The Gutenberg galaxy.* Toronto: University of Toronto Press.

McLuhan, M. (1964). *Understanding media.* New York: McGraw-Hill.

McLuhan, M. (1969, March). Interview. *Playboy,* pp. 53–54, 56, 59–62, 64–66, 68, 70.

McLuhan, M., & Fiori, Q. (1967). *The medium is the message.* New York: Random House.

McLuhan, M., & McLuhan, E. (1988). Culture and communication: The two hemispheres. In *Laws of media* (pp. 67–91). Toronto: University of Toronto Press.

Mead, G. H. (1934). *Mind, self, and society.* Chicago: University of Chicago Press.

Media Education Foundation. (1994). *The killing screens: Media and the culture of violence.* Northampton, MA: Media Education Foundation. 37 minutes.

Media Education Foundation. (1997a). *The electronic storyteller: Television and the cultivation of values.* Northampton, MA: Media Education Foundation. 30 minutes.

Media Education Foundation. (1997b). *The crisis of the cultural environment: Media and democracy in the 21st century.* Northampton, MA: Media Education Foundation. 24 minutes.

Media Studies Journal. (1994). Special issue: Race—America's rawest nerve. Vol. 8.

References

Merritt, B. (2000). Illusive reflections: African American women on primetime television. In A. González, M. Houston, & V. Chen (Eds.), *Our voices* (pp. 47–53). Los Angeles: Roxbury.

Messinger, S., Sampson, H., & Towne, R. (1962). Life as theater: Some notes on the dramaturgic approach to social reality. *Sociometry, 25,* pp. 98–110.

Meyrowitz, J. (1995). Mediating communication: What happens? In J. Downing, A. Mohammadi, & A. Sheberny-Mohammadi (Eds.), *Questioning the media: A critical introduction* (2nd ed., pp. 39–53). Thousand Oaks, CA: Sage.

Mitchell-Kernan, C. (1972). Signifying, loud-talking, and marking. In T. Kochman (Ed.), *Rappin' and stylin' out* (pp. 315–335). Urbana: University of Illinois Press.

Montgomery, B. (1993). Relationship maintenance versus relationship change: A dialectical dilemma. *Journal of Social and Personal Relationships, 10,* pp. 205–224.

Mulac, A., Wiemann, J. M., Widenmann, S. J., & Gibson, T. W. (1988). Male/female language differences and effects in same-sex and mixed-sex dyads: The gender-linked language effect. *Communication Monographs, 55,* pp. 315–335.

Murphy, B. O., & Zorn, T. (1996). Gendered interaction in professional relationships. In J. T. Wood (Ed.), *Gendered relationships* (pp. 213–232). Mountain View, CA: Mayfield.

Nakayama, T. (1995). Continuing the dialogue of evidence. *Western Journal of Communication, 59,* pp. 171–175.

Natalle, E. (1996). Gendered issues in the workplace. In J. T. Wood (Ed.), *Gendered relationships.* Mountain View, CA: Mayfield.

National Television Violence Study, (1996). *Scientific report.* Thousand Oaks, CA: Sage.

Newcomb, H. (1978). Assessing the violence profile studies of Gerbner and Gross. *Communication Research, 5,* pp. 264–282.

Nofsinger, R. (1991). *Everyday conversation.* Newbury Park, CA: Sage.

Nussbaum, M. (1992, October 18). Justice for women! *New York Review of Books,* pp. 43–48.

O'Connell, L. (1984). An exploration of exchange in three social relationships: Kinship, friendship, and the marketplace. *Journal of Social and Personal Relationships, 1,* pp. 333–346.

Ogden, C. K., & Richards, I. A. (1923). *The meaning of meaning: A study of the influence of language upon thought and of the science of symbolism.* New York: Harcourt, Brace, & World.

O'Keefe, B., & Sypher, H. (1981). Cognitive complexity measures and the relationship of cognitive complexity to communication: A critical review. *Human Communication Research, 8,* pp. 72–92.

Owen, W. F. (1984). Interpretive themes in relational communication. *Quarterly Journal of Speech, 70,* pp. 274–287.

Owen, W. F. (1985). Thematic metaphors in relational communication: A conceptual framework. *Western Journal of Speech Communication, 49,* pp. 1–13.

Owen, W. F. (1995, July). Personal communication.

Pacanowsky, M. (1989). Creating and narrating organizational realities. In B. Dervin, L. Grossberg, B. O'Keefe, & E. Wartella (Eds.), *Rethinking communication: Paradigm exemplars* (pp. 250–257). Newbury Park, CA: Sage.

Pacanowsky, M., & O'Donnell-Trujillo, N. (1982). Communication and organizational cultures. *Western Journal of Speech Communication, 46,* pp. 115–130.

Pacanowsky, M., & O'Donnell-Trujillo, N. (1983). Organizational communication as cultural performance. *Communication Monographs, 30,* pp. 126–147.

Park, M. (1979). *Communication styles in two different cultures: Korean and American.* Seoul: Han Shin.

Pearce, B. (1989). *Communication and the human condition.* Carbondale: Southern Illinois University Press.

Pearce, B. (1992, November). *Bringing news of difference: An application of systemic and social constructionist communication theory in conflict consultation.* Paper presented to the Speech Communication Association, Chicago, IL.

Pearce, B. (1994). *Interpersonal communication: Making social worlds.* New York: HarperCollins.

Pearce, B., & Cronen, V. (1980). *Communication, action, and meaning: The creation of social realities.* New York: Praeger.

Penelope, J. (1990). *Speaking freely: Unlearning the lies of the fathers' tongues.* New York: Pergamon Press.

Perry, D. (1993). "Jamaica Kincaid." *Backtalk: Women writers speak out* (pp. 127–141). New Brunswick, NJ: Rutgers University Press.

Peterson, E., & Langellier, K. (1997). The politics of personal narrative methodology. *Text and Performance Quarterly, 17,* pp. 135–152.

Petronio, S. (1991). Communication boundary management: A theoretical model of managing disclosure of private information between married couples. *Communication Theory, 1,* pp. 311–335.

Phelan, P., & Lane, J. (Eds.). (1998). *The ends of performance.* New York: New York University Press.

Philipsen, G. (1975). Speaking "like a man" in Teamsterville: Cultural patterns of role enactment in an urban neighborhood. *Quarterly Journal of Speech, 61,* pp. 13–22.

Philipsen, G. (1992). *Speaking culturally: Exploration in social communication.* Albany: State University of New York Press.

Philipsen, G. (1997). A theory of speech codes. In G. Philipsen & T. Albrecht (Eds.), *Developing communication theory* (pp. 119-156). Albany: State University of New York Press.

Phillips, G. M., & Wood, J. T. (1983). *Communication and human relationships.* New York: Macmillan.

Planalp, S., Rutherford, D., & Honeycutt, J. M. (1988). Events that increase uncertainty in personal relationships, II: Replication and extension. *Human Communication Research, 14,* pp. 516–547.

Pollock, D. (1990). Telling the told: Performing *Like a Family. Oral History Review, 18,* pp. 1–36.

Pollock, D. (Ed.). (1998). *Exceptional spaces: Essays in performance and history.* Chapel Hill: University of North Carolina Press.

Pollock, D. (1999). Personal communication.

Popkin, R., & Stroll, A. (2002). *Skeptical philosophy for everyone.* Prometheus Books.

Postman, N. (1985). *Amusing ourselves to death: Public discourse in the age of show business.* New York: Penguin.

Potter, J. (1996). *Representing reality.* London: Sage.

Potter, W. J. (2001). *Media literacy* (2nd ed). Thousand Oaks, CA: Sage.

Prins, K., Buunk, B., & vanYperon, N. W. (1993). Equity, normative disapproval, and extra-marital relationships. *Journal of Social and Personal Relationships, 10,* pp. 39–54.

References

Pryor, J. B., & Merluzzi, T. V. (1985). The role of expertise in processing social interaction scripts. *Journal of Experimental Social Psychology, 21,* pp. 362–379.

Puka, B. (1990). The liberation of caring: A different voice for Gilligan's different voice. *Hypatia, 5,* pp. 59–82.

Putnam, L. (1982). In search of gender: A critique of communication and sex-roles research. *Women's Studies in Communication, 5,* pp. 1–9.

Putnam, L., & Kolb, D. (2000). Rethinking negotiation: Feminist views of communication and exchange. In P. Buzzanell (Ed.), *Rethinking organizational and managerial communication from feminist perspectives* (pp. 76–104). Thousand Oaks, CA: Sage.

Rakow, L. (1992). "Don't hate me because I'm beautiful": Feminist resistance to advertising's irresistible meanings. *Southern Journal of Speech Communication, 36,* pp. 11–26.

Rawlins, W. (1983a). Negotiating close friendships: The dialectic of conjunctive freedoms. *Human Communication Research, 9,* pp. 255–266.

Rawlins, W. (1983b). Openness as problematic in ongoing friendships: Two conversational dilemmas. *Communication Monographs, 50,* pp. 1–13.

Rawlins, W. (1988). Adolescents' interaction with parents and friends: Dialectics of temporal perspective and evaluation. *Journal of Social and Personal Relationships, 5,* pp. 27–46.

Rawlins, W. (1989). A dialectical analysis of the tensions, functions, and strategic challenges of communication in young adult friendships. *Communication Yearbook, 12* (pp. 157–189). Thousand Oaks, CA: Sage.

Rawlins, W. (1992). *Friendship matters: Communication, dialectics, and the life course.* New York: Aldine de Gruyter.

Real, M. (1984). The debate on critical theory and the study of communications. *Journal of Communication, 34,* pp. 72–80.

Reinelt, J. (Ed.). (1996). *Crucibles of crisis.* Ann Arbor: University of Michigan Press.

Richards, I. A. (1936). *The philosophy of rhetoric.* London: Oxford University Press.

Richards, I. A. (1955). *Speculative instruments.* Chicago: University of Chicago Press.

Richards, I. A. (1968, February 3). The secret of "feedforward." *Saturday Review,* pp. 14–17.

Rideout, V., Foehr, U., Roberts, D., & Brodie, M. (1999). *Kids and media@the new millennium.* Menlo Park, CA: Kaiser Foundation.

Riessman, C. K. (1990). *Divorce talk: Women and men make sense of personal relationships.* New Brunswick, NJ: Rutgers University Press.

Risman, B. (1989). Can men mother? In B. Risman & P. Schwartz (Eds.), *Gender in intimate relationships* (pp. 155–164). Belmont, CA: Wadsworth/Brooks-Cole.

Risman, B., & Godwin, G. (2001). Twentieth-century changes in economic work and family. In D. Vannoy (Ed.), *Gender mosaics* (pp. 134-144). Los Angeles: Roxbury.

Robbins, B., & Ross, A. (1996, July/August). Mystery science theatre. *Lingua Franca,* pp. 54–57.

Rogers-Millar, E., & Farace, R. (1975). Analysis of relational communication in dyads: New measurement procedures. *Human Communication Research, 1,* pp. 222–239.

Rohlfing, M. (1995). "Doesn't anybody stay in one place anymore?" An exploration of the under-studied phenomenon of long-distance relationships. In J. T. Wood & S. W. Duck (Eds.), *Understanding relationship processes, 6: Off the beaten track: Understudied relationships* (pp. 173–196). Thousand Oaks, CA: Sage.

Roloff, M. (1981). *Interpersonal communication: The social exchange approach.* Beverly Hills, CA: Sage.

Rosenwasser, S. M., Lingenfelter, M., & Harrington, A. F. (1989). Nontraditional gender role portrayals on television and children's gender role perceptions. *Journal of Applied Developmental Psychology, 10,* pp. 97–105.

Rowland, R. C. (1989). On limiting the narrative paradigm: Three case studies. *Communication Monographs, 56,* pp. 39–54.

Ruberman, T. R. (1992, January 22–29). Psychosocial influences on mortality of patients with coronary heart disease. *Journal of the American Medical Association, 267,* pp. 559–560.

Ruddick, S. (1989). *Maternal thinking: Towards a politics of peace.* Boston: Beacon Press.

Rusbult, C., & Buunk, B. (1993). Commitment processes in close relationships: An interdependence analysis. *Journal of Social and Personal Relationships, 10,* pp. 175–204.

Rusk, T., & Rusk, N. (1988). *Mind traps: Change your mind, change your life.* Los Angeles: Price Stern Sloan.

Russell, D. E. H. (Ed.). (1993). *Feminist views on pornography.* Colchester, VT: Teachers College Press.

Sadker, M., & Sadker, D. (1986, March). Sexism in the classroom: From grade school to graduate school. *Phi Delta Kappan,* pp. 512–515.

Sallinen-Kuparinen, A. (1992). Teacher communicator style. *Communication Education, 41,* pp. 153–166.

Samovar, L., & Porter, R. (Eds.). (2000). *Intercultural communication: A reader* (9th ed.). Belmont, CA: Wadsworth.

Sarup, M. (1989). *An introductory guide to poststructuralism and postmodernism.* Athens: University of Georgia Press.

SCA (Speech Communication Association). (1993). *Pathways to careers in communication.* Annandale, VA: Author.

Scarf, M. (1987). *Intimate partners: Patterns in love and marriage.* New York: Random House.

Schaef, A. W. (1985). *Women's reality.* St. Paul, MN: Winston Press.

Schiller, H. (1996, June 3). Off the chart. *The Nation,* p. 16.

Searle, J. (1995). *The construction of social reality.* New York: The Free Press.

Searle, J. R. (1976). *Speech acts: An essay in the philosophy of language.* London: Cambridge University Press.

Seligman, M. E. P. (1990). *Learned optimism.* New York: Simon & Schuster/Pocket Books.

Sexism in the schoolhouse. (1992, February 24). *Newsweek,* p. 62.

Shailor, J. (1994). *Empowerment in dispute mediation: A critical analysis of communication.* Westport, CT: Praeger.

Shank-Krusiewicz, E., & Wood, J. T. (2001). "He was our child from the moment we walked in that room.": Entrance stories of adoptive parents. *Journal of Social and Personal Relationships, 18,* pp. 785–803.

Shannon, C., & Weaver, W. (1949). *The mathematical theory of communication.* Urbana: University of Illinois Press.

Shapiro, J., & Kroeger, L. (1991). Is life just a romantic novel? The relationship between attitudes about intimate relationships and the popular media. *American Journal of Family Therapy, 19,* pp. 226–236.

Shattuck, T. R. (1980). *The forbidden experiment: The story of the wild boy of Aveyron.* New York: Farrar, Straus & Giroux.

Shimanoff, S. B. (1980). *Communication rules: Theory and research.* Beverly Hills, CA: Sage.

Shimanoff, S. B. (1985). Rules governing the verbal expression of emotions between married couples. *Western Journal of Communication, 49,* pp. 147–165.

Shotter, J. (1993). *Conversational realities: The construction of life through language.* Newbury Park, CA: Sage.

Shuter, R. (1994). The Hmong of Laos. In R. Porter & L. Samovar (Eds.), *Intercultural communication: A reader* (pp. 213–219). Belmont, CA: Wadsworth.

Sights, sounds, and stereotypes. (1992, October 11). *Raleigh News & Observer,* pp. G1, G10.

Signorielli, N. (1990). Television's mean and dangerous world: A continuation of the cultural indicators perspective. In N. Signorielli & M. Morgan (Eds.), *Cultivation analysis: New directions in media effects research* (pp. 85–106). Newbury Park, CA: Sage.

Signorielli, N., & Morgan, M. (Eds.). (1990). *Cultivation analysis: New directions in media effects research.* Newbury Park, CA: Sage.

Skinner, B. F. (1971). *Beyond freedom and dignity.* New York: Knopf.

Smith, A. D. (1993). *Fires in the mirror.* New York: Anchor Books.

Smitherman, G. (1977). *Talkin' and testifyin': The language of black America.* Boston: Houghton Mifflin.

Sokal, A. (1996a, May/June). A physicist experiments with cultural studies. *Lingua Franca,* pp. 62–64.

Sokal, A. (1996b, Fall). Transgressing the boundaries: An afterword. *Dissent, 43,* pp. 93–99.

Sokal, A. (1996c). Transgressing the boundaries: Toward a transformative hermeneutics of quantum gravity. *Social Text, 46/47,* pp. 217–252.

Sokal, A. (1998, April 18). Truth, reason, objectivity, and the Left. *Economic and Political Weekly* (Bombay), pp. 913–914.

Sokal, A. (2002). http://www.physics.nyu.edu/faculty/sokal/ling (accessed July 8–12, 2002).

Sokal, A., & Briemont, J. (1998). *Fashionable nonsense: Postmodern intellectuals' abuse of science.* New York: Picador.

Sontag, S. (1966). *Against interpretation.* New York: Stein and Day.

Spelman, E. (1988). *Inessential woman: Problems of exclusion in feminist thought.* Boston: Beacon Press.

Spencer, T. (1994). Transforming personal relationships through ordinary talk. In S. W. Duck (Ed.), *Understanding relationship processes, 4: Dynamics of relationships* (pp. 58–85). Thousand Oaks, CA: Sage.

Spender, D. (1984a). Defining reality: A powerful tool. In C. Kramarae, M. Schultz, & W. O'Barr (Eds.), *Language and power* (pp. 195–205). Beverly Hills, CA: Sage.

Spender, D. (1984b). *Man made language.* London: Routledge & Kegan Paul.

Spitzack, C., & Carter, K. (1987). Women in communication studies: A typology for revision. *Quarterly Journal of Speech, 73,* pp. 401–423.

Sprecher, S. (2001). A comparison of emotional consequences of and changes in equity over time using global and domain-specific measures of equity. *Journal of Social and Personal Relationships, 18,* pp. 477–501.

Sprecher, S., & Felmlee, D. (1997). The balance of power in romantic heterosexual couples over time from "his" and "her" perspectives. *Sex Roles, 37,* pp. 363–379.

Stacey, J. (1991). Can there be a feminist ethnography? In S. Gluck & D. Patai (Eds.), *Women's words: The feminist practice of oral history* (pp. 111–119). New York: Routledge.

Stacks, D., Hill, S., III, & Hickson, M. (1991). *Introduction to communication theory.* New York: Holt, Rinehart & Winston.

Statistical Abstract of the United States: 1999. (2000). Washington, DC: Congressional Information Service.

Steele, J., & Brown, J. (1995). Adolescent room culture: Studying media in the context of everyday life. *Journal of Youth and Adolescence, 5,* pp. 550–571.

Stewart, J. (1991). A postmodern look at traditional communication postulates. *Western Journal of Speech Communication, 55,* pp. 354–379.

Stewart, L. P., Stewart, A. D., Friedley, S. A., & Cooper, P. J. (1990). *Communication between the sexes: Sex differences and sex role stereotypes* (2nd ed.). Scottsdale, AZ: Gorsuch Scarisbrick.

Stoller, D., & Karp, M. (Eds.). (1999). *The bust guide to the new girl order.* New York: Penguin.

Storey, J. (1996). *Cultural studies and the study of popular culture: Theories and methods.* Athens: University of Georgia Press.

Storey, J. (1999). *Cultural consumption and everyday life.* London: Arnold.

Storytelling and narrativity in communication research. (1985). *Journal of Communication, 4,* special issue.

Strine, M. S. (1992). Understanding how things work: Sexual harassment and academic culture. *Journal of Applied Communication Research, 20,* pp. 391–400.

Strine, M., Long, B., & HopKins, M. (1990). Research in interpretation and performance studies: Trends, issues, priorities. In G. M. Phillips & J. T. Wood (Eds.), *Speech communication: Essays to commemorate the 75th anniversary of the Speech Communication Association* (pp. 181–204). Carbondale: Southern Illinois University Press.

Striphas, T. (1998). The long march: Cultural studies and its institutionalization. *Cultural Studies, 12,* pp. 453–475.

Striphas, T. (2000). Cultural studies, "so-called." *The Review of Education/Psychology/Cultural Studies, 22,* pp. 27–45.

Suitor, J. J. (1991). Marital quality and satisfaction with the division of household labor across the family life cycle. *Journal of Marriage and the Family, 53,* pp. 221–230.

Sunnafrank, M. (1986). Predicted outcome value during initial interactions: A reformulation of uncertainty reduction theory. *Human Communication Research, 13,* pp. 3–33.

Tannen, D. (1990). *You just don't understand: Women and men in conversation.* New York: William Morrow.

Tannen, D. (1994). *Talking from 9 to 5.* New York: William Morrow.

Taylor, B., & Conrad, C. (1992). Narratives of sexual harassment: Organizational dimensions. *Journal of Applied Communication Research, 20,* pp. 401–418.

Taylor, D., & Altman, I. (1987). Communication in interpersonal relationships: Social penetration processes. In M. Roloff & G. R. Miller (Eds.), *Interpersonal processes: New directions in communication research* (pp. 253–285). Newbury Park, CA: Sage.

Television Bureau of Advertising. (1991). *Media comparisons* (SRI Rep. A9055–4). New York: Author.

Telling our stories: Special symposium. (1992). *The Journal of Applied Communication Research, 20, pp. v, vi, 349–418.*

References

Thibaut, J., & Kelley, H. H. (1959). *The social psychology of groups.* New York: Wiley.

Ting-Toomey, S. (1991). Intimacy expressions in three cultures: France, Japan and the United States. *International Journal of Intercultural Relations, 15,* pp. 29–46.

Treichler, P. A., & Kramarae, C. (1983). Women's talk in the ivory tower. *Communication Quarterly, 31,* pp. 118–132.

Trice, H., & Beyer, J. (1984). Studying organizational cultures through rites and ceremonials. *Academy of Management Review, 9,* pp. 653–669.

Troemel-Ploetz, S. (1991). Review essay: Selling the apolitical. *Discourse and Society, 2,* pp. 490–499.

Tucker, R. (1999). (Ed.). *Marx-Engels reader* (2nd ed.). New York: W. W. Norton.

Turner, V. (1975). *Revelations of divination in Ndembu ritual.* Ithaca, NY: Cornell University Press.

Turner, V. (1986). *The anthropology of performance.* New York: PAJ Publications.

Urgo, J. (2000). *In the age of distraction.* Jackson: University Press of Mississippi.

Value of children's shows is questionable, study finds. (1999, June 28). *Raleigh News & Observer,* p. 5A.

Van Lear, C. A. (1992). Testing a cyclical model of communicative openness in relationship development: Two longitudinal studies. *Communication Monographs, 58,* pp. 337–361.

Van Maanen, J. (1973). Observations on the making of policemen. *Human Organization, 32,* pp. 407–418.

Van Maanen, J., & Barley, S. (1985). Cultural organization: Fragments of a theory. In P. J. Frost et al. (Eds.), *Organizational culture* (pp. 31–54). Beverly Hills, CA: Sage.

van Yperen, N., & Buunk, B. (1990). A longitudinal study of equity and satisfaction in intimate relationships. *European Journal of Social Psychology, 20,* pp. 287–309.

Vavrus, M. D. (2002). *Postfeminist news.* Albany: State University of New York Press.

Vocate, D. (Ed.). (1994). *Intrapersonal communication: Different voices, different minds.* Hillsdale, NJ: Lawrence Erlbaum.

von Bertalanffy, L. (1951). *Problems of life.* New York: Harper & Row.

von Bertalanffy, L. (1967). *Robots, men and minds.* New York: Braziller.

Vorda, A. (1993). I come from a place that's very unreal: An interview with Jamaica Kincaid. In A. Vorda (Ed.), *Face to face: Interviews with contemporary novelists* (pp. 77–106). Houston: Rice University Press.

Walsh, F. (1993). Conceptualization of normal family processes. In F. Walsh (Ed.), *Normal family processes* (2nd ed., pp. 3–69). New York: Guilford.

Wander, P. (1983). The ideological turn in modern criticism. *Central States Speech Journal, 34,* pp. 1–18.

Wander, P. (1984). The third persona: An ideological turn in rhetorical theory. *Central States Speech Journal, 35,* pp. 197–216.

Warnick, B. (1987). The narrative paradigm: Another story. *Quarterly Journal of Speech, 73,* pp. 172–182.

Watzlawick, P., Beavin, J., & Jackson, D. (1967). *The pragmatics of human communication.* New York: W. W. Norton.

Weedon, C. (1987). *Feminist practice and poststructuralist theory.* London: Basil Blackwell.

Weigel, D., & Ballard-Reisch, D. (2002). Investigating the behavioral indicators of relational commitment. *Journal of Social and Personal Relationships, 19,* pp. 403–423.

Weiner, N. (1967). *The human use of human beings.* New York: Avon.

Wenzhong, H., & Grove, C. (1991). *Encountering the Chinese.* Yarmouth, ME: Intercultural Press.

Werner, C., Altman, I., Brown, B., & Ginat, J. (1993). Celebrations in personal relationships: A transactional/dialectical perspective. In S. Duck (Ed.), *Understanding relationship processes, 3: Social context and relationships* (pp. 109–138). Newbury Park, CA: Sage.

West, C. (2001). *Race matters.* New York: Beacon.

West, C., & Zimmerman, D. (1987). "Doing gender." *Gender and Society, 1,* pp. 125–151.

West, J. (1993). Ethnography and ideology: The politics of cultural representation. *Western Journal of Communication, 57,* pp. 209–220.

West, J. (1995). Understanding how the dynamics of ideology influence violence between intimates. In S. W. Duck & J. T. Wood (Eds.), *Understanding relationship processes, 5: Confronting relationship challenges* (pp. 129–149). Thousand Oaks, CA: Sage.

Whan, K. (1997, August 10). UNC study observes link between health, loving support. *The Chapel Hill Herald,* p. 7.

White, J., & Bondurant, J. (1996). Gendered violence between intimates. In J. T. Wood (Ed.), *Gendered relationships* (pp. 197–210). Mountain View, CA: Mayfield.

Williams, P. (1992). *The alchemy of race and rights.* Cambridge, MA: Harvard University Press.

Williams, S. (1989). *A description of the rules for the performance appraisal interview utilizing the coordinated management of meaning theory.* Unpublished master's thesis. University of Northern Iowa, Cedar Falls, IA.

Wiltshire, B. (1977). Role playing and identity: The limits of the theatrical metaphor. *Cultural Hermeneutics, 4,* pp. 199–207.

Wolf, N. (1991). *The beauty myth.* New York: William C. Morrow.

Wong, W. (1994). Covering the invisible "model minority." *Media Studies Journal* (Special issue: Race—America's rawest nerve), pp. 49–60.

Wood, J. T. (1982). Communication and relational culture: Bases for the study of human relationships. *Communication Quarterly, 30,* pp. 75–84.

Wood, J. T. (1986). Different voices in relationship crises: An extension of Gilligan's theory. *American Behavioral Scientist, 29,* pp. 273–301.

Wood, J. T. (1992). Narratives as a basis for theorizing sexual harassment. *Journal of Applied Communication Research, 20,* pp. 349–363.

Wood, J. T. (1993a). Bringing different voices into the classroom. *National Women's Studies Association Journal, 5,* pp. 82–93.

Wood, J. T. (1993b). Diversity and commonality: Sustaining their tension in communication courses. *Western Journal of Communication, 57,* pp. 367–380.

Wood, J. T. (1993d). Enlarging conceptual boundaries: A critique of research on interpersonal communication. In S. P. Bowen & N. J. Wyatt (Eds.), *Transforming visions: Feminist critiques in speech communication* (pp. 19–49). Cresskill, NJ: Hampton Press.

Wood, J. T. (1993e). From "woman's nature" to standpoint epistemology: Gilligan and the debate over essentializing in feminist scholarship. *Women's Studies in Communication, 15,* pp. 1–24.

Wood, J. T. (1994a). Engendered relations: Caring, connection, responsibility, and power in close relationships. In S. W. Duck (Ed.), *Understanding relationship processes, 3: Social context and relationships* (pp. 26–54). Thousand Oaks, CA: Sage.

References

Wood, J. T. (1994b). Saying it makes it so: The discursive construction of sexual harassment. In S. Bingham (Ed.), *Discursive conceptions of sexual harassment* (pp. 17–30). Westport, CT: Praeger.

Wood, J. T. (1994c). Gender and relationship crises: Contrasting reasons, responses, and relational orientations. In J. Ringer (Ed.), *Queer words, queer images: The construction of homosexuality.* New York: New York University Press.

Wood, J. T. (1994d). *Who cares? Women, care, and culture.* Carbondale: Southern Illinois University Press.

Wood, J. T. (1994e). Gender, communication, and culture. In L. Samovar & R. Porter (Eds.), *Intercultural communication: A reader* (7th ed., pp. 155–164). Belmont, CA: Wadsworth.

Wood, J. T. (1995a). Feminist scholarship and the study of personal relationships. *Journal of Social and Personal Relationships, 12,* pp. 103–121.

Wood, J. T. (1995b). Practicing theory, theorizing practice. In K. Cissna (Ed.), *Applied communication in the 21st century: Report of the Tampa conference* (pp. 157–167). Mahwah, NJ: Erlbaum.

Wood, J. T. (1995c). The part is not the whole. *Journal of Social and Personal Relationships, 12,* pp. 563–567.

Wood, J. T. (Ed.). (1996a). *Gendered relationships.* Mountain View, CA: Mayfield.

Wood, J. T. (1996b). She says/he says: Communication, caring and conflict in heterosexual relationships. In J. T. Wood (Ed.), *Gendered relationships* (pp. 149–162). Mountain View, CA: Mayfield.

Wood, J. T. (1998a). An exchange about exchange: A reply to Bernard Murstein. *Psychological Reports, 82,* pp. 1057–1058.

Wood, J. T. (1998b). *But I thought you meant: Misunderstandings in human communication.* Mountain View, CA: Mayfield.

Wood, J. T. (1998c). Ethics, justice, and the "private sphere." *Women's studies in communication, 21,* pp. 127–140.

Wood, J. T. (2000). *Relational communication: Change and continuity in personal relationships* (2nd ed.). Belmont, CA: Wadsworth.

Wood, J. T. (2001). The normalization of violence in heterosexual romantic relationships: Women's narratives of love and violence. *Journal of Social and Personal Relationships, 18,* pp. 239–262.

Wood, J. T. (2002). A critical assessment of John Gray's portrayals of men, women, and relationships. *Southern Communication Journal, 67,* pp. 201–210.

Wood, J. T. (2003). *Gendered lives: Communication, gender, and culture* (5th ed.). Belmont, CA: Wadsworth.

Wood, J. T., & Cox, J. R. (1993). Rethinking critical voice: Materiality and situated knowledges. *Western Journal of Communication, 57,* pp. 278–287.

Wood, J. T., Dendy, L., Dordek, E., Germany, M., & Varallo, S. (1994). Dialectic of difference: A thematic analysis of intimates' meanings for differences. In K. Carter & M. Presnell (Eds.), *Interpretive approaches to interpersonal communication* (pp. 115–136). New York: New York University Press.

Wood, J. T., & Dindia, K. (1998). What's the difference?: A dialogue about similarities and differences in the communication of women and men. In K. Dindia & D. Canary (Eds.), *Sex differences and similarities in communication* (pp. 19–39). NJ: Erlbaum.

Wood, J. T., & Duck, S. (1995a). Off the beaten track: New shores for relationship research. In J. T. Wood & S. W. Duck (Eds.), *Understanding relationship processes, 6: Understudied relationships: Off the beaten track* (pp. 1–21). Thousand Oaks, CA: Sage.

Wood, J. T., & Duck, S. (Eds.). (1995b). *Understanding relationship processes, 6: Understudied relationships: Off the beaten track.* Thousand Oaks, CA: Sage.

Wood, J. T., & Inman, C. C. (1993). In a different mode: Masculine styles of communicating closeness. *Journal of Applied Communication Research, 21,* pp. 279–295.

Wood, J. T., & Lenze, L. F. (1991a). Gender and the development of self: Inclusive pedagogy in interpersonal communication. *Women's Studies in Communication, 14,* pp. 1–23.

Wood, J. T., & Lenze, L. F. (1991b). Strategies to enhance gender sensitivity in communication education. *Communication Education, 40,* pp. 16–21.

Woods, B. (1999, January 18). One body, many voices: Anna Deavere Smith's one woman shows are fusions of America's fractious voices. *Raleigh News & Observer,* pp. 1C, 3C.

Yerby, J. (1995). Family systems theory reconsidered: Integrating social construction theory and dialectical process. *Communication Theory, 5,* pp. 339-365.

Zorn, T. (1991). Construct system development, transformational leadership, and leadership messages. *Southern Communication Journal, 56,* pp. 178–193.

Zorn, T. (1995). Bosses and buddies: Constructing and performing simultaneously hierarchical and close friendship relationships. In J. T. Wood & S. W. Duck (Eds.), *Understanding relationship processes, 6: Understudied relationships: Off the beaten track* (pp. 122–147). Thousand Oaks, CA: Sage.

Zuckerman, M. B. (1993, August 2). The victims of TV violence. *U.S. News & World Report,* p. 64.

Name Index

Vocate, D., 15
von Bertalanffy, L., 162–63, 166
Vorda, A., 219

Walker, G., 318
Walsh, F., 266
Waltman, M., 156–57
Wander, P., 310
Wartella, E., 247
Watzlawick, P., 161–62, 169
Weaver, W., 32–34, 40, 44–45, 46
Weedon, C., 283, 293, 294, 296
Weigel, D., 203
Weiner, N., 33–34, 40, 44

Wenzhong, H., 320
Werner, C., 182
West, C., 53, 213
West, J., 38, 310, 317
Whan, K., 12
Widenmann, S. J., 66
Wiemann, J. M., 66
Williams, P., 213
Williams, S., 150
Wiltshire, B., 123
Wolf, N., 318
Wood, J. T., 16, 17, 22, 24, 25, 32, 37,
    53, 68, 69, 71, 85, 86, 108, 135, 144,
    147, 167, 173, 175, 177, 179, 182,

189, 195, 199, 202, 204, 205, 206,
211, 216, 217, 219, 220, 223, 224,
225, 226, 228, 260, 261, 263, 264–65,
266, 267, 270, 281, 310, 317, 319
Woods, B., 136
Wright, P., 154

Yerby, J., 203

Zimmerman, D., 53
Zorn, T., 21, 157, 159, 173, 182, 224,
    266
Zuckerman, M. B., 246

Subject Index

Cool media, **242**
Coordinated management of meaning
    (CMM) theory, 141–52, 311, 312,
    315, 316, 318
   critical assessment of, 150–52
Corporate stories, **228–29**
Correlational explanations, **40**–41
Costs, **192**
Critical analysis, **71**–72
Critical race theory, **213**–14
Critical theories, **259**–84, 317–18
Cultivation, **245**
Cultivation theory, **244**–56, 312,
    317–18
   assumptions of, 249–52
   critical assessment of, 252–56
Cultural impact of communication,
    13–14, 210–11
Cultural mainstream, **250**
Cultural patterns, **144**–45
Cultural studies, **260,** 273–83, 317, 318
   critical assessment of, 281–83
Cultures, **275**–76
   organizations as, 227

Description, **32**–34
   thick, **124–25,** 232–33
Descriptive statistics, **65**–66
Determinism, **52**–53, 243–44
Developmental theories, **185,** 200–207
   critical assessment of, 206–7
Dialectical moments, 174
Dialectical theory, 172–82
   critical assessment of, 180–82
Dialectics, 173–74
   relational, 34, 175–78
   responses to, 178–80
Differentiation, 155–56
Discursive structures, **301**–2
Diversity, 218–20, 225
Domestic violence, 315–19
Dramatism, **97**–104, 311, 312
   critical appraisal of, 102–4
Dramatistic pentad, **101**–2
Dramaturgical model, **118**–19
Dramaturgical theory, 117–24
   critical assessment of, 122–24
Dramaturgy, **117**
Dual perspective, 85
Dynamic equilibrium, 166

Education as career in communication,
    27
Effect, cause *versus*, 254–55
Electronic epoch, 239–40
Episodes, **142**
Epistemic relativism, 302–4
Epistemology, **56,** 312–13
Equilibrium, achieving, 165–66
   dynamic, 166
Equity, **195**–96
Erotica, 317
Etc., 82–83
Ethics in communication, 34
Ethnography, **70**–71, **124**
   misuse of, 131–32
   performance, **117,** 124–32
Exchange theory, 312, 318
Experience, muted, 268–69
Experiments, **68**
Explanations, **34**–35
   causal, **40**–41
   correlational, **40**–41
   law-based, **40**
   rules-based, **41**–42
Expression, 177–78
Extensional orientation, **80**
External validity, **72**

Facts, brute, 62
Facts, institutional, 62
Fantasy themes, **17**
Feedback, in communication,
    33–34
Feedforward, **84**
Feminist theories, **259,** 260–67
   critical assessment of,
    265–67
Fidelity, 109–10
Fragmented self, 293–96
Frames, **118**–19
Free will, 47, 53–55, 313
Front stage, **121**–22

Gender, 53, **260–61,** 266, 282
Generalized other, **92**
General semantics, 75–88
   critical assessment of, 85–86
General systems theory, 162–66
Grand narratives, **288,** 290–92
Group communication, 17

Guilt, **98–99,** 103
   purging, **100**

Hermeneutic circle, **126**–27
Heurism, **44**
Heuristic value, 197–98
Hierarchy, **99**
   of meanings, **141**–45
Homeostasis, 165
Hot media, **242**
Humanism, **62**
Human nature, views of, 52–55
Human relations as career in commu-
    nication, 28
Hypotheses, **64**–65

I, **91**–92
Identification, 98
Ideological domination, **276**–77
Ideologies, **274,** 282–83, 320
Impression management, **119**–21
Inclusion stage, **264**
Indexing, 83–84
Individualism, 320
Inequity, **195**–96
Institute of General Semantics, 86
Institutional facts, **62**
Integration, 176
Intensional orientation, **80**
Interactional theory, 161–72, 318
   critical assessment of, 171–72
Intercultural communication, 21–22,
    187–89
Internal validity, **72**
Interpersonal communication, **16**–17
Interpretive analysis, 69–70
Intrapersonal communication, **15**–16

Knowledge, 55–59
   multiple ways of, 263–65
   situated, **214**–15

Language, 210–11, 262, 299–300
   misrepresentation of character of,
    85–86
   muted, 268–69
Laws, **59**
   of behavior, 185
   explanations based on, **40**
   universal, 59–60